Concubines and Power

Concubines and Power

Five Hundred Years in a Northern Nigerian Palace

Heidi J. Nast

Foreword by Hausatu Abba Ado Bayero

University of Minnesota Press | Minneapolis | London

Published by the University of Minnesota Press
111 Third Avenue South, Suite 290
Minneapolis, MN 55401–2520
http://www.upress.umn.edu

Library of Congress Cataloging-in-Publication Data

Nast, Heidi J.
    Concubines and power : five hundred years in a Northern Nigerian palace / Heidi J. Nast.
        p.   cm.
    Includes bibliographical references and index.
    ISBN 0-8166-4153-6 (hc : alk. paper) — ISBN 0-8166-4154-4 (pb : alk. paper)
    1. Women—Nigeria—Kano—Social conditions.   2. Concubinage—Nigeria—Kano.
3. Kano (Nigeria)—Politics and government.   4. Kano (Nigeria)—History.   5. Human
geography—Nigeria.   I. Title.
    HQ696.7.N37 2004
    305.42'09669'78—dc22

                                                                        2004020159

Printed in the United States of America on acid-free paper

The University of Minnesota is an equal-opportunity educator and employer.

12 11 10 09 08 07 06 05   10 9 8 7 6 5 4 3 2 1

To Hajiyya Abba Ado Bayero

and

in memory of
John Bradbury (1944–1988)
John Lavers (1936–1993)
Nehemia Letvzion (1934–2003)

Contents

Foreword

Hausatu Abba Ado Bayero

The publication of *Concubines and Power: Five Hundred Years in a Northern Nigerian Palace* marks the culmination of a journey started about fifteen years ago when Dr. Heidi J. Nast was a doctoral student at McGill University in Montreal. She first came to me in the palace to discuss her research plans. For those of us involved with the project in various ways since its beginning, our satisfaction and relief at the materialization of a book at the end of it all are matched only by similar feelings of the author. Several people whose names or words appear in this book have died since Heidi met them, especially those who were already advanced in age at the beginning, such as the late Hajiya 'Yar Mai-Tilas, daughter of the last precolonial emir of Kano ('Aliyu dan Abdullahi) and wife to the late Emir Abdullahi Bayero. Among royal slaves, several including Sallama Daku and *dan ciki* have also passed away. Those of us who are still alive by God's grace find ourselves fifteen years older today than we were when the project started.

Being myself a princess from Katsina and a granddaughter of a concubine, the subject of concubines and their historical role in the palace presented me an opportunity to satisfy my own curiosity. Indeed, I am in the awkward position of being an object of discussion, even as I participated in the act of producing the work. My mother was a daughter of Emir Dikko of Katsina, born by a concubine, but was herself a free princess and wife. The discussions in the introductory chapter on princesses and their being produced through conquering acts, plenished in the wombs of concubines, and cultivated within palace walls to nourish the emirate through marriage, could well have applied to my own mother. As one of the emir's wives, I am also a subject in the discussions on the relationship between wives and concubines. For me, therefore, the work has a personal intensity; perhaps this intensity kept me animated and engaged throughout these long years.

A work of this nature combines information from many sources. The writer contributes experiences she has had elsewhere, inferences drawn through comparative studies, and theoretical frameworks and paradigms for sorting out and explaining the information gathered. My personal opinion (which is, for obvious reasons, not an expert one) is that Dr. Nast has done an excellent job of bringing this work to fruition and raising a number of interesting questions, shedding light on the history of the palace in an unprecedented manner. I am impressed by the manner in which she has revealed the role of women in the palace, in so doing dispelling the stereotype of the Hausa woman as an idle, disenfranchised subject with no political and economic role in traditional society. I have no doubt that this work will set the stage for further research into this interesting area of the history and society of northern Nigeria.

I congratulate Heidi for her achievement and express once more my joy and the joy of all of her sources and research assistants in the palace at the successful completion of this enterprise. I trust that this end marks a new beginning, and thus look forward to what promises to be an intriguing period of further research.

I recommend this book to all those who are interested in the result of intensive, often complex fieldwork and research that seeks to broaden the frontiers of our present knowledge.

Kano
20 November 2003

Acknowledgments

After completing my cultural geography dissertation on sociospatial changes in the Kano palace circa 1500 to 1990, I was uninspired to publish it. It was heavily empirical and emphasized the importance of geographical methodologies in eliciting new data, and it lacked theoretical verve and focus. Over the next ten years, I would sift through much unused data, reconsider the data in different theoretical ways, and eventually return to Kano (in 2000 and 2003) to discuss my ideas with palace inhabitants, palace community members outside the palace, and local scholars. Along the way, I realized that the story of concubines needed to be told, since concubines historically occupied and controlled the vast majority of palace space but were largely secluded, making their history opaque to a world of academia, which was composed largely of men. This book, then, has emerged out of the ashes of its former self, taking on much additional information and a more steadied empirical and theoretical frame.

That said, I have quite a task here: to thank the many people who helped me gather my thoughts and data over a period of fifteen years. It would be impossible to list all of those persons whose encouragement or assistance were essential to the original and later work. I will not duplicate the lengthy list of names of those who helped me in procuring dissertation materials, many of which provided background data for this study and are listed in the dissertation itself (Nast 1992). Instead, I focus on those who helped bring this particular work to fruition after the dissertation had been completed.

Most important, I thank the palace community. While I obviously did not meet every palace community member, and was undoubtedly liked by some and disliked by others, their collective patience with my persistence and their collective assistance with this work are remarkable. I am especially grateful to His Highness Alhaji Ado Bayero, who never seemed to mind my inquisitive traipsings about and my many requests for interviews; and to Hajiyya Abba Ado Bayero, a historian in her own right who helped shape the direction of this work in many ways. Sadly, most of the elders whom I had interviewed for the dissertation had passed away by the time I returned in 2000; nonetheless, I met many new people who graciously participated in new rounds of questioning, for which I am most thankful.

I also met old friends and made new ones at the Kano State History and Culture Bureau and the new Centre for Research and Documentation in Kano (CRDK), where I was invited to give a jointly sponsored seminar on my research findings in November 2000. Malam Auwalu Hamza of the CRDK was particularly gracious in arranging the logistics for this event. The scholarly input I received from both groups was invaluable in helping me to decipher key bits of palace data. Similarly, the opportunity to present some of my findings at the British Council (BC) in December 2003 as part of a jointly sponsored monthly lecture series of the BC and CRDK provided me with a great deal of local feedback. While in Kano in November 2000, I met with Philip Shea, who freely offered his thoughts about Kano palace life and about the passages of writing that I gave him to read. His scholarly thoroughness and love of writing meant that he often wrote comments superceding in quality and quantity the material I had given him to review. I could not have carried out my research in 2000 without the assistance of Rahbi, the stepdaughter of the former slave titleholder, Maje Sirdi, and I am obliged to Tahir and Diana El-Khayal for graciously lodging me in their home at this time.

In 2003 I met other persons in Kano who took a considerable amount of time to discuss the ongoing work with me, comment on a recent draft or part of the manuscript, discuss material of related interest, or collect new data. These include Alhaji Ado Sanusi, the fourth eldest son of the late Emir Sanusi (1953–63) under whom he served as the Dan Iya of Kano; Mamman Siya Abubakar, the newly hired historian for the Daura palace; His Highness Alhaji Muhammad Bashir, emir of Daura, and his first wife, Hajiyya Kilishi, whose hospitality was invaluable; and Alhaji Yusuf Maitama Sule (dan Masani), a respected Kano politician who lived in the slave household of Madakin Kano, a high-ranking aristocrat, but his grandmother was a palace *baiwa* [*sing.*

slave]. Alhaji served as a prominent northern politician, first in NEPU and then in the NPC during the First Republic. During the Second Republic, he served as Nigeria's ambassador to the United Nations. He proudly emphasized that he came from a *bayi* (slave) household and bemoaned the fact of the aristocracy's political demise. When I left his chambers after an interview, his waiting hall was filled with those seeking his advice and patronage. His Highness Alhaji Sunusi, emir of Dutse, allowed me access to the old Dutse palace where the remainder of his deceased father's household resides, in one instance leading several of us (Sadiya, Aisha, Sophia, and I) on a tour of the old palace, showing us various structures and explaining how the palace functioned historically. He later spent some hours with me discussing Dutse's relationship to Kano and helping me think through some comparative Dutse-Kano palace data; he also gave me a diskette of the data for his Web site on the history of Dutse (see www.dutse.emirate.org). I am thankful to his wife, Gaji, for her hospitality, camaraderie, and warmth at these times, and to Aisha and Sophia for introducing me to Gaji and for accompanying me (with Sadiya) during a field excursion to abandoned indigo-dyeing yards, one located along the River Jambo and the other behind the village of Limawa. I am grateful to the Babban Jakadiya Hadiza of the old Dutse palace for informing and directing us to the indigo-dyeing areas, to Sallaman Dutse's son (Bello Ismail) for taking us to those places, and to Mallam Nuhu Limawa for accompanying us to the Limawa dyeing yard and telling us about its history. Thanks also to Sallaman Dutse Muhammad Ismail for leading us on a second tour of the old Dutse palace and for answering our many questions.

Much credit must also be given to Sanusi Lamido Sanusi, grandson of former Kano emir Alhaji Sanusi (1953–63), and a scholar, intellectual, and friend whose palace landscape insights I have much valued. I prevailed on him many times to review and comment on renditions and parts of the book manuscript, in person and via e-mail. I am equally indebted to his wife, Sadiya Ado Bayero, in whose home I stayed in 2003 and who became a close friend. She accompanied me on fieldwork trips to Daura, Dutse, and Limawa, leavening our times with humor and anecdotes about palace life and history. She also worked with me during many palace interviews, helping to videotape certain parts of the palace landscape.

Many others challenged me to think with greater rigor and to write with greater ease. I am indebted to the Social Theory members at the University of Kentucky, where I held a postdoctoral fellowship in geography from 1992 to 1994. I am especially grateful to John Paul Jones, Susan Roberts, Rich Schein, and Dick Ulack for their intellectual stimulation and support. It was at the University of Kentucky that I began to think about centering this book around state formation and royal concubinage. Since 1998 I have been fortunate to be a fellow at Northwestern University's Program of African Studies (PAS), one of whose perks has been my own small office in one of the best African-ist libraries in North America. I am thankful to Jane Guyer, who was director of PAS in 1998, and to her successors, David Schoenbrun and Richard Joseph, for renewing annually my fellow status. I presented two papers dealing with this work at PAS lunchtime seminars and gave an evening seminar for the University of Chicago's African Studies Workshop; all resulting input was appreciated and formative. I am especially indebted to John Hunwick, whom I first met in 1989 through John Lavers, and who has periodically checked in with me, taking considerable interest in my progress and work. Similarly, I thank Sean O'Fahey, a visiting professor at PAS who took a great deal of time out of his own research schedule to discuss my work regularly. Most of all, I thank LaRay Denzer, who read many early versions of this work and was a bulwark of constructive criticism and support. She encouraged me to think through my findings in comparative regional context.

I also appreciate the feedback of Hausa scholars at the interdisciplinary colloquium "Identity and Marginality in West Africa: Historical and Anthro-pological Perspectives on Hausa Society," organized in 2001 by Adeline Mas-quelier and Steven Pierce at Tulane University and of scholars of royal court women at the interdisciplinary colloquium, "Palace Women around the World," organized in 2004 by Anne Walthall at the University of California Irvine. The colloquia allowed me to present earlier renditions of chapters 1 and 2 respectively, and to engage collectively with scholars working in related areas.

Others have provided long-distance encouragement. I thank Michael Mortimore and Jay Spaulding, who read early drafts of this work and offered wonderfully in-depth commentary. I am additionally thankful to Jan Hogen-dorn for his comments concerning certain of my hypotheses about grain tax-ation. Carrie Mullen of the University of Minnesota Press provided strong guidance throughout, for which I am most grateful. Thanks also to her assis-tant, Jason Weidemann.

I am particularly indebted to the College of Liberal Arts and Sciences and to DePaul University's University Research Council for giving me significant amounts of monies over the years to return to Nigeria to carry out new work and to prepare this manuscript for publication. I completed the later field-work and writing during several leave periods between 1998 and 2003. Tahir and Diana El-Khayal graciously lodged me in their home during my field-work tenure in Kano in 2000, while Sadiya and Sanusi Lamido Sanusi did so during my 2003 stay.

When I was first conducting fieldwork in 1988, my dissertation supervi-sor at McGill University in Montreal, the economic geographer John Bradbury, died unexpectedly. He was a remarkable man, capable of guiding new graduate students in ways that were inspiring and affirming. I have never forgotten his gentle ways and his commitment to use his skills to work for social justice. Even though I moved away from economic geography toward more cultural interests, John supported and encouraged me, his calming ways inspiring me long after his untimely death. I hope one day to become as inspiring a teacher as he was.

That same year, I was fortunate to meet Professor John Lavers. Like John Bradbury, John Lavers supported and encouraged my work, taking much time to review my field data and to discuss with me his own ideas about the palace, suggesting readings and mentoring me thoughtfully. Given my advisor's death, I was especially soothed and stimulated intellectually by his acumen and kindness. I have often reflected on his encouragement when I doubted the feasibility of this present study and was much saddened after he, too, died at a young age.

I met Professor Nehemia Levtzion in 1997 when he served as discussant for an African Studies Association panel where I gave a paper (Nast 1996). Like John Bradbury and John Lavers, he read my work thoroughly and engaged with it receptively and considerately. Over the years he kept in sporadic contact and he would later become one of several readers for this manuscript. His thoughtful and scholarly style motivated me to finish the final necessary revisions. I am indebted to each of these three men for teaching me that social science scholarship is about people and that scholarship and scholars are best cultivated mindfully and with care.

While there are many people to consider and thank, my gratitude should not be taken to imply that any of the persons mentioned here agrees with me in whole or even in part. Rather, I express my indebtedness to those who took the time to engage and to challenge.

Prologue

T his work presents a historical geographical account of royal concubinage in the monumental palace of Kano, Nigeria, built circa 1500 and
today inhabited by over one thousand persons (see Figure 1). The text
is based on extensive field research in the Kano palace between 1988 and 2003.
The palace of Kano is the largest in existence in West Africa and the most
important of its kind. When first built, it hosted about fifteen hundred persons
and was designed specifically as an Islamic place, serving as a key geographical
node for the dispersion of Islamic political culture, however syncretically, into
the region. Accordingly, Islamic seclusion, royal concubinage, and eunuchism,
all typical of extant sultanates, were implemented on a massive scale in the
palace interior. At the time, Kano, Fez, and Cairo were the three most important cities of Africa, Kano later evolving into the leading commercial entrepot
of Hausaland, a region extending from southern Niger into central Nigeria,
and from Cameroon westward toward Dahomey (Sutton 1979).

The work is pioneering in several overlapping ways. First, the work
demonstrates how *human geographical methods* can be developed and used in
contexts such as the Kano palace, where no archaeological work has been
accomplished and no relevant primary sources exist, to elicit new sources and
data about the past. Aerial photographs of the palace and city, for instance,

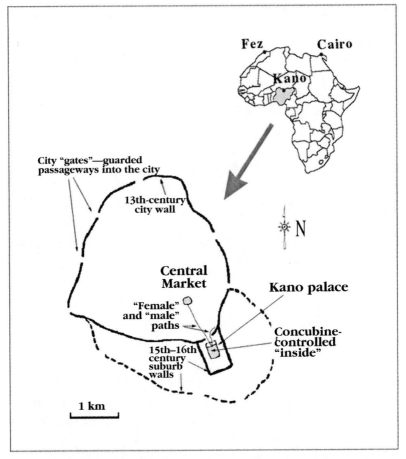

Figure 1. Kano, Nigeria: city walls in the sixteenth century. The palace was built as a rectangular suburb onto the preexisting circular city walls.

were examined to discern how settlement patterns changed over time, while detailed field mapping of all interior place names and structures in the palace, including ruins, was used to discern gendered differences in the naming, historical use, and cultural coding of palace space. These methods are especially important given the vast areal extent of the palace, a walled enclosure measuring nearly 260 meters in width and 540 meters in length, within which hundreds of structures are situated. Dozens of palace community members from different age groups worked intensively with me (in the field research and in my writing) to help reconstruct how the landscape of concubinage changed over the centuries.

The book is similarly pioneering in its *theoretical* premise, namely, that in agrarian-based state contexts reproduction moves history. The text subsequently begins by questioning who fed the palace population, a question heretofore not addressed, a few scholars instead asserting (in passing) that agricultural slave estates were dedicated to state needs, as embodied in the palace, or that Kano's early state revenues consisted of a grain tax. My work, in contrast, studies the logistics and geopolitical importance of feeding one thousand to two thousand persons daily. Drawing on my detailed ethnographic work and mapping data, for example, I assemble considerable human geographical evidence that concubines were key players in the assessment and collection of the state's primary tax, grain, and that they constituted a complex and powerful hierarchy that managed grain proceeds and marketing. The data also show that royal concubines served as territorial representatives of the place from where they were initially taken as prisoners of war, providing important links between capital and conquered hinterland. Royal concubines and their natal place additionally had much to gain from the fact that Islamic law guaranteed freedom to concubine children, meaning that any concubine son could become king (many did) and any of their children could be used in political marriages.

A third pioneering aspect of the work has to do with the new *empirical finds* occasioned by the geographical method. Through mapping exercises, for instance, I located an extensive indigo dyeing field in the concubine section of the palace and documented palace practices linking indigo symbolically to royalty and female fertility, associations common in other parts of West and North Africa. The data controversially suggest that royal concubines monopolized indigo cloth dyeing as early as the sixteenth century, overseeing its production in the palace confines and using the cloth initially as a political currency circulated among regional courts and persons of importance. Heretofore, it has been assumed that indigo cloth dyeing in the region was a nineteenth-century affair run solely for economic purposes by men. My work instead shows that dyeing was a much older and symbolically laden endeavor wrested away from royal women and placed squarely in the male public and commercial domain centuries later. By thus reassessing the importance of reproduction and, particularly, fecundity in state imaginaries and practices situated in agrarian places, a different history of state formation emerges, one guided by practical considerations of, for example, food production and the geopolitics of royal marriages and local systems of exchange.

While state concubinage was from the outset a formidable political institution, it has largely been ignored in scholarly accounts of state formational processes in Hausaland. Part of the oversight in Kano has to do with the fact that, even today, royal women are secluded strictly in the palace interior and accessible only to other women (or children), such persons having, first, to pass through guarded labyrinths to reach them. Today, eleven concubines remain—all of slave descent—nothing comprehensive having been written about them. This book, in contradistinction, shows how geopolitically central the institution of concubinage was, and that it strongly shaped state imaginaries, rituals, and symbolic practices for over five hundred years. By offering a distinct political economic and cultural geographical account of the rise and place of royal concubinage in the sixteenth century and its subsequent decline over the following centuries, I resist the marginalization of women in normative accounts of African geopolitics and history.

My work complements that of many scholars operating across a number of fields. Most notably, it builds upon the scholarship of Edna Bay (1998) on royal wives in the Abomey palace of the West African kingdom of Dahomey in the eighteenth and nineteenth centuries and Nakanyike Musisi's (1991) pathbreaking work on elite polygyny and state formation in Buganda. My work also builds upon that of Beverly Mack (1988, 1991, 1992) and Rufa'i (1987) on nineteenth- and twentieth-century royal women in Kano, and on that in Flora Kaplan's (1997b) edited collection on women's powers in Africa, primarily, though not exclusively, in the twentieth century. At the same time, the work is inspired by Ifi Amadiume (1997), who retheorizes matriarchy in Africa, generally, and asks us to place more analytical attention on acephalous, agrarian contexts. This project builds upon Musisi's and Amadiume's by looking at centralizing states dependent on agriculture, using geographical methods to extend the historical reach of scholarship on women in West Africa centuries further into the past.

Geography Matters

Geography as a discipline is not well understood by nongeographers, perhaps because it spans such a wide swath of the human and physical sciences and because it is limited in the popular imagination to maps and map-making. Moreover, in the United States at least, geography is not mandated to be offered as part of elementary or high school curricula, being subsumed under the rhetoric of social studies. Between the 1960s and 1990s, the discipline went into decline, many geography departments being closed or threatened with closure.[1] Popular and academic ignorance of the discipline is abetted by the commercial sector, most bookstores, for example, not having distinct geography sections. Most books written by geographers are instead shelved under anthropology, cultural studies, political science, history, meteorology, geology, and the like. Geography and geographers are hence obscured in popular and academic imaginations, especially in the United States, despite the fact that geographical research has had a tremendous impact on physical and social science scholarship.

Because so much of this book's content and methodology center on geography and spatial analysis, and because of popular confusion in the United States about what constitutes geography, it is important to state from the outset how and why this work is a geographical one. The primary engine behind the sequencing of events reproduced here, for example, is not historical questioning per se. Rather the work grows out of spatial questions concerning landscape changes in a remarkable West African place—the royal interior of the massive Islamic palace of Kano. Accordingly, aerial photographs, settlement pattern maps, and field maps of palace landscape features, including palace ruins, architectural styles, floor topographies, and place names (varying over time and along lines of gender) were analyzed for spatial characteristics. Likewise, ethnographic data, local myths, primary and secondary sources, and linguistic data were mined for clues into spatial change over time. I also conducted a cursory comparative study of the nearby Dutse palace of Dutse emirate, a palace built in 1807 with a sociospatial layout strikingly similar to the Kano palace. My reliance on spatial information proved crucial in developing new, if unfamiliar, sources with which to interpret life in the palace-core of what was then the early city-state of Kano. The new sources are especially important since no archaeological work has ever been done on the palace, inhabited since it was first built.

Wherever possible, the data were sifted, sorted through, and interpreted with the help of numerous community members. These included sons and daughters of the last precolonial ruler, Emir Aliyu (1894–1903), children and concubines of the first colonial ruler, Emir Abbas (1903–19), and the concubines, wives, servants, and children of subsequent emirships, especially those of His Highness Emir Ado Bayero. His Highness Alhaji Nuhu Muhammad Sanusi of Dutse Emirate and his Sallama (a leading palace slave titleholder, traditionally a eunuch) provided me with information about the landscape of, and concubines' sociospatial organization in, the old Dutse palace. Elderly women there directed me to places nearby wherein were located the remains of extensive dyeing yards run historically by women.

In all cases, analysis of the landscape was geared toward discerning how social and political relations were expressed spatially and how they changed over time. In contrast to, say, a historian, I asked questions such as: Who/what is located where and to whom/what are they connected? What is the name of this place and what is the logic of its name? Did the name change over time? And if so, why? What practices or rituals were carried out in this place? What spatial associations does this place hold for different social groups? Who uses a particular place—and how, when, and why? Who is advantaged or disadvantaged by a particular spatial placement? How does the organization of a landscape (or portion thereof) work to channel social practices, allowing certain interactions to occur with ease and others not? What happens when a particular nodal place of social interaction and production is disrupted? How is this disruption evinced in the landscape? Who precisely was/is affected? How? Why? Why is the architectural style of this structure older than the styles surrounding it? Why is the ground floor of this structure so much deeper than the floor heights of surrounding structures? This human geographical questioning was bolstered by years of geological training and field mapping, the methods of both disciplines working to educe new facts about royal concubine life in Kano city-state over a five-hundred-year period, circa 1500 to 2000.

The data show that the symbolic economy and material sustenance of Kano as a nascent city-state centered around concubine bodies, lives, and practices. Over the next three centuries, the importance of concubinage waned, in part as a result of a nineteenth-century Islamic reform movement led by the Fulani. Concubine fortunes declined further during British colonial rule (1903–60) and after postindependence. This study presents spatial evidence for this rise and decline, in the process providing important new details about concubinage and the royal workings of a key polity in West Africa over a *longue durée*. The work temporally and empirically broadens the horizon of scholarship on women and gender relations in West African royal or state contexts, the majority of which addresses the nineteenth and twentieth centuries (e.g., Awe 1992; Coles and Mack 1991; Johnson 1937 [1921]; Kaplan 1997b; Lovejoy 1988, 1990; Mack 1988; Matory 1994; and Sweetman 1984; but see Bay 1998; Kaplan 1997a; and Lebeuf 1969).

The study questions how childbearing and palace food production activities, controlled by royal concubines who were linked to grain tribute and taxation processes, were collectively essential to geopolitical consolidation and centralization. The pivotal importance of kinship ties to the hinterland and food production in the growth of Kano city-state and, by implication, the importance of concubines and grain taxation has been largely overlooked in studies of regional state formational processes. Thus this work provides new data with which to begin comparative work on state concubinage, gender relations and slavery in Hausaland, and other early centralized Saharan and Southwest Asian state formational contexts (e.g., Necipoglu 1991; O'Fahey 1980; Spaulding 1985).[2]

Circuitous Beginnings

I gained access to the palace community in a circuitous way. I arrived in Kano in 1988 as a geologist about to begin doctoral fieldwork in human geography on the backward and forward economic linkages of a Nigerian national brick works program geared toward low-income housing provision. I anticipated working closely with the Nigerian Mining Corporation, the parastatal organization responsible for mining clay minerals needed in manufacturing bricks. Never having visited Kano before, I unexpectedly found myself drawn to the beauty of the adobe-based structures in the old walled city of Kano, rather than the brickworks. Geologist and geographer, I was struck by the many ways in which the sixty-year British colonial presence had so clearly and forcefully imprinted itself spatially and architecturally on the old city, disrupting and insinuating itself into the fabric, rhythm, and material substance of old city life.

But the crookedness of the story begins even before this. While first en route to Kano from Montreal (where I was a doctoral student at McGill University), via London, our plane experienced electrical problems. Though halfway to our destination, we were forced to return to London's Heathrow Airport. Upon deplaning, I met a fellow passenger, a young Lebanese woman, Rebecca Abd, related through her maternal grandfather, Joseph Raccah, to Miriam Sielah, who until recently cooked the evening Ramadan meals for the titular Islamic rulers of Kano, including Abdullahi Bayero (1926–52), Muhammad Sanusi (1953–63), and His Highness Emir Ado Bayero (1963–).[3] We continued our Kano-bound journey together and kept in regular touch with one another for two years thereafter.

About two months after my arrival, impressed by the magnitude of colonial changes I observed in the old city, I decided to change my research direction and study them. With this in mind, it became important for me to ask permission from the emir to enter and work in the city, his traditional stronghold. Despite the rescindment of traditional rulers' formal powers after national independence in 1960, the emir holds considerable political and cultural urban and regional sway. Moreover, the palace was central to the history and political processes of colonial change.

Rebecca kindly arranged for me to visit Miriam Sielah, known affectionately in the palace as Uwar Gida or Titi Raccah, who quickly saw to it that I had a formal audience with the emir. On the appointed day, accompanied by Miriam's Libyan husband and Rebecca's Lebanese servant, we met in the most massive of the several throne chambers, Soron Ingila (Hall of England), built more than fifty years earlier after the emir's precursor and father visited England. Today it is used for audiences with foreign dignitaries and other persons seeking official sponsorship or help. The emir welcomed the work, consequently giving me permission to work in the old city. The titleholder, Madakin Kano, was put in charge of arranging for me to interview knowledgeable builders and titleholders in the old city for an initial survey. Six months later, I returned to Montreal, having finished preliminary work on the historical geography of Kano city.

Another unexpected twist in the research direction occurred early on during my second visit to Kano in the fall of 1988 after I entered the office of the emir's private secretary located in the public area of the palace. I intended to deliver, through him, a greeting from a U.S.-based scholar to one of the emir's wives, Hajiyya Abba. At that time, Hajiyya was the third most senior wife (Islamic law allows a man to have up to four wives). Hajiyya's grandmother had been a concubine-slave of Emir Diko in the Katsina palace, in Katsina city, the center of a historically rivalrous city-state northwest of Kano city. In Islam, concubine children are freeborn; hence, Hajiyya's mother was a freeborn princess, a royal daughter.

As I sat in the secretary's office writing a message to Hajiyya on a piece of paper that would eventually be carried to her quarters in the palace interior, her soon-to-be son-in-law entered and introduced himself, Sanusi Lamido Sanusi, a grandson of the former emir of Kano, Muhammad Sanusi. When he heard that I was writing to Her Highness, he insisted that I greet her personally. We left the public area of the palace and entered one of two guarded palace labyrinths emptying out into the most extensive part of the palace, the secluded interior of royal women and children; this was an area off-limits to adult men and most visitors. I was immediately struck by what I saw: massive and intricately detailed traditional structures and a relatively quiet, if busy and intense, life of royal women and children.

For centuries, royal wives have served as patronesses to female visitors and strangers to the city, accommodating, counseling, and assisting a plethora of often very cosmopolitan visitors. Hajiyya Abba was thus perhaps more prepared than I was for our first meeting, and we visited for some time. As I left she asked if there was any way she could assist me in the research. Given that no geographical research had been done on the palace, I asked her about the possibilities of studying the palace landscape and changes to it over time, something in which Hajiyya herself expressed interest. Hajiyya would later be instrumental in helping me to obtain a second audience with the emir, whereupon I was given permission to map the palace interior comprehensively and to study its spatial history.

What I thought would be a relatively circumscribed study of the palace past, eventually linked into a larger study of the old city, became something much less manageable and more significant. From its outset, the palace had been a complicated node of political leadership and control, such that changes in its interior were tied to political and cultural changes well beyond the palace's confines. For the next year and a half, I collected many stories and materials about palace life. And over the next ten years I would rethink my data in a comparative context, one centered on concubines and early states. In 1999 I began writing a work that centered on concubines, by now convinced that the story of this early city-state emerged out of an agrarian context in which fertility of women and earth were key parts of the state imaginary.

In November 2000 I returned to Kano to discuss my interpretation of the data with Nigeria-based colleagues and members of the palace community. Once again, Hajiyya Abba became a central player, listening patiently while I read out loud to her most of an initial manuscript draft. Where she disagreed with an interpretation, we stopped at length to argue and discuss it, for the most part coming to some sort of consensus or an explicit agreement to disagree. We decided to signal our divergent interpretations in the final text via a note outlining our positions. Where she or I felt we needed more data, we suspended reading the text until we could find evidence to support an argument one way or the other. Typically, this involved doing additional fieldwork in the palace or the city and its environs, or our interviewing persons who might be able to offer crucial bits of information. Overall, it was a very heartening and exciting time, since the spatial information I had collated previously pointed to stories that for her and others seemed to make a lot of cultural sense and which became largely vindicated by our work.

Sanusi Lamido Sanusi and his wife, Hajiyya Sadiya Ado Bayero, were instrumental in helping me carry out additional work in 2003. Malam Sanusi read and commented on most of the book chapters, offering important correctives and additional information, a process of overview that he commenced months prior to my visit and continued up to weeks before the work went to press. Moreover, Hajiyya Sadiya accompanied and assisted me in fieldtrips to Dutse, Daura, and the two rural women's dyepit sites in rural Dutse. She accommodated me in her Kano home where we consistently discussed and debated the significance of the data, with her offering many insights into palace life and the work at hand.

Book Organization

Each chapter is organized around a particular finding that allowed previously collected and somewhat fragmentary data to fall into some kind of geographically coherent place. Chapter 1, for example, is structured around the moment when I discerned sixteenth-century pathways connecting the palace-suburb to the city on aerial photographs. These connections helped me to establish baseline landscape features of the first palace layout, something important for temporally and historically situating other relevant information, especially that involving the orientation of the palace when it was first built and the presence and placement of palace grain treasuries destroyed during the colonial period. Chapter 2 is more historically and empirically wide-ranging in that it speaks to the importance, and limits, of spatial data, picking apart in some detail two empirical finds: a eunuch colony built in the late

1500s adjacent to the king's quarters in the palace interior, and an extensive indigo dyeing yard in the royal women's area that may have been operated by female slaves or eunuchs on behalf of concubines as early as the 1500s.

Chapters 3 and 4 center around changes that occurred in the nineteenth century, signaled by a dramatic change in the gendered composition of palace grain hierarchies and the shutting down of the palace dyeing yard. These changes occurred following the Islamic holy war or jihad led by an ethnic group having pastoral origins, the Fulani. Following their occupation of Kano, they instituted numerous changes in the royal landscape. The first part of the nineteenth century hence saw the dissolution of assumedly non-Islamic Hausa sites in the palace (chapter 3), while the second half of the century saw their re-emergence and re-elaboration in a political context wherein concubine powers were somewhat revived but still much reduced (chapter 4). In particular, the palace concubine area was halved, the excised area reassigned to a palace cemetery (built atop the former dyeing yard) and to male slaves, including a cadre of male slaves who partially usurped concubine authority over grains, the novelty of the cadre raising questions as to who held grain responsibilities in the past.

British colonization (1903–60) hastened the demise of concubinage, a theme developed in chapter 5. In integrating the Nigerian economy with that of Britain, they mandated that taxes be paid in pounds sterling, in the process outlawing payments of taxes to the Crown in cowries and grains.[4] By stripping the emir of the right to wage war, one of the main sources for concubines (prisoners of war) disappeared. At the same time, colonial abolition of slavery made it difficult to locate a second major source of concubines: the female children of former slave women, children still considered to hold slave status and therefore legitimately (according to Islamic precedents) enslave-able. Concubinage, though reduced in extent, continued during the colonial period, British officials effectively ignoring it as a form of slavery. Nonetheless, palace concubinage went into decline, its demise paralleling the diminishment of royal entitlements, authority, and power.

Finally, the conclusion describes the structural remnants of palace concubine life today, and conjectures what sort of future palace concubines have. I also suggest ways for retheorizing the centrality of concubines in state formational processes in agrarian contexts.

Fieldwork Resources

Fieldwork was carried out over a twenty-two-month period in Kano between February 1988 and August 1990 and during two month-long visits in November 2000 and November and December 2003. Certain sociospatial characteristics of the palace and city of Kano lent themselves well to historical geographical inquiry. Besides the fact that the palace and old city had strikingly different formal geometries—the city circular, the palace rectangular (Figure 1)—aerial photographs indicate that the high walls surrounding the palace date from circa 1500, forming a remarkable baseline of historical-material continuity within which to work.

In working to identify changes in the sociospatial organization of the palace landscape I benefited much from architectural plans of the palace, drawn by Bello Nuhu Ahmed (1988), a northern Nigerian architectural student. Disallowed entry into parts of the palace interior, Ahmed approximated the disposition of some interior structures using aerial photographs and inside palace contacts. Similarly, Mrs. Rufa'i's 1987 study on palace life provided useful information with which I could work, including a census of present-day palace inhabitants (see Table 1) and an overview of contemporary palace slave hierarchies. I include Rufa'i's table here to demonstrate the continued vitality and size of the present-day palace community.

I also profited from the photographic resources of Kenting Air Photos, a Canadian aerial photograph company with an office in Kano, where I obtained aerial photographic maps of the palace and city. And, in London, colonial photographs in the archives of the Royal Geographical Society (RGS) and the Foreign Commonwealth Office Library proved invaluable to the research, many of the photographs of the city and palace not yet catalogued, identified, or documented. Early on I ordered copies of relevant RGS photographs, these consequently forming the basis for individual and group discussions with elderly palace inhabitants. The most valuable photographs were those taken in 1903 after Kano's defeat, when Lord Lugard temporarily set up office inside the palace. Almost all of the photographed structures no longer exist, yet were identifiable by elderly women and men residing in, or associated with, the palace.

A plethora of methods were used in the collection, analysis, and interpretation of data. Fifty to sixty persons collectively helped in data collection and interpretation. Largely through Hajiyya's assistance and social network, I worked with roughly ten young persons in various capacities as field assistants, mostly but not all royalty. These included Hajiyya's three daughters (Salamatu, Zaineb, and Sadiya), a daughter (Hasiya) of the then first wife (Hajiyya Maryam Odé), a son (Ujudu Sanusi) of the previous emir Sanusi, one of Sanusi's grandsons (Sanusi Lamido Sanusi), and several persons associated with the palace slave community. These persons collectively helped me arrange interviews and think through what sorts of resources were available; they were also immensely helpful in carrying out the logistics of mapping and in helping me document the details of the palace interior.

Rather than pursuing a single method, I focused on particular spatial questions, pursuing responses to these in whatever methodological manner I

Table 1. Census of palace inhabitants

Kofar Arewa, the Northern Area

	Female	Male	
Adults	111	100	
Children	181	194	
Total	**292**	**294**	**(586 persons)**

Kofar Kudu, the Southern Area

	Female	Male	
Adults	89	93	
Children	139	146	
Total	**228**	**239**	**(467 persons)**

Cikin Gida, the Interior Area

	Female	Male	
Sarki/Emir (the king or emir)		1	
Wives	4		
Sadaku (concubines)	16		
Children[a]	60	54	
'Yan Fulani (elderly royal women)	24		
Kuyangi (unpaid domestic servants of slave descent)[b]	16		
Matan fada (concubines of former kings or emirs who chose to remain in the palace even though they bore children and are juridically free after their husband's death)[c]	19		
Slaves[d]	27		
Jakadu (unpaid guards and messengers of slave descent)	8		
Old women	7		
Total	**181**	**55**	**(236 persons)**
Grand total	**701**	**588**	**(1,289 persons)**

Source: Rufa'i (1987).

[a] *In 2000, several royal daughters counted the number of the emir's children and informed me that he has 69, not 114, children. I was told that it was inappropriate to ask an emir outright how many children he has, since he is symbolically understood as the father of all. Perhaps royal women inflated their numbers to impress Rufa'i, or she may have confused the many children who come to play in the palace as palace inhabitants.*
[b] *Rufa'i (1995, 178) defines kuyangi as "female slaves of the palace," a definition with which I am largely in agreement. I might add that kuyangi were traditionally slaves who carried out more rigorous chores, and it is debatable whether kuyangi would be considered slaves today.*
[c] *If a concubine does not bear her master a child, she remains a slave and can be inherited by the next emir if he is not the former emir's son, father, or uncle.*
[d] *I am uncertain here as to whom Rufa'i (1995) is referring, as kuyangi and jakadu are the main female slave categories in the palace ciki.*

could improvise or develop. The study was integrated into the lives of many palace inhabitants, however marginally, because the emir had given me permission to work inside the palace interior and because of the personal relationships I developed with community members. What this meant is that the research process rarely felt as though it was under my control. I might begin to interview an elder, for example, and one of her friends might enter, actively joining in. Or an elder with whom I was talking might announce she was tired and get up and leave. I can also recall two fieldtrips with elders who became visibly disdainful about the long time it was taking me to sketch and record details about ruins they were pointing out to me. In both cases, they exasperatedly left me far behind. When the research took a sudden empirical turn upon finding new evidence, as it did when I began to document nineteenth-century palace pastoral activities, some female elders became skeptical or chastised me for going off in yet another different direction, admonishing me that at the rate I was going I would never finish.

Hajiyya, having historical interests of her own, became driven by the research questions and pursued certain questions of interest after I had left for the day. Hence, often she would arrange for appropriately knowledgeable persons to visit her quarters for formal discussions with us. I would then be introduced and "told" what we were doing, when, and why. Her initiative, skills, and intellectual acuity in these contexts were invaluable to the study.

Group discussions were the most lively and informative. They involved minor and major disagreements, collective processes of memory jogging, and the expressing of different speaking and knowledge positions that reflected variability in age, stature, personality, and experience. Group discussions were largely limited to the women's domain and tended to involve all sorts of persons, many of whom might be there just to listen. Such discussions led me in unanticipated research directions. In contrast, the men I interviewed were rarely interrupted in the continual way women were, be it by visitors, children, cooking chores, itinerant trading, and so on. Thus, my interviews with men were more temporally linear and perhaps more thematically focused. Most times I recorded interviews, but not always. Sometimes impromptu discussions would emerge and I would have to run and find a paper and pen to record as best I could. And often, I would be shown places and things involving forays impossible to capture on tape. In these contexts, I summarized, mapped, sketched in notebooks, photographed, and/or in 2003 videotaped, where possible annotating along the way or soon after the fact, usually the same day.

Upon reflection, I see that the nonlinearity of the work brought me to think through the geography of the palace in a "nodal" way, that is, to see a particular place, person, object, or body part as a node through which all sorts of practices, meanings, politics, and economies passed (Nast 2001). I hope that this book captures some of the ways that geography complicates our thinking about sociospatial processes and meanings in an agrarian context wherein reproduction shaped the geopolitics of state formation and cultural change. I hope the work also points to the impossibility of mapping out any essentialized trajectory of Islam over the centuries. Instead, it explores how Islamically syncretic social and spatial practices played out dynamically over time as discerned within the limits of my person, time, and place.

Introduction

Royal concubinage in the West African city-state of Kano, in what is today northern Nigeria, was a historically formidable institution that is today largely defunct. In the 1500s and 1600s royal concubines numbered in the hundreds, were organized into complex labor hierarchies, and collectively—if indirectly—commanded considerable power throughout the state. Concubine power derived from concubines' centrality in a primarily agrarian world that celebrated and depended upon fertility, both human and earthly; from the disparate knowledges that they brought with them; and from the many activities they carried out in reproducing the royal household, a control center of the early state. The emergence of state-supported concubinage coincided with Kano becoming one of the three most important sixteenth-century cities in Africa, alongside Fez and Cairo, a coincidence that I argue was foundational to the city-state. By the late 1500s, Kano was a center of power and learning linked into trans-Saharan networks of the Islamic world.

The emergence of large-scale state concubinage of Kano was tied to the elaboration of a slave-based administrative hierarchy of the state in which eunuchs were key. Such slave institutions emerged after the Islamic palace-exurb of Kano city was built circa 1500. The palace was the first state center

1

to be built in the region, effectively anchoring the city-state to one place, allowing for centralized territorial and political control. It also hosted a royal stable out of which the first state cavalry system developed. Secondary evidence suggests that a similar kind of Islamic palace existed in sixteenth-century Gao, the capital city of the Songhay empire, though the palace no longer exists. Leo Africanus, writing circa 1510, indicates that

> [t]he king has a special palace set aside for a huge number of wives, concubines, slaves and eunuchs assigned to watch over these women. He also has a sizeable guard of horsemen and foot soldiers armed with bows. Between the public and private gates of his palace there is a large courtyard surrounded by a wall. On each side of this courtyard a loggia serves as audience chamber. Although the king personally handles all his affairs, he is assisted by numerous functionaries, such as secretaries, councilors, captains and intendants [sic]. (Hunwick n.d., 1)[1]

There is presently no way to discern which palace was built first, or if one inspired the other. The Abomey palace of the kingdom of Dahomey may have existed as early as the 1710s, though little is known of its architecture or layout (Bay 1998, 27, 40).[2] What is known is that thousands of women governed the Abomey palace along with lesser numbers of slave men and eunuchs, all collectively known as *ahosi* or wives. The term did not connote conjugality, but subservience to the king, a kingly ahosi being any person "owned" by the king, including artisans (male or female) he might bring to the kingdom to serve him.

In contrast to a dearth of information on early Sudanic palaces, considerable historical detail exists concerning the Islamic palace that may have served partially as a template for the Kano palace: the massive (nearly 600,000 square meter), rectangularly shaped Topkapi palace built by Sultan Mehmed II in Constantinople following that city's defeat in 1453 (Necipoglu 1991). Founded in 1459, Topkapi would become the early ruling center of the Ottoman universe some forty years before the founding of the palace at Kano. As in the Kano context, the palace was commissioned to be built along with a new mosque and was to be so magnificent that it "should outshine all and be more marvelous than the preceding palaces in looks, size, cost and gracefulness" (Necipoglu 1991, 8). And like the Kano palace, the Topkapi palace was home to numerous concubines and eunuchs who at times wielded considerable geopolitical influence, though not enough historical information is available to make detailed comparisons.[3] While much is known about Topkapi's internal layout and history, little is known about concubine divisions of labor or the political life of concubines.

This study, by comparison, explores the details of Kano concubinage in the context of the palace's changing historical layout. It centers on the political importance of state-sponsored concubinage in the Kano palace where for the first time a separate and massive interior place of Islamic seclusion was created within which the royal family, including concubines, lived and for centuries flourished. As O'Fahey and Spaulding point out, "The veneration and seclusion of the monarch, the concealment of his bodily functions, and the belief that he bestows life upon his subjects, or withholds it, are all beliefs common to the broader conceptual pattern of Sudanic kingship," making kingly seclusion not peculiar to Islam (1974, 18).[4] What Islam allowed for was a transregional religious codification of concubinage and concubine seclusion on a large scale for patriarchal state purposes, especially geopolitical consolidation and control over biological, political, cultural, and social reproduction. Concubine children, for instance, could be used in marriages to forge territorial alliances, since Islamic law dictated that concubine children were freeborn; hence the children of palace concubines were princes and princesses, as were the children of freeborn wives.[5] And royal concubines helped collect, organize, distribute, and use the proceeds of the first form of state tax: grain. There is also evidence that some palace concubines served as informal representatives of the territories from which they were seized and, conversely, as sources of information about those places. Concubinage became central, moreover, to a political imaginary based on royal patrimonial rights over food, kingly provisioning of food being emblematic of the right to rule. Through their control and political use of state grains, in particular, royal concubines expressed kingly provisioning powers at a scale heretofore unknown. By contrast, Islam would make few inroads into everyday vernacular life of city and countryside until the nineteenth and twentieth centuries.

The largeness of the area lived in and controlled by Kano's royal concubines indicates that the palace exurb was the largest material marker of state acceptance of Islam. Providing over 140,000 square meters for monumental religious expression, the palace was a massive theater wherein the political cultural centrality of Islamicized, patriarchal state control over reproduction and knowledge was staged. Thus, while concubinage had existed in various forms in the region for centuries prior to Islam, Islam codified and elaborated upon the institution in ways that allowed for monumental politicized expression of it across the Saharan region.[6]

Kano palace's royal concubines realized their powers through the overlaying of Islamic laws regarding concubinage onto pre-existing cultural codes and customs, allowing the state to accumulate, centralize, and use women's fertility and knowledge resources in instrumental ways. At the same time, the laws gave concubinage an institutional permanence that allowed for a great amount of flexibility and creativity within it, the institution, of course, changing dynamically along with Islamic sensibilities over the centuries. As in any agrarian context, fertility was especially valued, as indeed was the case for most precolonial non-Islamic groups throughout West Africa (e.g., Amadiume 1997).[7] Yet, while both non-Islamic and Islamic groups prized female fertility, Islam opened up new ways for the state to capitalize on it in particularly patriarchal ways and for women to utilize it for their own agendas (Amadiume 1997).

Islamic rules concerning concubinage in Kano were taken both directly from the Koran and from the tenets of the Maliki School, especially the rules codified by the renowned North African scholar of Maliki jurisprudence, Sidi Khalil in his work, the *Mukhtasar*.[8] Here, explicit legal and status distinctions were outlined differentiating between the persons of freeborn wives and concubines. Most importantly, only four wives could be married by a single man (Sura IV.3),[9] whereas any number of concubines could be owned, with the proviso that an owner be able to provide adequately for all of them.[10] Concubines who bore children held at least one advantage over wives. A master could not divorce the former (they were not technically married) and he was bound to provide adequately for a concubine until her death, barring bankruptcy.[11] In contrast, a man could divorce his wife, whether or not she had borne him a child.[12] Concubines who bore their master a child also held an edge over other kinds of slaves: By law, they were to be freed upon their master's death. As written in the *Mukhtasar*, "The slave who has become a mother by the act of her master is known in law as *umm walad*, 'the mother of offspring,' and has henceforth the right to enfranchisement on the death of her master and as a first charge on his estate. . . . The status of 'mother of offspring' is established from the moment that the father has acknowledged his child" (Ruxton 1916, 368).[13]

The juridical status of the children of concubines is of great importance, especially in the context of Kano palace life where concubines were in abundance and served the state indirectly and directly. Concubine children were legally born free, assuming their father's status instead of the slave status of their mother, a fact with profound political and territorial implications (below). Yet it is key to recall that these considerable rewards (freedom upon the master's death and the automatic freedom of their children) applied only to those women who bore children. Those who could not or did not could legally be inherited, given away, or sold.

The premising of concubine prerogatives on childbirth belies the importance children held in an Islamicizing state context where paternity and ownership of persons were central to structuring a new *paterfamilias* and asserting male control over childbearing resources. For in order for a slave woman to gain the rights and status of a concubine, she had to be impregnated by *her owner*. If a slave woman were to be impregnated by any other man—slave or free—she and her children remained the owner's property, saleable and inheritable after the master's death. In this way, Islamic tenets regarding concubines mapped fatherhood onto ownership in a way that made them coterminous with one another, rewarding both owner and owned with some sort of privilege: For the man, his right to her children; for the woman, her freedom and the freedom of her children. Sexualized social relations of ownership, then, were what defined the rights and obligations of concubine and master, and were central to gendered hierarchies amongst the palace slave community. In keeping with the monumentality of the palace institution, the political importance of concubinage in shoring up the paterfamilial basis of the state was heightened.

Given the slave status of concubines, royal concubine powers must be seen as exceptional, even extraordinary, given that most concubines were spoils of war. A territory would be pillaged and women and men taken as prisoners of war and enslaved. Slave-prisoners were divvied up between soldiers and nobility, the king having the privilege of first choosing those men and women he desired to serve him and his household. If a woman slave was taken sexually by the king and bore him a child, she became, de facto, a concubine. A concubine might also have originally been given as tribute to the king. This form of tribute was an especially judicious choice for slave families already living in the palace and seeking political favor with their royal master (Stilwell 1999, 2000). Nineteenth-century data show that many royal concubines at that time came from palace slave families. Unlike the hundreds, if not thousands, of slaves captured and brought to the palace, these slaves' families constituted a large in-house community, one divided into competing and powerful households.

The giving away of a daughter by slave households was useful not only because it expressed their trust in and allegiance to the king, but because it ensured that through their daughter's procreative power, slave and royal lineages would be linked. A slave daughter who bore a child for the king gave her parents an invaluable gift; they became grandparents of royalty; and if she bore a son, her parents became grandparents of a potential future king. Slave men and women hence had much to gain from personally and politically investing in the concubinage system (cf. Stilwell 1999, 2000). At the same time, the exchange of information between the households of king and slave client would have been indispensable to procuring political intelligence beneficial to both parties (see Guyer and Belinga 1995).

Fertility and the Territorial Fruits of Concubine Provenance
The rights and privileges awarded childbearing concubines worked in tandem with the great value afforded a person's birthplace and kinship network to the

territorial and political benefit of the state. The place from whence royal concubines derived (either through slave lineages in the palace or through capture) mattered, as did the subsequent geographical and political placement of their children. Ironically, it was the Islamically assigned rights of and laws regarding concubines as slaves that allowed them to become political resources for the state. For not only could they now be massively accumulated and centralized in the capital city, but they and their children were now associated with royalty, facilitating regional pacification (below). Given that Kano city lay at the center of a highly productive agrarian region, the transference of reproductive powers to the palace opened up substantial opportunities for female fertility to take symbolic and material hold at many political levels. At the same time, concubines shared and synthesized invaluable knowledge derived from their many disparate places of origin.

That concubine provenance was valued politically is deduced mainly from nineteenth-century palace data indicating that royal concubines captured from a particular place were sequestered together in an interior palace "ward" (*unguwa*) often named after the place from whence the majority of concubines living in that ward came. Circa 1900, for example, four concubine wards held the place names of the regions from which they were captured, including Kacako, Garko, Unguwar Bare-bari (Ward of Bornoans), and Nassarawa. Following British colonization in 1903, after which local rulers were prohibited from waging war, the names of these and other wards were "frozen," new territorial recruits now being forbidden.

Remarkably, though British rule meant that concubine accumulation through war was forbidden, collective memories about particular concubines and slave provenances were sustained in a number of ways.[14] Following Abdullahi Bayero's (1926–53) accession to the throne, for instance, concubines in Unguwar Bare-bari (Ward of the Bornoans), whose antecedents had come from Borno, visited their natal place with great fanfare. The highest-ranking concubine administrator recalled with pride the circumstances of the visit: a concubine of Emir Abdullahi, whose ancestors had been captured from Maiduguri, was taken to visit her people. She presumably went with a retinue of other Borno or Bare-bari concubines, there being many concubines at this time with that ancestry, most of whom lived in Unguwar Bare-bari. While in Maiduguri she was met and ritually honored by her Bornoan kin, later planting a seed of a *kuka* (baobab) tree to record her visit, a tree associated historically with divine kingship.[15] In a similar vein, the mother of Emir Muhammad Sanusi (1953–63) was a concubine whose ancestors had been captured from the town of Garko. When Sanusi came to the throne, he spent one night in Garko town to honor his maternal ancestors. His mother was also sent to Garko with an entourage, all the women of Garko ritually coming out to greet and honor them.[16] Even more striking is the story of the most renowned nineteenth-century concubine-turned-wife, Shekara, a royal daughter captured from a palace in Daura. Her pedigree was deemed so important that she was freed and married by Ibrahim Dabo (1819–46); three of her sons succeeded one another as king. Her Kano palace location made her renown in Daura as well, both palaces marking her importance by building a formal "Room of Shekara" in her memory that still exists today.[17] Another story, relayed to me on the condition of anonymity, deals with the freeborn parents of a small girl captured in Niger generations ago in a war waged by the leader of a city-state near to Kano. In this case, the freeborn parents, after searching for their daughter and learning that she had been made into a palace concubine, went to see her and were sent home feeling relieved and honored.[18] Moreover, nonroyal female slaves in the region, especially concubines, knew their natal places well, as evidenced by the fact that many ran away from their masters to their home and kin in the first decade of colonial rule, the British sending "patrols and messengers to induce them to return" (Lovejoy 1988, 249). Lovejoy's perusal of northern Nigerian court records of the colonial period also reveals that "[e]thnic awareness [among slaves, generally] was well developed," later averring that colonial court records and oral testimony of slaves showed that the "ethnic backgrounds of concubine mothers were remembered well . . . but the significance of that identity . . . seems to have been slight" (254, 263). Again, historical and sociopolitical context here is needed. First, royal concubines were often collected in great numbers from a single place, making their connections to their places of origin much stronger and of a collective nature. Secondly, palace concubines held much greater authority than did their nonroyal counterparts, making the utility of ethnic identity in the former of greater importance.

What these stories suggest is that concubines never forgot where they came from; nor was a concubine or her parents necessarily prevented from maintaining contact after the former was captured. Indeed, status hierarchies among palace women, with wives ranking the highest, followed by concubines and, last, nonconcubine slave women, facilitated geographical lines of communication and knowledge flows between places. A female slave messenger or person hailing from the same or nearby place of a royal concubine, for instance, could easily have been sent as an emissary of a palace concubine to carry messages to those she wanted to tell of her whereabouts. The stories additionally imply that the geographical origins of a royal concubine were significant politically, concubines in a sense representing their places of origin. Accordingly, a concubine's presence in the palace assisted in pacifying the place from which she was taken, that area now formally invested and represented in palace life through her person and reproductive capacities. The king could also tap into the knowledge resources of concubines about the regions from where they came, and concubines could potentially use their knowledge of and position in the palace to benefit their natal place.

That palace concubines served as political and kin representatives of the place from which they were captured resonates with what Guyer and Belinga have called, in the context of Equatorial Africa, "Wealth in People as Wealth in Knowledge," wherein political authority stems as much from cultivating the material and social resources of disparate peoples as from simply accumulating their lineage lines and labor (1995). That concubines held such capacities has been well documented for other nearby regions. In eighteenth-century Dahomey, for example, Bay avers that palace women's slave status never negated their allegiances or connections to their places of origin and related kinship networks (1998, 145). Indeed, high-ranking palace slave women in Dahomey maintained and even cultivated contact with the towns and villages of their birth, some, for example, moving their kinsmen to the capital or establishing estates that could be bequeathed to their blood relations. And in one case, Dahomean battles against the Mahi people were held in abeyance during the reign of a king whose appointed Queen Mother (a slave "wife" of a former ruler) hailed from that region, the Mahi claiming they were kin to the king (152). Bay's work in fact suggests that concubine mobility and the monumentality of Dahomean palace concubinage served the state well. Whereas men were committed to serving their own lineage upon marriage, young girls (concubine or free) customarily learned the art of dividing their loyalties between the lineages of their parents and those of master or husband. A palace slave "wife's" allegiance to her master (the king) would have been even stronger given that geographical distance from her family heightened her dependence on him. Thus, in the Abomey palace, popular tradition holds that the most powerful titleholding woman of state, the Queen Mother or *kpojito,* was always a slave (144), a scenario similar to the Kano palace where the most powerful palace women were concubines whose children frequently became king.

Musisi's work shows similarly that women captured in war in Buganda after the thirteenth century were divvied up by the army, with the king retaining rights to the greatest number of women (1991). These women, "married to the king," became representatives of their place, their reproductive capacity enhancing his status. Women were, in this way, signs of their owner's military prowess and virility:

> One of the strategies the king used for effective control over the clans of the conquered or subdued territories was to link himself by marriage to

these populations. This encouraged polygyny on a large scale. As in other despotic societies, the king and his bureaucrats monopolized polygyny. Expansionist warfare with plunder increased the potential for wealth dif- ferentiation among men and enhanced men's ability to acquire extra wives. Moreover, all the women captured in war were distributed by the generals who left most of the warriors empty-handed or with "small change" such as goats. As women became signs and objects of prestige and class, polyg- yny stratified men. The more wives a man had, the higher his status on the political and social ladder. . . . [T]he king and the chiefs found themselves with tremendous numbers of women, whom they housed in high reed fence enclosures. (Musisi 1991, 772)

In Kano, the geopolitical importance of concubine provenance derived not only from the body and provenance of the concubine, but from the fact that according to Islamic precedents concubine children are freeborn. Con- cubine children therefore had the same status and rights as those of freeborn wives. Status equalization among the king's children meant that any one of them could be used in marriages designed, as they were, to consolidate geopo- litical and economic alliances in the city and hinterland. Royal children were, in this sense, a primordial form of currency, their bodies forging transactions that worked to centralize the polity.

Status equalization also meant that *any* royal son could succeed to the throne. That concubine sons often became king can be explained in a num- ber of ways. First, concubines far outnumber wives, which means that there are simply more concubine children from which to choose a king (since the nineteenth-century *jihad,* referred to as an emir). In other words, it is sta- tistically more probable, all else being equal, that a concubine son would succeed to the throne. However, the playing field was far from equal. Well- established slave families, for example, held great political sway and the first Islamic state council was made up of eunuchs. It was in the interest of these slave councilors, military leaders, and officials to lobby for a leader who was one of their own, perhaps a son of a slave daughter they had previously given to the king as tribute. Additionally, the lineages of recently captured palace concubines were, unlike those of royal wives, disentangled from long-stand- ing regional webs of political intrigue, making the accession of their sons much less politically fraught. Because a king could *choose* his concubines they and their sons may have been differentially favored.[19] Moreover, the status of the captured slave woman apparently also mattered: She might hail from a powerful ruling family from a nearby city-state, as did Shekara, for example, in which case her political importance might rival that of a wife. Last, royal wives were married off at a tender age, arriving in the company of a slave retinue, including women who might be taken by the emir as concubines. These concubines stayed on with the wife, serving as her guardians and caretakers, one effect of their duties and their age being that they were more savvy about palace life and more politically influential.[20] And in any case, concubines collectively brought with them a wealth of information about the places from which they were captured and about innovative practices therein.

If a particular concubine son became king, the woman's community of provenance had much to gain, at least to the extent that the son, like a son of a royal wife, considered the place from where his mother and her kin derived with special regard. This and other potentials for privilege from the capital—produced through concubinage—would not have been lost on those in the hinterland, their allegiance undoubtedly obtaining partly from knowing that one of their own resided in the palace. Indeed, concubine powers negotiated through kinship could be extraordinary (cf. O'Fahey 1980, 38). In the nineteenth-century sultanate of Dar Fur, royal concubinage redeemed a formerly ostracized and semi-servile tribe on the territory's margins, known as the Beigo. Apparently, a Beigo slave woman became the sultan's favorite concubine, her son subsequently becoming sultan upon her master's death. As a result, the Beigo were "freed from their semi-servile status, their chief was entitled 'sultan' and various Beigo achieved positions at court" (38).

Similar sorts of territorial benefits accrued from the eighteenth century onward through the bodies of slave women accumulated in the Abomey palace. Bay relays, for example, how territorial conquests resulted in kingly accumulation of female slave ahosi in the central palace; most of these captured women were permitted to "keep in touch with their home areas and kinspeople, the palace function[ing] literally as a vehicle of political and social integration" (1998, 143). Moreover, opportunities were "granted to those newly conquered women to become part of the monarchy—to join the small group of persons closest to the king who wielded a certain amount of power in his name" (76). She notes how a slave ahosi might rise to power in subsequent reigns, one particular woman successfully counseling a successor king to wage a retaliatory war on a village where her son had been captured and killed.[21] Bay suggests that ahosi indeed cultivated lineage connections after capture, requiring that they balance state and lineage interests, interests that ultimately were linked (97).[22] Additionally, a king's daughters (many being children of female slave ahosi) married into important households where they might serve as spies for their father's interests (63).

The territorial benefits that accrued to a group as a result of its connections with the palace were in some Sudanic contexts extraordinary. Recall, for example, the benefits that accrued to the Beigo in nineteenth-century Dar Fur. At the same time, most palace concubines' powers would have been evinced at quotidian levels through their social networks, skills, and allegiances. In 1918, for instance, the British accused a Dutse palace concubine of mobilizing local youth to ambush their colonial appointee from Kano.[23]

The Royal Granary-Treasury and Concubines as State-Household Managers

Kano palace concubines were not only useful in representing and cultivating territorial links with the hinterland. They were central to an innovative and complex slave hierarchy that administered palace life. Most important, royal concubines surveyed and controlled the entirety of the secluded palace interior which, from circa 1500 to the mid-1800s, made up most of the palace area. Moreover, they administered the production of food for over one thousand persons daily, a monumental activity requiring that they have ready access to a large and consistent grain source.

Field evidence discussed in chapter 1 shows that massive amounts of grains were stored in state granaries located in the secluded female interior, and that the granaries were controlled by royal concubines. At least in the sixteenth and seventeenth centuries, most of these grains presumably derived from state taxation of surrounding farmland, with taxes tendered primarily in grain. Over subsequent centuries, as larger proportions of taxes were paid in nongrain goods and currencies, royal grain sources were supplemented and finally replaced in large part by produce from slave estates dedicated to palace reproduction.

Chapter 1 also shows that the considerable needs of the palace community for grain meant, in practice, that concubines participated in the process of grain taxation, indirectly and directly. Grains owed the state were not brought to town all at once, but were collected on a geographically rotating basis, depending upon harvest times and relative farm sizes and locations. In this way, a semi-regularized stream of grains filled the palace granaries. These grains, like royal concubine children themselves, served as vital political *and* economic currency. Since pre-Islamic times, the kingship was linked to the ability to provide enough food for the people, and, in the palace, grain-based foods were prepared elaborately to impress and entertain important guests. Grains were additionally bartered for one another and in the distant past may have been used as a currency in markets.

The Decline of Concubinage

Royal concubine fortunes waned over succeeding centuries, apparently in tandem with the declining political economic importance of grain and the declining importance of concubines as territorial representatives—and of royal concubine children as instruments through which (via marriage) territorial linkages were forged. As the territory was consolidated, as the economy diversified, and as merchant (exchange) relations began to dominate the economic landscapes of Kano, other currencies and in-kind goods, such as cloth and, later, cowries and European currencies, came into play, developments that registered strikingly in the palace interior.

Field evidence establishes that royal concubines were originally well positioned to compete in the diversifying market economy of Kano, but eventually their opportunities were curtailed by other economic and political interest groups. For example, it appears that concubines controlled a large cloth-dyeing enterprise in the palace interior, adjacent to the most powerful concubine ward. The finding, based on geographical and linguistic evidence, is of enormous importance in that it shows that the lucrative, male-run indigo cloth-dyeing industry of the nineteenth century grew out of earlier cloth dyeing-practices of royal women (chapter 2). In conjunction with other field data, the finding also suggests that palace concubines may initially have had a monopoly over the creation and use of indigo-blue dyed cloth, a highly prized item that circulated as an important trans-Saharan currency since at least the sixteenth century.

There is some evidence that palace concubines may have attempted to break into commercial cloth-dyeing endeavors in the 1600s and 1700s. Perhaps it was the threat this posed to male control over currency production and long-distance trade that forced the permanent closure of the palace dye field in the early 1800s. It also related to the first Fulani emir's pressing need to give Kano malams an industry that would allow them to support themselves and their students after the early nineteenth-century jihad. From then on, men living outside the palace, supported by successive Kano rulers, were given exclusive license over indigo dyeing practices. This nineteenth-century gendered takeover of dyed cloth production, coupled with the earlier influx of cowries and other monetary currencies into the region; the rise of male-run urban and rural industries; and the lessened geopolitical importance of grains and concubine children, would certainly have displaced fertility as the central organizing principle of the state. Such a displacement, perhaps not coincidentally, intersected the nineteenth-century Fulani-led religious reform movement, leading to a sharp decline in the number and power of concubines, detailed in chapters 3 and 4.

Chapter 5 discusses how concubine losses were compounded during British colonial rule, from 1903 to 1960. Concubine sources were directly attacked when the British disabled the accumulation of concubines through war. British abolition of nonconcubine forms of slavery also meant that fewer slave men married slave women, such that fewer slave daughters were born and, hence, available to the king as tribute. Moreover, the British eventually forbade the payment of taxes in anything other than pounds sterling, an act that eroded a foundational part of concubine identity and power, namely control over royal grain.

In 1960 Nigeria became an independent state. Initially, local rulers could hold elected public office, such that many northern elites continued to govern and hold colonially instituted powers over prisons and the local police. All of the latter were successively curtailed after the military coups of 1967 and 1976, these and other curtailments affecting negatively the ability of the emir to sustain concubine life in the palace. Moreover, from the 1970s onward, a number of scholars led an attack on concubinage in northern Nigeria as practiced by wealthy merchants and the aristocracy. These scholars, particularly Abubakar Gumi (Grand Qadi of Northern Nigeria), had a lasting impact on the younger generation of princes and the wealthy. Today, no Kano princes have concubines.[24] The last chapter thus surveys royal concubine life today and discusses the future viability of the institution.

The spatial analyses presented in the chapters that follow are theoretically tied to and depend upon a much larger conceptual framework of interiority, as described by many scholars writing about the creation and ontological, political, and phenomenological consequences of interiority in different cultural and historical contexts (e.g., Boddy 1989; Butler 1990; Grosz 1990; Lefebvre 1991; Lingis 1994; Nast 2000; and Wigley 1992). I argue that interiority, as a concept of spatial organization, was created in a new way in Kano through the Islamic institution of female seclusion.[25] Hence, I discuss below how interiority expressed itself in the palace through language, architecture, and sociospatial practice.

Children as Grains: The Palace Ciki

Geographical analysis of the palace suggests that concubines lived a secluded life in a special interior place, known as the palace *ciki* or "inside," pronounced syllabically with a high-high intonation pattern. Eliciting the spiritual, cultural, and political significance of the ciki came from relating its many practical and symbolic links to the bodily "stomach," also known as *ciki,* though syllabically intoned using a high-low pattern. These two differently intoned words are etymologically linked and, as I will argue below, helped create a sense of interiority traversing bodily and architectural domains.

All of royal family life was contained in the palace ciki, this space becoming the place wherein the large, dynamic, and Islamically informed universe of spatiality, meaning, and practice unfolded itself. As the largest and most significant part of the palace landscape, the ciki was a formidable material force shaping an Islamic universe of interiority, bodily and spatially. Here, state-led domestication of territory and reproduction (in short, law and order) were imagined and materially expressed. Territories conquered "out there," with all their human and earthly potential for fertility, were reproduced physically through an interiorized ward system of concubinage, the names of towns conquered "without" being re-presented physically, and by name, in the palace "inside" or ciki. More generally, the ciki (interior), tied up as it was in a complex of material and linguistic practices, was itself a sociospatial *practice* constituting and holding within itself all that which had been conquered, tamed, cultivated, and (most important) made fertile. As such, the ciki was where paternal orders and creative acts were shaped and inscribed—the place where fertility was captured and centralized through conquest and paternally guided labor.

Fertility was embodied practically and symbolically in the ciki by royal children (the product of the domesticated and fertile royal concubine body) and royal grain (the produce of a domesticated and fertile maternal earth). Tellingly, conquest and fertility-related signifiers are rendered in Hausa through the main verb associated with eating, *ci*, and through signifiers associated with the main interior body-place that contains and digests food, namely, the stomach, *ciki*. Hence, conquest is connoted by the word *ci*, in this case translatable as "to eat up" or "consume." Making love is also deemed *ci* in the vernacular; a pregnant woman is called *Mai ciki*, or "to have a stomach," pregnancy is *ciki* or "stomach," and the womb is called the "stomach of woman" *(ciki na mace)*.

The equivalences and associations between signifiers of architectural and bodily interiors, on the one hand, and conquest, lovemaking, and eating, on the other, have additional associational effects. The main product of conquered and domesticated land is grain, for example, just as the product of conquered and domesticated slave women are children. Grains are eaten *(ci)* and initially repose in and nourish the body through the stomach *(ciki)*, making one feel full, *cika*. Similarly, royal children, analogously produced through conquering acts *(ci)*, initially repose and are plenished in the royal concubine womb *(ciki)*, and are later cultivated in the palace interior *(ciki)*, so as to eventually nourish (through marriage and political deployment) the monarchical state.

Thus, by plenishing the bodily ciki (high-low intonation) or stomach/womb, grains and children served to sustain the extra-bodily interior ciki (high-high intonation) of the palace. In turn, the latter became the metaphorical body of the state, a domesticating and digestive place where paternal law and provision pronounce themselves. One vibrant expression of the political equivalences between children and grain discussed in chapter 2 is worth repeating here: That all royal children were born in a special granary-like building located in the compound of the most powerful concubine in charge of royal grains, Master of the Granary.[26] Masquelier (forthcoming) speaks of similar metonymic associations in more recent work with Mawri women in nearby Niger, albeit in the context of mortar and pestle symbology:

> While the vision of the pestle next to the mortar had potent sexual implications during the wedding, in the daily act of pounding [grain], the woman thereafter symbolically reenacted the fecund union of complementary elements (mortar = womb/pestle = penis) so crucial to the viability of marriages and the vitality of society because of what it produced (food = child).

Vernacular Dispersions of Interiority

That the meaning of interiority is today intelligible through constellations of vernacular signifiers connoting fertility across human and earthly maternal domains suggests that at some point the architectural and linguistic forces associated with its palace expression became commonplace. That is, architectural and linguistic practices embodying and shaping fertility and interiority in royal contexts eventually filtered into everyday architectural and linguistic imaginaries and practices. This scalar filtering of inside-outside distinctions, passing from stomach and womb to conquered world and back again, is remarkably consistent with the Islamic context described by Janice Boddy (1989, 70–72) of the Hofriyati in Sudan. Here, the interior place of the household is known as the *hosh* and is symbolic of the womb, an equivalence of body and place that works itself outwards across scales and materialities. The hosh and/as womb define a spatially dichotomous universe comprised of that which is inside and civilized (cultivated, seeded, conquered, interiorized, reproduced, and paternally made lawful) and outside and uncivilized.

One supposes that after interiority in the palace was established, its form was incorporated into aristocratic and merchant households. Indeed, during the nineteenth and twentieth centuries, the Kano palace division of "inside-outside" was found in many compounds across Hausaland, its universality developing over centuries. Such architectural mimicry not only would have flattered the king, but would initially have created formal affinities between power seekers and the royal household, though no one dared build a household of royal size or demeanor (cf. Sa'ad 1981, 130). Over time, other social groups adopted the palace "house" form, though many rural households did not employ the ciki for wife seclusion until the twentieth century (Hill 1977, 84).

But the palace was not the only force shaping vernacular architectures and senses of space. Widespread adoption of a core household place for female seclusion was undoubtedly shaped by the fact that Kano was connected increasingly to a West African universe of trans-Saharan trade fueled largely by the interests of Islamic scholars and merchants from North Africa. Just as the adoption of Arabic literacy and numeracy facilitated financial transactions of Islamic merchants and clerics operating across the Saharan region, the adoption of Islam and its relevant cultural mores and forms, including wife seclusion, would have provided traders with important cultural capital. After all, while the interiorized morphology of the palace was initially unique to Kano royalty and the merchant classes, it was certainly common in other Islamic contexts with which Kano was, through trade, connected. This is not to say that Islamic practices remained static, but that seclusion remained an organizing principle within which much change occurred over time.

Pre-Islamic Divides in Regional Context

Adoption of the ciki as a place of female seclusion raises major questions about how palace morphology impacted a diverse universe of pre-Islamic cultural constructions and morphologies of "space." How was "space" envisaged and organized previously by different ethnic groups? If interiority was not a key organizing principle of pre-Islamic households, was interiority expressed at a different scale? In other ways? Or not at all? And if interiority was not central to household organization, how and why did the palace become a primary node of symbolic and practical diffusions—a staging ground for promoting Islamically gendered spatial arrangements, divisions of labor, and sumptuary codes?

Moreover, how did the architectural creation of palace interiority inform how concubine bodies, pregnancy, fertility, and paternity were culturally, politically, and spatially understood and deployed? How did the state's centralized accumulation of fertility (through concubinage and conquest) inside the palace ciki shape political and phenomenological understandings of the pregnant body? Obversely, how did the materiality of the pregnant body (earthly and human), and the uses to which it was put, shape paternity itself, both at the level of the Islamic paterfamilias and household, and the larger monarchical state and royal state-household? Why and how was the Islamically informed drive to centralize the state geographically, and through slave-based paternity, embodied in practice and metaphorically by the enclosure of the interior stomach-womb?

The historical origins of interiorized state life can be deciphered partly by comparing early Kano palace morphology to the morphology of extant pre-Islamic or non-Islamic households. The scant evidence that exists suggests that prior to Islam women were not secluded in any special interiorized place.[27] And, since no permanent house of state in Kano had previously existed in Kano (Last 1979, 71), there would have been no corporeal or territorial place emblematic of an established political core or "inside" at the state household level. Accordingly, equivalences among the stomach, womb, paterfamilias, and state could not have existed previously in the architectural ways it did following the Islamization of Kano political culture. By contrast, architectural interiority *did* develop in non-Muslim contexts where the state similarly asserted centralized state authority over women and their reproductive capacities. By the late 1500s, for example, non-Muslim Bugandan chiefs usurped clan rights over land, centralizing land authority instead in the person of the king. This transition occurred contemporaneously with the creation of "elite polygyny" wherein the king "married" hundreds of freeborn and enslaved women from the territories conquered, forcing the coalescence of other clan lines into his own. As Musisi writes, "elite polygyny . . . revolutionized the architecture of the dwellings of the elite men who had to enclose their homesteads with high reed enclosures . . . so as to keep an eye on their numerous women" (1991, 783).

My theorizing of the co-emergence of and equivalences between bodily and state-territorial notions of interiority should therefore not be taken to imply that gendered divisions of labor and space never existed in West Africa prior to Islam. Indeed, some sort of sexed spatial divisions of labor are present in all cultures.[28] In West Africa, one of the most documented spatial instances of sexed divisions relates to the architectural practices of the agrarian Dogon of Burkina Faso and Mali, a cultural group originating in the Bandiagara region in the thirteenth or fourteenth century (Dieterlen 1982, 9). Dogon house forms traditionally caricatured the human form, understood as *emblematic* of universal order. Different sculptural and functional parts symbolized maleness and femaleness, an anthropocentric practice anathema to Islam.[29] Dogon patriarchs lived communally in a compound in the village center, all compounds built to resemble anthills, symbolic of primordial order (Azuonye 1996, 10–11). While gendered divisions of labor and gendered ways of symbolizing the universe existed, Dogon women were never secluded.

While gendered asymmetries may have existed in Kano prior to the building of the palace and consequent Islamization in the region, once the context of their creation and sustenance changed, they could not mean the same thing. In Islamicized Kano the territorial inside was nested and represented sociospatially and linguistically in the house-inside, in turn likened to a womb-inside, both "insides" marking paternal conquest and patriarchal social order. Thus, whatever sexed cosmological divisions existed in Kano prior to the coming of Islam, palace divisions had to speak through them, mapping a different logic onto pre-existing ones.

Wives versus Concubines

It will be noticed that I do not discuss royal wives in any depth. I do not do so, first, because I am concerned with the much larger institution of palace concubinage and, second, because I do not believe that royal wives were as foundational to state formational processes as concubines, either in terms of their contribution to state imaginaries of fertility or to territorial representation and state management. While there were undoubtedly exceptionally powerful wives, such as Auwa, the freeborn wife of King Rumfa (1463–99) whom Last (1983) surmises was the daughter of the Askia Muhammad of Songhay, palace concubines seem to have had a more global externalized reach. The reasons I would argue concubines had more influence is that (1) they were more numerous and represented (and had knowledge of) many far-flung regions; (2) their lineages had no prior established history of lineage-rivalry with the king, which meant they were often more trusted (to wit, many concubine children became king); (3) as a "class" they had the support of the powerful state slaves; (4) many were chosen by the king and hence, his personal favorites, unlike wives who were typically chosen for him; and (5) their children were freeborn and, hence, of equal status to the children of freeborn wives. The last point meant that status differences between these two groups of women were of limited *duree,* since both groups of women produced royal children who, upon accession to the throne or marriage to powerful persons, would honor their biological mothers.

This is not to say that status differences among the four wives and hundreds of concubines did not exist: They did. Concubines prostrated before royal wives and served them, and royal wives decided the marriage fates of concubines' female children. Concubines were also the palace's managerial class, whereas royal wives were leisured. And wives had their own private estates inside the cikin gida, whereas concubines mostly lived communally in wards or in the estates of wives whom they served. Nonetheless, these differences are not significant enough to argue that wifely authority was greater than that of concubines in state formational processes, especially when in many cases the status differential between wives and concubines could be exchanged over a single generation: the daughter of a palace concubine might become a royal wife to a nearby king, or, like Shekara, a princess might be enslaved. Such interchangeability was also apparent in Buganda after the fifteenth century, when "[p]easant girls or women taken in war as captives became wives as easily as the daughters of the wealthiest chiefs," the difference being that in non-Muslim Bugandan, the king could have as many high-birth as low-birth or enslaved wives as he desired. The ease with which the Bugandan king could take wives did not, however, mean that there were no status distinctions or unequal divisions of labor among them. Indeed, a similar sociospatial hierarchy obtained between Bugandan wives: Untitled wives (of lowly birth or slave status) lived communally in sections controlled by a special wife-administrator, whereas titled wives (of high birth) lived individually in their own enclosures (Musisi 1991, 779). Unlike the Kano context, titled wives held substantial geopolitical authority over territorial administration and taxation. These powers were enabled by the fact that, unlike the Kano context, high-ranking wives were numerous. That is, the Bugandan king could have hundreds of titled wives, who formed an important state managerial class, something not possible in Kano where Islam restricted the number of wives to four.[30] For a number of reasons, then, not least of which was the sheer number of concubines, concubine history forms the core of this work. It was only in the 1800s, when concubine numbers declined greatly, that I posit the importance of wifely provenance and powers increased relative to concubines (chapters 4 and 5).

Early Historical Sources

No early historical sources exist that describe Kano palace life and spaces in any sustained way. A few texts, dating from the nineteenth and twentieth centuries, allude to the palace, but none of these address life in the palace ciki per se. Nonetheless two sources provided useful clues about early palace morphology, the *Kano Chronicle* (KC) and the *Crown of Religion Concerning the Obligation of Princes* (CR) discussed in turn below.

The KC is a king-list; it lists the name and numbers of years that Kano kings reigned. It also reports at some length on events taking place during each king's reign. Originally written in Arabic, the KC spans the period from Barbushe, a pagan king who supposedly lived on Dalla Hill in present-day Kano city sometime before the tenth century, to the reign of Emir Bello (1883–92).[31] The original text contains no dates, dates first being provided in Palmer's 1967 English translation of the text, which he derived by working backwards in time from a known date (the 1807 Fulani overthrow of the last Hausa King of Kano, Alwali) using the regnal lengths stated in the KC.

Until recently it was believed that the KC was a compilation of mostly written materials, the first portions being recorded sometime in the mid-sixteenth or mid-seventeenth centuries (Last 1983; Smith 1983). It has since been argued based on information unearthed by Starratt that the text is much younger (1993, 126, 153). That is, it is based largely on oral traditions compiled in the late nineteenth century to bolster the claims of a particular dynastic line of the Fulani, either by one or more malams collaborating with one or more senior slave officials in the palace (Starratt 1993; Lovejoy, Mahadi, and Muktar 1993; Hunwick 1994).[32] While the potential recency of the document makes it difficult to ascertain the exactitude of many historical details described, Hunwick asserts that the chronology of events, "at least back to c. 1500, has been corroborated by dates from other sources for events mentioned in the KC" (1994, 14).

The dates that Palmer deduces, for example, indicate that al-Maghili, the renowned cleric from Tlemcen (Algeria), visited Kano sometime between 1463 and 1499, during the reign of Muhammadu Rumfa, the king who built the Kano palace.[33] This timeframe is corroborated by Ahmad Baba, who wrote Al-Maghili's biography in the early 1600s (Hunwick 1994). Based upon this and other intertextual evidence, Hunwick surmises that the KC is most accurate from Rumfa's reign onwards, and that it was during his reign, or a little earlier, that Islam began to become well established in Kano.

This is not to say that the KC contains no historical errors or omissions from Rumfa's reign onward—or that it does not reflect the political interests of its writers. Other sources show that the KC conflates al-Maghili's visit to Kano, for example, with that of another Arab scholar, Abd al-Rahman, who probably visited Kano after al-Maghili's departure (see Hunwick 1993). Last, especially, has been careful to point out the problems of relying on this document alone (1983). Disclaimers notwithstanding, he and other scholars draw extensively on the KC in exploring Kano's early history.

In contrast, the CR is a primary source document that was written for King Muhammadu Rumfa by al-Maghili, purportedly at the king's behest. The text contains information on proper Islamic rule and is of a genre of Islamic political literature called "Mirrors for Princes." According to Gwarzo, Bedri, and Starratt 1974/77, "Mirrors" are essays that "describe the qualities and behaviour of good Muslim rulers and equate the welfare of the ruler with the welfare of his domain" (16), akin in content and inspiration to the political treatise of Machiavelli, *The Prince,* written in 1513.

While most scholars deal with these two texts in terms of political history, comparing them to other texts and oral traditions, they are used here for clues into the spatial organization of the palace. Information in CR, in particular, showed how much the palace, though inspired by local practices, was a place built to officiate and facilitate Islamic custom and rule.

CHAPTER 1

Grain Treasuries and Children: Royal Concubines in the 1500s and 1600s

In early November 1989 I purchased a large-format aerial photograph of Kano city to analyze macro-scale palace features and to see if I could discern spatial connections between the palace and the old city. As a geologist I had been trained to examine aerial photographs for evidence of geological movements (such as faults and folds) and their temporal sequencing, the latter determined through analyzing crosscutting relationships between them. A large fold in the geological terrain would represent an older event, for example, if it was crosscut by a fault, but if the linear surface expression of the fault was folded, it would follow that the fault had formed earlier than the fold. By thus mapping and analyzing geological details, I could determine, if only partially, the magnitude, kind, and timing of different movements. I planned now on applying these geological methods within a social geographical context: the extant urban fabric of Kano city. In this way, I hoped to discern spatial structures and crosscutting relationships between them, thereby establishing relative age-dates of palace-related places.

Analysis of the aerial photographs of Kano city provided crucial historical information concerning: (1) how the palace was originally oriented; (2) how the palace-suburb was placed in relation to the old city, the central mosque, the central city market, and the defensive moats and ramparts during the reign of King (hereafter referred to as Sarki) Muhammadu Rumfa (1463–99); and (3) the spatial extent of the earliest royal concubine-run interior. Because it was Rumfa who established the palace, market, and mosque, any evidence of linkages between these institutions and places beyond them would provide clues into the spatial logic of and practices associated with the palace exurb. Out of the ring road surrounding the central city market, for example, many roads radiate outward to marketplaces beyond Kano, places that would have been of some importance during Rumfa's reign. Their historical importance and the fact that many of them are visibly crosscut or obliterated by later roads and other structures, suggest these roads were contemporaneous with the market (see Figure 2).

One of the radiating roads especially important to this study is the one that leads directly to what had been the palace's northernmost retaining wall, passing through this wall, west of its centerpoint, to the northern perimeter of the secluded royal interior (see Figure 3). East of the palace wall's centerpoint, a second pathway radiated outwards to the northeast. The northeasterly pathway ran past the palace stables and merged with a city ring-road that during Rumfa's time had been an inner perimeter road to the city's defensive moats and ramparts.

The placement and relative positioning of the two roads convey a wealth of historical geographical information. First, their placement make it plain that the palace originally opened up, or faced, northward and that it had two entranceways tethering it to sites essential to the political health of the centralized monarchical state: the main city ramparts, and the central city market, the latter soon to become a regionally renown center of commerce.[1] Wedged in between these pathways and near the palace was the central city mosque, its presence ostensibly demonstrating that Islamic practices, relatively new to Kano, had become integral to state and public life.

Severing off the public and male slave-led domain from the palace labyrinth and secluded royal interior was a vast curtain wall, sited exactly at the point where the two palace pathways conjoin. A similar wall exists today. The curtain wall was of great historical cultural significance because it established a definitive break between royal and nonroyal domains. Henceforth, the emir's royal women and royal children would be cordoned off from the male-run slave households of the "public" north, adjacent to the city. As will be seen in subsequent chapters, the areal extent of the public northern area went virtually unchanged for centuries, unlike the private area of women to the south.

The pathway positions and convergence point, in tandem with other field data, show that the palace landscape was divided along two distinct, crosscutting axes. A north-south axis divided the palace into a western "female" and

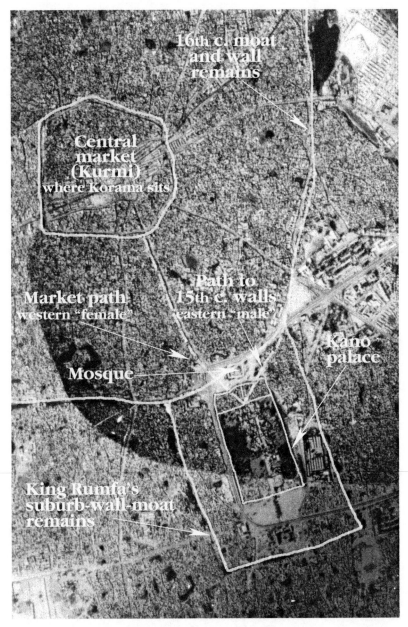

Figure 2. Aerial photograph of a portion of Kano city. The moat around the palace and city walls dating from the 1500s are still visible, as are the centuries-old connections between the palace and old city. Note the western "female" path leading out of the palace ciki (inside) toward the central market, and the eastern "male" path leading from the palace stable outward toward the first generation of city ramparts from the early sixteenth century. Other pathways radiate outward from the central market to various cities and places of importance beyond Kano.

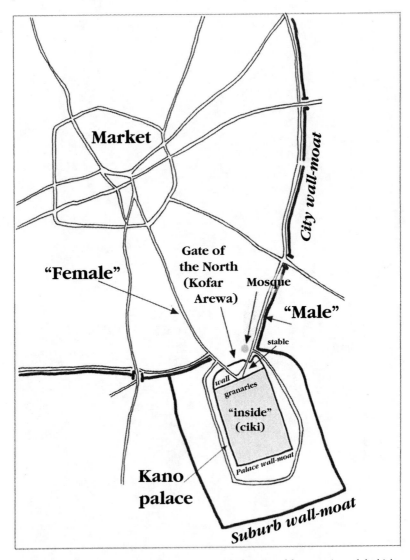

Figure 3. A schematic drawing of Figure 2, showing the location of the granaries and the high wall that separated the palace ciki (shaded) from the slave residential area to the north, today known as Kofar Arewa or Gate of the North.

an eastern "male" sector. The eastern pathway, for example, led to the city's ramparts linked in turn to palace military sites. The pathway cut past the royal stables created by Rumfa, an anchor for the polity's first state cavalry, and along the household of the powerful title-bearing male slave official. The official was responsible for stable upkeep, a portion of palace armaments, and the training of certain warriors, including cavalrymen.[2] The western pathway, in contrast, was market-oriented and "female." It led from what I would later discern to be a field of granaries located in the secluded palace interior, to the central city market where the single most important female market official presided over a considerable group of female grain sellers. An east-west axis, defined by the east-west trending curtain wall, divided the palace into a northern public sector (controlled and defined largely by male slaves) and a southern private sector (managed largely by female slaves).

The mosque would have been constructed prior to the central market or palace, providing laborers with a place of prayer while they worked to construct the latter two structures. Because men's prayers are rendered communally and in public, the positioning of the central mosque amid the two pathways would have been culturally and politically strategic: All persons must pray facing eastwards, toward Mecca; for men to avoid sexual thoughts during prayer, women had to be removed from their field of vision. The eastern pathway thus *had* to be male, for if the gendered geographical sequencing had been reversed, men gathering to pray would have looked eastward onto women going to and from the market.[3] The north-south orientation of the Kano palace and the number and gendered qualities of its gateways was replicated in the old Dutse palace built in the early 1800s. Though the palace is more oblong than rectangular and the entrances lead out from the southern wall, a western entrance was built for women that emptied out onto a southwesterly pathway which intersected another road leading eastward to the main market wherein a powerful female grain official, the Korama, sat; an eastern entrance was built for men and emptied out onto a southeasterly trending road, a mosque built just east of it, similar to the arrangement in Kano. The eastern entrance hall was called Soron Rakuma (Hall of Camels) because all tribute to the emir passed through it, some apparently loaded on camels.[4]

The rest of this chapter explores the sociospatial organization (or sociospatiality) of the secluded palace interior and the linkages between this area and places in the outside world. I argue that royal concubine activities, particularly grain procurement and administration, defined much of the contours of interior state life. By geographically tracing out historical sites of palace grain usage and grain-related labor hierarchies (most of which no longer exist), it will be shown that grains were formidable as both an effect and force of regional agricultural fertility and productivity, upon which palace life initially depended.

The Hall of Grain and the Sultanic Grain Treasury

There are many palace traces of a munificent grain past, yet they are difficult to discern in the present-day landscape. Most relevant social and spatial structures have been converted to other uses, have been destroyed, or are in a state of disuse. As a result, the history and significance of grain-related places are largely overlooked by researchers and contemporary inhabitants alike.

Demarcation of the grain sites evolved partly from analyzing the history of Hausa place names and concubine titles, many of which point to grain-related activities that are no longer of practical importance. By mining palace place names for information about each site's origins and history, it became clear that place names and functions changed over time, varying for men and women and among age groups. Usually only the most elderly of persons, residing inside and outside the palace, for example, knew the meaning of older palace place names and could tell stories about them. The oldest name- and place-related stories relayed by middle-aged persons, in contrast, were associated mostly with the colonial period (1903–60), whereas most young people did not know and were generally disinterested in palace place history.

One of the best-preserved spatial and linguistic remnants redolent of the palatial grain past is Soron Hatsi, literally, Hall of Grain. The morphology and structure of the hall are telling to the extent that the pillar and beam style reflects an archaic architectural form predating the mid-nineteenth century (Sa'ad 1981). At first, its name made no sense, given its contemporary use as a passageway into an area containing a modern health clinic and the largely abandoned concubine ward, Kacako. Individual and in-group discussions with one of the most erudite and intelligent of palace elders, the titleholder Gogo Mai'daki,[5] however, showed that Soron Hatsi had, since at least the nineteenth century, been a formal entrance hall into a walled complex of granaries holding unthreshed grain. The grains, still on their stalks, were tied into bundles called *dami*. The granaries located in the enclosure, I was told, were those set aside for dami collected as an Islamic tithe for the poor, called *zakat*. Malams distributed these dami to those in need on a discretionary basis. A much larger number of granaries containing dami existed outside this walled complex, and were dedicated for palace use.

The placement of the granaries at the terminus of sixteenth-century palace features and their utility and large number recommends that granaries, similar to those of the nineteenth century, existed circa 1500. There would presumably have been an even greater number of granaries at this time, since fortified towns, rural slave estates, and daughter palaces were built up and used for different purposes from the fifteenth through nineteenth centuries.[6] In this sense, the granaries functioned as the state's first permanent (agricultural) treasury, though the origins of the dami changed over time. This deduction makes sense when it is considered that concubines were responsible for feeding about two thousand persons daily, the majority of whom were relatively leisured, or at least not engaged fully in agricultural production.

Locating the state granaries beyond the confluence of the two main palace pathways tells us that granary placement was proprietary and strategic, their interior location intimating that the dami were largely administered and used by royal women for state-household reproductive purposes (Figure 4). That the granaries were located in the northern perimeter of the interior also suggests that the location was chosen to facilitate "quick release" of grains in an area relatively removed from interior palace life. Slave men, eunuchs, and slave women, in other words, could take from and replenish the granaries with great spatial efficiency in a periphery proffering little sociospatial disruption to inner palace life. At least up to the eighteenth century, dami would have been the main in-kind tax collected by the state. These grains would have been used to reproduce the palace community, additional grains deriving from dedicated royal slave estates. Nineteenth-century data collected by Giginyu insinuates that grains produced on the estates were dedicated largely to supplying fodder for the royal stables, horses eating considerably more than the average human (1981).[7]

The discovery of the presence, extent, and location of the granary fields is thus significant, demonstrating a substantial degree of early state centralization of grain taxation storage. Smith has argued, in contrast, that since Rumfa's reign *all* grains consumed by the palace came from slave plantations (1997, 125). Basing his conclusions solely on information from the KC, Smith recounts that just prior to Rumfa's reign, a powerful Kano titleholder went on massive slave-raiding campaigns, saturating Kano city and its environs with slave labor. The king at that time was a major benefactor, receiving enough slaves

> to establish twenty-one separate villages. . . . Dawuda's slave raiding capitalized and transformed the chiefship by investing it with substantial numbers of captured men as a versatile resource. Those twenty-one thousand slaves settled afield furnished annual tributes of grain and other crops that could support a large number of slaves and freemen employed at the capital in increasingly specialized political and military roles. (Smith 1997, 125)

Smith argues that there was never again such a large influx of slaves into Kano, hypothesizing that the slave population was so great that it perpetuated itself largely through biological reproduction. Smith does not address the fact, however, that grain taxes from the rural populace were collected and must have been directed *somewhere*—despite the difficulties of transporting something as heavy as grains, a difficulty making it easier to target farms close to the city. Moreover, he takes the KC at face value in terms of the number of slaves said to have been captured and distributed (1,000 in each of the twenty-one towns) even though the KC characteristically uses numbers as hyperbole

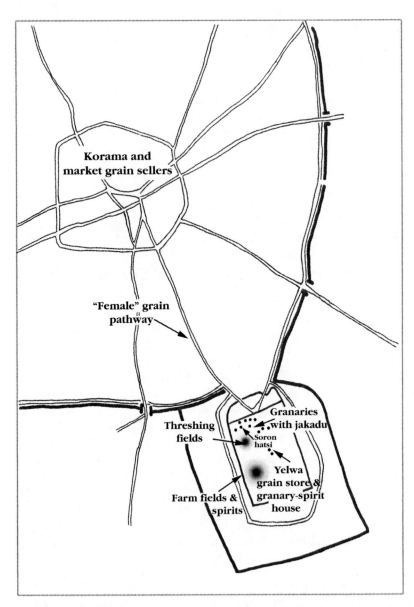

Figure 4. Royal grain areas within and outside the palace, including the pathway to the market that facilitated informational flows between royal concubines and Korama, the female grain official responsible for setting grain prices and regulating grain volumes to be traded in the city market. Note the association of the west with grain locations and the association of some grain locations with spirits.

rather than to relay empirical fact (it also notes, for example, that King Rumfa had 1,000 wives). If Smith's contention that these 21,000 represented only one-fifth of the war booty, the original number of slaves captured by Dawuda would have exceeded 100,000, which seems improbable. Given that Smith's argument is based exclusively on inaccurate numerical data from the KC and that he ignores other information in it, for example, the KC's assertion that grain taxation began with King Nagugi, his assertion that slave estates provided all palace grains for the considerable palace population is somewhat problematic.[8]

My preference for suggesting that grain taxes were the main impetus behind building the granaries derives partly from a mid-nineteenth-century account of Hausaland by the Kano-born malam, Imam Imoru (Ferguson 1973). Details in his text provide clues into the annual volume of grains given to and required by the Kano palace, volumes much more reasonably derived from a plethora of rural farm sources. His writings suggest that an average farm yielded about 200 grain bundles or dami. If taxation levels were approximately 10 percent of farm yield, each farm would have rendered twenty bundles.[9] Imam Imoru also relays that different sizes of granaries existed throughout Hausaland, varying from small ones in the compounds of poor commoners, to large ones in compounds of the wealthy, to enormous ones in the palaces of royalty.[10] It seems not unreasonable to deduce from information he provides that palace granaries were larger than normal, each one accommodating 500 bundles. If there were about twenty palace granaries in the interior, a number calculated roughly from assessing the size of the area dedicated to granary use, the total capacity for storage would equal 10,000 dami. Based on average farm yield data indicated above, full capacity would be reached if 500 farms tendered 20 dami (unthreshed) each. If each dami weighed roughly 100 pounds, each farmer would have contributed 2,000 pounds of unthreshed grain to the palace treasury. Assuming conservatively that the wastage to grain ratio was 3:1, the 2,000 pounds translates into about 650 pounds of threshed grain.[11] The 10,000 dami that the palace granaries is estimated to have accommodated, then, equaled 1,000,000 pounds or 500 tons of unthreshed grain, equal to 165 tons of threshed grain.

So much for crudely approximating palace granary *capacity*. To approximate palace demand, it is assumed that a minimum of one pound (less than two cups) of threshed, uncooked grain was sufficient to fill the caloric needs for all meals for one person daily.[12] Feeding 2,000 palace persons each day would then require 2,000 pounds (2000 × 1 lb.) or one ton of *threshed* grains daily. Given the estimated 3:1 wastage of a dami, feeding a community of 2,000, including the poor, visitors, and other clients, would have required three times that amount—three tons or 6,000 pounds—of dami. Given that palace granaries could accommodate at most 165 tons, the palace community could subsist for just over 50 days without refilling the granaries. Given that there are 365 days in a year, the palace granaries would have had to have been refilled about seven times annually, translating into taxation revenues collected from 3,500 average-sized farms, that is, the 500 farms needed to fill the granaries once, multiplied by seven. Refilling the granaries was probably not done all at once, but gradually, there being several mitigating factors, such as the existence of two to three harvests per year, additional palace storage facilities may have been located in rural areas, and there were differences in the travel distances farmers or royal messengers would have to traverse to arrive at the capital. It may also have been the case that some farms yielded threshed grains to the king, perhaps through the central grain market official, Korama.

In any event, 180 (30-lb.) bundles would have remained for the average farm (the 200-bundle average minus the 20-bundle tax), which translates into 1,800 pounds of threshed grain or 1,800 person-days of food, presuming one pound of uncooked grain per day per person. If these 1,800 person-days are divided by 365 (the number of days in a year), we arrive at a figure of 5—the number of persons per year for which an average farm could produce, wastage from the dami being used along with family grains to feed farm animals.

These figures are general and conjectural in the sense that there are no sure demographic data for the palace or the period from which to draw. I have also not calculated how much additional grain would have been needed to feed the hundreds, if not thousands, of royal horses, many of which were lodged in the palace stables, partly because Giginyu's work suggests, contra Smith, that slave estates were set up not to provide grain for people, but to supply fodder for horses, at least in the nineteenth century (1981). Moreover, I have not included the in-kind payment given over to local chiefs and administrators for arranging the forwarding of grains to the central palace. The amount of grain I have deduced for palace reproduction is therefore highly conservative. The largeness of the numbers demonstrates the monumentality of palace needs and suggests that such needs could probably not be met by rural slave estates alone, especially given that estates had their own reproductive requirements, including the provisioning of horses and farm animals. This hypothesis is more in keeping with the work of Hill, who avers that plantation slavery was not widespread in prejihadic Hausaland, plantations being something developed much later by the Fulani after the nineteenth-century religious jihad (1985). Cooper similarly points out that prejihadic slavery in Niger was not geared toward large plantation systems, but toward smaller scale labor inputs on farms and in the cities (1997, 6–7).[13]

Granaries functioning as state treasuries were not unusual features in the Sudan. In the seventeenth-century Islamic kingdom of Funj, east of Kano, for example, granaries were located throughout the kingdom, reflecting the fact that the state was perambulatory and less invested in commercial exchange. When the state was later seated permanently in the capital city of Sinnar and tied into Islamic networks of commerce and trade, grain storage was centralized.[14] Sinnar's trajectory suggests a similar scenario for Kano, involving a transition from dispersed to centralized grain storage after the palace exurb of Kano was built. In any case, the presence of extensive granaries in the Kano palace advises that grain tax revenues were first centralized circa 1500, ensuring the viability of palace-based administrative life. The fact that royal concubines administered granary contents shows that royal women were integral, vital parts of this state apparatus, womanly "domestic" duties in this case tied intricately to state reproduction.[15]

The location of the granary treasury complex at the terminus of the western, "female" pathway suggests that connections between women in the interior and the central market were of some political importance. Indeed, the pathway connected the palace ciki to the city grain market which was presided over by the most important female official of state, Korama (see Figures 3 and 4).

Korama, Market Grains, and Palace-Market Links

Korama is a historically intriguing and greatly under-studied state official. Sa'id, for example, refers to Korama simply as an official who served in "the Hausa administration" (1983, 117), while Smith records that Korama existed up through the reign of the last Hausa ruler, Alwali (1781–1807) (1997, 63). The title, however, was originally the most important and powerful one associated with Kano's central market. While Korama's powers declined in the mid-1800s, she served the Fulani administration throughout the nineteenth century, the title only dying out in the mid-1900s (chapter 5).

Korama's pre-nineteenth-century powers were extraordinary, encompassing the regulation of all city grain prices and volumes.[16] Accordingly, she occupied the single most important economic office created by Rumfa. Singularly honored among female titleholders, she was awarded a caparisoned horse, and wore masculine attire, in particular a robe and an *alkyabba* or mantle. Her wearing of the alkyabba is significant in that it was typically reserved only for the highest-ranking male court officials (Lavers 1985).[17] Field data show that Korama reported daily on the status of grain sales and regional grain supplies at daily palace court sessions, up through the reign of Abbas (1903–19), whereupon she reported only weekly. Wherever she traveled, she was attended to by her retinue, including subordinate female grain sellers of the market, her procession characterized by considerable pomp and circumstance. All informants who relayed information to me about the title-holder spoke of her tremendous power and might, evinced by her large entourage, magnificent clothing, and her superior mode of travel by horse-back.[18] The consistency of her praise was unlike anything I had encountered previously in informant descriptions of any other freeborn or slave officials. Curiously, the considerable powers of this female titleholder have gone rela-tively unnoticed for over a century by Kano travelers and scholars from the west. Her title appears to have been widespread across Hausaland, though there has been no detailed comparative historical or geographical study of it.

The KC first mentions the Korama title with regard to Sarkin Abdullahi Kisoki's reign (1509–65) and his successful routing of the Sarkin Borno, a for-midable enemy to the east:

> In the next year the Sarkin Bornu came to attack Kano, but could not take the town and returned home. Then Kisoki said to one of his men, Dunki, "Mount the wall, and sing a song in praise of the Sarki and his men of war." Dunki went. The song that he sung was this: "Kisoki, physic of Bornu, and the Chiratawa." He sung it again and again, and after that he praised all those who were present at the fight . . . about forty in all. Dunki said their praises for forty days. After these he celebrated anyone else he thought was worthy, as Madaki Koremma [Korama], Dagachi, Alkali Musa Gero. . . . The Madaki Auwa, because she was the grandmother of Abdu-lahi [and wife of Muhammadu Rumfa], was also celebrated, in a song beginning: "Mother! Kano is your country. Mother! Kano is your town."

Here, Korama is the *first* title and person mentioned after the king's warriors (Palmer 1967 [1928], 113). Field and secondary evidence indicate that the title may be pre-Islamic, predating the building of the palace exurb and cen-tral market. The title would have gained considerably greater political and economic importance after Rumfa centralized taxation storage and grain sales through establishing the palace and a central market. In this sense, Korama's pre-Islamic significance was strategically recognized and expanded upon as a strategy to bring grain, the mainstay of Kano's agrarian economy, under centralized state control.

It is tempting to conjecture that early on Korama's marketplace served as a clearinghouse for grains to be taxed by the state, perhaps from areas further afield than those where the heavier dami could be transported to the palace with relative ease. I suggest this because all farmers who wanted to sell grain were required to deposit their goods with the Korama in a large collection area in the market interior. Korama's attendees would record the volume brought by each seller and then stockpile the grains together in large mountain-like mounds. Only the Korama and her designated assistants knew who had brought what grains and only the Korama and her designated assistants could sell them; the farmers would return later to collect their due.[19]

The word *Korama* is interestingly redolent of grains, linked etymologically to images of earthly fertility. As Bargery notes, *korama* means a large stream flowing through fertile land, and only secondarily refers to the female title-holder, as in "2. (Kano and Zaria) The head woman trader in cereals and foodstuffs which are sold by measure" (1934, 623).[20] Besides asserting parenthetically that the title was present in both Kano and nearby Zaria, Bargery avers that similar positions were held by female titleholders, known as *saraki*, in two states north of Kano, the nineteenth-century Fulani sultanate of Sokoto and the adjoining and rival Hausa state of Katsina.[21] Smith writes likewise that the office of Korama existed in Daura, though the status and grain-related responsibilities of the office may have varied (1978). Since at least the 1700s in Daura, for example, Korama was an elderly free woman appointed by, and subordinate to, the Chief Butcher (Sarkin Pawa). She presided over grain sellers, volumes, and prices, and she collected portions of articles sold by measure from market vendors as tax (117). The Daura Korama also diurnally collected grain tributes from vendors, the tributes used to feed single women, *karuwa* (a term at times translated uncritically as "prostitutes"),[22] and *bori* spiritual mediums for whom she was responsible. The latter two groups had overlapping membership. Smith avers that by the early nineteenth century the Kano Korama was similarly assigned by the market's Chief Butcher, an assignation vehemently denied by informants (1997, 63). The Korama, they insisted, was elected to office and had the greatest of respect of her peers, having achieved considerable recognition, respect, and status in her trading career. This electoral process is similar to what Jaggar describes in terms of how the Kano city's Chief Blacksmith was selected, namely that "[t]he candidate should be generally popular with his fellow craftsmen and a man of experience, good sense and sound judgment" (1973, 18).[23] Indeed, the present emir of Daura and the Daura palace's official historian (Alhaji Muhammad Bashir and Mamman Siya Abubakar, respectively)[24] maintain that the Daura Korama was the eldest daughter of the king and that it was she who appointed the lesser, rural Koramas. Smiliarly, the emir of Dutse asserts that his region, too, boasted a Korama with related grain and responsibilities and the ability to appoint rural Koramas.[25]

My research shows that the Kano Korama had powers similar to those obtained in Daura and Dutse, but that she was independent of the Chief Butcher. The data also indicate that traditionally every market in Kano city and every village market had a titular Korama (or her equivalent), though the Korama in Kano's central market reigned supreme.[26] In the latter instance, the king confirmed the election of the Korama by her peers through a ritual turbaning. In return for her services, the Korama was allowed to take a portion of the goods she regulated and sold by measure. The last Korama of the central Kano market was turbaned by Emir Usman (1919–26) and died in about 1950. Today, grains hold little of the cultural, economic, or political importance they did historically, explaining partly why no Korama has since been reappointed to any of Kano's or Dutse's central markets.[27]

The spatial linkage effected between Kano's central market and the palace interior by the "female" pathway (similar to what was noted for Dutse) is striking and insinuates that it forged strong social ties between palace concubines and Korama. Because Korama's position made her privy to information on regional grain production, the pathway surely also transmitted her judgments concerning taxation amounts and the differential abilities of certain regions or farmers to pay, not only to the king during her daily consultations with him, but to royal concubines who ultimately controlled and monitored grain flows into the palace.[28] In this sense, royal concubines were aware and part and parcel of grain taxation processes. And certainly Korama could have used the market pathway to send royal concubines and wives tributes of grain collected (or extorted) from market vendors. Indeed nineteenth-century information shows that Korama interacted regularly with royal concubines. Many palace informants averred, for instance, that the leading concubine administrator, Uwar Soro, regularly requisitioned Korama for female laborers to carry out the most arduous of interior tasks, the threshing of grain foremost among them. The palace threshing tasks assigned to Korama indicate that the workforces of Korama and palace concubines revolved around cooperative management of incoming grain. Might the shared tasks intimate that the market was also a tax collection site, if not for all city-state inhabitants, then for those who had not paid up but who were intent on selling their goods—a site of confiscation, if you will? And, as suggested above, for farmers from distant places, threshing grains beforehand made sense, given the distance from the central market.

The market pathway in any event would have helped streamline the acquisition and storage of grains deriving from the market, either as tax, tribute, or purchase, particularly when palace reserves were low or depleted. It is not unreasonable to conjecture that the minions of palace concubines used the pathway additionally to barter palace grains for other grains in the market as needed.[29] Some etymological evidence indirectly supports this hypothesis. In particular, the palace entrance hall for the western palace pathway has for at least a hundred years been called Kofar Kwaru (the Gate of Bartering). Unlike the word *ciniki*, which refers to trading more generally, palace informants insisted that *kwaru* refers to a kind of trading specific to women, that is, the bartering of grains.[30] Perhaps early on the grains also served as a kind of currency with which palace concubines could pay for other items, such as cloth, indigo, salt, or spices. Spaulding's work on the Sudanic Funj kingdom of Sinnar is instructive here, in that it documents how, beginning in the 1600s, units of grain (as well as iron, cloth, salt, cattle, and gold) were employed in some marketplaces as currency (1985, 110).

Other nineteenth- and twentieth-century data indicate that still other sociopolitical and labor linkages existed between Korama and concubines. Royal concubines regularly called on Korama to send workers to the palace to pound the palace interior floors *(dabe)* into a hard, cement-like surface, and the last Korama, whose name was Ai, married a palace *bauwa* (slave).[31] Ai's children held lucrative positions in the palace slave hierarchy: One daughter became a palace concubine, while one of her sons became the emir's driver, his son in turn inheriting the position.[32]

In the 1500s and 1600s, then, it appears that the centralization of grain collection and distribution through the granaries and central market were two of the most important, if not *the* most important, political and economic activities of the reorganized state. Tax centralization and marketing, moreover, effected crucial and highly politicized sociospatial linkages between palace concubines and Korama.

In a sense, Korama's title and position, like that of a certain royal concubine (below), incarnated linkages between femaleness and the fertility, of earth and humans. Korama's connection with royal women and royal granaries in tandem with the fertility-related meaning of her title is redolent of other pre- and non-Islamic contexts where grain marketing and fertility concerns were interconnected and the preserve of women. Especially striking were the labor and status parallels that existed between Korama and the Sonya or Lelu, two market-related female titles of urban and rural contexts, respectively, in nearby Nupeland, titles that operated from at least the 1500s onward.[33] The title *Sonya* derives etymologically from the Nupe root, *So,* meaning head or chief, and is equivalent to the Hausa term for queen, *sarauniya.* As Nadel explains:

> Among the Bida women of low birth, the wives and daughters of commoners, we find another women's rank, *Sonya*. She is, as the Nupe put it, the "*Sagi* [a royal female title] of the poor": what the royal princesses do for the women of the nobility the *Sonya* does for the women of her own class: she advises them and arbitrates in their quarrels, taking, however, the more serious cases to the [royal] *Sagi*. The *Sonya* might almost be called a female officer of state. All large-scale women's work that is done in Bida by order of the king is organized and supervised by her—for example, *the beating of*

the floors in the houses of the king and the royal nobility: The *Sonya* is, above all, entrusted with the *supervision of the market*. She is elected by the Bida women who are regular traders on the market, and her rank is confirmed by the *Etsu* [king]. The respect and deference with which all Bida women greet their *Sonya* illustrates the importance of her position. Formerly she was a royal fief-holder on a small scale, holding land of her own; *she was also allowed to levy a small due on all business transacted on the market.* Of this levy, the *Sonya* returned one-third to the *Sagi* or *Nimwoye* [a royal woman's title] as a symbol of her submission to the highest authority of these royal princesses over the women of Bida. Today the *Sonya* is still supervising. (1965 [1942], 148; my emphasis)[34]

Like Korama, then, the Sonya was of nonroyal birth and was elected by female peers in the market. And, as in the case of Kano, the king confirmed her appointment, and she organized the labor needed to pound palace floors. Nadel's work suggests, moreover, that Korama liased with, and was answerable to, a titleholding female relative and appointee of the king, that she received some form of tribute from market transactions she oversaw, handing over a portion of these to royal women, and that she held her own lands. In villages of Nupeland, the Sonya's duties were held by the titleholder, Lelu, a replication paralleling Kano women's assertions that every Kano market, rural or urban, had a Korama. Nadel found that village Lelu were much valued for their abilities in magic, akin perhaps to the Korama's association with fertility and spirit possession practices (Nadel 1965 [1942], 148).

Yet another female titleholder with duties similar to the Korama existed at about the same time in Yorubaland, the so-called Eni-oja who, according to Reverend O. Johnson, was the "chief administrator" of the king's market and "head of all devil worshippers," the latter probably referring to fertility-related possession cults (1937 [1921], 66). Like Korama, the Eni-oja wore "a gown like a man" and the king would ritually lean on her arm once a year, on the day he accompanied her to worship in the market and "to propitiate the deity that presides over markets" (66). Unlike other documented cases of female grain officials, the Eni-oja controlled the market in tandem with the third highest-ranking palace eunuch, both receiving remuneration ("emoluments") from their administrative activities (59).

There is some evidence that similar market-related associations between female palace officials and eunuchs obtained in Kano and extended into the domain of taxation. Kano palace eunuchs, for example, held treasury-related titles (chapter 2) and were available to royal concubines and Korama. Moreover, eunuchs of lesser status assisted physically in the storage and dispensation of grains in the palace interior. At any rate, eunuchs traversed royal female domains and, therefore, like the royal female messengers (*jakadu*), made for ideal palace/outside world go-betweens. Eunuch responsibilities for early forms of grain taxation in Kano are intimated in Fika 1978 (10 n. 42). Based on ethnographic information, Fika asserts that some eunuchs appointed by Rumfa oversaw tax collection from farmsteads, paralleling eunuchs' revenue collection duties in Oyo (Bay 1998, 113). Like other scholars, however, Fika never explores women's official capacities in this regard or the internal grain needs of the palace that compelled women's involvement, including Korama, in state grain procurement processes. In light of the sociospatial data presented above, it is tempting to surmise that eunuchs indeed participated in tax collection, but under the direction of, or in tandem with, Korama, palace concubines, and jakadu. The partnership of concubines and eunuchs, with concubines in some instances outranking eunuchs, may help explain why one of the wives or concubines of Rumfa's successor and son, Abdullahi (1499–1509), established a eunuch market after her son Kisoki came to power (East 1971 [1930], 33).

The genealogy of the Korama title is complicated by research showing that the title may derive from an ethnic group, known as the Kurama, who lived near the Kurmi market, prior to the nineteenth-century Fulani takeover. This may be an instance where the name of a geographical place (the market) instituted by Rumfa became transmogrified into the name for an ethnic group, for though the Kurama lived alongside the Hausa, they were apparently not absorbed, but remained separate, calling themselves the Akurmi (Forest People), after the name of the market, Kurmi (Nengel 1988, 245). From the 1500s through the 1700s this group must have dispersed itself widely, since by the 1800s the Kurama were concentrated southeast of Kano, in the highlands and plains of Jos and eastern Zazzau where they engaged mostly in agriculture. In any case, their earlier association with agriculture and marketing in Kano suggests that the Korama title harks back to a time when the Akurmi operated in and near the Kano market and were valued for their farming and grain marketing abilities. Perhaps they assumed control over the agricultural parts of the market, taking the market name of Kurmi as their own, additionally deriving a title (Korama) from it, a title alloyed with farming and fertility. More interesting is the fact that during the nineteenth century the title of Iyan Kurama was created in Zazzau, the holder of which was responsible for collecting taxes from non-Muslim Kurama (252). The first titleholder was the son of the Fulani emir, Malam Yamusa (1821–24) who, as royalty, resided in Zaria, sending out jakadu on his behalf. His taxation responsibilities are thus reminiscent of what I suggest obtained among the Korama, Mai-Kudandan, palace eunuchs, and female jakadu.

It seems more likely, however, that the origins of the Korama title derived etymologically from the word *Kurmi*. Such a connection is discerned by Shea (1986) in an unpublished work that, drawing on an unpublished paper by the linguist Schuh (1983), avers that the name of Kano's central market (Kurmi) derives from the proto-Chadic etymological root *k-r-m* that is at least two thousand years old. This root is related to a constellation of signifiers associated collectively with different kinds of grains (especially millet and guinea corn), plant parts (particularly the leaves of bean and corn plants), grain trading, and various senses of plenitude: [35]

> The most important and obvious word concerned with grain sales which seems as if it might have some connection with our earlier terms is *kwarami*. Bargery gives the principal meaning of this word as: "trading in corn, buying in villages and selling in towns." And Abraham concurs. The main function of the central urban market, such as in Kano City, would have been for the selling of grain which had been bought in villages, and perhaps it is not too far fetched to suggest that at one time such a market might have been called *Kasuwar 'Yaa Kwarami* or even *Kasuwar Kwarmi*. If indeed this is part of the explanation of how *Kasuwar Kurmi* got its name and *how its officials got their titles,* then what would have distinguished the market from others would have been that this was an organized, disciplined grain market with appointed officials answerable to the *Sarkin Kano* (the King) and who enforced the use of standardized measures to ensure fair trading and justice. In the fifteenth century this would no doubt have been a boon to the ordinary consumer and would have encouraged people to patronize such a market. (Shea 1986, 5; my emphasis)

Shea goes on to summarize the historicity of the Hausa root *k-r-m* and its Arabic counterpart, *karim,* and closes by arguing that:

> the new market established by Mohammed Rumfa in the fifteenth century was named *Kurmi* because it had one or more of the following connotations for the people of the time: grain, quality, abundance, wealth and generosity (and perhaps thus justice). This new market was thus distinguished as one where one could get fair measure for grain, as a disciplined, ordered and just market and one where there were responsible officials appointed by the King and answerable to him to ensure justice.
>
> . . . Mohammed Rumfa is remembered especially for introducing orderly government on the Islamic model. . . . It would be expected that if he instituted a market at this time that he would have followed Islamic injunctions about insuring fair and just measures in the market. (9)

In light of the fact that only women traded grain in Kano's central market, that the palace gate of Kwaru spoke to women's monopoly over grain bartering generally (kwaru), and that Kofar Kwaru was the state's linchpin linking the Korama (and grain trading in the Kurmi market) to palace concubines (and the interior granaries), I would make the case that Shea's analysis be extended. In particular, I would reason that his constellation of signifiers speak specifically to a feminized symbology of fertility, both earthly and (by association) human.

Whatever the case may be, my elaboration of market-palace alliances between women based on sociospatial data and grain-based practices begs questions of precisely which concubines were responsible for grain storage and use inside the royal interior and who determined taxation amounts and ensured that grain taxes reached the palace interior. Both questions are addressed, in turn, below.

Mai-Kudandan—Master of the Granaries

Field discussions and the mapping of palace structures imply that grain storage and use were controlled by a powerful concubine, bearing the title Mai-Kudandan (Master/Owner of the Granary). The last such titleholder died in the late 1980s, and a new appointment was never made.

The meaning of *Mai-Kudandan* was inferred from geographical information in tandem with etymological clues and data from secondary sources, especially Rufa'i (1987). The word *kudandan,* as translated by Robinson, means a hut made with mud walls (1925). More important, he proffers two additional Hausa equivalents: *kudandami* and *kwandandami, dami* reminiscent of the manner in which grain taxes were brought to the palace granaries, that is, as unthreshed grain bundles or dami. Might the particular hut to which the word *kudandan* was originally applied have been those used to store grain, that is, kudandan of dami? It would seem so, especially given that *Mai* translates as "Master" or "Owner," which would then make her full title, Master/Owner of the Granaries.[36] Indeed, Bargery's definition tells us that a kudandami is specifically "a corn [guinea corn] bin built of clay, the walls being continued upwards and inwards till only a small circular opening is left" (1934, 623). Abraham's definition additionally relays that a kudandami was a permanent variety of grain-storage facility for ears of guinea corn or millet or threshed grains (1962). At least in the nineteenth century, a kudandan sat typically on large stones, keeping the contents dry and protecting the grain from insect encroachment.

Sociospatial evidence suggests that the administrative duties of Mai-Kudandan and her staff circa 1500 were extensive. The etymology of her title and nineteenth-century practices suggest that she was directly responsible for ministering the storage of all of the palace's incoming grains, which were carried to the palace granaries by slave workers, especially slave boys and eunuchs. Recall that the same title and grain-related responsibilities existed in the old Dutse palace and that a similar position obtained in the Abomey palace of Dahomey; in the latter case, a powerful "wife" of the king held the keys to the king's storehouse-treasury until the early 1700s when she participated in an unsuccessful coup against the king. As a result of her treason her responsibilities were handed over in perpetuity to a male official (Bay 1998, 88).

Whatever the case, Mai-Kudandan administered the daily distribution of grain portions to specific concubine emissaries. Nineteenth-century titles and divisions of labor suggest the following labor scenario: Daily, Mai-Kudandan visited the granaries to oversee cadres of concubines and slave women, presumably under directives issued by Uwar Soro, who as chief palace concubine knew how much grain was needed daily. Unthreshed dami was first handed over to slave women known as *kuyangi,* administered by the leading *kuyanga (sing.),* Uwar Kuyangi (mother of Kuyangi), who lived in the central concubine ward of Yelwa (Abundance), along with all the other chiefly female titleholders.[37] The kuyangi, at times assisted by Korama's recruits, threshed the dami in open fields located in the westernmost part of the palace interior (Figure 4).[38] The threshed grains were then brought to Yelwa, wherein was located a massive threshed grain-storage facility and kitchen. Here, Mai-Kudandan would sit and preside over her minions as they used specially calibrated calabashes to distribute the grains to concubine representatives from all the concubine wards and wifely places. These representatives, known as *iyayen waje,* were answerable to the concubine titleholder, Babba Uwar Waje (the *big* woman of the place), who likewise resided in Yelwa. It was the task of the iyayen waje to oversee the carriage of their respective grain allotments (by *kuyangi*) to their represented place *(waje),* to which they were dedicated as chief domestic manager. Thus, the uwar waje *(sing.)* of the first wife collected her portion on behalf of her mistress, as did the uwar waje of the second wife, and so on.

While grains destined for consumption in wifely sectors and some communal concubine wards were sent directly to those places, most grains were kept in Yelwa and cooked for the palace community as a whole, which included royal children, slaves, malams, and many guests and visitors. Mai-Kudandan and the leading concubine, Uwar Soro, supervised food preparation in Yelwa through an elaborate concubine and slave hierarchy.[39] Different qualities and quantities of food were produced for different status groups of persons, according to their sociopolitical standing. Royalty and nobility received the highest quality foods, whereas Islamic scholars and menial slaves received the lowest. Social standing was underscored further by the fact that the differently hierarchized food types were prepared by different status groups of women: Slave women cooked for scholars and slaves, royal wives and high-ranking concubines cooked for the emir and his special guests, and concubines cooked for royal children and others.

Food hierarchies were similarly evident in wifely quarters where concubines accomplished the heavier kinds of labor involved in cooking, whereas the wife remained seated, watching over the concubines' actions with care, lest they put "magic" *(magana)* in her food. Such surveillance demonstrates the tenuousness of master (wife)–slave (concubine) relations. While concubines were subservient to wives, wives depended on them, with concubines having ways of negotiating some sort of fair treatment. Status hierarchies between the two groups were also evident in the fact that only a wife could apportion and distribute food in her compound.[40] And there is evidence that wives, not concubines, helped determine the marriage partners of royal children, especially young girls.

Most food cooked in Yelwa was prepared in the centrally located Soron Tuwo (Hall of Porridge). Many palace women and men relayed how concubines and slaves traditionally sat atop large tortoises while stirring their respective pots, the tortoises sopping up food bits that dropped on the ground.[41] As it did in many areas throughout West African, the tortoise presumably held spiritual significance, embodying notions of femaleness and fertility.[42]

Intriguing evidence from the nineteenth century indicates that Mai-Kudandan may not only have officiated over treasury grains, an embodiment and symbol of earthly fertility, but over royal childbearing itself: To wit, royal woman were expected to give birth in Mai-Kudandan's quarters, quarters built in the shape of a kudandan (granary, an arrangement identical to that obtaining in the old Dutse emirate palace nearby).[43] Through her position, place, and person, then, royal children and grains became symbolic and practical equivalents. On the one hand, royal children were born in a kudandan reminiscent of the royal granary/treasury that Mai-kudandan controlled, these children, like grains, being important markers of kingly wealth and virility.[44] On the other hand, royal children were the fruits of female fertility that, like grains borne from the earth, were essential in materially and culturally reproducing the state over the *longue durée*. Children not only ensured kingly succession but, like grains themselves, served as a kind of currency, in this case, deployed in marriages to build up kinship links with those of importance in and outside the capital. Children of lesser chiefs and kingdoms were similarly deployed, forming complex cultural and social webs of kinship and connection.[45]

Beside her many grain-children responsibilities, Mai-Kudandan presumably helped tend to the "house" of the most important female palace spirit residing in Yelwa, today referred to as Aljanna (Arabic for "spirit"). In similar fashion, probably as early as the late 1500s, the favorite "wife" of the king of Buganda cared for the goddess of power and fertility (Musisi 1991, 782). In the Kano palace, the female spirits lived in two separate structures built in the form of granaries. The first was located in the central concubine ward, Yelwa, in the western side of the palace, just like the granary-like spirit-house for the aljanna of the nineteenth-century palace of nearby Dutse emirate. Both of the latter granary houses were built adjacent to sacred kuka (baobab) trees, far from the main entrances. Today, the Kano palace kuka near Yelwa is enormous and much feared by palace women who would never deign to cook with its leaves; the Dutse palace kuka and spirit kudandan, by contrast, were demolished by the present emir of Dutse, who forbade the practice of bori and abandoned that palace to build a new one, leaving his father's entourage there; intact. The Dutse palace's kuka-kudandan focal point marked, as was the case in the Kano palace, the site for concubine-led bori practices.[46] The other Kano palace site of a female palace spirit was probably built in the nineteenth century and was located inside the king's compound, about one hundred meters to the east of the granary house in Yelwa. Until recently, concubines collectively cared for the spirit homes and ensured that the spirits were well fed (cf. Rufa'i 1987), the house in Yelwa the former focal point of concubine-supported bori practices.[47] This spirit-grain-fertility connection was reiterated in other contexts. Recall, for instance, that Mai-Kudandan lived in a granary structure wherein all royal children were born and that she controlled the state granaries. Recall, additionally, the dual grain-spiritual responsibilities of Korama, her titular associations with fertility, and her obligation to feed single, sexually active women not otherwise provided for (karuwai) and female spiritual mediums of bori. These latter were often called upon to intervene in cases of infertility (Barkow 1972, 326) and would have been indispensable to palace bori practices centered around Yelwa's spirit house.[48] A particularly potent expression of bori's concern with fertility was described and photographed by Starratt during the Shan Kabewa (Drinking Pumpkin) Festival of 1989 at Rijiyar Lemo, Kano. In a caption to her photograph, she writes:

> The Bori celebrant is standing on an inverted grain mortar with a large pumpkin (kabewa) in front of him. He will jump and land feet outstretched, crushing the pumpkin with his buttocks. Participants will rush to grab a piece of the vegetable to use in preparing medicines for the coming year. Formerly a Harvest Festival, Shan Kabewa is now performed annually before Ramadan. (1993, 143)

Similar connections of spirits and agricultural fertility were evinced in the western palace farmfields used only by slave women and controlled by spirits.

Six ciki (interior/stomach) sites helped shore up and disperse Mai-Kudandan's authority and power: the northern granaries; the northwesterly threshing grounds; the central kitchen or Soron Tuwo; her personal chambers where all royal children were born; the threshed grain storage facility; and granary-like places for palace spirits, most of these located in Yelwa (see Figure 4). In some senses, the religious and managerial powers of Mai-Kudandan surpassed those of the leading concubine administrator, Uwar Soro, leading perhaps to rivalries between them, though such feuds remain in the realm of conjecture.[49] At least in the twentieth century, Uwar Soro monitored portions of grain treasury contents on the king's behalf. Specifically, dami delivered to the palace as tax or religious tithes were first arranged in front of the king's secluded residential quarters under her direction. After she announced the name of the respective contributor, the allotment would be brought to the king's quarters for inspection, a scenario once again demonstrating the intimate knowledge and involvement of royal concubines in the tribute process.[50]

Given the centrality of grain to the early polity, and Mai-Kudandan's powers over the granary treasury, it is hard to imagine that Mai-Kudandan's political reach did not extend beyond the palace interior and city market. Indeed, some evidence suggests that she and her female slave cadres, including special emissaries known as jakadu, were implicated in the process of grain taxation itself.

Tax Collection and Female Jakadu

According to Smith, prejihadic tax collection was tended to by the *male* kin, clients, or slaves of ruling chiefs and officials *(hakimai)*, many hakimai residing in the city (1997, 77). The taxation agents were collectively called jakadu, which loosely translated means "messengers" or "emissaries."[51] Following nineteenth-century Fulani reforms, the jakadu institution was altered substantially, though it remained a powerful institution of men, one eventually abolished during British rule (chapter 5). Yet, there is no reason to think that because male jakadu dominated taxation processes just prior to and after the jihad, that they always did so.[52] I propose instead that a palace cadre of female slaves, also known as jakadu, did so with the assistance of eunuchs. These latter may later have served, or been the precursors to, the male jakadu to whom Smith refers in the context of the late 1700s.[53] Before outlining my reasons for proposing female jakadu's historical importance, I want to outline in some detail their nineteenth-century responsibilities, which I think point to much larger spatial and political ambits in the past.

Throughout the nineteenth century female jakadu held numerous palace positions and carried out security-related and ambassadorial tasks on behalf of the king and royal women. Some of these tasks are still accomplished today.

Perhaps most important, the jakadu served as the king's bodyguard while he remained in the palace ciki. What this meant is that when the king left or entered the palace interior, jakadu escorted him to his male guard, which awaited him at the outermost labyrinth gates to escort him to "male places." Conversely, the jakadu ritually received him from his male guard upon his return. Wherever the king traveled in the ciki, female jakadu preceded him in formation, proclaiming his presence loudly and slowly by the chorus, "tak-ka-wa san-nu" (walk with care), a means of telling others in the interior that they should remove themselves from his direct path and view. In keeping with these guard functions, female jakadu were posted to and lived in checkpoint-houses located in the labyrinth passageways leading to the palace ciki.[54] Female bodyguards serving similar kingly and palace gate functions were noted by European travelers to the Abomey palace of the nearby kingdom of Dahomey as early as the 1700s, suggesting that such bodyguards were not unusual.[55] Bay notes that the presence of the bodyguard indicated how much more the royal palace was than simply a large-scale polygynous household (1998, 69).

The female jakadu that lived and worked in the palace labyrinth ensured that visitors entering the ciki were properly dressed and of the proper demeanor, age, and gender; or if the sarki (king) was praying or consulting with his imam or councillors nearby, the jakadu would detain visitors until he was finished (see Figure 5). These jakadu were older, loyal adherents to

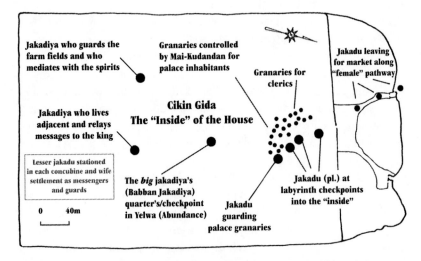

Figure 5. *Jakadu* locations in the early palace. Lesser *jakadu* were stationed in each concubine and wife settlement as messengers and guards. The granaries for clerics would have been walled off, with Soron Hatsi (Hall of Grain) perhaps serving early on as the guarded entrance hall.

palace life and order. At night, they each locked their own labyrinth door, separating the interior from the rest of the palace and world beyond and securing the safety of the king and the royal family. Other jakadu guarded strategic sites associated with grain use and/or pre-Islamic spiritual practices. Some, for example, were posted to the main granary area or small farms in the western agricultural fields worked by and for slave women. In the western fields, at least one jakadiya *(sing.)* was responsible for guarding against spirits believed to inhabit the fields. If she felt there was danger, a slave woman intent on farming would not be allowed to enter.[56] These many jakadu-guarded grain sites would have been of far greater importance prior to the nineteenth century, when grain taxes and earthly fertility held greater political and spiritual sway.[57]

Still other jakadu were stationed in passageway-residences at the mouth of each concubine ward and wifely sector. Besides carrying out guard duties, they served as that section's messenger. Given royal wifely seclusion and the dispersed administrative structure of royal concubines, messenger services were many and varied. A jakadiya or her underling might be sent to another interior section to relay goods or messages; or she might relay messages from the "outside" to inhabitants of her section. Alternatively, she might be sent to the market or a distant village. Today, only one such guardswoman remains, an elderly woman who sits in the entrance hall of the central concubine ward of Yelwa, the titular head of all female jakadu, Babban Jakadiya (The Big Jakadiya; in Hausa, the word "big" is tonally emphasized). Historically, Babban Jakadiya ruled all female jakadu, and it was presumably she who received the kola nuts and gifts (their main remuneration) from powerful male titleholders on her charges' behalf. Similarly, an elderly Babban Jakadiya (Hadiza) lives in the old Dutse palace; it was she who knew of women's village-based indigo-dyeing practices and where they were located, presumably because of her spatial freedoms and responsibilities.

One of the most important emissarial tasks of jakadu was to lead kuyangi in an annual procession to the homes of landholding nobility, bearing great quantities of food prepared by royal wives and concubines, the foods were carried in very large covered containers.[58] Female jakadu had many slave women (kuyangi) at their disposal, suggesting that they held higher status than kuyangi, a relative position that may also have obtained for the female guard of the Abomey palace of Dahomey (Bay 1998, 205).

The ritual provisioning of food to the ruling classes was presumably a means of asserting the king's superior provisional abilities and a means by which royal women demonstrated their control over grain resources and their skills in transforming the grains into something transactionally powerful and useful.[59] Similar provisioning of food was an integral part of the annual kingship ritual in Dahomey known as the Customs. An eighteenth-century visitor described, for example, that food and locally brewed beer were prepared in the palace and later "carried in procession by palace women and distributed 'not only among the more distinguished guests, but even without the camp, where the vulgar partake plentifully'" (Dalzel, cited in Bay 1998, 125). In Dahomey, young armed female soldiers were paraded at Customs, there being four or five distinct female corps (Bay 1998, 129–35).[60]

Cooper, summarizing the scant evidence from secondary sources, describes nineteenth-century jakadu equivalents in nearby Gobir, Damagaram, and Ader (1997, 67–68). In all cases, the women seem to have served primarily as court messengers and diplomats, though none of the works she cites could be considered a comprehensive study about jakadu. Drawing on the work of Last (1967, 92) for example, Cooper notes that "[w]hen Sokoto captured Jekadiya [sic] Iyargurma Faima of Gobir during one of Bello's raids [of the nineteenth-century jihad] on the recusant forces of Maradi, she owned forty slaves of her own and was a valued messenger" for the king of Gobir (1997, 67). And that in eighteenth-century Ader, the jekadiya (assumed to be only one person) "announced important visitors, maintained the fire in the sarki's entryway where men gathered, and was sent on special diplomatic missions" (67). In a different vein, the jekafadu (it is unclear if this is one person or many) of Damagaram acted as an intermediary between the sultan and his wives, a relationship that may have also obtained in the Kano palace: Perhaps the jakadu who lived in the entrance-residences of each of the palace sections of royal concubines and wives intermediated between these women, the king, and the women's natal communities, helping to cultivate crucial political geographical ties. Certainly this appears to have been the case in Maradi where Cooper asserts that "[t]he wives of the sarki of Maradi today come from all over the region and reflect ties with strategic interest groups: maintaining those marriages and ties [through the jakadu] is an important part of maintaining his support more generally" (68).

In any event, the many nineteenth-century security and emissarial tasks of Kano palace jakadu and their assumed intimate involvement in grain-related concubine tasks begs an important historical question: What was the geographical extent and political range of jakadu activities during the 1500s and 1600s? From and to where, for example, and from and to whom, did jakadu bring royal messages and orders? Were the messages solely personal salutations levied among women within and outside of the palace, or were the jakadu important emissaries, effectively strengthening ties between palace concubines' and wives' communities and the king? Might jakadu also have worked in tandem with eunuchs in carrying palace concubine mandates, sanctioned by the king, to chiefs responsible for certain grain-taxable lands in the context of an early agrarian economy? If in the nineteenth century jakadu served as official go-betweens between Korama and palace concubines, ritual emissaries to the households of nobility, royal guards and messengers, and intermediaries with high-ranking eunuchs, might they have wielded their powers historically in more significant ways? After all, the nineteenth century was a period of decline for women, suggesting that all palace women had operated historically in larger and more economically and politically powerful ways than those circumscribed by the female pathway and palace interior.

The data collectively make it possible to hypothesize that Mai-Kudandan and Uwar Soro worked together with the Korama, ultimately directing eunuchs and female jakadu in early forms of grain tax administration, male jakadu taking over taxation roles sometime in the eighteenth century when cowries began to replace grains as the taxation currency.[61] In this sense, female jakadu's largely ceremonial functions today as the king's bodyguard, their ritual guarding of the palace labyrinths, their running of errands for palace concubines and wives, and their leading of annual food processions to the houses of powerful men are relics of much larger historical responsibilities.

Royal Women and Grain Taxation in Regional Context

Comparative regional information suggests that the two northern palace gates originally served as filters for different species of in-kind taxes entering the palace proper. Grains entered the western "female" gate into the interior preserve of women; recall that the western palace pathway led from the Korama-controlled central grain market to the concubine-controlled centralized grain treasuries in the ciki. By contrast, nongrain items entered the eastern "male" gate into the preserve of slave men. A similar taxation scenario operated in the rectangularly shaped palace built in the eighteenth century in the Sudanic sultanate of Dar Fur (O'Fahey 1980, 24–28). Here, the "male" entrance was located in the north, instead of the east, and led directly to a palace domain considered to be public, as was the case in the Kano palace. Moreover, just as in the Kano palace, the male, public area hosted royal stables and households of slave warriors, eunuchs, and other palace slaves. The "female" entrance to the Dar Fur palace, narrower and located in the south, led to royal private and familial domains. Each of these palace gates received different types of taxation and tribute. Grain, cloth, or animal tributes were carried through the women's gate because the items were intended for domestic palace consumption, though much of the grain received through this gate was grown on royal slave estates. Beyond the female gate were interior areas where slave women and concubines prepared foods, located similarly to the Kano palace granaries and threshing grounds. Obversely, revenues intended to support military and administrative endeavors were brought through the male gate. As in the Kano context, state revenues were not brought all at once to the capital. O'Fahey notes similar gendered symmetries and gate positions in the nineteenth-century palace of Wadai, west of Dar Fur and east of Kanem-Bornu, described by Barth and al-Tunisi (O'Fahey 1980, 169 n. 57).[62]

Women's official involvement in taxation is not unheard of, though it is commonly assumed to have been of relatively minor importance. In the nineteenth-century breakaway Hausa state of Maradi to the north, for example, the titleholding woman Iya (Mother) was key to non-Islamically derived spirit (bori) initiations and public ceremonies, one of these involving market renewal rites. Iya was characteristically the sister or aunt of the Maradi ruler who was the chief arbiter among women of the aristocratic class, additionally mediating for rural women, and judging disputes among largely rural female practitioners of bori; she also levied grain from market vendors and taxes from "prostitutes" and bori specialists, though her bori responsibilities may have developed only after the nineteenth-century jihad (Cooper 1997, 25, 27; Smith 1967, 108).[63] Her limited control over taxation in the context of bori, markets, and grain defines a context analogous to that controlled by Korama in Daura and Kano, described above. Mack (1991, 112–13), summarizing the work of Dikko (1982), notes that the Iya title also existed in Katsina and that the titleholder intermediated between lesser chiefs and rulers, arranged marriages for former rulers' widows, and ministered to palace feast preparation. That the Iya oversaw the latter suggests that she, too, held some control over grains. She was assisted in this duty by the Sarauniya, a title typically awarded to a ruler's eldest daughter.

Magajiya, another female titleholder in Maradi, similarly levied taxes in village lands awarded to her (Smith 1967). Cooper avers, in fact, that it was the Magajiya and not the Iya who originally administered "prostitutes" in Maradi (1997, 27), Eschard claiming similarly for the Nigerian case of Ader (1991, 216). In Daura the Magajiya was the first daughter to be born in the palace. Like the Maradi Iya, she helped settle women's matters and disputes, the king's eldest daughter (made Korama) handling grain-related matters.[64] The case of Maradi is especially important because it was the Hausa successor state to Katsina, which succumbed in the nineteenth century to Fulani jihadic reforms, many negatively affecting women. Accordingly, state organization in Maradi provides clues into how prejihadic states were structured.[65]

Nadel's work on female titleholders in Nupeland, southwest of Kano, even more provocatively shows that women occasionally controlled or held the power of taxation (1965 [1942]). In Bida, the market Sonya, who controlled the central market and whose equivalent in Kano was Korama, for example, was a fief-holder who levied dues on all business transacted in the market, one-third of which was returned to two royal titleholders, the Sagi and the Nimwoye, female elders related to the king who were powerful in their own right. As Nadel explains, they, along with a third royal titleholder, "occupied an extremely influential position at the court. They took part in the king's council, they could join in the war with their own troops of slaves and serfs, they held fiefs and owned land. Theirs was the position of 'kings over the women of Nupe'" (147).

Similarly, Johnson writes about many tiers of royal female titles in ancient Yorubaland (1937 [1921]). Most of the highest-ranking titles (eight in all) contained the word *Iya* ("Mother" in Yoruba) in them and all of the titlehold-ers had palace compounds.[66] Several titleholders were feudal heads of towns, including the Iya Oba (the Queen Mother), the Iya kere, and the Iyalagbon. The responsibilities of the first two are strikingly similar to those of two Kano palace titleholders, Mai-Babban Daki (the Queen Mother) and Mai-Soron Baki, the concubine titleholder in charge of the king's private chambers who arranged all domestic audiences with the king (Nast 1996). In Kano, the Mai-Babban Daki is said to have administratively controlled limited state lands and related tribute and revenues. What the Yorubaland data suggest, though, is that the Mai-Soron Baki may also have been entitled to land. In *rural* Yorubaland, the most powerful female official was the Iyalode, a titleholder who controlled a hierarchy of female officials. Johnson writes, "Some of these Iyalodes command a force of powerful warriors, and have a voice in the coun-cil of chiefs" (1937 [1921], 77).

Lebeuf describes similar scenarios for three nineteenth-century principal-ities in Kotoko, east of Kano, in what is today Cameroon (1969). There, three titled women ruled alongside the reigning prince: the Gumsu or first wife; the Magira, his biological mother; and the Rolanduma, his oldest sister or a pater-nal aunt. Just as in Kano, the prince was allowed four wives of nonservile birth (the *ngabdelle* or *maram*, depending on the principality) and as many concu-bines as needed or desired (*surien* or *kilime*). The most powerful wife, the Gumsu, commonly the prince's first paternal cousin or paternal niece, was installed using the same ceremonial accorded the prince himself. According to Lebeuf:

> She is in his attendance at all official meetings, she is in charge of nomi-
> nating one of the highest state dignitaries, the Chef des Armees, and she
> actively engages in juridical affairs. She also gathers taxes *(redevances)* from
> a number of places, naming their representatives to the central govern-
> ment; these places include Guedaba, Nkarse et Guechi in Logone-Birni,
> and Klessoum in Kousseri. But her principle function is to be at the dis-
> posal of the Prince whenever he so desires. (1969, 127)[67]

Because of the latter, she resided in quarters facing the personal chambers of the prince and set apart from the residences of other wives and concubines. Moreover, she was forbidden from bearing children and was forced to abort should she become pregnant, since pregnancy would take her attentions away from the prince. The Kotoko case is important in that it indicates a high-ranking palace woman not only collected principality taxes, but also held political oversight over the regions from which her taxes were collected, powers perhaps similar to those Mai-Kudandan held. What is different, here, is that in Kano, palace concubines held most female positions of power, whereas in Kotoko the four freeborn wives did. The Gumsu's taxation duties, for example, would in the Kano case have been handled by the concubine Mai-Kudandan, just as the Gumsu's responsibility of devoting all attention to the king's bodily well-being (to the point of living opposite his sleeping chambers) was in Kano assumed by the palace concubine Mai-Soron Baki.

Murdock avers that many such powers were held by royal women in Sudanic states and that these powers were unusual in non-Sudanic Africa, the only known precursor to women's powers obtaining in Pharonic Egypt (1959, 146). Using comparative information, he identifies three prototypical female positions of power in Sudanic contexts: a Queen Mother, a Queen Consort (a powerful wife or concubine), and an office for the eldest sister of the king.[68] Murdock believes that the uniqueness of Sudanic women's state powers in relation to other state systems in the world is the best evidence to date for claiming Egyptian influence in the Sudan.

Musisi's work on Bugandan state formation, however, shows that women served in powerful state capacities south of the Sudan, albeit in an area having Sudanic influences. Her work describes in some detail royal women's participation in taxation. Intriguingly, Musisi avers that such powers accrued only after the thirteenth-century incursion of Nilo-Saharan peoples. By the late 1500s, freeborn women were, like Kano concubines, collected en masse in the king's household and were given political responsibilities over regional chiefs and taxation. These *abakyala* ("ladies" or titled aristocratic wives) controlled most Buganda chiefs, including the prime minister. As Musisi explains,

> The senior wife . . . had five chiefs under her, including a county chief . . .
> and the chief gate guard. . . . [Another of the ladies] had eleven chiefs
> under her, including two county chiefs. *The chief tax collector was also*
> *responsible to her.* . . . [Another lady] had nine chiefs under her. . . . In total,
> the forty-two titles wives (the *abakyala*) had some eighty six chiefs under
> them. (1991, 780–81; my emphasis)

These titled "ladies" were set apart from wives who were untitled peasants or enslaved women. All, however, were considered "elite wives," the king having no restrictions on him concerning how many women he could take from any of the categories.

The data show, then, that palace women in various Sudanic (and Sudanic-influenced) kingdoms served as titleholders, controlling state lands from which they were allowed to collect taxes and tribute, and that they could serve in any number of state capacities, including kingly bodyguards and as soldiers. Moreover, there is evidence that female officials in a number of kingdoms worked in tandem with eunuchs in market and tax-related activities. In Kano, grain taxation fed into the "domestic" needs of palace concubines, palace concubinage in turn linked firmly to an imaginary of earthly and human fertility embodied in grains and children. Despite their "public" grain-related responsibilities royal wives and concubines maintained seclusion by using jakadu and eunuchs as go-betweens, these persons effectively overseeing the collection and storage of grains entering the palace through the western "female" gate, Kofar Kwaru which served as a fulcrum between the palace interior and Korama.

Yelwa and Royal Control over Food in Comparative Context

The concubine ward of Yelwa (Abundance) was paramount to interior palace life and lay at the sociospatial and symbolic core of the palace-universe (see Figures 4 and 6). Like Korama, much of what is known about Yelwa is based on oral testimony. These testimonies suggest that, unlike other concubine wards, the name, location, and function of Yelwa remained unaltered across the centuries, though its extent, internal configuration, and architectural style would have changed over time. Sa'ad's informants claim that Yelwa was the name, perhaps a nickname, of the original palace (1985). This would make sense, given that palace life emerged symbolically and literally out of (the interior ward of) abundance. Information relayed to Rufa'i suggests that Yelwa was given its name during the reign of Sarki Muhammadu Zaki (1582–1618) (1995, 50). At the very least, the archaic pillar and beam architectural style of the main and massive cooking hall (Soron Tuwo) tells us that the structure probably predates the early nineteenth century, similar to Soron Hatsi and Kofar Kwaru. No female palace elder could remember a historical time when Yelwa or its name did not exist.

Significantly, the communal cooking hall is positioned in nested fashion in the center of Yelwa, placing it effectively in the geometric center of the rectangularly shaped palace ciki. Its central location was discerned after ascertaining and subtracting southern land portions of the palace added on to, or built up in, the nineteenth and twentieth centuries. I interpret Yelwa's centrality as an intentional rather than serendipitous spatial feature, a way of symbolizing the centrality to palace life of grains and the concubines who oversaw

Figure 6. Soron Tuwo (Hall of Porridge): (a) exterior and (b) interior views of the monumental palace cooking hall circa 1990, by which time it was largely abandoned. Soron Tuwo lay in the precise center of what would have been the full extent of the palace *ciki* in 1500. Its location indicates the symbolic and practical centrality of grains and fertility in palace life. Its interior is cored by two massive pillars, a technology used in building massive structures prior to the early nineteenth century.

them. That is, in the center of Yelwa (Abundance) in the center of the ciki (the palatial stomach, womb, inside), grains were transformed into food and, subsequently, into life itself. Yelwa's location incubated and evoked cultural practices that interrelated and identified human and agricultural fertility, fertility additionally being registered in its name. To the degree that Yelwa was the hub of fertility, childbearing, and food production, it served as an umbilical site anchoring the palace universe of fertility to and within itself.[69]

All the most important female slave managers lived in Yelwa, including the concubine titleholders Mai-Kudandan, Uwar Soro, and the Mai-Soron Baki, who oversaw audiences with the king conducted in his chambers. Mai-Soron Baki also guarded over the king's personal treasury and armaments and maintained his quarters (Nast 1996). Babbar Uwar Waje (The Big Uwar Waje), chief concubine administrator of the uwar waje, and Uwar Tafiya, the chiefly concubine who mobilized and organized concubines accompanying the king on military expeditions, also lived in Yelwa.[70] The leaders of lesser female nonconcubine slave cadres likewise lived in Yelwa, though in considerably more modest circumstances. These included the Babban Jakadiya, leader of the female jakadu and Uwar Kuyangi, the head of all kuyangi (domestic servants). Yelwa was the primary center for pre-Islamic spirit possession practices, known as bori,[71] concerned mostly with earthly and human fertility, but also concerned with the vitality of all humans and human endeavors, including markets.

The importance of food in kingly political system, incorporated in part through the names and locations of Yelwa and Mai-Kudandan, cannot be underestimated. Food's centrality was tied not only to earthly and humanly fertility per se, but to provision, a kingly concern and a prerogative ritualized and symbolic of chieftancies, kingships, and sultancies throughout West Africa. Indeed in Sinnar, kingly provision of food was the mythical centerpiece of early kingship. The first leader, it is said, heroically gathered up all the food in the territory to distribute it justly amongst the peoples for which reason he was venerated and made king (Spaulding 1985, 127).[72] A similar mythology exists in Kano, evident in an annual kingship ritual that only recently died out: until the 1970s, upon the first seasonal rains the Kano ruler would go to his ex-urban farm, followed by thousands from the city. Originally, one supposes that his public presence was announced by drums, though in the twentieth century his departure was announced by the booming of guns. Upon reaching his farm, the emir planted the first seed of the planting season, thereafter sitting under a tree, those who followed him continuing to plant until the sun reached its zenith. The next day, everyone would go to their own farms and begin planting.[73] What these scenarios again hint at is that what is currently called *reproduction* lay at the core of political life: *fertility, along with the kingly control over it,* was the linchpin of rule.

Ritual pronouncements of the king's superior ability to provide food is alluded to in the nineteenth-century work of Malam Imoru, a trader and malam born in Kano in 1858. He claims that Uwar Soro, as the most important female palace official, could be asked at any time by the king to prepare food for a guest to impress him. Not fulfilling his wishes were grounds for her dismissal (Ferguson 1973, 213). In a similar vein, Hajiyya Abba, descended from Katsina royalty (Katsina was a rival city northwest of Kano), relayed that the culinary abilities of the Uwar Soro in the nearby Katsina palace were historically legendary, her gastronomic prowess proclaiming the greatness of a king. Recall also that royal wives and leading concubines of the Kano palace ritually sent specially prepared food to titleholding officials in abundance, an act declaring not only the skill and fertility power of royal women, but the bounty of the king.

Fertility Power and Palace Women

The earliest palace, then, seems to have been organized sociospatially around considerations of fertility—earthly (grains and granaries) and human (children), both associated with the activities, places, and bodies of royal concubines. Childbearing and fertility, generally, were venerated. As Amadiume points out, African societies have always placed great value on women's abilities to bear children, women having historically used kinship relations to construct and sustain strongly gendered and separate domains of power (1997). Fertility's importance was, if anything, sociospatially disrupted and manipulated by Islamic practices of seclusion, allowing for state-patriarchal centralization of fertility's powers.

The importance of fertility in non-Islamic mythologies was and is evident throughout the region. In Igbo mythology of southeastern Nigeria, for example, the highest deity is Ala, an earth goddess whose fertility encompasses earth and humanity. She is often depicted surrounded by numerous children and grandchildren. A lesser deity amongst the Igbo of Owerri is the water goddess Ekunochie, similarly associated with fertility and commonly shown in the presence of single women who, seemingly positioned outside an economy of fatherhood (they are not obviously owned), is celebratory of female fertility powers.[74] Riverine Igbo, like the Oru, who migrated from Benin centuries ago, historically worshipped water goddesses associated with the fertility of both earth and women (Jell-Bahlsen 1997). The Oru considered one riverine creature in particular, the tortoise (which were numerous in the palace ciki), to be sacred in its liminality—passing with relative ease from earth to water and back again.

In the Islamic context of the Kano palace ciki, where hundreds of concubines were supported, children of concubines and wives were considered king's property and were used to benefit the city-state's monarchical centralization. The existence of the palace ciki was thus a powerful spatial means for structurally corralling women's fertility into the service of a centralized, patriarchal state. Non-Islamic practices in the palace nevertheless continued, including bori, a form of spirit possession and worship centering on fertility. Continuation of bori practices was enabled, ironically, by the fact that the Islamically informed segregation of women into western portions of the ciki helped to place women beyond the scrutiny of male clerics.

The next chapter presents evidence that palace concubines tried to keep up with changes in the regional political economy during subsequent centuries, engaging in large-scale cloth dyeing for the practical and political needs of the palace and perhaps even as a means of generating some economic currency. At the same time, eunuchs assumed greater importance, eventually moving from residences in "male" parts of the palace into residences located in the concubine-run interior, a move that created social tensions and awarded new functions and meaning to male castration.

CHAPTER 2

Fecundity, Indigo Dyeing, and the Gendering of Eunuchs

T he story of early Kano palace life relayed thus far has relied on interpreting early sixteenth-century spatial patterns of the city and palace
in light of linguistic data and nineteenth-century information. These
data suggest that concubines were vital players within an explicitly (even if
syncretically) Islamic state. Spatial methods and analyses partially compen-
sated for the lack of archaeological data, producing key insights into state formational processes in what was largely an agrarian place. Unfortunately, no
primary documents or other secondary sources are available to refine my
analysis of the sociospatial processes that shaped this important early crucible
of Islamicized state life. Much more nineteenth- and twentieth-century information was available, including recent scholarly works on Kano palace life
and architecture, and archival photographs and documents dating from the
colonial period, permitting greater elaboration on sociospatial changes in
palace life during those centuries.[1]

The many difficulties involved in identifying material changes in the
palace landscape during the sixteenth through eighteenth centuries were
overcome partially also through spatial methods. These methods were crucial
in identifying and mapping out two important interior sites, both dating possibly from the sixteenth century. The first site consists of a large open-air field

controlled by concubines and abutting the central concubine ward in the palace interior or ciki wherein locally produced cloth was dyed with indigo. Though indigo-dyeing technology would change greatly over the centuries, women's dyeing practices endured until 1807 when the interior field was abandoned, eventually to be converted into a dynastic burial ground for Fulani rulers. The second site consists of a large defense-related eunuch colony built in the ciki in the late 1500s to surround the king's quarters, following a successful coup. The colony, redesigned and rebuilt in the mid- to late nineteenth century, was later razed in the 1990s to accommodate a large modern business complex. This chapter examines these two sites to show how they helped constitute distinct and early political cultural practices. Both sites provide important new empirical and analytical directions for researching the geopolitical dynamics of early states as well as the changing political meaning and dynamism of state eunuchism and concubinage. As such, the sites offer rare opportunities to theorize the changing importance of fertility in the political economic imaginary of the state and region and how these changes affected the innermost workings and tensions of the state household, especially those between concubines and eunuchs.

Just as chapter 1 demonstrated the utility of spatial data and geographical methods in discerning sociospatial features of the first palace landscape, this chapter shows how other spatial information can be used to gain insight into palace life in the centuries that followed. Before describing my findings, however, I digress at some length to overview the Islamization of Kano, thereby placing my findings more firmly in regional historical context. Along the way, I examine the provenance of palace eunuchs and concubines and the gendered and status-based conflicts and alliances between them. I also explore how the Queen Mother's powers and the political importance of women and fertility might have been impacted by Rumfa's introduction of state concubinage, eunuchism, and an all-male state council.

Islamization and Kano's "Arab King"

In the 1300s, when Mali was at its economic and political peak, Malian scholars and merchants known as the Wangarawa arrived in Kano, then known as Dalla after the central city hill of Dalla.[2] The Wangarawa played an important part in solidifying early state structure by assisting in the conversion of kings and by helping to defeat rival hill settlements, particularly Santolo and Fangwai to the southeast, derogated as centers of "pagan" life (Figures 7 and 8). Throughout the 1300s, Kano's rulers engaged in large-scale Islamically sanctioned slave raiding in newly conquered areas, expelling sizable numbers of nonbelievers. In doing so, they facilitated centralized territorial and political control and aided the state in acquiring a great amount of labor.

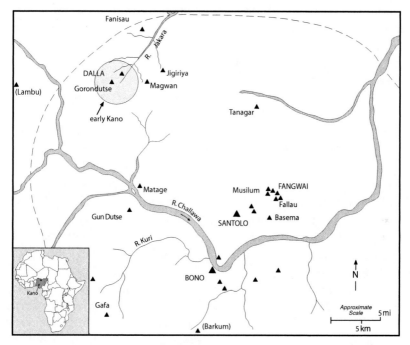

Figure 7. Challawa River bend settlement sites. Prior to palace building, Kano was known as Dalla. (Adapted from Last 1979, 19.)

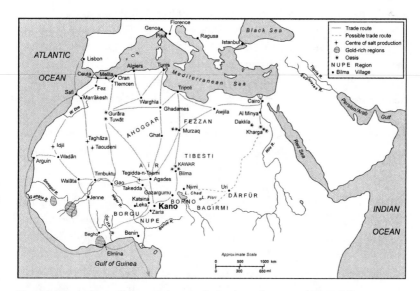

Figure 8. Principal long-distance trade routes in the sixteenth century. (Adapted from Hunwick 1985, 333.)

During the 1300s and 1400s Islamic trade networks expanded in two directions out of Dalla, to the east and north, and to the south and west. The different trade networks were tied loosely to two opposing political factions that King Rumfa (1463–99) would bring together during his reign. Trade to the east and north accelerated in the early 1400s when Kano became tributary to the Islamicized kingdom of Borno. It was probably through Bornoan trade routes to Egypt that Dalla leaders acquired chain mail coats, iron helmets, and quilted armor, given that the Hausa word for armor *(lifidi)* derives from an Arabic one *(libd;* Hunwick 1985). Participation in Islamic trade networks allowed Dalla to upgrade its army and thus gain regional military prominence facilitating the acquisition of larger numbers of slaves. As Hunwick points out, "captives taken . . . and made into slaves could then be used in building, agricultural and other manual labours, while some could be exchanged for further horses" (1985, 330). Dalla forged additional and important trade connections to Egypt and North Africa through trade with the kingdom of Air to the north.

Trade to the south and west passed southward through Zaria (a Hausa state) and Nupeland to Gonja (in what became known as the Gold Coast), a source of kola nuts and gold on the Volta River. Wangarawa merchants and scholars in Dalla and Katsina (a rival Hausa state to the northwest) may have built this trade route as a means of seeking a shorter route to Gonja where they had been trading since the latter part of the 1300s. Construction of the road, later immigration to Dalla by Arabs (principals in trans-Saharan trade), and the prevalence of salt there (the commodity used by the Wangarawa to trade for gold) suggest that gold was common in Dalla by the mid-1400s.

It is not known when the Dalla Hill settlement gained preeminence over the regional hill system or when the town became popularly known as Kano. By the 1500s Dalla had gained ascendance over the Fangwai/Santolo settlement systems; the Dalla Hill settlement had been walled; trade connected Dalla to Egypt and sahelian West and North African kingdoms; and craftspersons, Islamic scholars, and merchants, including the Wangarawa, Bornoans, Tuaregs, Nupe, and Kwararafa, had migrated into the walled settlement of Dalla Hill. In-migration, along with increases in productivity resulting from the use of iron implements in farming and hunting, diversified and increased the population of the Dalla settlement system. The total population of Kano city circa 1500 was probably around 25,000 persons, not including the 1,500 to 2,000 or so persons who lived in or were supported in large part by the Kano palace.[3]

The name *Kano* first surfaces in the late fifteenth- and early sixteenth-century Arabic sources of the cleric al-Maghili and the traveler Leo Africanus, while Borno sources of the same time period employ the name Dalla. At least until 1450 or so, Dalla (Kano) was not a permanent capital, the nascent state not restricted to a single place.

Islamic scholars had arrived in Kano in the 1300s as part of an immigration wave that included Islamic traders and missionaries who, from about A.D. 1000 to 1600, migrated from Southwest Asia and North Africa to much of West Africa in search of gold, salt, and other tradable goods. With trade came proselytization and the partial Islamization of West Africa, with concomitant adoption of Islamic cultural practices. According to the KC and oral tradition, King Muhammadu Rumfa firmly established Islam as Kano's state religion, facilitating its acceptance (though not necessarily its adoption) throughout the kingdom.

Last contends that decades prior to Rumfa's reign, two itinerant political factions tied loosely to the two distant trade networks competed against one another in the region (1983). A Muslim faction lived near Dalla Hill and was associated with the Wangara scholars and merchants who traded to the south and west. The faction derived from the reign of King Yaji (1349–85) who converted to Islam and, with the Wangarawa's assistance, defeated the Santolo "pagans." The second faction derived from the reign of Yaji's son, King Kanajeji (1390–1410), an itinerant warlord who reinstated pagan practices and allied himself with the Tuareg and Sao to the north and west (see Figure 7). During Kanajeji's son's rule (Umaru, 1410–21), Kano was made tributary to the kingdom of Borno to the east. While Rumfa's exact origins remain unknown, Last conjectures that he was a Muslim who came from Berber or Tuareg regions north of Kano. If so, Rumfa's epithet as relayed in the KC, "The Arab King," is not metaphorical. Even if he shared *ethnic* ties and, hence, alliances with Kano's non-Muslim Kanajeji faction, *as a Muslim* he was acceptable to allies of Kano's Muslim Wangarawa. As Last notes: "he seems to have been a 'new man' not strictly identifiable with any particular role or group" (72).

Rumfa, Islam, and the "Male" Eastern Side of the Palace

Rumfa is cited in the KC as the greatest of innovators, a man who instated twelve reforms expanding the king's material might and presence.[4] First, he built the Kano palace, contained by a high rectangular retaining wall that made plain the massiveness of the royal household. A specially built rectangularly shaped exurb with high retaining walls (Rumfa's second innovation) contained the walled palace (see Figure 2). I use the term *palace-exurb* to indicate the tightly nested quality of the monumental palace within the large ex-urban place. Rumfa later re-expanded the city walls by building circular ramparts that looped southward around the palace-exurb (see Figure 1). If the KC is to be believed, Rumfa completed the palace-exurb walls and circular wall extensions before moving into the palace. At any rate, the southern walls of the rectilinear palace and exurb were aligned to Mecca, the palace possibly placed outside city limits to disavow spirit worship practices associated with the city (Fika 1978, 23).[5] Rumfa also created the Kano central market (his third innovation) wherein the most powerful regulator of regional grain sales was placed, the female titleholder Korama (chapter 1).

The palace-exurb's spatial qualities were remarkably innovative. Its rectangular shape and Mecca-bound orientation were atypical of sub-Saharan settlements, its geometry reminiscent of the square suburbs of Tlemcen (Algeria). The palace was also the first place that accommodated Islamically sanctioned *seclusion* of massive numbers of royal women (Rumfa's seventh innovation), the KC euphemistically boasting that Rumfa had one thousand wives (his sixth innovation).[6] This is not to say that monumentality of the palace or state concubinage was regionally unique. European observers noted in the early 1700s, for example, that the largest palace of the Dahomey kingdom (located in the capital city of Abomey) was "as big as a small Town" and governed by the king's "wives," who numbered well over two thousand (Bay 1998, 67). The Abomey palace, unlike the Kano palace, however, was not shaped or oriented for Islamic purposes, and Abomey "wives'" status and activities were not defined by Islamic law.

Lavers (1981) suggests the palace-exurb's rectinilarity and alignment on an axis toward Mecca was inspired by al-Maghili, the renowned Islamic cleric from Tlemcen invited to counsel King Rumfa (see Starratt 1993). Al-Maghili wrote a tract for Rumfa titled "The Crown of Religion Concerning the Obligations of Princes," in which he advised the king on broad issues of state, including Islamic taxation and vernacular forms of Islamic decorum. He insisted on distinct sumptuary prerogatives and physical separation between men and women and admonished the king to "adorn your body and sweeten your odour, and embellish your clothes as far as (Muslim Law) permits the adornment of men, without the imitation of women" (Gwarzo, Bedri, and Starratt 1974/77, 20). He also counsels the king not to concern himself with the domestic and the feminine, where at best he could be a "rooster," but to concern himself with the properly masculine affairs of state, thus becoming an "eagle." This counsel is significant in that it suggests that Islam (if not al-Maghili per se) heightened and reshaped pre-existing gendered norms and gendered spatial divisions of labor into something ostensibly more patriarchal. The creation of visible differences in gendered subjects is underscored by the introduction of clitoridectomy into the region at this time, a procedure some have argued was created as a means of differentiating more dramatically the anatomical differences between men and women.[7]

As head of state and of the royal family, King Rumfa resided in places symbolically, spatially, and practically set apart from those of royal women. The practice of seclusion was widespread throughout West Africa prior to Islamization and expressed the divinity of kingship. Nonetheless, pre-Islamic practices of kingly seclusion in Kano at this time took on new Islamic meaning and sanction: great numbers of royal women were also secluded and the king was to separate himself from them in most official state and religious matters, allowing only the most "pious and trustworthy to come near" (Gwarzo, Bedri, and Starratt 1974/77).[8] Several prominent structures were thus built near the king's chambers. The Kano palace landscape thus amalgamated pre-Islamic and Islamic forms of seclusion on an impressive scale.

Field research suggests that Rumfa's quarters were located in the eastern part of the palace interior and were positioned to be spatially opposite the quarters of royal women (see Figure 9) and perhaps adjacent to a ritual dwelling for a female palace spirit, a second spirit residence located in the central concubine ward of Yelwa (chapter 1).[9] Unlike those of royal women, Rumfa's personal chambers were tethered to the outside world via a pathway that ran along the eastern interior periphery, through the royal stables, into the public slave area, and out through the "male" palace entrance hall onto the path leading northeasterly to the city walls. The placement of the king's

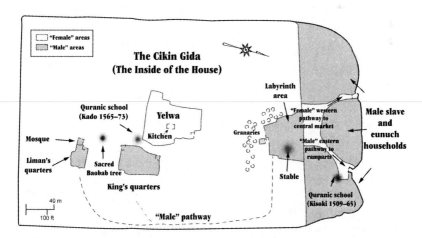

Figure 9. King Rumfa's personal chambers in the eastern part of the palace *ciki* alongside other male domains, such as the mosque, study areas for princes, and the liman's quarters. The Quranic school referred to in the *Kano Chronicle* and built by Kado (1565–73) is here assumed to be in the same location as the school that the KC states was later rebuilt by Bawa (1660–70) in the place known as Soron Faggachi (Palmer 1967) or Soron Pugachi (East 1971 [1930]). The KC refers to the Quranic school set up even earlier by Kisoki (1509–65) as being in the "portico."

residence and the "male" pathway leading to the outside world reinforced the gendered east-west division defined by the eastern male and western female entranceways (chapter 1).

Yet Islam cannot be said to have been singularly responsible for the east-west gendered symmetry in the Kano palace interior. Rather, the symmetry was worked out syncretically through pre-Islamic spatial traditions. Many African cultural groups, Islamic and non-Islamic alike, have had spatially gendered households, often along linear axes. In sixteenth-century Mossi, a non-Islamic kingdom south of Songhay, for example, the eastern part of the palace was "female" and associated with darkness, the past, and death, whereas the western part was "male" and associated with the life and the well-being of the kingdom (Zahan 1967, 167). The nineteenth-century Islamic palace or *fashir* of Dar Fur, east of Lake Chad, was similarly gendered; albeit along an east-west axis, which produced north-south symmetry. O'Fahey writes:

> The *fashir* [palace] was the Fur household writ large; the male and female entrances, the arrangement of the huts, the *diwans* or places of audience, the messes where men ate communally—all were common to royal palace and prosperous households alike. The sexual division, or better the divide between the public and the private domains, was fundamental; the *fashir,* typically aligned north/south, was divided into a northern male and a southern female sphere, entered by . . ."the men's gate" and . . ."the women's gate" . . . respectively. The [men's gate] . . . led to the public domain which housed the officials, servants and slaves of the sultan, the . . . [women's gate led] to the quarters of the royal women, concubines and some of the eunuchs. (1980, 24)

These gendered structures and symmetries of the Dar Fur palace are strikingly similar to those of the Kano palace.

Such divisions existed elsewhere at smaller palace scales. A large palace courtyard built for audiences with the king in the Dahomey palace, for example, was divided spatially into two: The king's side (the right side) of the palace was associated with royalty, maleness, and insider status, whereas the women's (left) side was associated with femaleness and commoner, outsider status. Perhaps the Kano palace's innermost symmetry reflected similar ontological divisions between royalty (the right or easterly side) and commoner (the left or westerly side), many concubines deriving from nonroyal lineages (see Bay 1998, 11).

However informed by pre-Islamic practices these gendered spatial patterns may have been, they assumed new *Islamic* meanings and uses: a mosque and quarters for a liman (the scholar-official accompanying the king on military expeditions) were built in the easterly "male" parts of the Kano palace next to the king's quarters, alongside other male religious domains that would be built up over the next century (see Figure 9). Spatial data from the Kano palace and the KC also indicate that two of Rumfa's successors built Quranic study areas. Abubakr Kado, son of Rumfa and the powerful Auwa, built one site close to his personal chambers where his sons could engage in religious study. Rumfa's grandson Kisoki (1509–65) also constructed one, but outside the royal ciki next to the eastern "male" entranceway. Their construction suggests that religious education had important political functions. Indeed the palace of the Sudanic sultanate of Dar Fur in the eighteenth century had an on-site school from which state bureaucrats were recruited, this practice possibly harking back to Egyptian Mamluk and Ottoman practices (see O'Fahey 1980, 27).[10] Such schools trained students in literacy and numeracy in Arabic, key skills for state treasury officials, accountants, and traders, among others. Eunuchs appointed to Kano's state treasury (Rumfa's twelfth [and last] innovation) would have needed such skills.

The Kano Nine and Royal Women

The KC credits Rumfa with instituting the first council of state (his eighth innovation) called the Tara-ta-Kano or "Kano Nine," in reference to the number of men serving on it. The council, originally made up entirely of eunuchs, displaced the Queen Mother from accession decisions, although these women continued to hold significant informal power. The political influence of King Rumfa's wife, Auwa, for example, whom Last surmises was the daughter of the Askia Muhammad of Songhay, spanned no less than six reigns (1983).[11]

Kings over centuries married daughters of important personages, but none achieved Auwa's political longevity. As Rumfa's widow, she successfully affected kingship decisions, directly and indirectly through her offspring, over a period of one hundred years, exercising political prowess and acuity. Rumfa was succeeded by Auwa's son, Abdullahi (1499–1509), for example, and, later, by her grandson Kisoki. When Yakufu (1565) and Dauda Abasama (1565), succeeded Kisoki, she used her influence to have them deposed, paving the way for another of her sons, Abubakr Kado, to take the throne, though he, too, would eventually be deposed.[12] Indeed the KC records that Kisoki did not reign alone or even with his councilors but, rather, "with his mother Iya Lamis and his grandmother Madaki Auwa."[13] The Kano Nine therefore constrained, but did not efface, royal women's participation in accession decisions. In a dramatic expression of this gendered shift in power, the Kano Nine drove a Queen Mother known as Fasuma, either a wife or concubine of King Shekkarau (1649–51), out of the palace because of her role in her brother's unsuccessful attempt to put her son in power.

Musisi writes of a similar devolution of women's powers to male authority structures in the state formational context of Buganda after the thirteenth century (1991, 771). As the kingship became more centralized and male clan heads' powers were diminished, women were denied access to leadership positions and land. Instead, they became important objects of exchange, their reproductive powers used to re-enfranchise clans that had formerly held power; in particular, women's bodies were used by the king to produce children who could then be married off to clan leaders whose family lines would then be linked and subordinated to the king's.

The eunuchs of the Kano Nine complicated dynastic state politics and spatial organization. They not only held important administrative posts associated with the state council, they held landed estates, administered other palace slaves and the northern "male" palace slave area, saw to the well-being of official guests, and managed the palace stables.[14] Four additional eunuchs controlled the state treasury, different types of treasury goods presumably being accounted for separately, such as livestock, valuables taken in war or given from other rulers to the king, and grain. In this respect, the title of one of the Kano Nine eunuchs, Maaji (Treasury) is telling: His title suggests that he represented the four treasury officials to the state council, reporting on state holdings, a post that would have required accountancy skills. He may also have been the official who worked with Korama and leading royal concubines to meet diurnal royal household grains needs and to supervise grain taxation (chapter 1).[15]

By virtue of their office, the nine eunuchs of the Kano Nine held powers much greater than those of the king's male kin. At the same time, their powers eroded the influence of royal women over accession. It is reasonable to surmise that politically ambitious women cultivated eunuch alliances to increase their sons' chances of accession. Alternatively, they may have helped displace eunuchs from the Kano Nine. Kisoki's mother (Lamis), conceivably a concubine of Abdullahi, for example, lobbied successfully to have one of her sons placed on the Kano Nine council. To accommodate the son, the titled eunuch, Barde, was expelled (Palmer 1967, 113). Maintaining and consolidating power, then, also required that eunuchs cultivate quasi-kin communities of support, especially among the slave population.

While the eunuch composition of the Kano Nine shored up kingly authority, producing a centralized, nonkinship-based state bureaucracy, eunuch castration simultaneously made the palace a peculiar theater of struggle. On the one hand were palace women, particularly concubines whose politics were mediated through kinship networks, or what might be called a "politics of fertility." On the other hand were powerful state eunuchs whose networks were not centered on procreation per se, but on the patronage and political powers they wielded as an effect of their office, constituting what might be called a "politics of infertility."

Both eunuchism and concubinage in any event would have destabilized the pre-Islamic institution of the Queen Mother and free women's affinal powers. Matrilineages no longer factored into political power as had been the case previously; women no longer shared formal royal decisionmaking with men; and traditions honoring freeborn women's matrilines, common in pre-Islamic African contexts, would have disappeared. Instead, concubines from hundreds of disparate lineages produced children uniquely united and made socially equal through their patrilineage to the king. In this sense, *concubines dispersed and centralized lineage powers away from each other and the Queen Mother.* Matrilineal relationships established between a concubine's birthplace and the capital, while of local significance, were weak in a comparative or regional sense, given that a myriad of other royal concubines were similarly forging localized kinship links. Such rotation of kingship opportunities through women from radically different matrilines is likewise noted for Buganda where at least since the late 1500s "the kin ties and role of the *bakembuga* [elite wives of the king having either freeborn or slave status] became of crucial importance because they were the axis along which the kingship rotated to different clans" (Musisi 1991, 780). Geographical centralization and lineage competition, facilitated through concubinage, depended to some extent on each conquered settlement being invested politically in seeing their "son" on the throne. What tied these far-flung matrilines together was that their children were now the freeborn children of a powerful king, ownership of concubines providing concubine children with legitimate rights to the throne. The Queen Mother, free wives, and concubines were thus compelled to develop different kinds of negotiation skills with one another and the king, given the newly instituted Islamic apparatuses of state.

The Queen Mother's symbolic and practical displacement might reasonably be adduced to have created structural tensions between those invested in pre-Islamic systems of matrilineally derived powers (the "grandmothers") and those invested in a plurality of nonaffinal powers negotiated through the territorially far-flung institution of concubinage (individual sons), buffered politically by the fertility-neutralizing forces of eunuchism. For concubines, their disparate geographical provenance and their ability to cultivate territorially cohering kinship links to the king assumed political significance.[16]

An Assassination Attempt and "Male" Eunuch Invasion of the Ciki

We do not know the provenance of Kano palace eunuchs or what sorts of skills they had, though their manufacture in sub-Saharan Africa for centuries prior to their deployment in Hausaland is well documented (Hogendorn 2000; cf. Ayalon 1979). The KC writes that Queen Amina, sovereign of the rival Hausa state of Zaria, was the first ruler in Hausaland to own eunuchs, these having been given to her as tribute by the king of Nupeland, southwest of Zaria. Little is known about Queen Amina except that she was powerful and militarily adept.[17] The KC writes simply that "[a]t this time [1421–38] Zaria, under Queen Amina, conquered all the towns as far as Kwararafa and Nupe. Every town paid tribute to her. She first had eunuchs and kolas [kola nuts] in Hausaland" (109). While information provided in the KC implies that she did not place these men in state positions, perhaps she used eunuchs in ways to circumvent kinship-based intrigues and thus stabilize her position, as did Rumfa. That Queen Amina's eunuchs derived from Nupeland suggests that Kano palace eunuchs also came from that place, which is not to say that Nupeland was the sole source of Kano eunuchs. Nupeland was located along the Niger, a plausible trade route for eunuchs exported out of the declining Malian empire.[18]

In West Africa eunuchs were rarely manufactured where they were captured. While slave men were often captured in a belt-like region spanning the Sudan from Mossi (Mali), through Damagaram (Niger) and Ningi (Nigeria) territories, into present-day Chad and Sudan, the sites of eunuch manufacture were less numerous. As Hogendorn notes:

> In West Africa, there were places of castration in Mossi country to the south of the Niger River bend (present Burkina Faso), in Damagaram (Niger Republic), in Borno (northeast Nigeria), and especially in Baghirmi (Chad). Just as in eastern Africa, depots on slave export routes were also the provenance of castrations, as for example at Marzuq and Kebabo (southern Libya). (2000, 49)

Palace field data suggest that, at least in the nineteenth century, Damagaram was well known as a place of eunuch manufacture. Eunuchs from Damagaram had only their testicles removed, in contrast to more radical and dangerous North African surgeries.[19]

In 1989 I began to reconstruct where a group of eunuchs had lived in the palace historically. The process began after learning that one of three remaining palace "eunuchs" (a hermaphrodite), bearing the epithet *dan ciki* (son of the inside), held the once-formidable eunuch title Turakin Soro, a title derived from one of the first state titles (Turaki) awarded by King Rumfa to eunuchs. I later visited Turaki's traditional compound, which at that time abutted a modern business complex in the southeasterly part of the palace. Later, while discussing with elderly royal Fulani women palace landscape features evident in photographs taken just after the 1903 British conquest of

Kano, I learned that Turaki's compound had once been part of a very extensive eunuch colony.[20] Though informants averred that the Fulani emir,
Abdullahi dan Dabo (1855–82), had built the colony after expropriating
about half of the royal women's quarters for male dynastic and military use,
KC data suggested that he had actually only *re*built the colony that King
Muhammad Zaki (1582–1618) had instituted centuries earlier. The photographs thus provided valuable evidence for the existence of an important sixteenth-century site which, when rebuilt, was placed inside a newly created
second labyrinth. Drawing upon information derived from the archival photographs, spatial and informant data, and the KC (Palmer 1967), I would
reconstruct the colony's history in this way:[21]

> During Rumfa's time, eunuchs lived mostly in the central and west-
> ern households of the northern palace slave area, today known as
> Gate of the North (Kofar Arewa; Figure 3). During King Muhammad
> Shashere's reign (1573–1582), two of his most trusted eunuchs, San
> Turaki Mainya (the Turaki of Princes)[22] and San Turaki Kuka (Turaki
> of the Baobab Tree),[23] gained renown when they, unlike other sol-
> diers, did not desert the king in a difficult and protracted battle
> against the rival Hausa state of Katsina. One day, San Turaki Mainya
> overheard a plot by the king's brothers to assassinate the king and his
> liman. Turaki Mainya counseled the king not to leave his chambers.
> The Turaki then donned the king's clothes to impersonate him, and
> went to the mosque at the normal time for prayer, with a retinue of
> disguised guards and soldiers in tow. But the ruse was unsuccessful.
> Turaki, nine of his own slaves, and twelve of the king, were slaugh-
> tered, and the king was overthrown.

> The new King, Mohammed Zaki (1582–1618), decided to guard
> against such a thing ever happening to him by building a defensive
> eunuch colony onto his residential quarters. Heretofore, palace
> eunuchs had only ever lived in the northern male slave domain or
> beyond it, the colony hence embodying a drastic change in palace
> interior life. Before making the changes, the new king buried the
> assassinated Turaki Mainya beneath the mosque's grounds where he
> had been killed and built another mosque nearby. The new Turaki
> Mainya was relocated close to both the king's quarters and the new
> mosque, along with other eunuch compounds (Figure 10). Still other
> eunuchs were placed in special quarters in and around the king's
> chambers to perform security-related, "male" functions in keeping
> with their easterly placement. Though the Fulani abandoned the
> colony in the early 1800s, Abdullahi dan Dabo resurrected key parts

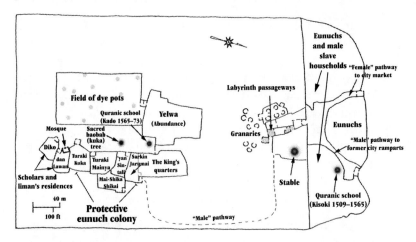

Figure 10. The eunuch colony in the *ciki* built after the assassination attempt on King Shashere (1573–82). Eunuchs were previously concentrated in the northern central areas of the "male" slave domain, Kofar Arewa (Gate of the North). The indigo dyeing yard abutted the central concubine ward of Yelwa (Abundance) to the south.

of it in the mid-1800s; these resurrected portions were those the British photographed in 1903. Most of the grounds were demolished within decades thereafter, the remnants of the colony lived in by dan ciki demolished for new construction in the 1990s.[24]

Muhammad Zaki's decision to build eunuch residences in the palace interior invites speculation. Were female guardswomen or *jakadu* ineffective in detecting or preventing Zaki's coup? Were they implicated? Certainly in Dahomey, in the absence of a kingmaker's council, women in the Dahomey palace worked in tandem with ambitious princes to place their favorite candidate or son in power. During the reign of Agaja (who died in 1740), for example, a palace "wife" who controlled the treasury sent gifts secretly to the king of Oyo, entreating him to help her place her son in power. The coup was unsuccessful, leading Agaja's successor, Tegbesu, to prohibit any woman who had borne the king a son from guarding the treasury (Bay 1998, 83). Later, a palace woman poisoned a king, possibly a "wife," having been promised by a high-ranking official that she would be catapulted to power if she supported him in his coup (160). Some women may have felt they would be at risk if they did *not* support a coup. Again, in the Dahomey context, the entire female bodyguard of one palace section was killed when it resisted a successful nineteenth-century palace coup (174). At any rate, it is doubtful that Kano palace concubines or slave women wanted the eunuch compounds in the interior, given that these eunuchs eroded their heretofore-unchallenged authority over and access to the palace interior and body of the king.

That the coup took place indicates that the eastern interior sector lacked adequate security, or that palace insiders—including palace concubines—were involved. The possibility of the latter may explain why only the most trusted slaves (eunuchs) were posted in the interior, nearest to the king. The deployment of eunuchs within palace slave women's terrain probably set in motion or heightened pre-existing gendered political tensions. [25]

Domiciling eunuchs in the palace ciki would have changed the meaning of castration and, hence, of eunuch bodies. When eunuchs lived outside the royal "inside," their castration demonstrated forfeiture of the ability to procreate, a limit on their ability to form personal kinship networks. This sociopolitical sacrifice made plain their allegiance and corporeal dedication to king and royal family. Spatially relocating eunuchs to the "inside" altered the importance and social valence of the sacrifice. The inability of eunuchs to threaten kingly paternity rather than corporeal dedication became central to the politics of these men's bodies. Through relocation, in other words, a different sort of "male" body was made. Eunuchs could now be prized for their ability to reside among and assert a de-sexed-male authority over royal women. [26]

Castration hence became not only important in relation to the king, for whom it signaled complete corporeal submission to lineage and person; it also became important in relation to secluded palace women, allowing eunuchs regular interior access to women. The sexual impotence of eunuchs now held special (de)sexualized value, proof of a biological inability to threaten kingly centralized and sexualized authority over women rather than corporeal submission in the larger sense. Given that castration now made it possible for *both* men and women to forge political alliances with eunuchs, political intimacies and intrigues among eunuchs and all palace dwellers were heightened, facilitating complexly gendered, competing webs of patronage, allegiance, and power. Capturing the loyalty of powerful eunuchs most certainly also heightened tensions and intrigues among royalty as much, if not more, than it did among the slave community.

"Female" Eunuchs

Castration meant that not all eunuch duties and bodies were necessarily gendered "male." Rather, certain eunuchs were dedicated to the service of palace women, carrying out a variety of domestic labors. Royal women had long employed and used eunuchs. Recall that Queen Amina of Zaria was given eunuchs as tribute from the king of Nupeland. I also hypothesized in chapter 1 that eunuchs worked intimately with the most powerful palace concubines to administer state grain taxation and the state grain treasuries, duties simultaneously domestic (tied to the reproduction of palace life) and extra-domestic (tied to state taxation and the reproduction of the core apparatuses of the state). These men, in turn, were responsible to the four titleholding state treasury officers, all of whom were eunuchs appointed by Rumfa. Eunuchs may also have worked with the state grain official, Korama, not un-like with the partnership between eunuchs and the female grain official in Yorubaland. In Kano, moreover, Lamis, the daughter-in-law of Auwa (Rum-fa's wife and possibly daughter of the Songhay Empire's Askia Mohammed) and holder of the title Iya,[27] reportedly established a eunuch market soon after Rumfa's reign, a market Last believes was located west of the palace (1983, 69).[28] Given the westerly "female" placement of royal palace women, the westerly location of the market may indicate that eunuchs sold there were intended largely as domestic servants for wealthy or powerful secluded women—or simply that the market was a royal female domain.[29] Symboli-cally registering royal women's dominion over a potentially powerful group of men, the market would in any case have provided a venue for disciplining (through sale) insubordinate eunuchs. The market may also have siphoned off especially promising eunuchs into the king's service.[30]

The gendered use of eunuchs within the palace division of labor informed, and was informed by, the meaning and placement of eunuch bodies. A eunuch's function—domestic or military/state—affected his gender-coding and geographical placement. Recognizing sociospatial and gendered differ-ences among eunuchs became crucial in interpreting the historicity and func-tioning of the field of indigo dye pits I found in the women's section of the palace.[31] While the indigo dyeing industry in Kano has been documented as an exclusively nineteenth-century male affair, field data show that palace con-cubines ran a large pre-nineteenth-century indigo dyeing yard in the midst of palace concubine terrain.[32]

Royal Concubines, Eunuchs, and the Royal Dyeing Fields

I became aware of the dyeing field when, in the process of analyzing the nom-inative content of palace place names, elderly palace members were asked why the palace cemetery was known as karofi, dye pits. They asserted that a field of dye pits had existed previously in a large open field south of, and abutting, the central concubine ward of Yelwa. Further research showed that the built-in, ground-level pits were preceded by large above-ground pots, and that the Fulani abandoned the area after they assured power in 1807 (chapter 3). The field's large size and its location in the midst of concubine territory intimates that concubines used the field prior to the Fulani takeover to produce palace clothing on a large scale. The area may also have served as a kind of royal mint.

Indigo-dyed cloth from Kano had been valued as currency throughout the Sudan since perhaps the 1500s, and dyed cloth in other nearby areas had served as valuable political and cultural currency for hundreds of years before that, especially in Yorubaland to the southwest.

Colleen Kriger's work suggests that since at least the fourteenth century two distinct indigo-dyeing systems existed around the Niger-Benue Rivers' confluence (1993). A "southern" system centered in Benin and Yoruba states was linked to European coastal trade and involved mostly women who spun, wove, and dyed cloth in clay pots using the indigo variety *lonchocarpus.* These women's participation in commercial textile-related activities heightened in the 1600s and 1700s. In contrast a "northern" system, of which Kano was part, was centered in Kanem, Borno, and Nupeland and was run by men who dyed in large pits using the variety *indigofera.* End products were exported outside the area through Muslim trade networks. Imam Imoru offers a corrective here, asserting that nineteenth-century Kano dyers used both kinds of indigo: a wild variety (*talaki,* corresponding to Kriger's "southern" *lonchocarpus*) and a domesticated variety that was more popular (corresponding to her "northern" *indigofera*) (Ferguson 1973, 81, 113). Indeed the latter variety translates as "indigo of the household," suggesting that this indigo was historically used in household-based production. This domestic association is congruent with my palace findings and suggests a revision of Kriger's analysis. That is, royal women developed dyeing technology in the northern system centuries earlier, using clay pots and both indigo varieties, their dyeing activities later assumed by women outside the palace as well (see Kriger 1993, 366, 369).[33]

Philip Shea has done the most comprehensive study to date on indigo cloth-dyeing in Kano (1975). His work shows that the industry took off suddenly in the nineteenth century, after pit technology was developed. Here large dye pits were dug into the ground and lined with locally manufactured cement. Shea conjectures, using field evidence, that predecessors to the large pits were large freestanding pots and, before that, small pots. He does not, however, query when pot technology-based dyeing began, or if women had any part in the technology's creation and development, as was—and is—the case in all of West and North Africa. Shea instead focuses on how rapidly expanding commerce, among other factors, spurred the transition from dyeing in pots to dyeing in pits. High demand from outside the region, he suggests, triggered innovations in dyed cloth production. Not only were dye pits easier to build and repair, they were larger than pots and able to accommodate large amounts of cloth. They also served as a catchment for large quantities of a mordant byproduct that precipitated out of the solution. The mordant could be collected after one batch of dyeing was completed and used in the next round of dyeing. All of these qualities permitted the "mass production" of indigo-dyed cloth in the nineteenth century, fueling a highly lucrative export-based industry in the city and, especially, in its rural environs.

Finding the field of palace dye pits compels a rethinking of when pit technology in Kano was introduced. My research shows that early pit technology evolved out of women's pot-based cloth dyeing and palace women's domestic activities. How far back royal women's cloth dyeing extends is unknown. It is not unreasonable to surmise that indigo dyeing was done in small batches in pots since the very beginning of palace life, in keeping with the ancient pedigree of indigo-based cloth dyeing in Yorubaland in southwestern Nigeria. Comparative information provided by Plumer shows that women historically controlled pot-based indigo dyeing activity in all documented areas of West Africa (1971). Among the Ashanti, for example, women tie-dyed with indigo, the color blue representing female tenderness and, commonly, the rule of a Queen Mother.[34] Women from many other ethnic groups across the Sudan also dyed in pots, including the Bambara of Mali, whose indigo dyed cloth was dedicated exclusively to royalty. Mende women of Sierra Leone and Liberia, as well as Songhay and Soninke women of Mali, began dyeing cloth with indigo with the advent of Islamization. Clark asserts that it was slave women in Soninke villages of the Senegambia region who historically dyed with indigo, slave men weaving the cotton cloth that the women dyed (1997, 1999).[35] Slave women prepared and used both the wild and domesticated varieties of indigo. As Clark explains,

> An important textile-related industry, dyeing, occupied female slaves [of the Senegambia region], particularly among the Soninke. To produce the most highly valued color, women gathered leaves from wild or domesticated indigo, which they pounded, dried and boiled in a complicated process that lasted about one week. The resultant liquid was sun-dried and shaped into small balls of loaves for sale or local use. Besides indigo . . . women used kola nuts for yellow, acacia tree fruit for black and millet seeds for red colorings. . . . Dyeing considerably increased the price of cloth. (1999, 73)[36]

The work of Balfour-Paul (1997) affirms the findings of Clark, albeit in the context of Soninke and Toucouleur dyers in the Senegal river region of southern Mauritania. Here women similarly monopolized the indigo dyeing industry, using wild and cultivated indigo. A 1970s revival of indigo dyeing involved both men and women although women, intriguingly, tended "to be the best overall bosses" (113). Balfour-Paul's comprehensive research on dyeing practices throughout North Africa and the Middle East shows that women historically ran the indigo dyeing industries of rural Morocco and Mauritania.

In the Arab world the dyeing of indigo has usually been a male preserve, *apart from small-scale domestic dyeing,* sometimes with wild indigo plants. This reflects the tendency worldwide for men to dominate large-scale commercial dyeing, leaving women to fulfill the demands of more local markets. The mere presence of women near the all-male dyehouses in Egypt and Syria was considered inauspicious; *yet the dyers of Mauritania, like the rural Berber dyers of Moroccan Atlas mountains, were always women.* . . . In many parts of South-East Asia too indigo dyeing is an exclusively female . . . job for those past the menopause . . . above all due to their infertility, which will not jeopardize the fertile dye vat. (1997, 75; emphasis added)

Comparing female Moroccan dyers (known as *id mm yy^w* man) with female Yoruba dyers in Nigeria, Balfour-Paul notes that the former were commissioned by male weavers "when they required blue or green. . . . [Moreover,] some of the dyers would travel for about five days, carrying on their backs an iron pot, *aqqzdir,* and their indigo, to enable them to bring their services to a client's home" (107).[37] This latter scenario suggests that at least some female dyers capitalized on their skills, though in the end, they were kept out of urban markets. Women also monopolized rural indigo dyeing in Tunisia (110), men again monopolizing the lucrative industry of towns.

The practice of pot-based indigo cloth dyeing by women in West Africa is perhaps most ancient in Yorubaland, where women dyed in a special yard constructed at the back of the extended family household. In some Yoruba contexts, cloth dyeing was linked to the worship of Iya Mapo, a goddess and protectress of female trades. Elisha Renne's study of the Bunu Yoruba of Northeast Yorubaland is especially provocative, indicating that Bunu women elders controlled pot-based indigo dyeing and held all proceeds from indigo-related sales (1995). These elders, akin perhaps to Kano palace concubines, directed the activities of young female labor; many girls, in fact, ran away because the labor was so difficult and because they did not control or benefit directly from cloth sale revenue.

The existence of a large pre-Fulani dyeing yard in the Kano palace invites historical speculation. Regional precedents in other West African contexts suggest that indigo dyed cloth was produced initially for royal needs only—Kano palace women, and royalty generally, monopolizing the use of the color blue. Shea points out that in sixteenth-century Kebbi, a kingdom to the west along the Niger River, for example, a royal wife is said to have owned a prestigious indigo-dyed headdress (1975). And in nineteenth-century Bamun (Cameroon), princesses were given indigo-dyed "Royal Cloth" to wear on their wedding day (Harris 1985, 259). A similar royal tradition is borne out in the contemporary Kano palace, where royal brides are ritually dressed in blue on their wedding day. The ritual begins on the Thursday prior to the wedding, when the bride is washed and dressed in an indigo-blue wrapper. The bride remains in her indigo-dyed wrapper until the next day when she is taken to her husband. In preparation for consummation, the bride lies atop her indigo wrapper, opening it from the front. Consummation consequently takes place on top of this special cloth, presumably to guarantee fertility.[38] By contrast, costly indigo-dyed "black" cloths were required for *all* marriage transactions in Bunu Yoruba contexts, and were worn by young women only *after* marriage rituals (Renne 1995, 65).

As early as the eighteenth century, if not earlier, the Jukun Court (northern Nigeria) drew upon the indigo dyeing expertise of non-Muslim Hausa to produce dyed Royal Cloth, suggesting a political and economic expansion of women's dyeing activities at this time:[39] The Royal (dyed) Cloth was used as commercial currency, but only by royalty (Harris 1985, 155). This usage suggests that dyed cloth from the Kano palace eventually came to hold economic (exchange) value.[40] The Royal Cloth production described by Harris dispersed swiftly through royal households across the West African grassfields. By the nineteenth century, it was used as royal bridewealth, ransom, tribute, gifts, marker of royal status, marker of court status, and in marriage and death rituals. All of these uses were reminiscent of earlier uses of the Cloth as a political currency reserved for royalty.

Hausa artisans introduced cloth-dyeing technology into other regions, though it is unclear in all cases whether or not these artisans were women. The last precolonial ruler of Bamun (Cameroon), King Njoya, brought male Hausa artisans to his kingdom to develop commercial-scale indigo dyeing works in his kingdom. Six pits were placed in front of his palace and worked exclusively by men, beginning an industry that would later move into the city. Even in nineteenth-century Bamun, however, certain indigo cloth remained associated with femaleness, royalty, and the divine. Two indigo batik pattern types in particular were reserved for Bamun royalty: The *ntieya* for the king and the queen mother; and the *ntiesia* or *nti shwo* for the king's maternal brother. Reserving certain patterns of indigo cloth for these two ruling matrilineal groups signals older associations of indigo-dyed cloth with royalty and lineality (kinship) generally. As indigo-dyed cloth grew in value, producing particular indigo-based nonroyal patterns or special kinds of cloths would have been a way to capitalize on its commercial value, while still speaking to older, political-religious values. Perhaps this was the case in the production of the "Benin cloth" of Benin and Yorubaland, three hundred to four hundred miles southwest of Kano. During the 1600s and 1700s large quantities of solid blue or blue and white striped Benin cloth were exported to the Dutch and the English, patterns that presumably held little (if any) royal value (Kriger 1993, 372).

The meaning of the color blue is key to interpreting the importance of indigo and that of pot-based indigo dyeing. The riverine Igbo of southeastern Nigeria regard blue and white as divine and identical, associating both with coolness and femaleness. Here women were likened to water: Both are fertile (the river floods its banks, fertilizing farmlands), vital to trade and communication, and fluid, liminal elements of the cosmos. Within this universe, women and water spirits are "at the crossroads between the ordinary and the extraordinary, between spirits and humans, life and death" (Jell-Bahlsen 1997, 129). In strikingly similar fashion, the floor of, and the carpets and blankets in, the female spirit house abutting the king's chambers in the Kano palace were and are all blue. A very fine, white riverine sand is mounded up in the center of the blue floor, suggesting the logic behind the identity of blue and white—water and riverbank—both pointing, as in the Igbo case, to liminality itself.[41]

Similarly for the Bunu, the color indigo is likened to black rain clouds, these clouds, like pregnant women, portending and producing life (Renne 1995, 71). Bunu women traditionally ingested the dregs of indigo from dyeing pots as part of medicinal fertility rituals, rituals that may have had counterparts in the Kano palace. Indigo was, in fact, felt to have such power over fertility that young Bunu women were not supposed to come near indigo dyeing pots. Perhaps similar beliefs about indigo's fertility powers were held in the palace, explaining why Kano palace dyeing activities were in the western ciki area furthest from the public (male) domains, at some distance from the king's eastern ciki enclave and near farm fields worked by slave women and inhabited by spirits. The fertility power of indigo also helps explain why the dyeing yards of Limawa village were located so far away from populated areas, in one case at the back of the village and, in the other, along a river bend where blue waters and white sand commingle. A somewhat tangential clue into indigo's fertility-related associations comes from the nineteenth-century Kano-born cleric, Imam Imoru (b. 1858). He relays that after a wife weans her child, she "plaits her hair and rubs prepared indigo in it; covers her hands and feet with henna, *lalle,* puts on perfume, and goes to her husband who sleeps with her" (Ferguson 1973, 254), though it is not clear if the indigo was singularly cosmetic or had fertility significance.

Nineteenth-century and contemporary data from the Kano context suggest that dyers could dye cloth in many colors, especially red, green, and yellow, none of which were associated with royalty or women.[42] By contrast indigo blue was associated with fertility, divinity, and royal women, as was the case for the Igbo and Bunu. Importantly, senior Kano palace concubines continue to enforce the rule that royal brides wear blue on their wedding day, a rule increasingly resisted by brides who find the prescription idiosyncratic.[43]

I propose, then, that perhaps as early as the sixteenth century, royal con-cubines in the Kano palace supervised female slaves, eunuchs, and/or slave boys in the production of indigo-dyed cloth, with dyeing skills completely in slave hands not unlike the situation described by Clark in Senegambia (1997). The dyed cloth was used at first primarily by royalty, its dispersal restricted to strategically created circuits of *political cultural exchange.* Perhaps the cloth originally functioned as political-religious currency tied ontologically to the divinity of fertility itself—of women and of earth. Royal concubines in this way created and controlled the exchange of a currency that gathered force and meaning from the fecundity of their own bodies. Possessing or wearing indigo cloth by royalty made their superior ontological status visible and distinct. Its circulation in the form of gifts, bridewealth, or ransom transferred political-religious value to the person(s) receiving it, and only secondarily (if at all) economic value. Thus, through its exchange with allies, indigo-dyed cloth announced and forged (through exchange with allies) the political-procre-ative powers of royalty.

The Jukun Court's employment of Hausa artisans during the eighteenth century suggests that dyed-cloth production in the Kano palace had by this time assumed limited commercial proportions. If so, Kano palace concubines transferred the political value of indigo-dyed cloth into limited (royal) polit-ical economic domains. In so doing, the originary fecundity-symbolics of the dyed cloth would have been partially abstracted and transferred into royal commercial sectors, not unlike Dahomey palace women who pursued com-mercial activities, including smithing, trading, and farming (Bay 1998, 147), a process of value transfer into realms of exchange that would be appropriated and expanded upon by female entrepreneurs prior to the nineteenth century and male entrepreneurs in the nineteenth century. This irruption into vernac-ular female domains helps explain the presence of the two large indigo-dye-ing yards set up by women near Kano, of which there were presumably many more in the past: (1) along the bend in the River Jambo near the village of Limawa and (2) behind the village of Limawa in nearby Dutse emirate. In either case, literally tons of pot shards and ash remain, defining plateau-like areas that speak of centuries of women's dyeing activities. In the case of Limawa village, a woman desiring to engage in dyeing consulted with a woman who oversaw the yard and, if she received permission, would work any num-ber of deep, cylindrically shaped pits.[44] An analogous transition from politi-cal cultural use value to economic exchange value is recorded for Brazzaville, in what is today known as Congo. As Martin explains, "In the pre-colonial era, the production and distribution of the most valued cloth had been in the hands of senior lineages and royal families who had seen this power diffused to a new entrepreneurial class with access to imported cloth" (1994, 495).

I might also conjecture that the nineteenth century saw the rise of gendered divisions of labor in the use of the two indigo varieties. Cooper points out that in Maradi, men monopolized domesticated indigo production (indigofera) grown on rich valley soils, to which they had singular access (1997, 50). Men's monopoly over the Kano dyeing industry throughout the nineteenth century, Imoru's assertion that indigofera was at this time much more popular, and Cooper's findings in the context of Maradi suggest that Kano women may eventually have been forced to rely on the wild indigo variety (talaki), at least until the state banned them entirely from the industry.

Dyeing, Birthing, Eating: The Fecundity of Pots

Palace women's control over indigo cloth dyeing was deduced initially by analyzing spatial data, the western location of the palace dyeing yard, and its positioning just behind the most powerful concubine ward. In November 2000 the elderly titleholder Maje Sirdi (Owner of the Saddles, a title historically associated with the cavalry and stable upkeep) Ibrahim provided details about women's dyeing activities, relayed to him as a young man by his mother, now deceased.[45] Hailing from a long line of palace slaves, she told him of a time before the Fulani (1807) when palace women dyed with indigo in the field adjacent to Yelwa, using massive pots, known as *kwatanniya* (also *kwatarniya*). With a mouth spanning about forty inches, almost twice its height of about twenty-four inches, which facilitated easy access to pot contents, the kwatanniya had a geometry that made it ideal for use in birthing ceremonies.[46] The word *kwatarniya* is similar to the word for calabash, *kwarya,* a vessel made from gourds and used for storing and measuring cooked and uncooked foodstuffs, especially grains. The relationship of birthing pots to calabashes speaks, again, to metonymic links between women, children, and grain. As Cooper avers with respect to her work with women in Maradi, "the *faifai* [a woven calabash covering] and calabash evoke the closure of the womb and the abundance of food produced by women: the internal . . . made external in consumption and public display" (1997, 65). The metaphorical equivalence of a grain-filled and the pregnant woman/womb is similarly described by Masquelier (forthcoming) in the context of Nigerien Mawri women for whom "calabashes summon images of fecundity and reproduction through their common association with the womb." *Kwarya* likewise refers to the shell of a tortoise; at one time the shells served as bowls or dyeing pots, particularly for royalty.

Historically, tortoises were numerous in the palace and roamed freely about the interior. Palace tortoises may have held additional spiritual significance. Jell-Bahlsen points out that the riverine Igbo of southeastern Nigeria, for example, regarded tortoises, crocodiles, and pythons as liminal and sacred creatures favored singularly by the water goddess, the most powerful female deity (1997, 107). These same creatures are carved into the early nineteenth-century wooden door leading to Ibrahim Dabo's (1819–46) Quranic study chambers. The last palace tortoise died circa 1995, following the tortoise population's precipitous decline after centralized, communal cooking in the Soron Tuwo (Hall of Porridge) ceased during the colonial period, though one tortoise more than a century old still lives in the Dutse emirate palace, their food now carried to them in bowls by elderly women.[47]

Palace concubines' control of early pot-based dyeing practices, and indigo and indigo pots' ritual and practical association with birthing, cooking, eating, and fertility, dovetail with the gendered qualities of the language of nineteenth-century dyeing technology. The *muciya*, the tool used by men to stir indigo in the large pits, is the same as that used traditionally by women to stir tuwo, the staple porridge of Hausaland. Historically, palace women daily cooked massive amounts of tuwo, in large pots, pot sizes and shapes presumably changing over the century to accommodate increasing demand. Not only would cooking pot innovations have influenced the size and shape of pots used in indigo dyeing, the large volumes of ash generated by the vast cook fires in the central kitchen were used as a mordant in the indigo dyeing process. The lightweight ash would have been transported with ease to the dyeing fields adjacent to the central kitchen. A transfer of innovations in pot technology from the kitchen to the dyeing yard helps explain why the term for a single dye pit (*tukunyar baba,* or "pot" of indigo), relies on the same term used to denote a kitchen cooking pot *(tukunya)* (Shea 1975, 157).

Royal concubines lived in a world that produced strong practical, spatial, and metonymic-symbolic connections among birthing, indigo dyeing, pot technology, grains, farming, and fertility. Shea's work suggests that such associations obtained in rural non-Islamic settings of nineteenth-century Kano where grains were pounded at harvest time *in dyeing centers* (1975, 226). The grains were cooked at the dyeing site and given out as alms. Shea also found large abandoned dyeing pots in a rural cornfield outside Kano. When Shea questioned his male informants about the pots, located at "some distance from any houses," they averred they knew nothing, perhaps because men never dyed in them; women did (174). Indeed, Madauci et al. in a pamphlet entitled *Hausa Customs* notes that "[women] in the villages still dye their clothes in indigo," though they do not specify where (1985, 58). This location at "some distance" is in keeping with the Limawa dyeing yard located in back of the village wall near farm fields; and with the River Jambo dyeing yard, rivers associated with women's divine fertility. Thus, perhaps indigo's fertility needed to be sequestered, its later public positioning in cities by men who appropriated the industry in the nineteenth century, speaking to indigo's fall from symbolic grace into the commercial secular.

The existence of fertility-grain-cooking-indigo associations outside the palace context, prior to nineteenth-century pit development, suggests that sometime between the eighteenth and nineteenth centuries dyed indigo cloth production in the Kano palace irrupted into vernacular Kano contexts. If so, the irruption may have signaled royal concubines' increasing participation in larger circuits of commercial exchange, involving a further emptying out of the originary, political-religious value of dyed cloth. Indeed in the eighteenth- and nineteenth-century palaces of Dahomey, women founded and managed a number of industries. Though Bay does not specify what these were, it is clear that they were engaged in it for profit (1998, 148).

Fulani Expropriation of Palace Concubines' Dyeing Practices

It is reasonable to suppose that when dyeing became more important in commerce across the Saharan region, palace concubines expanded the scope of their own domestic dyeing operations. Perhaps they expanded the dyeing fields or experimented with larger pots similar to those used in birthing rituals and communal cooking. At some point, though, pits were instituted in the palace yard, resulting in the current toponym of the yard, *karofi* (dye pits).[48] It may have been at this time that eunuchs were conscripted to carry out the labor, given the notorious arduousness of pit-based dyeing. If so, eunuchs were the first "men" to dye, using the largest of pot and pit technologies.[49]

Large-scale pot innovation may have heralded a new cultural openness to producing indigo-dyed cloth for nonpolitical, non-use-value purposes. Palace concubines' control over dyed cloth means that they would have been at the technological forefront of producing dyed-cloth currency in Kano. Palace concubines may even have been a major force behind production of the so-called Kano cloth used as a currency throughout West Africa, perhaps as early as the sixteenth century (see Shea 1975). In any case, widespread use of the cloth as political currency and, later, as an economic currency indicates that royal cloth production entered the abstracted domains of economic exchange, beyond the political-religious (non-Islamic) circuits of royal life.

The new regional-commercial uses of dyed cloth undoubtedly also signaled that the politico-cultural value of fertility, embodied in grains and grain exchange (taxation and tribute to rulers) and in children and marriage exchange (kinship cultivations between hinterland and central place), was changing. The palace's symbolic and practical universe of fecundity (royal children and grains) was transforming into a universe where the politico-cultural value of cloth and fertility decreased, exchange values being abstracted away from the cloth's royal deployment and use.

Innovations in pit technology initiated by palace eunuchs and concubines probably occurred in the eighteenth century, when the technology was exported to the Jukun kingdom. There is also evidence that by the end of the eighteenth century, women across the Kano region were engaging in dyed-cloth production. This peculiarly female industry was curtailed by male Islamic reformists after the Fulani takeover of Kano in 1807, though women in nearby Limawa continued to dye up until the Kano civil war (Shea 1975). In Kano many female state officials were removed from office after 1807 and palace women's powers over grains and cloth-dyeing were diminished. After the first Fulani occupied the palace, the dyeing yard was abandoned, a later ruler walling off the former yard area from the royal women's domain and converting it into a cemetery for dynastic clan heads (chapters 3 and 4).[50] The Fulani leadership also created laws specific to Kano that banned women from the industry. Nonetheless, some women in Kano's rural nineteenth century environs managed to retain dye-pit ownership. In these cases, men (slave or free) provided the labor, a gendered pattern I suggest had obtained historically in the Kano palace. Shea notes, for example, that a nineteenth-century woman in Dal town, south of Kano, owned three dye pits worked by five of her male slaves (1975, 161, 180–81). Another Dal woman possessed five dye pits. At the same time in a town outside the southern perimeter of Kano, a woman owned five dye pits and rented additional pits for her business, her sons dyeing the cloth in the pits she owned. In Rano, near Dal, women could inherit dye pits, but not work them, restricted instead to collecting rents obtained from leasing the pits to men. In one of these places an elderly informant told Shea that though women did not own dye pits, they had historically done so. My work offers a revisioning of Shea's data: that the indigo dyeing industry was expropriated from women and slaves at a time when it was becoming lucrative, the male-run Kano industry thus ultimately deriving from the palace's "female" interior.

Kano city seems in fact to have been the one place in Hausaland where women's participation in the industry was outlawed forcefully. Whereas previously royal concubines and women in the city and rural areas were the main purveyors of the indigo dyeing universe, Kano city women in the nineteenth century were expressly forbidden from owning dye pits (Shea 1975, 188).[51] This proscription apparently derived from the fact that there were considerable monies to be made in the industry, which, if concentrated in women's hands, might effect gendered asymmetries in wealth accumulation and spatial divisions of labor and social life. The reformist Fulani complained, for example, that women worked openly in public venues without paternal constraints. According to the reformist leader Shehu, "Among the innovations is the staying of men at home and the going out of women to market, competing with men; and it's a forbidden innovation and also an imitation of Christians. Their women sell and buy in the shops and the men (live) at (their) houses; and the law has prohibited imitating them" (Kaura 1990, 88).

Not uncoincidentally, closure of the palace dyeing yard coincided with strong state support for the establishment of male-run commercial dye-pit areas outside the palace, a process initiated by the first Fulani ruler, Suleiman (1806–19). An interesting regional analogy occurred in Yorubaland when the Oba Ohen purportedly punished women for selling royal cloth in the market by transferring royal weaving responsibilities from women to men (Kriger 1993, 373 n. 31). The finding that Kano palace concubines controlled large-scale indigo dyeing activities complicates Balfour-Paul's 1997 assertion that men monopolized indigo dyeing in cities across North Africa and the Middle East, whereas women controlled domestic production. In particular, it begs the question of who *initially* or historically began indigo dyeing in urban areas. The fact that small-scale domestic dyeing pervaded the Arab world and that some rural female dyers of Morocco were itinerant entrepreneurs suggests that women's commercial indigo dyeing activities in the region may also have been expropriated by men once they became lucrative. Thereafter, women were discouraged from frequenting dyeing yards—their mere presence being judged inauspicious.

In any event, the first male-run commercial dye pits in Kano were placed in the city ward known as "The Ward of the Nupe"—the Nupe being renown for their weaving and dyeing skills. The dyeing yard was subsequently relocated to the Ward of Takalmawa near the central market, along the western pathway leading out of the palace. Shea's field interviews show that the first labor force for these male-run dye pits was made up of slaves (1975, 121–23), just as I hypothesized was the case for the palace. Shea's informants also noted close joking relations between some dyers in the area and palace women, especially since the late 1800s. These dyers, it is said, enjoyed patronage from the palace, though their business was geared originally and primarily toward export. After Emir Abdullahi (1855–83) encouraged more Nupeland weavers to settle in the city, a dye-pit area was established in a ward called Bakin Ruwa west of the central market. This area was developed primarily for the dyeing of the blue thread used by the Nupe.

The Nupe may have been central to introducing indigo dyeing techniques into the palace, centuries earlier. Recall that the Nupe were among the major immigrant streams into Kano during Rumfa's reign and that Nupeland was located along a major trade route. Recall, too, that after Queen Amina conquered Nupeland, she received eunuchs as tribute from the king. Nupe dyeing skills may, however, have been derivative: Kriger notes that nineteenth-century women dyers in Nupeland were freed slaves of Yoruba origin (1993, 377). Given that Yoruba women had practiced indigo dyeing for possibly centuries before this, it is possible that Yoruba slave women introduced Nupe women to indigo dyeing. After all, Kano was connected by trade to both Nupeland and Yorubaland as early as the 1300s through larger regional trade patterns that ultimately connected Kano to Liberia to the west and Tripoli to the north (Hiskett 1981, 74, 78).[52] In any event, Emir Bello (1883–92) subsidized the dye-pit business of an Islamic teacher in the ward of Sudawa. One of the sons of the entrepreneurs cultivated his market niche by providing dyed cloth to palace women, the Queen Mother creating and conferring upon him the honorary title King of the Dyeing Center. These relationships point to the historical importance of dyeing for royal women and their patronage powers. Moreover, they show that local dyers provided palace inhabitants with dyed cloth once the palace dyeing yard ceased operations.

Local dyers became a commercial force with ideological-religious ties to the reformist Fulani. By favoring male commercial-Islamic interests over palace concubines', the Fulani leadership won out in a number of ways. It could now collect (nominal) taxes on city and rural dye pits (Shea 1975, 196); it gained political capital by supporting the male-driven commoditization of a product that involved encouraging the in-migration of skilled craftspersons; it secured the political support of Islamic scholars and students who were set up in the dyeing business; and it secured the political-religious support of reformist Fulani who objected to women operating in the marketplace. The benefits to be had by the leadership outweighed benefits to be had from palace women, whose value derived from fertility practices that were now of declining importance to the state.

Shea conjectures that the oldest Kano city dyeing centers are those that are the most lucrative today. These include two along the western "female" pathway leading out of the palace. Shea reasons that these dyeing centers were successful because they were close to the central market. Their success may also have derived from the fact that they were set up along the "female" pathway to cater to the palace-exurb's needs, needs no longer met by palace concubines.

In sum, the palace landscape holds clues that complicate our understanding of indigo dyeing in the region. Fulani leaders proscribed palace women's dyeing activities and those of women in the city and rural areas. The leadership instead supported male-based cloth-dyeing enterprises to expand greatly this lucrative commercial sector and gain political-religious capital. The Fulani's new legal and customary structures for cloth dyeing transformed it into a purely male industry, eroding the politico-cultural and spiritual uses of indigo and fertility in the state imaginary.

Conclusions

The creation of the eunuch colony and the cloth-dyeing fields speak complexly to the changing meaning and utility of fertility to the state and the importance of concubine knowledge to the success of the state. Whereas the new eunuch colony built in the eastern "male" part of the palace interior served security functions, I hypothesize that eunuchs also dyed in western "female" parts, under the direction of concubines. Differences in eunuch locations and related labor tasks show that castration allowed for eunuch bodies to be socially and politically fluid along distinctly gendered lines.

Based on spatial data I also hypothesize that royal concubines monopolized the production and distribution of indigo-dyed cloth as early as the 1500s, catering initially to royal needs and desires. I additionally suggest that pot size and technology used in birthing rituals and cooking informed the size and technology of pots used in the palace's indigo dyeing yards. Indigo's associations with femaleness, fertility, and spirituality reinforce the sense that the earliest state depended on the monarchical centralization of agricultural surplus and procreation, as well as the culturation of concubines' knowledge resources. The data intimate that palace women were the first dyers in Kano, assisted perhaps by slave women and/or eunuchs from Nupeland familiar with Mande or Yoruba dyeing practices. If so, concubines and eunuchs were the first purveyors of Kano's indigo dyeing technology, concubine knowledge being instrumental to state political culture. The dye pits' abandonment by the Fulani after 1807 raises the question as to whether Kano's Fulani leadership forbade women's dyeing practices because its profitability threatened the ability of men to assert their authority and identity as household providers.

Questions remain as to how and to what extent royal concubines administered the production of dyed cloth and when these activities became economically charged. Recall that concubines were central to early grain tax collection and disbursement when Kano state depended on the production and redistribution of grain, unlike the entrepot and industrial contexts of later centuries, especially nineteenth-century Kano. Might concubines have eventually participated in commercial cloth dyeing sometime prior to the nineteenth century because of grain's decreased importance to the state, particularly in relation to the emergence of regional currencies that facilitated palace links to actors and places involved in trans-Saharan trade? Whereas grains held considerable use value in the reproduction of palace life, dyed cloth had potential exchange value realizable in realms of trans-local exchange. With technological changes in dyeing and increases in slave labor available to them, royal concubines could have expanded their commercial activities in the 1600s and 1700s in ways that eventually challenged the gendered ideologies of nineteenth-century Islamic reformism.

CHAPTER 3

Great Transformations:
Expropriation and Fulani Rule

The Fulani Jihad and Early Palace Habitation

Between 1804 and 1809 an Islamic jihad, or reformist holy war, was waged by a number of Fulani clans across and beyond Hausaland. The Hausa had been deemed un-Islamic, though the extent and degree of their irreligiosity is debatable.[1] Led by the Fulani scholar Usman dan Fodio, most of the region was conquered, including Kano in 1806. As Last notes, "[T]he stereotype about the eighteenth-century governments and the Muslim elite of that time is a distortion of reality. . . . [T]he so-called 'Habe' rulers were [in fact] part of a more conservative Muslim reforming movement" (1987 [1974], 9–10). The jihad accordingly often involved negating the "Muslim-ness" of Muslim populations in conquered towns and villages (23–24). Last argues that the jihad's impetus evolved in the 1700s as Fulani pastoralists were increasingly restricted socioeconomically and geographically; concurrently, a Fulani-led populist reform movement was emerging with the dramatic regional increase in the numbers of Muslim scholars and students. At the same time, production of cotton and dyed and woven cloth for export intensified, alongside increases in slave exports for the trans-Atlantic slave trade, all of these activities bringing increased wealth and mobility to many. Last claims that these and other mobility-inducing changes loosened ties to locally specific "pagan" practices, facilitating regional Islamization: "Driven from the ritual sites of their ancestors, many, it seems, turned to Islam as a faith tied to no one particular place" (8). The not-uncommon exemption of Muslims from taxation provided further incentives to converts, heightening regional migrations. In households, Islamization disrupted traditional hierarchies, adult sons refusing to labor on their fathers' farms or to remain under their control. Thus, support for jihadic reform "did not grow so much out of the depths of despair as out of the need for a coherent way of understanding and organizing the new social realities of the eighteenth century" that operated at various social geographical scales (9).[2]

What followed was nothing less than "the transformation of a handful of pastoralist leaders and teachers into a political stratum ruling over great states" (Burnham and Last 1994, 313). The conquered area, extending from what is today northern Nigeria to southern Niger, and from Chad to southwestern Nigeria, was reorganized into a larger centralized administrative unit known as a caliphate (Figure 11).[3] Subjugated Hausa states were designated

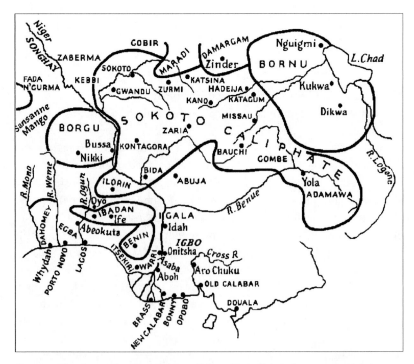

Figure 11. The nineteenth-century Sokoto caliphate. Heavy lines indicate states and their approximate limits at their peak. Names of a state or of a division of a state (e.g., an emirate in the Sokoto caliphate) are not repeated when it has the same name as its capital city (e.g., Kano). (Modified from Fage 1978 [1958], 41.)

"emirates," with those called upon to lead them deemed "emirs," after the Arabic *amir-al-mu'minin* or "leader of the faithful."[4] The caliphate was loosely consolidated and in 1812 was divided into two parts by the Shehu (Sheikh), Usman dan Fodio, the first caliph. Over one million square kilometers in area and hosting a population of about ten million, the caliphate became the largest nineteenth-century polity in sub-Saharan Africa, albeit one with no central standing army.[5]

The Shehu at first hoped to avoid what he saw as the un-Islamic excesses and hierarchies of Hausa rule, accordingly admonishing Fulani leadership to avoid adopting Habe[6] (Hausa) political ways:

> [D]o not follow their way in their government, and do not imitate them, not even in the titles of their king. . . . Address your chief emir as "Commander of the Believers," and the emir of each province as "Emir of such and such a province," and the emir of each place as "Emir of such and such a place," and the emir of each village as "Emir of such and such a village," and him who has charge of God's statutory punishments as "Emir of the statutory punishments."[7]

The larger western area of the caliphate was administered by the caliph's idealistic brother and vizier (counselor), Abdullahi, who after the Shehu's death, resided in Gwandu, an important military base for the Fulani. The eastern sphere was administered by the caliph's politically pragmatic son, Muhammad Bello, who was headquartered in Sokoto in 1809, a base camp during the jihad around which Bello eventually built city walls (Last 1987 [1974]).[8] As Burnham and Last aver, out of the old regional city-states, "only Kano, Katsina, and Zaria [all in the eastern sector] took over from the preceding dynasties both the physical urban structures and some of the political system," thus leaving much physical and political infrastructure intact (1994, 318). The emir whom the Shehu appointed in Kano was known as Suleiman, recollected popularly as a deeply religious scholar from the Mundubawa clan.

Within the Kano palace interior, ten years passed before significant rehabitation took place. Ethnographic data nevertheless make it clear that concubinage was organized soon thereafter along labor lines reminiscent of former Hausa rule, suggesting royal concubinage was reinstated using the knowledge resources of slave women and men familiar with interior administration. Palace rehabitation occurred in part because the Fulani leadership realized that it could not effectively maintain, much less govern, the Kano region without its new emir occupying the place that had since the sixteenth century been associated practically and symbolically with state rule. This realization led to a policy of urban settlement antithetical to the former rural bias of Fulani religious scholars who "traditionally lived in a rural *tsangaya*, a temporary 'camp' for students and their teacher, since urban life was considered inimical to study—and the Qur'an too 'potent' to keep in town" (Burnham and Last 1994, 326).[9]

Despite the Shehu's initial admonitions against previous political excesses, jihadic leaders in Kano were eventually given permission to expropriate the physical infrastructure associated with the leadership of the Hausa past, taking over the large state compounds of titleholders who had lived in the city, in the process claiming lands associated with the respective state office (Smith 1997; Last 1987 [1974]). The Fulani could not afford, however, to alienate those from whom they had taken over, especially those knowledgeable about how the state worked, particularly slave bureaucrats. The shifting over of state entitlements and power to the Fulani had therefore to be negotiated with some care, Dabo, the second Kano emir, and his successors developing new titles, political hierarchies, and opportunity structures for a wide array of political scions, all men. These included new Fulani power brokers and Islamic scholars, and former palace slaves and freeborn leaders of the *ancien regime*, the Fulani placing pressure on a system of state entitlements that had limited capacity for expansion.[10]

The new leadership accomplished the transition to Fulani rule successfully in part by negotiating away some of the most important powers of palace concubines and women more generally. The massive dyeing yard would be shut down, for example, and concubines' public grain duties would be greatly reduced, the benefits of these actions initially accruing mostly to male Islamic clerics and palace slaves, respectively. Such changes were entertainable, I argue, because fecundity was now expendable, given its decreased political-religious value at this time. The caliphate structure, in particular, provided an alternative model for political coherence that superceded (but did not entirely displace) the concubine-centered, kinship-based ways that territorial alliances had been legitimated and cemented in the past.[11] Despite caliphate centralization, city-states (emirates) enjoyed considerable autonomy. Bureaucratic slavery re-emerged along with the system of state entitlements. In Kano, over time, slaves would return to the palace to take up domestic and state positions (Stilwell 2000), slave girls and women playing the greatest part in rebuilding the most mundane parts of interior palace life upon which reproduction of the state household still depended.

This chapter focuses on changes implemented in the Kano palace interior (ciki) by the first three Fulani emirs, Suleiman (1806–19), Ibrahim Dabo (1819–46), and his son, Usman (1846–55), exploring how the state refashioned itself in relation to a previous symbolic and practical economy of fertility. The changes enacted were mostly negative ones, involving the abandonment of large tracts of palace lands associated with the fertility-economy and the rupturing of previously important spatial symmetries between men and women. The changes shaped and were shaped by a new state imaginary tied less to female and earthly fertility and more to asserting dynastic, male control, especially in relation to the new wealth generated by Kano's burgeoning nineteenth-century trade and industry.

Abandoning the Dye Pits

The Fulani initially shunned the Kano palace, associating it with what they saw as the state's previous excesses, including un-Islamic forms of taxation, forced conscriptions into the army, forced labor, non-Shari'a based adjudications, and the economic and spatial freedoms accorded women, especially in markets. Yet Suleiman knew he could not rule effectively unless he inhabited it, which he eventually did in about 1808.[12] Suleiman's reign was difficult. He was a scholar who remained in Kano city throughout the jihad, never entering the battlefield, for which reason he was discounted by other clansmen as a leadership contender. Yet, according to most accounts, his religiosity led the caliph to appoint him emir. In any event, he never gained the support of Kano jihadists and continually guarded against competing Fulani clansmen to uphold his position.[13] As Smith explains:

> Suleimanu commanded little respect among them. His poverty, his lack of land, cattle, a numerous following of kin and clients, slaves, and strangers appealing for support, coupled with his non-participation in the battles of the jihad, his personal failure or refusal to quit Kano and withdraw (hijra), and the modest status of his lineage, discredited him thoroughly among the ruling Fulani, who had already habituated themselves and others to their new aristocratic status. (1997, 214)

Though Suleiman did not accept his ostracism passively, he was unable to rule through consensus. He in fact forced his presence in meetings that took place regularly among Fulani clan heads in a mosque outside the palace; he also depended on eunuchs (considered especially trustworthy) to run a pared-down administration.[14] Despite the Shehu's injunctions against reinstating Hausa titles of the past (Smith 1997), Suleiman used many of them, (Lovejoy, Mahadi, and Muktar 1993) including one of the most important slave titles, dan Rimi, which he awarded to a eunuch named Yaoji.[15] The entitlements and powers of the dan Rimi office were apparently not used, suggesting that Yaoji worked mostly as a domestic servant (Stilwell 2000, 127).

Suleiman initiated the first major landscape change in the palace: Abandonment of the royal dye pits (Figure 12). In doing so, he dispossessed future royal women of a large place wherein they had controlled and benefited from dyed cloth production for centuries, these activities historically facilitating

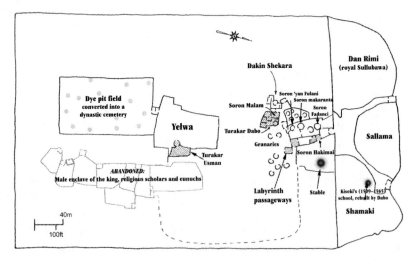

Figure 12. Early interior palace changes effected during the reigns of Suleiman (1806–19), Ibrahim Dabo (1819–46), and Dabo's son Usman (1846–55).

palace women's participation in both local and transregional universes of political, cultural, and economic exchange (chapter 2). Suleiman's decision was certainly in part incidental—the Shehu had initially forbidden the resurrection of former palace titles and many practices, and Suleiman did not have many slaves, much less concubines having the skills needed to run a large indigo dyeing yard. But abandonment of the area may also have dovetailed with religiously sanctioned retrenchments of women's socioeconomic and political cultural powers, a way of marking Fulani religiosity in contradistinction to the Hausa-led past. The Shehu was especially opposed to women participating in or attending public markets, which would have set women's production and marketing of a particularly lucrative commodity at odds with the masculinist religious sentiments of the state. Sheikh Usman dan Fodio's objection to women operating in or attending public markets was partly tied to a larger initiative of educating and secluding free women (now partly leisured due to the intensified use of slaves), the latter leading to an elaboration of low-level household-based craft production. But his sentiments regarding women in marketplaces also stemmed from his belief that women were responsible for acrimonious, competitive relationships with men. He denigrated their market presence as being akin to the "habits of Christians" and produced guidelines regarding women's participation in trade. Specifically, a woman could trade only if she had no male guardian or relation to trade for her. Elderly women were given special permission to trade, just as only elderly and "ugly" women could attend public mosques. In one text the

Shehu decries women's public presence as follows: "And among the innovations is staying of men at home and going out of women to market competing with men; and it's a forbidden innovation and also an imitation of Europeans [a mistranslation; this should read "Christians"]. Their women sell and buy in shop and the men (live) at (their) house; and the law has prohibited imitating them."[16] As Burnham and Last point out, little is known about how "Fulbe women, brought up in pastoralist camps, reacted to this radical change in living—an incident is recorded, though, when the Shaikh's [Shehu's] wife resisted his ban on her going to market. Manners of dress and entertainments had to change too" (1994, 327).

The Shehu in any event justified his proscriptions religiously, writing, for example, that the market "is as sacred as the mosque, and it should be maintained by learned men, as is the case with the mosque" (Sulaiman 1986, 96). While men and women were enjoined not to intermingle in public places for religious reasons (it might lead to illicit sexual relations), such restrictions must also have worked to increase men's market shares, on the one hand, reducing women to secluded workers of handspun cotton, while on the other hand controlling proceeds from the expropriated and much more lucrative production and sale of indigo dyed cloth. That is, the religious proscriptions benefited men politically and economically, especially given the market's centrality to Kano trade and industries. At the same time Suleiman undoubtedly gained political points with the caliphate leadership and economic points with male traders and craftspersons when he eliminated women's participation from indigo dyeing by both shutting down the palace dyeing yard and possibly initiating the juridical changes that made it unlawful for any Kano women to own dye pits. Shea, writing about Kano towns in the nineteenth century, notes that, "even if a woman inherited a dye pit from her father or husband she would have to give it away or sell it" (1975, 81–82). The outlawing of women from inheriting land (and, by juridical corollary, dye pits) would be reasserted by male emirate authorities as late as 1924 (see 180 n. 24).

Suleiman's shutting down of the palace dyeing yard and the creation of laws banning women from dyed cloth production and trade was accomplished initially to facilitate the transfer of ownership and control over the particularly lucrative indigo dyeing industry to male clerics and their (male) students; Suleiman subsidized specific commercial indigo dyeing yards in the city for Quranic scholars. Consequently, women's exclusion from lucrative commercial dyeing activities helped secure alliances between a number of male domains needed to keep Suleiman, and the Fulani generally, in power, Suleiman simultaneously shoring up the populist religious ideology of the times and occluding the real gains to be had by men.[17]

Problematically, the Shehu's and other's pronouncements about women's immorality and the need for and benefits of seclusion have characteristically been taken at face value by contemporary scholars rather than submitting the Shehu's claims to political economic scrutiny. Men's immorality, moreover, is remarkably never noted, jihadic men featuring mainly as saviors of women's virtues and champions of women's rights. Thus, for example, Last writes that the Shehu was so disturbed about the "drift of women into courtesanship," that he wrote "several vivid poems in Fulfulde about the immorality of women in his time" (1987 [1974], 8). Yet there is no evidence that women were any more "immoral" in the 1700s than they were previously. Similarly, Last writes that the Shehu forbade women from wearing makeup or from dressing their hair in ways that purportedly "made proper ablution or prayer impossible" (16), there being no question of what kind of hairstyle would make the washing of one's hands, feet, and mouth impossible. Or, again, that the Shehu objected to the seductive ways that women wore their wrappers. Sulaiman (1986) and Kaura (1990), along with Malami (1998) who largely summarizes Sulaiman's work, likewise summarize and interpret the Shehu's teachings and writings in relation to women. Kaura, for example, describes prejihadic women as debased (1990, 78–79): "Women both young and elderly, paraded the streets, markets and public places without *Hijab* (the outfit Islam recommends for women). It became fashionable for women to attend market places while men stayed at home as in the case of European countries" (1990, 78–79). This unrestricted intermixing between the sexes did not escape the watchful eyes of Shaykh Usman who observed that "They assembled at a place with evil intention, he who sees them (at this stage) has seen senselessness (by itself). Men and women thou laying down (half-naked) in the open; each of them with shameless dazzling eyes bulging out. Men and women thou keep on clapping their hands. Jumping up and down turning aside ways of staggering *[sic]*."

Kaura also remarks approvingly on the caliph's dictates that only "[o]ld and ugly women are allowed to attend the burial ceremony of a close relative. Similarly a woman is allowed to go to market and transact business when she could not get [a] second person of the position of either a husband or close relative or woman to do it on her behalf. The market should be within the locality since a woman is not allowed under the *shari'ah* to undertake a long journey without her husband or blood relations. . . . [W]hen women are allowed to go out, Shaykh Usman pointed out . . . 'that a woman shall go out in her uglier and thick dress.' . . . This is in addition to refraining from talking to or looking at men. The aim was to stop women [from] being attracted to men" (1990, 80).

Last asserts, in fact, that seclusion benefited women in the long run, enabling "women to be educated and not be mere domestic drudges," though he points out here and elsewhere (Boyd and Last 1985) that the Shehu emphasized religious education for women for practical political reasons: as educators of children, women were the most important carriers of the new reformist ideology. Any sustained critique of the Shehu's moralistic assessment of women is nonetheless lacking. Nor are Fulani directives about seclusions in Kano analyzed in terms of its "class" implications: only the most elite households could afford seclusion, secluded women in turn relying largely on a now enlarged workforce of slave women or the poor to provide the most arduous labor; most poor women continued to farm and engage in limited trade well into the twentieth century.

Abandoning the "East": Disuse of the Interior

The second site associated with Hausa rule that Suleiman additionally abandoned was the large male enclave inside the ciki that hosted the king's chambers, the protective eunuch colony, and the liman's residence and mosque. Suleiman would have built new quarters for himself elsewhere in the interior, possibly in the northwest, while the eunuchs and liman would have taken up residence in the sparsely populated slave male area in the north, or outside the palace altogether.[18] The departure of these latter from the interior made sociospatial divisions between male outsiders and palace women more pronounced.

The KC tells us that Suleiman moved in the palace after he paid a visit to the household of the mother of a powerful palace titleholder, Sarkin Dawaki (King of Horses; Palmer 1967 [1928], 127; East 1971 [1930], 60).[19] Nothing is relayed, however, as to how the palace ciki and, in particular, concubinage, fared initially after the end of Hausa rule. Did Suleiman incorporate any of the previous king's wives or concubines into his household, as would have been common practice? Was there any interest in revivifying female parts of the interior? Who had the skills needed to run the ciki, and who would have educated new wives and concubines about palace political culture?

Royal women's reoccupation and repopulation of the interior would have been accomplished in two main ways. First, the emir could have chosen concubines from among prisoners of war. Especially important would be the daughters, wives, or concubines of non-Fulani rulers and chiefs—women having expertise in running chiefly households. Ibrahim Dabo, for example, installed and honored the captured daughter of the king of Daura in the ciki.[20] Second, the emir could receive a concubine as a gift *(sadaka)*[21] from those currying his favor, either slave or free. In light of Suleiman's legendary modesty and attention to the Shehu's injunctions that leaders live simply, however, as well as his relatively short tenure and the initial disorganization and disuse of palace titles and spaces, it may be supposed that Suleiman did not cultivate concubinage or slavery. Most slave places, including concubine wards, were in all probability abandoned, the few persons living in the ciki having little knowledge and resources to sustain it. Female grain-related sites, such as the granaries, the jakadu-guarded farm fields for slave women, and the grain-house for the palace spirit in Yelwa would accordingly have fallen into disrepair. It may even have been that Suleiman had *no* concubines, especially since the caliph's brother, Abdullahi, during his brief residence in Kano just after its conquest, wrote a poem *(Tazyin al-Waraqat)* decrying the worldliness of Kano jihadists. Among the many activities he criticized was the "collecting of concubines and fine clothes."[22] The caliph himself only had one concubine, Mariya, one of whose daughters (Maryama) eventually married Suleiman's successor, Ibrahim Dabo (Boyd and Last 1985, 295).

Ibrahim Dabo and the Efflorescence of Concubinage

Prior to the jihad Ibrahim Dabo had been a malam living in Nupeland and Zaria, to the southwest. After the jihad, Dabo served as one of Suleiman's few appointed titleholders, the Galadima, becoming a trusted councilor. Through luck and intention, Dabo succeeded Suleiman as the second emir of Kano, in the process establishing the basis for dynastic succession, displacing Suleiman's lineage and clan from power.

Dabo recognized the centrality of state concubinage and male slavery in consolidating and enhancing his position, and cultivated both institutions accordingly. Like Suleiman's, his appointment had been contentious:[23] he had played no major role in the jihad, which caused widespread, clan-based resentment. Unlike Suleiman, however, Dabo secured his position early on by militarily quelling revolts led by Fulani clan leaders and by developing political means for consolidating his authority. He also created ritual and practical means for centralizing power, all of which directly or indirectly impacted the palace landscape. Upon his appointment to the emirship in 1819, for instance, he had a temporary passageway cut into the *southern* palace wall through which he walked in an accession ritual created specifically to symbolize his right to rule as a parvenu. And upon accession, Dabo wrote to the caliph, requesting permission to resurrect certain state titles—a request granted, allowing him considerable political latitude and maneuverability.[24] In particular, he could now award state lands and titles to Fulani clan leaders officially, the retention of which would be tied to clan support of him.[25] To underscore to these officials that their authority, office, and entitlements came from him, he established special turbaning rituals and reinstituted prostration before the ruler. Dabo also developed a special form of turbaning for males from his lineage. In particular, out of the top of the turban came two short ears of material, a way of visibly reckoning and honoring those from the ruling family (see Figure 13).

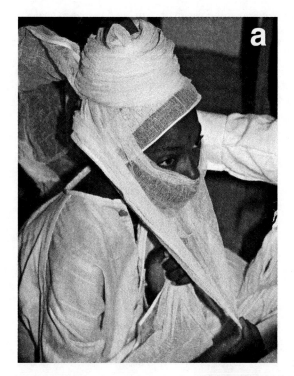

Figure 13. Dabo's turbaning innovation. Turbaning is a complicated process, and only those from the royal family may have two extensions extending from the top. (a) An older prince helps his younger brother on Sallah day. (b) Two properly turbaned princes are greeted by well-wishers on their wedding day (25 November 1988) in an open area just north of the palace, near the city mosque. Photographs by the author.

Like Suleiman, Dabo negotiated the prejihadic spatial order of the palace with little understanding of its past and with a desire to reshape the landscape in ways that would set him apart from his Hausa predecessors, still popularly represented as un-Islamic. Accordingly, he built himself a modest residential complex made up of two simple structures, both of which still stand today: A personal *turaka* (the designated sleeping quarters of a household head), known as Turakar Dabo, and a Quranic study hall—the so-called Soron Malam (Hall of the Teacher; see Figure 12).[26] In relation to the previous Hausa kingship site, Dabo's complex was unique on two counts: It was small and it was placed in the northwesterly part of the palace, diametrically opposite spatially to the massive southeasterly quarters that the Habe kings had occupied previously. These marked, spatial disjunctures registered publicly Dabo's aversion for the Habe past and ruptured the long-held female-male, west-east symmetry with which that past had been associated. His new quarters placed him squarely amid royal women and close to the public domain.

Dabo cultivated and used the kinship-producing powers of women to consolidate and centralize Fulani allegiances to him, though on a lesser scale than his predecessors had done, given the lesser numbers of women with whom he bore children. Early on in his reign, for example, he gave his daughter, Fatsamatu Zara, in marriage to a recalcitrant Fulani leader, Dabo Dambazau, a man who had much resented Dabo's and Suleiman's appointments, having lobbied for the emirship since the conquest. Fatsamatu's maternal pedigree was key: She was the daughter of Shekara, the most renowned nineteenth-century palace slave woman—and a princess from the Hausa palace of Daura whom Dabo eventually freed and married. The marriage gave Dambazau so many advantages that in time he would choose to become Dabo's greatest ally. Fatsamatu was given the title Magajiya, for instance, a title originating in Daura, the mythological center of the Hausa states. The Magajiya was the early queen-ruler of Daura, its devolution to Fatsamatu giving her superior political cultural value.[27] Dabo also included in her dowry a town near Kano, and he awarded Dambazau the title Sarkin Bai along with state lands, some of which were claimed by a rebel clan leader who eventually seceded to form his own emirate. Dabo would repeat the marriage-alliance gesture subsequently, giving at least half a dozen other daughters to clan heads to whom he also awarded state titles, cementing political allegiances through the traditional system of entitlements and kinship.[28] At the same time, Dabo married the caliph's daughter (Maryama), her son (Aliyu) eventually assuming the throne after the Kano civil war of the 1890s. Dabo's marriage to Maryama reflected the Shehu's ethnocentric desire to unite all Fulani groups through inter-marriage (Last 1987 [1974], 327) and indicated the new leadership's preoccupation with Fulani purity and hence freeborn (Fulani) wives rather than non-Fulani concubines per se (see Barth 1965, 525); the Shehu hence strove to create a culture wherein Fulani-ness and Muslim-ness were considered identical. Such attention to ethnic purity was anathema to pre-Fulani regimes wherein marriages were forged to cement territorial alliances across ethnic groups. This preoccupation with purity would surface en force during the reign of one of Dabo's sons, Abdullahi. Some of Abdullahi's slaves married daughters of Fulani nobility while he was away on a military campaign, these marriages causing considerable ethnicized political consternation (chapter 4).

The political importance of *daughters* is instructive. I hypothesized in chapter 1 that royal concubines were accumulated historically in the capital as a means of consolidating territory. Palace concubines captured from hinterlands became representatives of conquered territories, especially if they derived from important families. Based in the capital, they could negotiate indirectly on their territory's behalf; their children could be boasted as royalty; and any one of their sons might become king, further connecting the capital to the mother's place of capture. Dabo, though, did not need to consolidate territory through concubine accumulation per se. His problems were more political than territorial. The confederate structure of the caliphate meant that the conquered status of jihadic lands was not what was in question, though there were considerable threats at local levels often met by alliances between emirate leaders.[29] Most tensions came from political wrangling among jihadic leaders, their non-Fulani subjects either disaffected or disregarded in these negotiations (Smith 1997). What needed immediate consolidation was not land, but Dabo's authority and, hence, interclan support, both requiring he create a strong centralized administration.

Dabo's political use of his daughters in marriage makes it reasonable to surmise that procreation and, hence, wives' and concubines' *children* assumed special importance for Dabo, helping to explain why Dabo had so many children—thirty sons and twenty-two daughters. Likewise, the Shehu had thirty-seven children and his successor Bello seventy-three. The political deployment of daughters in marriages throughout the caliphate was in keeping with historical precedents with the caveat that now these daughters were seen to hold the extra caché of Fulani-ness. Thus, when the Shehu's son and successor (Muhammad Bello) gave his daughter to al-hajj Umar, Fulani leader of the Tijaniyya, a powerful rival Islamic brotherhood, the gift presumably held new ethnic values intended to bridge religious differences.[30]

Shekara and the Reinstitution of Interior Life

While concubine representation was not as pertinent as it had been in the past, there was one notable exception: Shekara, the captured daughter of the renegade "Hausa" king of Daura.[31] Her provenance was of signal political importance, for she came from a state long associated with the cultural origins of Hausaland (Smith 1978, 52). According to one informant, Shekara ran away from the Daura palace as a young girl, climbing out from under the palace's retaining wall. Though the details of her arrival in the palace are varied and sketchy, stories recalled indicate that Shekara was either kidnapped or captured early on in Dabo's reign. Upon learning of her royal status after a chance encounter, Kano political insiders purchased her from her captors and brought her to the Kano palace.[32] Even though she was of non-Fulani origin, Dabo acknowledged the superior advantages to be gained by purchasing her. He may also have freed her and made her his wife, though my sources are unclear on the point. Rufa'i avers, as did one of my informants, for example, that Shekara remained a concubine, whereas others asserted that her appellation as Uwar Dabo (Woman of Dabo), her expansive quarters, and her residential proximity to Dabo (their chambers were connected via a passageway) suggest that she was made his wife (1982). His decision would become key in consolidating his dynastic ambitions and indicates further that the Fulani valued free wives over concubines.

Shekara was herself a devout Muslim and apparently supported her husband's religiosity actively, visiting him in his Quranic study and at times staying with him during prayers. Unlike Boyd and Last's argument that Sokoto women were mobilized by Qadiriyya brotherhood interests after 1838 to serve as "agents religieux" promoting reformist ideologies amongst the populace-at-large (1985, 288), there is little evidence that Shekara or others (including Dabo's learned and religious Sokoto wife, Maryama) were mobilized for religious purposes in the Kano palace, where bori continued to thrive. What seems more salient is that Shekara brought with her considerable expertise about how a "Hausa" palace ciki functioned and she was honored accordingly.

Though Shekara lived separately in her own walled compound, as did the other wives, her quarters held a spatially superior position: they were anchored to Dabo's personal Quranic study hall via a passageway that later became known as Soron Kitso (Hall of Hair-Braiding) when it became detached from Shekara's quarters (after her death) and used as such. Given the political cultural prestige of Shekara's place of origin, the fact that she was freed by Dabo, her royal origins, and her superior palace location, it is likely that she served as a close informal advisor to the emir and his household concerning the reproductive workings of the palace, a presumption borne out in the many ways she influenced informally the working of the early reformist state. It was undoubtedly she, for example, who counseled Dabo to give her daughter state lands and the powerful Daura title of Magajiya as a dowry upon her marriage to Dabo Dambazau. Moreover, three of her sons succeeded one another to the throne. In total, Shekara's influence spanned seventy-four years, a record rivaled only by that of Auwa, Rumfa's wife.[33] Her dynastic influence is today evident in a palace poem proclaiming the greatness of Shekara's love for Dabo:

If someone loves Dabo (Ko wayansu son Dabo)
Not like Shekara (ba ya Shekara ba)[34]

Shekara's greatness was enshrined after Dabo's death in 1846, when her compound, known as Dakin Shekara (Room of Shekara) was incorporated into an accession ritual, the dynastic quality of which mirrored that of previous Hausa kingships (see Figure 12). Shekara's legacy and importance were similarly marked in her natal home, her room in her father's palace similarly enshrined Dakin Shekara after her departure. These two identically named monuments register powerfully how women captured for the king helped forge territorial connections and how such women did not necessarily forget from whence they came; that family members of these girls might spend years looking for their children—and find them; and that captured women's provenance was often of political importance for both the capital (where they were accumulated) and the women's place of capture—especially when the person captured might derive from the household of a local king or other important personage.

By the end of the nineteenth century, many pre-Fulani concubine hierarchies and Queen Mother institutions had been re-established, presumably as a result of Shekara's influence. It was probably she, for example, who as Queen Mother (during her sons' reigns) reclaimed the lands and residence associated with her office and reinstituted the practice whereby *hakimai* (the ruling chiefs) greeted her weekly in her residence *before* going to greet the ruler, a relict expression of how women's procreative powers had previously been venerated.[35]

Given Dabo's many military campaigns, most palace concubines at this time probably derived from the spoils of war. Others may have been given to Dabo as tribute, while still others would have been daughters of palace slaves given as concubine-tribute by those who had occupied important palace households prior to the Fulani takeover. Like Shekara, the latter would have been culturally indispensable to interior consolidation, having varying degrees of knowledge about how the interior worked, either because they or their kin had served in the palace during previous Hausa regimes and/or had been groomed to become concubines. They, along with Shekara, may have encouraged Dabo to readopt certain paraphernalia of state, such as the elaborate ostrich-feather slippers, ostriches being considered exotic creatures, living near the interior granaries.[36] The slippers harked backed to kingly

Bornoan practices that Rumfa and his successors imported to connote prestige and leadership (Smith 1997, 226).

The Triumvirate, Shamaki, and the Slave Estate System

Increases in the nonconcubine slave population far outweighed increases in concubine numbers. Many prisoners of war were brought into the palace system as slaves to help re-establish much of the previous centralized slave bureaucracy and practices. Two slave men in particular derived from the *ancien regime* and were of special importance: Nasamu and Barka. Dabo gave the former the title Shamaki (Stables) and the latter, dan Rimi (Son of the Silk-Cotton Tree).[37] These men had held these same titled positions during the last prejihadic regime of Alwali (1781–1807). Dabo also reinstituted the titled position of Sallama (Peace), traditionally held by a eunuch. In doing so he recreated the male slave triumvirate created by Kutumbi (1623–48), the next great state innovator after Rumfa.[38]

Exploring Kutumbi's reasons for innovating the triumvirate is important in that it provides clues into how the triumvirate was symptomatic of larger changes in the needs and desires of the monarchical state as embodied in the palace, changes upon which the Fulani would later elaborate. Last argues that Kutumbi's dynastic influence emerged, and Muhammadu Rumfa's (1463–99) house *(gida)* or dynasty declined, as a result of sixteenth- and seventeenth-century regional geopolitical shifts (1983).[39] Kutumbi's ascendancy in particular reflected a geopolitical realignment away from Borno (to the east) and toward the Wangara (in the west). With this shift came the championing of military exploits rather than state-supported scholarly endeavors, along with initiatives integrating the capital more intensively with the hinterland. Although much of Rumfa's power base had come from the western-located Wangara scholars and merchants, his dynastic successors were increasingly unable to defend them or their large state-awarded estates, largely because local armies had emerged against which local knights were defenseless. Estate protection for and clientage from the Wangara would also have declined because the Songhay empire was collapsing, making it difficult for state treasuries to benefit from the extensive trade networks through Songhay that had once existed.

Last suggests that Kutumbi was successful in the realigning process because his allies were kinsmen from and near the western areas under siege, especially that faction of the Mbau that converted to Islam in the fourteenth century through Wangara influence (1983, 76). Kutumbi was able to cultivate the loyalties of the Wangara scholarly community rather than the loyalties of Borno's scholarly factions despite Songhay's decline. Upon his accession, Kutumbi instituted a series of practices to stabilize his position, including the creation of the slave triumvirate Shamaki, Sallama, and dan Rimi. He also emphasized the importance of the military in state affairs, using ritual and ceremonial means. He created a special cadre of bodyguards, and he began using a processional standard of trumpeters and drummers, along with numerous eunuchs arrayed in ornaments of gold and silver. Most importantly, he used the office of Shamaki to oversee a greatly expanded and upgraded cavalry, deploying this new force in military campaigns. To facilitate military maneuvers, he established fortified outposts where horses could be watered and fed before and after a campaign, appointing the Shamaki as the officer in charge. As the KC relays: "[Kutumbi] built a house [plantation estate] at Gandu, and another at Tokarawa. In the latter he lived when he went to war, and waited there until his army had assembled before setting out. When he returned from war he encamped at Gandu, where he would spend the night. Kutumbi was a very mighty Sarki [King] in Hausaland" (Palmer 1967 [1928], 119).[40]

It has been suggested that Shamaki's outpost-estates were central to effective provisioning of the cavalry (Last 1983). I suggest that Shamaki and the estate system were additionally pivotal to the reproductive flipside of military activity, feeding the palace slave population. The importance of the estates' agricultural function is evinced in the fact that Shamaki not only attended to royal horses and armaments, but to the agricultural estates of the outposts and their resident slave populations. Grains grown on the estates were not only used and stored in situ, but were sent to the central palace granaries where they were used largely for horses, and less so for human consumption.[41] Shamaki's position, tied to an expanded military and agrarian estate system, allowed Kutumbi to offset what must have been net grain tax losses suffered by the state due to large increases in the palace-based slave population as a result of war and from the concomitant intensified needs of the cavalry.

Throughout the nineteenth century the Fulani would elaborate on both Shamaki's position and the estate system. In particular, they built numerous fortified frontier towns and rural estates, necessitating that Shamaki's powers and purview expand.[42] At the same time, grain sourcing had to have become increasingly problematic since the late eighteenth century when the cowry shell began to achieve widespread circulation as a regional currency; by the nineteenth century, the state was in fact collecting taxes in that form, though it is not clear what the ratio of cowries to grains were, or how this ratio changed, during the nineteenth century (Hogendorn and Johnson 1986, 104–5).[43] In any case, over time, the Shamaki, dan Rimi, and Sallama would develop separate households in the northern palace slave area and prove invaluable to Dabo in bringing to bear on his Fulani counterparts the weight of a highly organized slave bureaucracy with which Dabo was personally unfamiliar (Smith 1997, 235; see Figure 12).[44] The renewed presence of the triumvirate, moreover, attests to the resilience and flexibility of a palace slave culture attuned to centuries of political uncertainty and change (Stilwell 2000, 133).

The New Shamaki: Rural Estates, Male Jakadu, and Concubine Losses

Shamaki assumed special importance for Dabo when he reinstituted and adapted the previous treasury system. Following the caliph's lead, Dabo implemented a dual treasury structure. On the one hand was a private palace-based treasury system managed *by Shamaki*. As Smith writes:

> As the wealthiest state in the Fulani empire, Kano was also the most frequently called on by the caliph to honour and reward distinguished Muslim visitor, sherifs, sa'ids, marabouts and clerics, by similar substantial gift from its state reserves. To handle these imperial demands and his own recurrent and capital expenditures, Dabo . . . placed the greater part of his revenue under the Shamaki at the palace, and held him responsible for prompt fulfillment of all approved demands for supplies and disbursements. (1997, 246)

On the other hand was a public treasury system managed by a freeborn Fulani man from Katsina, awarded the new title Ma'ajin Gari (Treasurer of the Town), who was additionally placed in charge of city administration.[45] The treasury division thus created one new position for Fulani followers.

Shamaki's private treasury assignment dovetailed with his other responsibilities, which included collecting and storing war booty and controlling the outpost-estates. Whereas in chapter 1 I theorized that female slave jakadu had been historically instrumental in administering the state grain tax, in tandem with Mai-Kudandan (Master of the Granary) and Korama, Smith's work shows that by the late eighteenth century male jakadu controlled taxation (1997). According to Smith nobility and councillors (hakimai) residing in the capital ministered to their districts through appointed kinsmen or local chiefs (77). Taxes were assessed and rural news was shuttled between the latter and the capital through male kin, clients, or slaves known collectively as jakadu. If I am correct in my earlier hypotheses that a specialized hierarchy of women officials in the city and palace previously held key taxation responsibilities, what happened to shift these responsibilities to men?

The answer to this question is complex and involves several imbricated processes attendant with Fulani rule. Part of the answer certainly lies in regional patterns of monetization. Specifically, as a result of the expansion of regional trade systems and diversification of the economy in the eighteenth century, the political, symbolic, and practical use value of grains was superseded. State requirements shifted proportionately both to other in-kind, use value mediums such as craft goods, and to mediums that allowed for participation in larger universes of exchange, especially, cloth and cowries.[46] Whereas the previous grain taxation regime had directly supported palace life and served as a redistributive mechanism that centralized kingly authority and facilitated an economy of fertility controlled largely by women, the introduction of cowries and other currencies eventually rendered the system largely obsolete. Grain was, in other words, displaced in part by currency forms having exchange value, the powers of male jakadu rising accordingly. At the same time, Ibrahim Dabo and his successors had expanded the estate system, initially for military reasons, with walled towns known as *ribats* built near Kazaure and Maradi (north and northwest of Kano, respectively) as a primary line of defense. Such an expansion undoubtedly increased Shamaki's powers and duties, additionally intensifying his responsibilities over grain production for a growing estate-based population and cavalry, and the re-emerging central palace population, especially the slave bureaucracy. Population pressures, the relative stability of the caliphate, and the fact that the state needed to collect taxes in monetary form in order to engage ever increasingly in regional and transregional exchange help may explain why the Fulani never re-established palace concubinage on the scale it had previously enjoyed.[47] The palace population, historically fed by grain taxes and tribute, depended now more than ever on agricultural slave labor for its survival. Like Kutumbi's era, then, the estate system accommodated a burgeoning slave community and cavalry system, this time related partly to the construction of ribats and the additional sustenance needs of the central palace. This line of reasoning suggests a historicity in the kind of slave system upheld by the state and is in keeping with Hill's assertions that prejihadic "Hausa" and jihadic "Fulani" systems of slavery differed fundamentally, the latter invested much more intensively in agricultural production on large-scale, slave-based plantations (1985).[48] VerEecke's analysis of the nineteenth-century jihad of the Adamawa Fulani (waged in tandem with that of Sokoto) suggests that Fulani culture and the jihadist reformist ideology helped create this Fulani preference for slave plantations. She writes:

> Slavery, initially connected with the Fulbe [Fulani] objective of converting the pagans [during the jihad] became . . . an economic venture of warriors and entrepreneurs alike. Slaves . . . became a . . . commodity . . . [and] provided the bulk of agricultural labor for the Fulbe. As among today's nomads, the newly settled Fulbe lacked agricultural skills, and thus

depended heavily upon their slaves. This also enabled them to devote more time to Islamic scholarship and warfare. . . . Those with many slaves founded slave farms. . . . [S]laves lightened the workload for women and men alike. (1988, 57)

Though both sedentary and nomadic Fulani made up the jihadic forces of Kano, Fulani culture was not historically centered on farming, something that would later be made apparent when Emir Abdullahi (1855–82) created a large pastoral slave estate to serve the royal family's dietary needs (chapter 4).

Some taxes continued to be rendered in-kind as grain, however, along with zakat—10 percent of grain production rendered in-kind to the ruler in keeping with Islamic law. VerEecke surmises similarly that just after the Fulani conquest in Adamawa, "[f]oodstuff may have been obtained from indigenous agriculturalists, and those Fulbe who did farm were obligated to pay tribute in grain to their local Fulbe leaders. . . . Slaves [however, eventually] did most of the farm work" (1988, 58). In Kano, a portion of zakat was stored in a walled section of granaries in the palace set aside for malams. State granaries were therefore still useful, but the grains stored in them now partly derived from agricultural estates and were distributed through more circumscribed political circuits of consumption related mostly to palace reproduction and clientage.

The status and work of male jakadu was adapted to suit the needs of the new ruling class. In particular, jakadu positions were awarded to *free* office-seeking men, especially other Fulani. Male jakadu positions, like the public treasurer's post, were opened to loyal Fulani followers, thus co-opting them into Dabo's dynastic system. As Smith explains, the emir would instruct:

[I]ndividual [free] courtiers to serve as *jekadu* [*sic*] to particular villages under the *Shamaki* or *Dan Rimi*. Some but not all of these *jekadu* had honorific titles. Often such commissions were initiated *at the suggestion of the senior slaves,* following *requests by suitable Fulani clients at court.* By virtue of their influence . . . the *Dan Rimi* and *Shamaki* acquired considerable following *among office-seeking [Fulani] freemen at the capital,* whose relations of clientage obliged them to keep these senior slaves well informed about events and opinion in their respective city wards. (1997, 246; my emphasis)[49]

While the incorporation of free men into the jakadu system displaced male slaves from an important source of power and patronage, the transfer was done in such a way as to shore up and centralize the emir's authority and consolidate and increase the power of palace slaves.[50]

The Shamaki orchestrated the storage of palace-bound private treasury goods received from male jakadu, including cowries, grains, and nongrain taxes. Nongrain revenues were stored in the northern slave domain. Because the Islamic grain tax (zakat)—along with other taxes rendered in grain and grains from dedicated estates—was stored in the palace's interior granaries, the Shamaki's duties extended into the concubine's domain, perhaps for the first time. Shamaki also assumed the duty of divvying out the grains from the palace granaries, requiring that he shuttle between public male and private female sites.[51]

On the one hand, Shamaki's dual military estate and granary responsibilities logically extended out of Kutumbi's earlier improvements on efficient cavalry provisioning through building up an estate system. On the other hand, Shamaki's interior grain-related duties were out of place given both that he resided outside the palace interior and that he held public military duties. That he assumed what had been women's duties may help account for the general feeling at the time that his position had become much overextended. Smith recounts that during Dabo's reign he became somewhat of a "polite imperial joke" (1997, 246).[52] Unlike Kutumbi's strict military deployment of the Shamaki, the Shamaki position under the Fulani extended into larger political and domestic domains. Besides the outpost-cavalry duties envisaged by Kutumbi, Shamaki was now expected to: organize and send tribute from Kano regularly to the caliph in Sokoto; organize the corvee labor of craftsmen whose goods were needed by the army (tanners and blacksmiths); administer palace wards and organize communications with the royal estates; and supervise those living on royal lands, along with the dan Rimi. The Shamaki was given license over the palace granaries presumably because the grains increasingly derived from the slave estates he administered. Of equal importance was the fact that palace concubines and female jakadu were fewer in number than in the past, making it difficult for them to attend to what had traditionally been their purview.

The data suggest that while Shamaki's powers waxed, the number and powers of concubines waned, especially those of Mai-Kudandan. This may explain why Mai-Kudandan relied on the Korama to secure for her female labor needed to carry out especially arduous tasks in the palace interior, such as the processing of palace grains for cooking. I also surmise that the work of female jakadu became spatially restricted: they guarded the labyrinth, served as domestic couriers and messenger for royal women, and carried out ceremonial functions for the emir and royal women.

In all these palace innovations, Dabo was guided not only by slaves familiar with the past, but by those who either had been disaffected with the *ancien regime* or who desired to adapt to the new order (Stilwell 2000). One of the most important free men to counsel Dabo was Ciroma dan Mama, a high-ranking freeborn official from the last Hausa regime whom some say was the last Hausa king's son. Whoever he was, he had been politically disaffected during Alwali's reign, siding secretly with the Fulani during the Kano jihad.[53] After the jihad, he was awarded extensive lands and, during Dabo's reign, a significant advisory place.[54] Dabo's tutelage under the Ciroma dan Mama, Nasuma, Barka, Shekara, and others, allowed him to reinstitute prejihadic institutions of state slavery, including concubinage. These institutions were modified significantly to suit his dynastic needs.

Dyeing and Dying

Ibrahim Dabo's successor and son, Usman, was not a warrior or an innovator. He also had few children (Smith 1997, 285), suggesting that whatever small boost concubinage received during Dabo's reign, the institution declined during that of Usman. The only change I could discern was Usman's conversion of the dyeing yard, long abandoned, into a dynastic burial ground. Both his mother (Shekara) and his father were buried there; later emirs interred there included Shekara's son Muhammad Bello (who acceded the throne in 1882), Maje Garko Yusuf (Abdullahi dan Dabo's son, who initiated the Kano civil war when he challenged his cousin Tukur's right to the throne in 1892), and Dabo's grandson, also known as Usman (1919–26), though he was nicknamed "dan Tsoho" because of his advanced age and ill health when he assumed the throne.[55] Usman also relocated the emir's personal chambers to an even more feminine place, the central ward of Yelwa (Abundance), what had been in Hausa times the most important symbolic and practical center of royal concubine life (see Figure 12).[56] In this way, like his father, he breached the gendered east-west symmetry of the *ancien regime*, encroaching upon what was perhaps the most defining female space of the Hausa past. Rather than simply abandoning his father's residential complex (Turakin Dabo) and study hall (Soron Malam), he continued to use them, incorporating these structures and those of his mother's chambers (Dakin Shekara) into dynastic accession rituals.[57]

Conclusions

The sociospatial changes enacted by the first three Fulani emirs in the palace interior boldly departed from the sociospatial precedents of the prejihadic past. As concubinage went into decline, the east-west symmetry associated with a cosmology of fertility was ruptured, the dye pits were closed down and a dynastic cemetery was created in its stead. Moreover, Shamaki's powers were increased, along with freeborn male jakadu, while Mai-Kudandan's powers and those of concubines and female jakadu waned. The lesser number of concubines, I suggest, derived from concubines' lessened importance in consolidating territory in the context of a caliphate structure, and from the earlier partial demise of grain taxation and concomitant rise of the cowry currency. These latter changes informed the re-elaboration of a state system of agricultural slave estates dedicated to feeding the palace community and royal cavalry. Concubine numbers may also have declined as the new Fulani overlords became preoccupied with ethnic purity and as they gained greater benefits from marriages with daughters of other Fulani leaders. For it was through Fulani wives that the elite could secure dynastic (rather than territorial) marriage alliances, the new elite being "identified by others if not by themselves as a distinct, almost alien group, preferring endogamy, speaking a language of its own and making claims to superiority as better Muslims than those they dominated" (Burnham and Last 1994, 333).

As important as these changes were, they pale in comparison to those implemented by Shekara's second reigning son, Usman's successor, Abdullahi dan Dabo. During his reign, key parts of the older symmetry would be restored—this time, though, as a means of forcefully restricting royal women's powers. Over half of the secluded female domain would be expropriated and formally walled off, the space being subsequently developed to serve the emir and various slave men.

CHAPTER 4

Concubine Losses and Male Gains: Abdullahi dan Dabo

The new Fulani rulers adapted themselves to and transformed state organization using the prejihadic palace slave resources at their disposal. In the process, the palace landscape was reworked, the female ciki (interior) undergoing particularly radical change. Chapter 3 explored how many parts of the ciki fell into disuse during the first three emirs' reigns. This chapter describes how many of these same parts were resurrected and transformed by the fourth emir, Abdullahi dan Dabo (1855–82), another of Ibrahim Dabo's and Shekara's sons. As in the case of Abdullahi's predecessors, the transformations did not enhance palace concubines' powers but spatialized and concretized their diminishment.

This chapter focuses on Abdullahi's changes, showing how they were intimately linked to an efflorescence of slavery and to political economic changes of which gendered jihadic reforms were an effect and part. The changes effectively show how much fertility's value had lessened since prejihadic days. Instead of accumulating slave women in the palace interior as concubines to produce children and represent their places of capture, for example, much female slave labor was now redeployed on agricultural estates alongside slave men, decreasing the numbers of concubines historically serving in the ciki. Agricultural production on these estates by now assumed special importance since most taxes were no longer collected in grain and the military needs of the state had expanded. Moreover, Abdullahi's reign saw new cadres of male slaves deployed in political, military, and paramilitary capacities inside the palace, requiring that new spaces be created for them; the changes cut deeply into what had been concubine domains, while eunuch spaces, in particular, burgeoned.

Documentation of Abdullahi's landscape changes owes much to coming upon a set of photographs of the palace taken just after the British conquest in 1903. These were found while perusing the Royal Geographical Society's photographic archives in London in 1988. I subsequently purchased the photos and, along with other relevant photographs, used them in individual and group discussions with palace community members residing inside and outside the palace. The most productive encounters came from group discussions with elderly royal women and eunuchs, for whom the photographs generated considerable debate and excitement, especially among those old enough to recognize structures since demolished. While some of these photographs have been published previously, others have not been and none have ever been examined in the context of a detailed historical geographical reconstruction, as they are here. The photographs and discussions allowed me to reconstruct key areas of the nineteenth-century palace landscape.

The principal women who helped elucidate the content of the photos included daughters of the last precolonial emir, Alhaji Aliyu, especially Hajiyya 'yar Mai-Tilas and Gogo Kahu, and the first colonial emir, Alhaji Abbas, including Gogo Mai'daki (whose childless mother was inherited from Aliyu after the British takeover in 1903) and Gogo Dambatta Ita. Gogo Nani, a younger sister of the emir also helped. The principal men who discussed the photos with me included His Highness Alhaji Ado Bayero; Malam D'au, a son of Emir Aliyu; Sallama Dako, one of the three highest ranking titleholding palace slaves; a high-ranking nobleman (Madakin Kano Shehu); and Alhaji Baba dan Meshe, the last palace eunuch who had an "accident" during circumcision and was considered impotent. Most of these men and women, save the emir and his younger sister, Nani, have since died. Hajiyya Abba, then the third wife (now his second, after the death of his first), moderated and mediated in many of the conversations that took place in the ciki.

Before elaborating on Abdullahi's changes I discuss at length an enigma I encountered in collecting spatial information about nineteenth-century palace grain tasks, which caused me to rethink gendered labor divisions of the prejihadic past. Discussion of these data is important for two reasons. First, the material is especially fragmentary and provocative, qualities underscoring the interpretive difficulties and pleasures of this and indeed *any* social geographical reconstruction where limited archeological and primary information is available. Second, I gathered and interpreted the data within the context of data collected for other time periods, an interpolative necessity that calls attention to the methodological strictures and challenges involved in reconstructing a specifically geographical story.

An Enigma: "King of Grain" and the Diminishment of Mai-Kudandan

A major impetus for writing about the nineteenth-century landscape, and especially about the changes that occurred therein during Abdullahi's reign, came from puzzling over the tasks assigned to the Mai-Kudandan (Master/ Owner of the Granary) titleholders in the nineteenth and twentieth century and the reasons why the title was allowed to lapse circa 1987.[1] At the time when Rufa'i (1987) was interviewing the last titleholder she merely administered the contents of a small palace grain store, the capacity of which was clearly insufficient compared to what was needed (then or in the past) to satisfy diurnal and annual palace grain needs. My own questioning revealed that most contemporary grains were purchased in sacks *(taiki)* from outside markets, a postcolonial necessity. The contemporary insignificance of Mai-Kudandan's responsibilities and title became particularly striking when elderly informants showed me the contours of an extensive complex of granaries she had once controlled, razed decades after the British conquest. This and other information made it clear that the palace ciki had once hosted extensive grain-related sites and hierarchies, the spatiality of which extended well into the city and beyond.[2]

In tandem with these puzzlements was the perplexing find that Abdullahi dan Dabo had set up a special new male slave hierarchy to administer to the distribution and storage of grains gathered as taxes and collected from rural estates. A special slave title was appointed to lead it: Sarkin Hatsi (King of Grain).[3] The fact that the hierarchy was newly founded begged the historical question of who had carried out his palace grain duties previously, when grain duties were even more important—a line of questioning that in light of spatial and ethnographic data led to the hypothesis that it was Mai-Kudandan who had accomplished his tasks and others related to them in the past.

Despite Sarkin Hatsi's presence, the Korama's powers (the key female grain official woman charged with setting city grain volumes and prices in the central market) did not decline, and may have initially expanded. Koramas of lesser status were by now installed in most markets, their appointments made through the top-ranked Korama in the central market, Kasuwar Kurmi.[4] The central market Korama reported as always, directly and regularly to the emir with a large retinue. Her official regalia was slightly elaborated upon to include the broad-rimmed Fulani hat or malafa.[5] Perhaps Korama's position remained intact because Kano's city population had doubled since Rumfa's time, to 50,000,[6] requiring significant concomitant increases in agricultural production and intensified coordination of grain markets—and because grains were a domestic necessity considered a womanly preserve. Not much profit would ever be made from transporting and selling grains, grain sales consequently not posing a threat to male market-hegemony. Economic limits on the profitability of this female endeavor and the domestic and reproductive utility of grain may have dampened jihadic concerns about women marketing grains in public. Moreover, women grain sellers occupied a coherent section in the central market, set apart from men, another factor that would have assuaged jihadic concerns about men and women intermingling in markets.

Sarkin Hatsi was given all sorts of paraphernalia of state. Most important, he was awarded expansive and luxurious quarters in what had historically been the palace ciki, within which he lived with titled assistants and a large slave retinue made up largely of slave boys. His office also carried considerable ceremony; like Korama, he was ritually turbaned and given elaborate robes of state. He was additionally the keeper of a ritual cup of office, symbolic of the official grain measure, the *mudu* (see Figure 14). Questioning why Sarkin Hatsi's slave hierarchy emerged when it did, along with why he was positioned in female parts of the palace and assigned domestic (female) food-related tasks, pointed to a number of grain-related, nineteenth-century state transitions. While population growth meant an escalation in the volume of city grain traded, increasing the state's need for streamlining and controlling grain market sales and thus Korama's economic influence, cowries (not grains) were now the primary medium in which state taxes were paid, a fact that would have decreased Korama's and especially Mai-Kudandan's *political* importance, along with the latter's economic viability. Coincidental with the drop in grain taxation revenues, the number of grain estates dedicated to producing grain for palace horses and the palace community were increasing, Dabo having earlier reappointed Shamaki to manage palace production and labor on the rural slave estates. All of these factors were part and parcel of fertility's (in the form of grain and women) political cultural decline, helping to explain why concubine grain duties devolved to slave men.

Korama's powers and prerogatives borne largely by urban-regional commercial interests in grains must have diverged politically and spatially at this time from those of Mai-Kudandan whose influence derived historically from state interests in grain taxation and the fertility of earth and women. This divergence would, of course, be expected, given grain's commercial importance and its relative displacement by the cowry shell and other currencies (as the normative state tax form).[7] As will be seen below, Sarkin Hatsi's office was

Figure 14. (a) King of Grain (Sarkin Hatsi) in his robes of state. He bears the traditional marks of palace slavery: the uku-uku (three-three), three scarified lines extending outward from either side of his mouth. (b) A palace child of slave descent scarified with the uku-uku. Photographs by the author.

tied additionally to larger interior changes in the palace landscape and to the initiatives of the Shamaki, whose grain-related estate duties must have been overwhelming.

The Southern Ciki: Concubine Losses and Male Slave Gains

Perhaps the most spatially radical change that Abdullahi precipitated was the ciki's diminishment as a result of his commission of Nassarawa (Victory)—a vast palace and pastoral-farming slave estate, located just beyond the city's southeastern walls (see Figure 15).[8] The complex expanded the emir's private, domestic domain and allowed for a more streamlined accommodation of Fulani dietary needs. The pastoral estate provisioned the royal household with milk, a Fulani staple used to prepare a variety of foods central to Fulani life, while the farm *(gandu)* provided the palace with vegetables and some grain. [9] Abdullahi lived in the Nassarawa palace a few months yearly, during the dry season (Rufa'i 1987), for which reason he kept a small number of resident concubines there.[10] By contrast, many more slaves, about five hundred, worked on the estate and complex.

Creating the Nassarawa palace-estate complex was tied to a dramatic reorientation and internal reconfiguration of the main Kano palace. Most strikingly, a large southern entrance was built into the Kano palace with a path leading out of it to the new palace. Constructing the entrance entailed demolishing the central part of the southern palace wall and building a monumental entrance hall in its stead. Unlike the "male-female" entrances of old located in the north, only a single entrance was built in the south and used primarily by men—eroding the gendered bilateral spatial principles of the palace's prejihadic past. Henceforth, cattle passed daily from the extra-urban Nassarawa complex through the southern entrance and into the palace ciki to be milked, a practice eventually discontinued by Abdullahi's grandson and colonial ruler, Abdullahi Bayero (1926–53) (Nast 1992). Because the new arrangement threatened to place the ciki's royal female inhabitants in direct spatial contact with the new southern public domain, Abdullahi displaced the ciki northward, elaborating a new and large southern labyrinth as a buffer zone between the southern gateway and the now much-smaller ciki. Like the labyrinth that lay to the north, the one in the south hosted one male and three female slave-guarded passageways, the two labyrinths producing a north-south symmetry of spatial functions (see Figure 16). The ciki, 50 percent smaller, was now sandwiched between two male domains.

Elaboration of the new southern labyrinth was tied to another of Abdullahi's radical architectural decisions: recreating and reinhabiting the southeasterly living chambers of prejihadic kings. Abdullahi did not merely rebuild the old quarters; he altered them in ways that increased his own interior

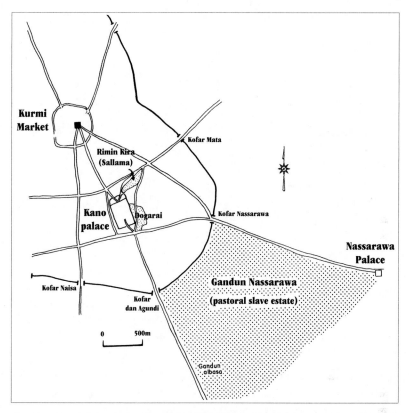

Figure 15. Map showing the location of the pastoral slave estate of Gandun Nassarawa (Farm of Victory) and its associated palace, Gidan Nassarawa (House of Victory). Gandun Albasa (Farm of Onions) was a smaller slave estate devoted to producing vegetables for the palace. The leading eunuch, Sallama (Peace), lived in the ward of Rimin Kira (the Silk Cotton Tree of Blacksmithing), where muskets would eventually be produced in the late nineteenth century. Abdullahi dan Dabo was the first emir to relocate some *dogarai* (bodyguards) from the city ward of Dogarai to the palace. The palace today is still known as Gidan Rumfa (the House of Rumfa) in reference to King Muhammadu Rumfa, who founded the palace. (Data from the Metropolitan Kano Planning and Development Board, *Map showing unguwa [ward] boundaries compiled from Local Government Survey maps*, ll.5.71, 1:4,800, and colonial contour map of Kano city at 1:12,500 [1932] from the National Archives Kaduna.)

presence and further separated women from men, including eunuchs. Rebuilding the prejihadic quarters anew was done with some fanfare, as is evident from the fact that Abdullahi commissioned the renowned Hausa builder Babban Gwani (*lit.* the Big Building Genius) to carry out the assignment. Unlike other structures, Abdullahi's quarters (dubbed Babban Soro or the Big Hall) were monumental and two-storied, allowing for armament storage on

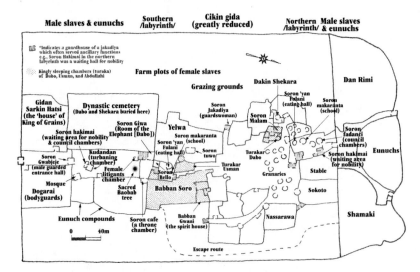

Figure 16. Palace landscape changes effected during the reign of Abdullahi dan Dabo (1855–82). During the reign of his father, Ibrahim Dabo, the three main slave officials in the northern palace slave domain were reinstituted, in keeping with prejihadic precedents. Hall of the Elephant (Soron Giwa) was probably built in honor of Abdullahi's father, who was known in praise songs as the "Bull Elephant," a term connoting great military prowess.

the second floor.[11] At the same time, Abdullahi kept the residences of his brother (Usman) and father (Ibrahim Dabo) intact, building a second story atop Soron Malam, these residences providing two additional living spaces. The increased number of kingly quarters and the two-storied quality of two of the chambers gave the emir a much larger visual and practical reach into the concubine interior.[12] From atop the second floor of Babban Soro, for example, Abdullahi could easily survey the central concubine ward of Yelwa (see Figure 17).

Contrary to what might be expected from a jihadic emir, Abdullahi also asked Babban Gwani to build a kudandan-house near Babban Soro for a female spirit, apparently unrelated to the one that lived in the threshed-grain granary structure in Yelwa (chapter 1).[13] The spirit dwelling was called Babban Gwani, after the architect, and may have been built because, like the other structures, it had existed there in the past.[14] Yet the fact that prejihadic kings lived next to the mosque and homes of Islamic clerics suggests otherwise; palace clerics of that time would not have permitted non-Islamic practices so close to a mosque. Alternatively, Abdullahi was currying concubine favor by employing practices they had long controlled. More likely, he was now accommodating spirit practices in which he himself believed and engaged, perhaps an effect of his having been raised in the powerful slave household of

Figure 17. A photograph taken directly after the British conquest in 1903 by Capt. C. H. F. Abadie from a vantage point at some distance east of the central concubine ward, Yelwa. Note the second story of the monumental kingly quarters that Abdullahi built for himself, Babban Soro. The second story overlooked the central concubine ward of Yelwa (Abundance), featured in the middleground. The considerable visual foreshortening in this photograph seemingly erases what would have been at least 20–30 meters separating the rowlike structure of Babban Soro from the rowlike structures in Yelwa. The fields in the foreground were cultivated by slave women. The bird droppings were from pigeons that would have been attracted by the massive amount of food cooked in Yelwa. (Photograph courtesy of the Royal Geographical Society, London, Picture Library, 068041, my annotations.)

dan Rimi Barka. The latter hypothesis is recommended by the fact that Abdullahi was accused publicly by his politically disaffected brother, Abdulkadiri (who had been given the highest state office of the time, the Galadima) of engaging in paganistic practices. Abdulkadiri is said to have circulated rumors that his brother had put a fetish in the palace and was engaging in rituals "to increase his physical and political capacities" (Smith 1997, 284). If Abdullahi was indeed guilty of fetish practices, he likely carried these out in the spirit's new granary dwelling connected directly to his chambers. It was perhaps to hide this kudandan-fact that a high wall was built to separate the emir's new spirit quarters from the palace mosque and clergy just to the south. Abdullahi is said to have been enraged by what he considered a brother's betrayal, and he indignantly wrote to the caliph and the caliph's religious advisor (the Waziri), proclaiming his innocence and asking permission to dismiss Abdulkadiri from office. Abdullahi's letter apparently won the caliph and

Waziri over, for the Galadima was deposed,[15] whereupon Abdullahi's son Yusufu assumed the Galadima post, thus putting Abdullahi's lineage in place for political ascent.[16]

Abdullahi's new chambers were not the only prejihadic structures that Abdullahi rebuilt. He also resurrected the sixteenth-century eunuch colony, mosque, and cleric's quarters that had once constituted the easterly male enclave of old, with one important difference. Instead of the places being integrated spatially with the emir's quarters, he placed the dividing wall between them (see Figure 16), stretching clear across the ciki, from Abdullahi's domain westward through the now much-reduced women's quarters. The wall's reach effectively partitioned off all southern "male" structures from a now exclusively "female" and kingly interior. This more stringent gendered arrangement was most striking in relation to the eunuch colony: Originally abutting the king's chambers, it now lay partitioned off, a short distance away in the new labyrinth. Nearby grew the monumental baobab tree, dating from the earliest days of the palace and associated in pre-Islamic mythology with chieftancy and, in Kano, with a eunuch title, Turaki Kuka (Turaki of the Baobab Tree; see Figure 18).[17] While it is unclear why Abdullahi placed eunuchs outside the formal ciki, it seems likely that he placed the clerics there to prevent them from witnessing the spirit worship practices in which he engaged near and in his quarters. As in the past, all of the "male" structures were located in the east, reinstating partially the gendered spaces of prejihadic days.

Abdullahi commissioned two other structures nearby: A waiting room for nobility called Soron Hakimai (Hall of Nobility) and turbaning chambers shaped like a granary, called Kudandan, which doubled as state council chambers (see Figure 19).[18] The proximity of the former structure to the baobab tree where prejihadic kings held court hints that Soron Hakimai replicated a much earlier structure. In contrast, Kudandan may have been an innovation. Recall that Abdullahi's father, Ibrahim Dabo, had asked the caliph to reinstate the entitlement system and that Dabo consequently reinstituted turbaning rituals, creating a special turbaning style for the royal family. Abdullahi may therefore have built Kudandan to situate and symbolize dynastic control over a turbaning process his father had begun. Alternatively, the chamber may have been one of those structures resurrected from the past to which the Fulani gave new dynastic meaning.[19] In any event, these two halls mirrored similar prejihadic structures in the northern labyrinth, bearing the same name and serving similar, if not identical, functions. As in the case of his predecessors' private chambers in the ciki, Abdullahi did not abandon the northern structures. Instead, he rotated state meetings between the two areas, holding daily morning council

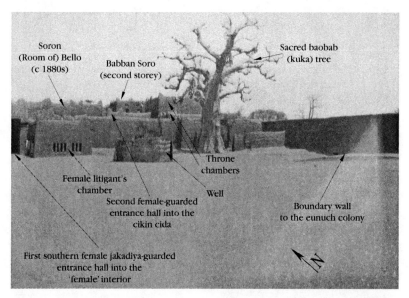

Figure 18. A northward-looking view of the southern part of the palace that Abdullahi dan Dabo (1855–92) reconstructed, photographed by Captain Fforde Searight, perhaps in 1904 or 1905. To the far right is the wall of the large rebuilt eunuch colony. To the far left is the first female-guarded entranceway into the new southern labyrinth; the second one is located slightly northward. The large circumference of the baobab tree suggests that it dates from Rumfa's reign. The baobab, associated with divine kingship, was cut down during the reign of Abdullahi's grandson, also known as Abdullahi (1926–53). Note that the female litigants' chamber contains slatted apertures at its base through which women relayed testimony to the eunuch Kilishi, who shuttled their testimony to the court, which was located further north in the labyrinth. An earlier photograph from the Foreign Commonwealth Archives, dating from 1903, shows that a wall would have separated these chambers from the area to the south. Soron Cafe (Hall of Plaster) was later rebuilt by Abdullahi's grandson (Abdullahi) in the 1930s and renamed Soron Ingila (Hall of England) after the then-emir's historic visit to England to meet King George V. (Photograph courtesy of the Royal Geographical Society, London, Picture Library, 068148; my annotations.)

meetings in the southern halls and daily evening meetings in their northern equivalents.[20]

Abdullahi commissioned two additional, completely new structures: a large complex of households for royal bodyguard or *dogarai* in the southeast corner of what had been the ciki, and luxurious quarters for Sarkin Hatsi (King of Grain) in the southwest. The dogarai were drafted from the larger dogarai community living in the city ward of Dogarai southeast of the palace.[21] The dogarai's decidedly "male" functions help explain their placement in the eastern side of the palace. Obversely, the western placement of

Acacia tree

Boundary wall to
eunuch colony

Entrance hall into
a eunuch compound

Kudandan:
Royal council/court chamber
and turbaning hall

Soron Hakimai:
Ante-chamber for nobility
awaiting royal court

Figure 19. The new waiting room for noblemen, Soron Hakimai (Hall of Nobility) and the tur-baning and council/court chamber, Kudandan, built in the new southern labyrinth during Abdullahi dan Dabo's reign and photographed by Capt. Fforde Searight. The wall to the right was part of the curtain wall of the eunuch colony rebuilt by Abdullahi, part of which is visible in Figure 18. The two structures had formal equivalents in the northern labyrinth. Daily coun-cil meetings were held in the southern chambers in the morning and in the northern chambers in the late afternoon. (Photograph courtesy of the Royal Geographical Society, London, Pic-ture Library, 068154; my annotations.)

Sarkin Hatsi's household speaks to the feminine quality of his grain-related labor tasks and the concubine structure to which his office was attached. Though ultimately answerable to Shamaki, Sarkin Hatsi took orders from Uwar Soro, the leading titleholding concubine to whom Mai-Kudandan also reported. Perhaps this arrangement obtained because Shamaki felt that his grain-related tasks, assumed since Dabo's time, had become too onerous given his many other responsibilities. It is not unreasonable to surmise that it was the Shamaki who suggested to Abdullahi that Sarkin Hatsi's position be created so as to relieve him of domestic-related grain duties. If so, Uwar Soro and Shamaki became ranked equivalents: Uwar Soro administered the inte-rior population, while Shamaki oversaw slave labor in "male" parts of the palace and on the agricultural estates. Their duties overlapped to the extent that each one was responsible for underlings having grain-related duties, Sarkin Hatsi's labor shared between them. Accordingly, Shamaki handled the labor involved in grain production on royal estates, with grain products siphoned into Sarkin Hatsi's care, while Uwar Soro administered grain distribution in the interior through Sarkin Hatsi and Mai-Kudandan. Because Sarkin Hatsi mostly worked with and was answerable to Uwar Soro, he was feminized by slave men and not considered part of the main male slave community.[22]

Sarkin Hatsi's duties were many. He supervised the collection and disbursement of grains from rural estates and grains gathered as taxes. Instead of receiving, stockpiling, and sorting grain procurements through the northern "female" gateway as had been done in the prejihadic past, grain activities were transacted through the southern gate. This reorientation of grain-related collection and storage activities belies the near irrelevance of grain in political, social, and economic transactions between Mai-Kudandan and Korama that had once characterized the palace's past.

Giginyu's work shows that the royal estates produced mostly sorghum, which was used to feed the royal horses (1981). My own data suggest that the agricultural surplus produced on the rural estates was used by both humans and horses, though the amount of feed needed for horses greatly exceeded the grain needs of palace inhabitants, due to the great number of horses and the fact that horses eat substantially more than humans. According to Barth, Emir Usman could "raise an army of seven thousand horses. . . . In the most flourishing state of the country, the Governor [emir] of Kano is said to have been able to bring into the field as many as ten thousand horses" (1965 [1857], 523). Abdullahi developed the cavalry even further (Ubah 1985, 31). If this was so, grains received as in-kind religious tithes (zakat) must have supplied the bulk of palace grains, with a small number of commoners (talakawa) apparently also rendering some of their non-zakat taxes in grain.[23]

The exact amount to be paid as zakat was determined by a male jakada just after harvest. Zakat grain revenues constituted 10 percent of farm yield and consisted mostly of guinea corn and millet. Zakat could only be collected from farms producing a minimum of five corn bundles (dami) or millet stalks (Garba 1986, 112) and was rendered in addition to the main farm tax, Kurdin Kasa, the vast majority of which was paid in cowries.[24] Zakat's importance is little understood, even today, partly because it was collected and used differently across the caliphate and because its religious character made it largely unintelligible to colonial officers attempting to study it (110–15). Nevertheless, a 1909 British colonial report claims that a Kano farmer "never knew when he might have to journey fifty miles with corn loads to the capital to convey the tax," a comment showing that the collection radius for the emir's household was extensive (Hewby, in Garba 1986, 110). Garba argues that the zakat was one of the easiest taxes to collect because its rate was fixed and because it held religious importance, some farmers even insisting that it be collected during the colonial era (1903–60).[25] Zakat proceeds were supposed to be used to support religious leaders and those in need. Given that the emir was by definition a religious leader and given the needs of his large household, his use of zakat could easily be justified. Indeed, *ulama* interviewed by Ubah in 1972 claimed that "the *zakka* [*sic*] was almost used up by the emirs and their officials instead of being given to the poor and needy," only a minor portion of the zakat used for the latter purpose (1985, 30).

This minor portion was apparently stored in a separate granary complex adjacent to but walled off from the main palace granaries. These were the preserve of Fulani malams or as Imam Imoru calls them, "palace malams," who served as palace advisors and expected to be supported by zakat revenues and to use these revenues to provide for those they deemed in need. These men held high status and were rewarded handsomely by the emir. As the Kano-born cleric Imam Imoru recalled:

> [P]alace malams are very learned and they tell the ruler the truth. The ruler provides them with their livelihood: their food, drink, animals to ride, and clothes to wear. He gives them everything, including servants, *bayi*, and female slaves, *kuyangi*. These malams wear expensive and elegant clothing like that of the ruler, and their saddles and horse trappings are like those used by the ruler. (Ferguson 1973, 227) [26]

Nevertheless, they did not allocate to the poor all that was their due: "The poor and the needy occasionally received presents distributed by the emir's agents such as the *Sarkin Shanu* [and Fulani malams], but they perhaps did not receive in full what the Qur'an provided for them" (Ubah 1985, 30). The origins of the "malam's" granary complex is not known, but they may have been built during the reign of the last prejihadic king, Alwali (1781–1807), who the KC avers established public granaries "in case of war and famine" (Palmer 1967 [1928], 127).[27]

At any rate, following harvests and the concomitant influx of tithe grains, palace slave boys received and sorted grain bundles in the southern labyrinth, later carrying them across the entirety of the newly delimited palace interior (ciki) to the granaries where Sarkin Hatsi, assisted by two slave underlings—Galadima Rumbu (The Galadima of the Granary) and Sarkin Tsani (King of the Ladder)—oversaw their storage. Sarkin Tsani would climb a large ladder placed on the granary to be filled. From here, he lifted the thatched granary roof with a special hook and directed slave boys as to where they should stack the dami. Galadima Rumbu was the liaison between the concubines and Sarkin Hatsi; slave women, on behalf of the wives and concubines, daily informed the Galadima Rumbu of their grain needs, whereupon Sarkin Tsani and his slave assistants would extract and distribute the requested amount of grains to them.[28]

The only site built for women in the new "male" south was a hall for female litigants, a small box-like adobe structure, set at some distance from an Islamic courtroom, also located in the southern labyrinth. The presence of the hall indicates that extant Islamic practices prohibited women from entering the all-male court presided over by the emir. Instead, they were to sit on the chamber's floor and give their oral testimony to a titled eunuch, Kilishi, through a small slatted window at the structure's base. Kilishi then acted as the go-between and shuttled the information to the court (see Figures 16 and 18).[29] Imam Imoru embellished on its modest qualities circa 1905 when speaking to the German administrator in Kete-Krachi, in what at that time was Togo. Specifically, he remarked that the women's hallway was a "very big shelter, with cool shade," going on to explain that this "is where the female plaintiffs sit, but they do not see the king, nor does he see them or hear their voices: the kilishi asks them about their complaints and tells them to the king" (Ferguson 1973, 238).[30]

Concubine Efflorescence and Sociospatial Organization

Despite the ciki's considerable diminishment, Abdullahi cultivated concubinage to a larger extent than had his father, Ibrahim Dabo, or his brother, Usman (1846–55). Smith records that Usman had few sons, whereas Abdullahi had numerous children, placing almost thirty sons in important positions of power (1997, 285). Palace informants claim that Abdullahi's children numbered 333, a figure undoubtedly more symbolic than real, a way of pointing out Abdullahi's virility and political strength.[31] In any event, palace concubines were by Abdullahi's reign organized complexly into a hierarchy of titled positions, collectively administering and reproducing the royal household. As in the past, title-bearing concubines were addressed by title and not by name, a way of connoting a concubine's cultural, political, and functional significance. Unlike the prejihadic past, the work accomplished by these women was contained by the interior.

Among the most important titleholding concubines who now ruled the ciki were Mai-Kudandan and Mai-Soron Baki. Now that Shamaki, through Sarkin Hatsi, administered the collection and storage of palace grain, Mai-Kudandan had only to attend to its internal distribution and processing, which she accomplished using female palace slave cadres. After receiving daily allotments of grain bundles through Galadima Rumbu, kuyangi threshed the bundles in the ciki's western fields. The chaff was used by the stables, while most of the threshed grain was sent to the central concubine ward, Yelwa. By the turn of the nineteenth century, concubines were paying local women to thresh some palace grain, suggesting that the amount of grain needing to be threshed exceeded what could be processed by slave labor internally. After threshing, most grain was brought to Mai-Kudandan in Yelwa where it was stored in a special granary or kudandan. By contrast, royal wives received their portion of dami (grain bundles) via special female slave delegates, iyayen wajeje. Threshed grains were measured with care, using three sizes of calabashes. Milk allotments were also collected each morning from Mai-Shanu (Master of the Cattle) and his assistants (who milked royal cattle in the easternmost palace fields) by slave women and iyayen wajeje who distributed it throughout the ciki.[32]

Uwar Soro (Woman of the [Emir's] Room) was the most powerful title-holding concubine at this time. Responsible for all concubines, including other titleholders, she served as personal secretary to the emir: Every day she met the emir in Soron Baki (the Room of the Mouth), the large audience hall inside Babban Soro, Abdullahi's monumental sleeping chambers. Here, after greeting him, she relayed news and messages concerning the ciki and its inhabitants, reporting additionally on births and deaths. Replies, instructions, or news from the emir to interior inhabitants were also relayed through her. She divvied up gifts and meats sent to the women by the emir or other persons, slave delegates or iyayen wajeje sharing out the goods to the various concubine wards and wifely places. Uwar Soro also counseled the emir on state-related matters and supervised cooking for the most important state guests.[33]

Mai-Soron Baki (Master of Soron Baki) was probably of equal or lesser rank than Mai-Kudandan. Her title refers to the fact that she lived in and was solely responsible for the emir's audience chamber for women and children, Soron Baki.[34] The title probably dates to the time of Rumfa (1463–99), when Al Maghili wrote him to hold daily audience with his household (Gwarzo, Bedri, and Starratt 1974/77). Malam Imoru describes how such daily household audience rituals were held, rituals that continued up through the early years of colonialism and that are still practiced on Fridays and special occasions:

> When morning comes he sits there [in room in the palace interior, the soron ciki] and the members of his household come to greet him, saying "May God give you a long life," *Allah ya ba ka yawan rai,* or "May your life be long," *ranka ya dade,* or "May God grant you success," *Allah ya ba ka nasara.* These are the greetings for a king throughout Hausaland. (Ferguson 1973, 209)[35]

Mai-Soron Baki accomplished many tasks. She ensured that the emir's quarters were kept clean, and that the emir was well served, especially while inside Soron Baki.[36] And every Friday, under her guidance, all royal women formed a procession to the audience chamber to pay homage to the emir, iyayen wajeje leading royal wives and concubines from their places and ward in order of these women's social rank.[37] Perhaps Mai-Soron Baki's most important task was requesting individual audiences with the emir on behalf of women and formally escorting them to Soron Baki upon the emir's consent. In all her duties she was assisted by 'yan soro, junior concubines whom she trained and administered.

The 'yan soro (children of the [emir's] room) were concubine recruits who lived in small rooms or taskoki inside Babban Soro. Lesser numbers of 'yan soro lived in taskoki in Soron Malam, the former residential quarters of Ibrahim Dabo. 'Yan soro were crucial to the social reproduction of ciki life. The least experienced and typically the youngest of concubines, they stayed inside the emir's quarters where they underwent intense training, part of which involved learning how to maintain the emir's compound and belongings, and how to minister to his person, the last task involving traditional massage or tausa. The 'yan soro were among those designated to summon concubines to the emir's chambers, which required that they learn who lived where in the ciki and how it was organized. They also retrieved armaments stored in the upper story of the emir's chambers when called upon to do so. Under Mai-Soron Baki's tutelage, the 'yan soro learned the essentials of administrative life, along with the intricacies of palace protocol. When and if these women bore children, they could ask permission to leave the taskoki to live in a concubine ward, allowing them to attend more fully to their children and to become more integrated into adult concubine activities. If permission was granted, new spaces opened up for newer 'yan soro recruits.

Mai-Soron Baki did not train all new concubine recruits. She trained only those obtained as prisoners of war or female domestic servants (kuyangi) later chosen or taken as concubines. Other young girls entered the ciki as the personal companions or laborers (kuyangi) of a new wife, that is, as property typically bestowed upon a wife by her father. If the emir took one or more of his wife's female companions as a concubine, he had to remunerate the wife. Alternatively, some wives arrived with concubines intended as gifts for the emir from their own fathers. In this case, the concubine resided in the place or waje of the wife, serving her as a companion and as a domestic servant—though of higher status than mere kuyangi.

The titleholding concubine Uwar Tafiya, or Woman (or Mother) of Traveling, was in charge of preparing a kind of mobile household for the emir when he went on military campaigns, ensuring that his creature comforts were met.[38] She chose which concubines accompanied him, she arranged for all his meals, and she attended to his personal needs. As Malam Imoru noted, throughout Hausaland a "king does not take his wives when he goes to war: he takes concubines . . . who ride on camels and mares and are accompanied by the eunuchs who guard them. Men dare not go near them: if they do they are beaten mercilessly, until they fall to the ground" (Ferguson 1973, 207). A similar situation obtained in Buganda where a "chief selected certain wives [there were no distinctions between wives and concubines] who were to accompany him in war. They guarded the war gods, cooked, sharpened spears or reeds, performed religious rituals, and at times attended to the wounded."[39]

The limited efflorescence of concubinage associated with Abdullahi's reign coincided with the reconsolidation of some of the most important pre-jihadic concubine spaces. Although the dyeing yard was never recovered, Yelwa again became the hub of ciki activity and palace reproduction. Most flour and milk, for example, were used in the central palace kitchen in Yelwa, known as Soron Tuwo, where four classes of food for four classes of persons were cooked in twelve enormous pots or *tukwane,* the food quality and the status of the women cooking, corresponding to the status of the person for whom the food was intended. Only wives (located in their respective wajeje or places) and concubines cooked for those of the highest rank—guests of the emir. Concubines typically cooked for the royal family ('yan Fulani), which included elderly or divorced royal women residing in the palace interior. Lower-status concubines and slave women prepared food for slaves, including eunuchs, stable-keepers, builders, and domestic staff. Only female slaves cooked for malams or the Islamic teachers. All told, concubines and slave women cooked daily for well over one thousand persons, most of them men.

Yelwa similarly became reinstated as the politico-religious center of ciki life: the female palace spirit, Aljanna, all the leading concubines, and the title-holding leaders of kuyangi and female jakadu, Uwar Kuyangi (Mother of the Kuyangi) and Babban Jakadiya (The *Big* Jakadiya), respectively, lived there.[40] Female jakadu guarded key interior checkpoints and carried messages for royal women, through their activities and powers were now greatly reduced.[41]

Abdullahi had good reason to cultivate concubinage and its spaces. Concubines from established palace slave households produced kinship links between his lineage and those of palace slaves, these links now holding special strategic importance for both parties involved.[42] On the one hand, the long-standing prejihadic slave community depended on Fulani rulers for their survival; by giving daughters and sisters to the emir, lineal structures and allegiances bled productively into another. On the other hand, Abdullahi depended on the support of these slaves to run the state and to remain in power, especially given his father's dynastic centralization of power. By taking a daughter from a slave household as a royal concubine, the emir accumulated considerable political capital: royal children borne by these concubines had grandparents who were palace slaves. The children thus had access to and could cultivate slave interests and intrigues, traversing both royal and slave communities and providing political intelligence indirectly and directly to emir and slaves alike. Concubines who derived from palace slave households were on the whole more valuable politically than those captured recently in war (barring slave women, like Shekara, who came from non-Fulani royal households) because they knew how to enculturate royal children into palace life, continuing a centuries-old, slave-led acculturation process.

The political importance of kinship links between the emir and his slaves was so great that even when royal children held no lineal connections to palace slave households, social ones were forged. Once royal sons reached puberty, for example, they were taken out of the ciki and placed in one of the three main royal slave households (Sallama, dan Rimi, or Shamaki) to be trained in political and military matters. Abdullahi's brother and predecessor, Usman, for example, had been sent by his father to live in the household of Shamaki Nasamu, while Abdullahi himself had been raised by dan Rimi Barka (Stilwell 2000, 142). In turn, Yusufu, Abdullahi's son by the caliph's daughter, who eventually initiated a civil war, was raised in the household of the head eunuch, Sallama.

The political benefits accruing from the imbrication of kingly and slave lineages stabilized the state. Stilwell writes that succession decisions depended on the blessings of powerful palace slaves who intensely, albeit informally, influenced kingmaking processes (2000). Indeed, slaves "often chose an Emir whom they thought would provide them with an opportunity to wield power and influence, and were unconcerned with how learned or pious he was" (143 n. 82). The insider knowledge of powerful slaves meant, moreover, that they had considerable political capital at their disposal with which to negotiate their interests:

> As "outsiders," royal slaves could do as they wished, protected from harm
> and censure by their ties to the royal household and the secrets to which
> they had access. Oral tradition relates that should royal slaves be displeased
> with the Emir, they often approached his mother (who could be their
> daughter or sister) for redress. Likewise, the Emir often turned to his
> mother for advice and guidance. (Stilwell 2000, 145)

If the palace slave community was so important and if Abdullahi's military successes were so great—allowing him to build up male slave spaces, especially those of eunuchs—why did concubine numbers decline? The answer to this question is not known, though some reasoned conjectures can be made. Abdullahi may have preferred obtaining knowledgeable women from pre-existing palace slave populations, for example, rather than accumulating large numbers of concubines through conquest. Such a strategy would have laid a surer groundwork for state household reproduction, given the political cultural ruptures that had obtained with the Fulani conquest of 1807. Concubine numbers in the Kano palace may also have declined slightly with the reassignment of small numbers of concubines to daughter palaces, such as Nassarawa. Especially since the time of Dabo, many fortified towns and royal estates had been built, a few having palaces with a very limited number of royal concubines managing the respective interiors. More important, the labor needs of royal agricultural estates may have meant that female slave labor was now preferentially deployed in farm fields. Finally, the increased geopolitical security afforded by the caliphate structure meant that most political energies could be spent on cultivating Fulani alliances rather than on territorial conquest per se. In this sense, the children of concubines were used to forge kinship links among a more limited number of Fulani clans, rather than among smaller chiefs of differing cultural backgrounds—a change that would have required lesser numbers of children. Smith notes, in fact, that Fulani nobility refused to marry their freeborn daughters to non-Fulani, who were considered heathen (1997, 295); if Abdullahi acted similarly, the population pool on which he could bestow freeborn progeny would have decreased. It appears, then, that having many children (and, hence, many concubines in postjihadic time) was somewhat of a liability.[43] In other words, intermarriages among Fulani might have placed a downward pressure on the number of royal children (and, by extension, concubines) needed by the dynastic state. Some evidence that not as many children were needed comes from the work of Smith, who avers that Abdullahi had difficulty placing his sons politically (285). To accommodate them, he removed some of his own brothers (e.g., Abdulkadiri) from power along with his brother's and predecessor's (Usman's) sons. At the same time, Abdullahi presumably had much to gain from bestowing concubines upon his Fulani clansmen as an act of patronage, that is, giving slave women away rather than keeping them for personal use.

In contrast to the comparatively lessened value of palace concubines, the political, economic, and cultural value of freeborn wives increased.[44] With the onset of Fulani rule, for example, most emirs vied to have a daughter of the Sokoto caliph, what I refer to as a "Sokoto wife." Among nineteenth-century rulers awarded Sokoto wives were Suleiman (1807–19), Ibrahim Dabo, and Abdullahi. Being given a Sokoto wife was especially crucial to the legitimacy of at least two Fulani rulers: Suleiman's marriage to the caliph's daughter (Sandata) increased his authority in the resentful eyes of his many detractors and was undoubtedly one reason why he remained in power; while Abdullahi's marriage to the caliph's senior daughter was arranged to heal a rift that developed between Kano and Sokoto when Abdullahi forcefully took the throne in 1855 (see Smith 1997, 273).[45] Ibrahim Dabo's Sokoto wife (Maryama) was a well-known poet and Islamic scholar, and in later life served as an informal councilor to Emir Bello (1883–92).[46] In all cases, Sokoto marriages enmeshed the ruling Kano lineage with that of the caliph. A recent praise song created for the wedding of the present-day emir of Kano to his Sokoto bride, Princess Saude, documents the Sokoto wife tradition:

Refrain:

Gwaron Giwa, sa maza gudu
Gwarzon mallam masu duniya
(Oh Elephant! [an honorific title signifying military strength] that makes warriors run away; Courageous malam whose world it is)

Ni Alhaji Musa Dankwairo
Zan yi tariki na gaskiya
Saraken Kano da suka auro Sakkwatawa
(I, Alhaji Musa Dankwairo [the Kano praise singer who wrote this poem], I will tell a true history of the emirs who married Sokoto princesses)

Sarkin Kano Mallam Sule
Ya auro diyar Sarkin Musulmi Malam Bello
Yarda Alla ta sadu da suwa
([The first Fulani] King Malam Suleiman married the daughter of the Caliph Malam Bello. May God's pleasure meet up with them)

Sarkin Kano Malam Dabo
Shi ne ya auro Maryama
Wace cika kira Uwar Daje, diyar Shehu
Yarda Alla ta sadu da suwa
(The Ruler [lit. King] Malam Dabo married Maryama, the daughter of the Shehu, who was called Uwar Daje. May God's pleasure meet up with them)

Sarkin Kano Abdullahi Maje Karofi
Shi ne ya auro Saudatu
Diyar Sarkin Musulmi Alu
Ta haifa mai [masa] Sarkin Kano Malam Alu
Kuma da wani nai [wani nasa]

Yardar Allah ta sadu da suwa
(The Ruler Abdullahi Maje Karofi [1855–82] married Saudatu, the daughter of the Ruler of all Muslims [the Caliph] Alu. She delivered for him the [future] King of Kano, Aliyu. And later delivered another [son] for him. May God's pleasure meet up with them)

Sarkin Kano Mallam Usuman
Ya auri diyar Sarkin Musulmi Maiturare
Yarda Allah ta sadu da suwa
(The Ruler Malam Usman married the daughter of Sultan Maiturare. May Allah be pleased with them)

Sarkin Kano Mallam Usuman bacin ya rasu
Sanusi Chiroman Kasar Kano
Ya aure ta ya rabu da ita tun gaban shi sarautar Kano
Yarda Allah ta sadu da suwa
(After Usman died, the Ciroma of Kano Emirate, Sanusi [1953–63], he married her. He separated from her before he became emir. May God's pleasure meet up with them)[47]

Sarkin Kano Alhaji Ado yanzu ya auro
Saudatu, diyar Sarkin Musulmi Abubakar
Jikar Shehu mai martaba
Zumunci sai karuwa yake
(King Alhaji Ado [1963–] now marries Saudatu, daughter of the Sultan Abubakar, granddaughter [descendant] of the holy Shehu [the leader of the jihad]. The bond strengthens.)[48]

Also, one of Abdullahi dan Dabo's daughters was given to the sultan of Sokoto as a bride. Her son, Ibrahim Narabala, became the father of the next Sokoto sultan, Ahmadu Bello. Thus, Abdullahi's daughter became the paternal grandmother of the sultan. Later, one of Sarki Sanusi's (1953–63) sons (Abubakar, Wombai of Kano) married one of Sultan Ahmadu Bello's daughters. Bello's mother, in turn, was a princess from the Kano palace.[49]

Ibrahim Dabo pronounced the signal importance of the Sokoto marriages by building a special waje (place) for his Sokoto wife in the ciki called Wajen Sokoto (Place of Sokoto). The premises were hence maintained and used to accommodate all subsequent emirs' Sokoto wives. Abdullahi elaborated on Wajen Sokoto's significance by initiating two rituals that continue through the present day: visiting "Sokoto" every Friday to offer his Friday prayers, the Sokoto bride being given formal guardianship over the emir's Friday prayer mat by the concubine Mai-Soron Baki, who just after their marriage ritually delivers the mat into her care; and writing a formal greeting from "Sokoto" to the caliph during or after the Islamic festival Id-el-Fitr.[50] The Sokoto marriages and the rituals and spaces associated with the Sokoto waje, then, symbolized the palace's political geographical ties to caliphate rule.[51] Unlike the naming of concubine wards after the concubines' place of capture—symbolic of how what was formerly wild or unconquered had been domesticated—the Sokoto waje's name represented a sought after and elite politico-religious pact.

Abdullahi's marriages to other free women may have been used to cultivate lineal ties to commercial and industrial endeavors. Informants recalled, for example, that the first colonial emir, Abbas, married the chief blacksmith's daughter, Halima 'yar Makera.[52] Intriguingly, Aliyu had earlier resurrected the fifteenth-century royal slave estate at Dorayi (which contained about fifty slave men and women) near the smaller estate of Kano's Sarkin Makera (Chief Blacksmith), indicative that long-standing historical and social links between Kano rulers and the Sarkin Makera were still being cultivated (Hill 1977, 214). Blacksmithing was especially important for it was central to asserting military primacy in the region (weaponry), and agricultural productivity (hoes), for which reason Abdullahi induced Sankara warriors to emigrate to Kano city, many settling near the central market to take up their blacksmithing craft (Jaggar 1973, 14). Abdullahi may also have created (or perhaps only resurrected) a blacksmithing enclave in a city ward just northeast of the palace, Rimin Kira (below).[53]

The drastically reduced number of concubines, reflecting decreased status and value, may have led, in turn, to a secondary devaluation: reduced numbers meant that fewer concubines now had to work more intensively to carry out or administer labor tasks similar in scope and intensity to those of the pre-jihadic past. Tasks included those demanded by the higher status wives.

Eunuchs, Blacksmithing, and Devalorization of Female Slave Reproduction

By at least the nineteenth century, a large palace household and blacksmithing facility had been set up in the ward of Rimin kira, which loosely translated means "the silk cotton tree of smithing."[54] The military- and agricultural-related facility was placed strategically alongside the eastern pathway built by Rumfa that led out of the palace towards the city walls, passing along the palace stables and Shamaki's compound. During Abdullahi's reign, Sallama Barka, a "eunuch" who had become particularly powerful, controlled the area, which effectively constituted a third eunuch stronghold (Palmer 1967 [1928], 131).[55] The other two included the new eunuch colony in the southern palace labyrinth and a eunuch community concentrated in the palace's central northern region of the "male" slave domain. Sallama Barka's black-smithing household served as a depot for much of the iron-based war gear, including spears, swords, bows and arrows, and, eventually, guns. It also contained the umbrella of state and the quilted armor used to protect horses and foot cavalry.[56] Sallama's control over the manufacturing site and depot helps explain how it became possible for him to wage a coup (unsuccessfully) against Abdullahi's successor and brother, Bello, who had turned him out of office (Palmer 1967 [1928], 131; Fika 1978, 57).[57]

That Sallama's responsibility and geographical reach was so extensive indicates how much more powerful eunuchs were than concubines, something already indicated in their relative numbers. Never again would concubine numbers increase to prejihadic levels. The importance of reproduction within the palace slave community as a whole ostensibly also waned, evident in the fact that Abdullahi gave palace slave men permission to marry free women. This prerogative not only curried favor by grafting slave men's lineages onto freeborn ones, but it potentially blocked the emir from taking these men's daughters as concubines, given that Islamic law forbids taking a free woman's daughter as a slave. These marriages were controversial and may be the reason that Abdullahi began scarifying slave newborns with the *uku-uku* (three-three), three small marks cut whisker-like into both cheeks (see Figure 14b).[58]

Scarification

Sumptuary codes had always been a common means for distinguishing between slave and free persons and among different status groups.[59] Among men, Kano slaves had historically worn loincloths instead of robes, for example, and Ibrahim Dabo had developed the special turbaning style for men of the royal family.[60] It is therefore not clear why Abdullahi felt compelled to go beyond sumptuary means and institute scarification.[61] Scarification is, of course, a common African practice that allows different status and cultural groups to be visually distinguished, yet it had never been used before in the palace. Its ubiquitousness in other contexts does not explain *why* Abdullahi so marked palace slave children. What might have been the importance and meaning of scarification for Abdullahi and/or for the slave community at this particular point in time?

One reason may have had to do with one controversy that marked Abdullahi's reign: his support of palace slave men's marriages to free Fulani women. As in many other West African places, such as the kingdom of Dahomey, free women who wanted a divorce or who did not want to marry the men to whom they were betrothed could come to the palace to seek a ruler's counsel and support (Bay 1998). If the ruler was away, the women could stay until his return, incidentally becoming available for courtship with local men. This indeed happened when Abdullahi was away on military campaigns southeast of Kano; free Fulani women, some of whom were aristocracy, came to the palace to complain about the free men they were expected to marry. While they waited in the ciki for Abdullahi's return, they were courted by palace slave men, some of the women marrying these men, causing considerable consternation among the women's Fulani male kin. As Smith explains:

> To Fulani aristocrats, who had steadfastly refused to marry their daughters to free Hausa or Habe, whatever their official status, knowledge of these marriages to throne slaves must have been especially humiliating, and their powerlessness to prevent or punish them even more so; and since they reasoned that such slave insolence was only possible by virtue of the emir's protection and complaisance, Fulani aristocrats and commoners alike held Abdullahi personally responsible for authorising or permitting such unions. Some still do so in Kano to this day. (1997, 294)

Despite Fulani complaints, Abdullahi stood by his slaves, refusing to divorce them of their aristocratic wives. His decision effectively meant that free Fulani women and their freeborn children now resided in the palace's slave quarters. Hence within these quarters, these children might be mistaken by outsiders for palace slaves. Abdullahi may therefore have invented the uku-uku at this point to assuage the feelings of his Fulani detractors, that is, marking only palace slave women's children and not those of freeborn Fulani women, creating visually accessible social distinctions despite shared living quarters.[62] One of Yunasa's male informants relayed that the scar design (three small marks on either cheek) was chosen arbitrarily, various male councilors suggesting to the emir different designs (1976, 47). Women informants from this study argued otherwise: that the design derived from that fact that slave infants are scarified, their tonsils are removed, and they are circumcised three days after birth, the uku-uku underscoring this unusual timing.[63]

The importance and meaning of scarification would have differed among age groups, between men and women, and over time. In the established male slave community, for example, scarified adults signified "history," the scars informing newcomers that these persons were born in the palace.[64] To newly captured slaves or those given to the emir as gifts or tribute, slaves bearing the uku-uku were recognizably senior and superior in status to them. Scarification would also have assisted palace slave men in carrying out duties outside the palace, for their high status and provenance were now discernible at a glance. Scarification additionally allowed the palace community to distinguish among children born to free Fulani women and the emir's freeborn children and those born in the slave community. Lastly, scarification incidentally allowed runaway slaves to be identified and returned to the palace.

The scarification of girls who became palace concubines was a special case. Not only would women bearing the uku-uku hold superior status in relation to new palace recruits, but slave girls bearing the uku-uku and given away by the emir to men of wealth or status carried on their person a palace trademark that informed all who saw them of their superior provenance, one effect of which might be that they were given higher rank in their new households.[65] It is tempting to conjecture that Abdullahi was particularly generous in concubine gift-giving as a means of placating his detractors, which would also explain why palace concubine numbers never grew to prejihadic numbers. That is, many marked slave girls were given away as a form of state patronage, a trademarking and exoticization of palace concubinage that heralded its political demise. Once valued for their usefulness as political players in domains of fertility, they were now perhaps more valued in the realm of patronage exchange.[66]

Conclusions

Expropriating over half the "interior" grounds, Abdullahi elaborated and transformed Hausa kingly spaces and practices, establishing a new Fulani palace landscape that would remain largely intact until the British conquest of 1903. The remaking of the southern half of the ciki into a *male* slave domain points to a historic shift in the relative cultural and economic value and utility of palace slave men versus slave women. On the one hand, resident slave numbers outside the ciki swelled, with many slaves settled in "male" palace areas or dispatched to rural estates and adjacent areas of the city. On the other hand, concubine numbers declined, with Abdullahi asserting the seclusionary tenets of and surveillance over royal women with greater intensity than had any of his predecessors. What the sociospatial changes suggest is that the symbolic and practical importance of concubine fertility no longer worked in the same cultural, political, and economic ways that it had in the past. Rather than fertility accumulating within the interior in the form of grains, concubines, and royal children—all centrifugally consolidating territorial ties with the outside—it seems that fertility was conserved and redirected. Female palace slaves would have been in greater demand as agricultural and menial laborers, for example, as well as for their symbolic content. It is therefore conjectured that many were sent to work on rural estates or were given away to nobility, clerics, and powerful merchants as concubines, cementing alliances now more economic and patronage-oriented than territorial. Lesser numbers would also have been taken as royal concubines to smaller rural palaces, or sold.[67]

The importance of freeborn palace wives may have increased at this time, reflecting a shift in emphasis from territorial to political and economic consolidation. Many Fulani emirs, for example, married daughters of the caliph, marking both their political allegiances and religious and ethnic ties to a new central authority. Emirs might have also used marriages to cultivate industrial or commercial interests, which were greatly expanding in part because the nineteenth century caliphate structure had assuaged pre-existing political rivalries, allowing merchants and craftspersons to travel with greater ease (Tambo 1974, 16).

The radical qualities of Abdullahi's spatial changes show how concubines' sociospatial privileges and powers were central bargaining tools in postjihad negotiations among Fulani commoners, merchants, clerics, overlords, and the male slave community-at-large. On the one hand, the religiously justified removal of women from cloth dyeing and the market (other than in the domain of grains) opened up commercial avenues for free tradesmen, Fulani clerics not least among them. Indeed, by the 1890s, male artisans of indigo dyeing in Kano had profitably brought their skills southeast of the Benue River to Foumban (present-day Cameroon) where they were integral to King Njoya's (1895–1924) efforts to set up dye works in front of his palace. As in Kano, King Njoya used the dye works to spawn commercial indigo businesses in the city (Harris 1985, 165, 169). On the other hand, new Kano palace slave hierarchies and spaces for men were set up on former female grounds at a time when many prejihadic male slave entitlements were being resurrected but shifted over from slaves to Fulani elites. Rumfa's first state council, the Tarata-Kano (the Kano Nine) had consisted solely of slaves; now, no slaves sat on the council, all positions instead filled by various Fulani clansmen.[68] Recall, too, that many male slaves lost their jakadu positions, and that new political positions, such as the Ma'ajin Wateri (Public Treasurer), had been created for free Fulani, remaking the Shamaki's treasury responsibilities as "private" ones. Creating male slave positions like that of Sarkin Hatsi and recreating large spaces for palace eunuchs and the military on former ciki grounds recuperated some male slave losses, if only ceremonially. The decline in palace concubine numbers and spaces, then, hints at larger political and economic changes in the region, one effect of which was the falling importance of fertility (as children and grain) to the state's functioning and imaginary.

Abdullahi's reign was followed by a tumultuous civil war, with his son by his Sokoto wife, Aliyu, eventually gaining power—the last Fulani emir to rule before the British conquest of 1903. The only structure I could find postdating Abdullahi's reign was a room built in the new southern labyrinth by Abdullahi's full brother and successor, Muhammad Bello in honor of himself, Soron Bello (Hall of Bello). Bello attempted in many ways to rein in the power of male slaves. He outlawed and annulled their marriages to free Fulani women, for example, marriages formerly condoned by his brother Abdullahi, and he awarded one of the most important eunuch titles (San Turaki) to his own son (Palmer 1967 [1928], 132; Fika 1978, 57). The price of Bello's alienation of key palace slave sectors registered in part when Sallama Barka led an unsuccessful slave revolt against him.[69]

Interestingly, Soron Bello abuts another honorific building, one raised earlier by his brother Abdullahi in honor of his father's many military successes, Soron Giwa (Hall of the Elephant), the elephant regarded as a strong and valiant creature.[70] Both structures record elite male accomplishments and both were built on grounds once controlled by palace women (see Figure 16). Fulani reinstitution of prejihadic slave practices would grind to a halt with the British conquest of the region, whereupon structural barriers would ultimately prohibit concubinage's cultivation, the subject of the next chapter.

CHAPTER 5

British Colonial Abolition
of Slavery and Concubinage

I n 1903 the British conquered Kano as part of the much larger project of
European imperialism in Africa. The conquest of Kano city was decisive
in establishing British rule in northern Nigeria, and the takeover of the
Kano palace finalized the city's colonial demise. According to Colonel Morland, who led the attack, he and his troops entered the city through a cannon-
made breach in the southwesterly city wall nearest to the city gate called Kofar
Kabuga, whereupon they proceeded through the largely uninhabited western
portion of the city to the palace. Then, "[a]fter forming up near the inhabited
portion, no further opposition being met with, I marched and occupied the
King's palace, which is a large series of buildings covering fifty acres, and surrounded by a high wall, and is in itself a stronghold."[1]

At the time Emir Aliyu (1894–1903) was returning to Kano from Sokoto,
where he had gone to greet the new caliph or Sarkin Musulmi (King of Muslims), a close relative and friend. Palace informants aver that the British-
officered West African Frontier Force (WAFF), made up of Hausa mounted
infantry and foot soldiers unsympathetic to Fulani rule, attacked the palace
from the northeast, from where they eventually entered and made their way
into the palace interior. Near the northern edge of the cikin gida there was
a "last stand" in which all the emir's forces left behind to the defend the

palace were killed (cf. Fika 1978).[2] WAFF soldiers went on a rampage: prayer mats were burned, the large clay cooking pots and calabashes of the women's sections were shattered or broken, a number of the massive hand-carved wooden doors were removed and carried away, and many compounds were burned or vandalized.[3] Palace inhabitants fled and the palace became deserted.

Upon hearing the news that Kano had fallen, Emir Aliyu abandoned his returning army but was soon captured and handed over to the British who exiled him, along with members of the royal household, to Yola and, later, Lokoja.[4] Thereafter the palace was transformed into temporary colonial headquarters, it being the most easily defensible area in the city and the symbolic and practical center of rule. Sir Frederick Lugard was placed in charge, arriving shortly after the conquest, and set up his office in one of the rooms of Babban Soro, formerly the personal quarters of the emir. The palace was additionally used to house WAFF soldiers, which for Colonel Morland was a logistical expedient: "All soldiers and carriers being quartered inside the King's palace, I am able to prevent them getting loose in the town. No town taken by assault has ever been less looted and injured."[5]

Abbas, Emir Aliyu's brother who had surrendered with his followers outside the city walls and who was seen as conciliatory toward the British, was chosen to succeed Aliyu. A British-styled installation ritual took place in the southern labyrinth, a former palace stronghold.[6] Abbas was compelled to swear formal allegiance to the king of England and was given a staff of office, whereupon he was permitted to live in the palace with his household and to head a colonially appointed hierarchy of "native" officials, the so-called Native Authority.

Under cover of apparent continuity in Fulani rule, colonialism eroded palace slave institutions and powers, though at first it did not eliminate them. A series of proclamations had been (and would be) issued that collectively made slave trading and raiding illegal, abolished the legal status of slavery, made all children of slaves free, prohibited all transactions in slaves, and ruled that compensatory payments to slave owners for slaves freed in British-sanctioned courts were unnecessary. Yet none of these prohibited slavery per se (Hill, 1977, 200; Lovejoy and Hogendorn 1993; Ubah 1985). They couldn't: on the one hand, there were too few British personnel to enforce abolition measures or to rule directly; and on the other hand, the colonial administration knew that palace slaves would be central to indirect rule. Without palace slavery, the state could not exist. Or at least it would be so altered that it could not be held up as a model of what the colonizers presented to the British public, namely, a system that worked indirectly and respectfully through local rulers and their hierarchies.

Palace slaves were not disinterested players of colonial rule, but negotiated it along strongly gendered lines. This chapter explores how colonialism reworked the palace landscape, the patriarchal spatial arrangements of the past infusing and accommodating a colonial and patriarchal present. In the end, palace slavery would be invaginated, slaves compelled to enter and negotiate a hostile colonial world.

Reconstituting the Ciki

By the end of the nineteenth century, royal wives clearly held more status than concubines. They were treated as a leisure class and engaged in no communal labor, except for the rotational cooking of the emir's food, as prescribed by Islamic law. Because of their higher status, wives had the least spatial freedom, each wife restricted to a large personal compound or "place" (waje). During Abbas's reign, these separate "places" included Bayan dan Soro, Sararin Garke, Sokoto, and Unguwar Fulanin Uwargida.[7] In contrast to wives, palace concubines were a managerial class that mostly lived communally in wards or *unguwoyi (sing. unguwa)*, moving throughout the cikin gida in the course of carrying out their duties (Nast 1993; Figure 20).[8] The differences between concubine and wifely settlement patterns is probably as old as the palace itself; royal wives traditionally arrived in the palace with large slave entourages, any young females being considered potential concubines. The fifteenth-century royal household of the Buganda king was organized along similarly hierarchical lines: Untitled wives (typically of lowly birth or slaves) lived communally in sections controlled by a special wife-administrator

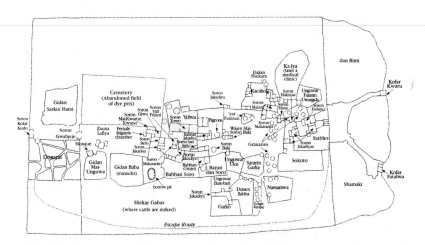

Figure 20. Palace landscape circa 1903 showing ward names and the location of pastoral activities.

whereas titled wives (of high birth) lived individually in their own enclosure (Musisi 1991, 779).

At the turn of the twentieth century, about fifty *sadaku*, or concubines, were secluded in the Kano palace, most living in eight densely populated wards:[9] Yelwa (Abundance), Kacako, Ka-Iya (You Can Do It), Nassarawa (Victory), Dutsen Babba (The Big Hill), Unguwar Bare-Bari (Ward of the Bornoans), Unguwar Uku (Ward of the Three), and Garko.[10] Additional palace concubines included those who arrived as companions and menial laborers (kuyangi) of a royal wife and who stayed with their mistress, though they, too, could circulate throughout the interior, and the 'yan soro—newly minted concubines who lived in small rooms (taskoki) inside the emir's personal quarters.[11]

Social hierarchies in the cikin gida were reconstituted during the colonial period, though the specifics of concubine duties and powers changed. As in the past, wives held greater status than concubines, and most administrative matters in the cikin gida were carried out by three senior titleholding concubines, Uwar Soro, Mai-Soron Baki, and Mai-Kudandan, each woman called by her title, not her birth name. The concubine delegates or uwar wajes (women of the places) from each unguwa and waje were answerable to them, with slave women carrying out the heaviest labor for both wives and concubines. Besides attending to grain duties and domestic chores, iyayen wajeje *and* slave women each morning collected milk from the titleholding male slave, Mai-Shanu (Master of the Cattle) and his untitled male slave assistants, who daily milked cattle arriving from the nearby palace-estate of Nassarawa in the easternmost palace fields of Shekar Gabas. Some cattle were tethered at night inside concubine wards in the eastern part of the cikin gida and after milking in the early morning were led with the others through the southern cikin gida, back to Nassarawa.[12]

Uwar Soro was the most powerful titleholding concubine who served as a personal secretary to the emir, and she also counseled the emir on matters of state.[13] She coordinated all food-related activities and was responsible for all concubines, including other titleholders.[14] Mai-Soron Baki lived inside Soron Baki, a round audience hall in the emir's large personal compound of Babban Soro, for which she was entirely responsible.[15] Her most important duty was to request audiences with the emir on behalf of women who wanted to see him. She also escorted female audience seekers to the emir's throne chambers.[16] Mai-Kudandan worked closely with Sarkin Hatsi (King of Grain), a titleholding male slave from the southern male slave community, to organize grain disbursement in the palace interior.[17] As in the past, most flour and milk were used inside the palace kitchen, Soron Tuwo, in the central concubine ward, Yelwa (see Figures 6 and 20). Here, high-status concubines cooked high quality foods for people of rank, while lower-status concubines and slave women cooked lower quality foods for persons of lesser rank.

Kuyangi (domestic slave women) and jakadu (messengers and guards) were also reinstalled. Most kuyangi were probably daughters of slaves already owned by the emir or by royal women, or were recent prisoners of war not taken by the emir as concubines. There were no more than sixty or seventy kuyangi inside the cikin gida after the British conquest, all under the jurisdiction of Uwar Kuyangi (Mother of the Slave Women). Kuyangi formed the lowest-ranking slave labor group and carried out the most strenuous and spatially extensive tasks. They threshed palace grain in the western open fields of the cikin gida, for example, and ground palace grains using large mortars and pestles, an activity typically done in open courtyards. They also washed clothes, another labor-intensive task accomplished in open areas. Kuyangi not taken as concubines married other palace slave men. While married kuyangi stayed at night with their husbands and families outside the cikin gida, unmarried kuyangi slept and ate in the entrance halls or rooms of concubines or wives whom they attended, some working their way up to becoming royal concubines. Many kuyangi had farm plots in the western palace field, Shekar Yamma (Field of the West).[18] Both kuyangi and jakadu could be sent to relay messages to persons in other parts of the palace, city, emirate, and so on, or to run market-related and other errands. Accordingly, both groups had access to all palace areas except the personal quarters of the emir.

Jakadu were administered by Babban Jakadiya and probably numbered no more than twenty-five just after the conquest. Jakadu were generally older women and may have served previously as kuyangi. Most had experienced marriage and had borne children, prerequisites of adulthood. Their age and experience signaled a maturity, discipline, and toughness required of them in their duties. The relative lack of external domestic demands made it possible for them to dedicate their lives to their work. Such dedication was necessary because they lived in the passageways they guarded, a placement that would have overwhelmed younger women with small children.

Jakadu generally worked alone and guarded areas in and near the cikin gida, effectively keeping men out of the interior and royal wives and concubines in. The most important areas secured by jakadu were the six entrance halls that doubled as the palace's checkpoints into the interior. These halls, three bordering the interior to the north and three to the south, formed the vertebrae of southern and northern palace labyrinths, a dense network of walled courtyards, open spaces, and buildings crucial to state life. The royal stables were located in the northern labyrinth, for example, along with a Quranic study hall for the emir, a dining room for royal male children and aristocracy, and several court chambers used as Islamic law courts and meeting halls. For a person to enter any of these areas, let alone the interior, he or she would have to pass the inspection of the labyrinth jakadu, a process typically involving formally greeting her and some kind of tribute. These jakadu were vigilant that visitors follow royal protocol and would keep persons out of the Quranic study hall or court chambers when the emir was nearby, making certain that those entering the area removed their shoes, a sign of respect. At least two of these women's chambers served state functions: The second northernmost jakadu chamber doubled as a waiting hall for nobility attending the emir's daily court, leading to its popular designation, Soron Hakimai (Hall of Nobility); while the second floor of the northernmost jakadiya's chambers doubled as a small arsenal (cf. Ahmed 1988; Rufa'i 1987). Each labyrinth-jakadiya secured and locked nightly the large gates leading into and out of her labyrinth passageway.

Additional jakadu lived in the entrance halls of each place (waje) and ward (unguwa) of the wives and concubines, respectively, protecting against illicit entry by men and running errands and carrying messages for inhabitants therein (Rufa'i 1987). Two other jakadu lived in and policed two passageways located at the interior's eastern and western perimeter, one leading into Shekar Yamma and the other into Shekar Gabas (Field of the East). The fields were formally accessible only through these passageways, each serving a strategic function: The guardswoman in Shekar Yamma monitored the moods of spirits inhabiting the fields, safeguarding the well-being of kuyangi who farmed there;[19] the jakadiya in the eastern passageway delivered messages to nearby concubines on behalf of the emir, providing an escort service for concubines he requested attend him in his chambers.[20]

A few jakadu guarded the clusters of granaries in the northern cikin gida that contained grain levies and grain from the royal slave estates. The grains included millet, guinea corn, rice, and wheat, each stored separately.[21] The openness of the granary grounds facilitated public surveillance of the area, helping to ensure that grain was not stolen or hidden. One cluster of granaries in the interior's northwest was surrounded by a high wall and had its own separate guarded entrance hall known as Soron Hatsi; the granaries were managed by malams who distributed the granaries' contents to the poor on a discretionary basis, at least during the first decade or two of colonial rule.

As in the past, Yelwa was the center of administrative and spiritual life. Uwar Soro and Mai-Kudandan lived there and Mai-Soron Baki had a second home for her children nearby that abutted Yelwa to the south. The female spirit's quarters were also in Yelwa. To enter Yelwa one had to pass through an entrance hall that served as a checkpoint guarded over and lived in by the administrative head of domestic slave women, Uwar Kuyangi. Nearby was the compound of Babban Jakadiya, her presence enhancing security in the area.

Within several years the social fabric and spatial organization of palace slavery would undergo strikingly gendered transformations. The erosion of slave women's places occurred somewhat later than that of men's and for dif-ferent reasons. These differences derived from the patriarchal structure of both traditional and colonial cultures.

Early Colonial Changes

The first slave institutions and places to be effaced were male ones associated with the aristocracy's ability to wage war and levy taxes.[22] The standing slave army in the palace was disbanded, for example, along with the emir's personal bodyguard, and palace munitions were confiscated (see Figure 21).[23] Then, in 1908, after the British forced the nobility into the countryside, the powers of

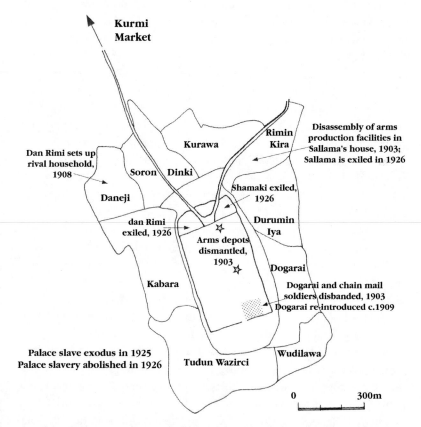

Figure 21. Map showing early changes to the landscape of male slavery following the British conquest of 1903. (Ward boundaries taken from Metropolitan Kano Planning and Develop-ment Board, *Map showing unguwa boundaries compiled from L.G.A. Survey maps, 1971.*)

two of the most influential male slaves living in the northern male slave realm were increased and realigned to undermine the emir's authority. One slave, the dan Rimi, was made into the Waziri, a key advisory position to the emir, filled traditionally by a Fulani freeman chosen by the emir (Ubah 1985). The pre-empting of the emir's authority and the consequent rise of dan Rimi's power (especially among slaves) produced such turmoil in the palace that dan Rimi moved out of his extensive palace premises to a large house in the city. At least 150 slaves left with him, including his extended family and male "client" slaves and their families, reshaping the spatial and social dynamics of the northern palace landscape (Nast 1992).

Shamaki suffered special losses under colonial rule because his powers stemmed from war and slavery: It was he who had helped the emir's forces prepare for war, particularly the cavalry, and it was he who controlled slave labor on the king's rural estates. Now the emir could no longer wage war, and palace slavery was being forced into decline. Even more vulnerable than Shamaki were the thirty or so palace eunuchs. During the nineteenth century eunuchs had served as formal and informal state and personal advisors, had managed the arms production facilities near the palace, and had carried out important domestic duties. With the outlawing of slavery, these eunuchs were the last of their kind. Despite dispersal of the palace militia and the exodus of dan Rimi and his clients, most palace slave men who remained were loyal to Abbas since they still had something to gain from a system of royal patronage that entitled them to, among other things, homes, farming tools, clothing, food, and, for those most powerful, horses, land, and political office.

The residential stability of the slave population, weakened by dan Rimi's exodus in 1908, was again challenged in 1909 when the British created the Native Treasury as the repository for Native tax revenues. In contrast to earlier colonial years, when the emir could directly access his 50 percent share of tax revenues, tax revenues were now controlled and dispensed in ways that eroded the emir's authority. The emir and so-called District and Village Heads, for example, were placed on set salaries along with religious officials in charge of newly instituted rural and city courts and various male slaves, now employed in the Native administration. Other "Native" monies were earmarked for colonial land surveys (used to determine taxation levels with greater precision) and "public works" projects that promoted western education, the institution of medical clinics and "charity and entertainment" initiatives. According to Bello, by 1910, "out of a total of £69,460 in the [Native] treasury, £41,460 was paid as salaries to the Native Authority officials. A total of £16,027 was also paid for capital projects. There was thus a reserve of £12,027," which were siphoned off to benefit the colonizers. By 1912, for example, all of the reserves were invested in Britain through Crown Agents, a process "whereby money capital was removed from the colony and invested in Britain" (Bello 1982, 127).[24]

These changes meant that the emir and other nobility were less able to dispense patronage directly to royal clients, leading them to develop indirect or mediated patronage methods through colonial structures instead. While the emir could still offer some traditional in-kind benefits to palace slaves, such as palace residence, food, and clothing, he had gained some authority to transition palace "slave" men into publicly funded, waged labor positions, a transitioning the British welcomed. For these men, political attachment to the emir now meant that they had better access to a number of waged colonial jobs, the indirect patronage benefits accruing from these posts allowing the emir to continue enjoying strong male "slave" loyalty or *biyayya*.[25] The Shamaki, Sallama, and dan Rimi thus continued to carry out traditional functions in addition to new ones, but were paid wages for their labor. These men remained the most powerful and retained many of their prerogatives of state office, such as horses, estates, land, and access to palace resources. Other slaves' traditional duties changed significantly. Some of the emir's bodyguards, for instance, became members of the waged Native Authority police force (Ubah 1985, 91), while high-ranking palace builders became waged contractors for and supervisors of labor used on colonial public work projects.[26] Still others served as horse attendants to British officers (Giginyu 1981, 150) or (like certain members of the ruling class) were conscripted into the colonially created "native" bureaucracy, the Native Authority.

British officials soon resented male slaves' powers and believed that because their powers were so great, they were acting in a rude and insubordinate behavior. Their insouciance was tolerated by Resident Temple to maintain harmonious relations with the emir, something that had been jeopardized when dan Rimi had been elevated to Waziri, against the emir's wishes and in gross violation of custom (Ubah 1985, 66–68), but the tolerance would soon change.

Because both the aristocracy and the British considered palace women's labors to be outside the domain of formal value, slave women were disallowed from the system of colonial waged labor. Slave women also had little power to confront colonial directives directly and were marginalized from the political processes reshaping the palace interior. There were, in fact, no formal opportunities for women to help stage the changes negotiated by British and local men.

The spaces and powers of women most affected initially by the colonial presence were those having to do with grain. In particular, the declining legitimacy of slavery and the progressive outlawing of in-kind taxes were doubly problematic for palace reproduction. On the one hand, with a decline in the slave population, grain production on palace estates decreased and, on the other hand, grain tax flows into the palace were restricted. Whereas the British colonial government had claimed a quarter of local taxes in 1904 (paid mostly in cowries, but also in grain, especially the zakat), in 1906 the percentage was increased to 50, a significant amount of grain in either case being siphoned away from palace premises and use.[27] Moreover the British decreed in 1906 that taxes (levied only on men) were to be paid in sterling. Given that most people at the time had little access to British currency, it was agreed that cowries and grains collected in the interim would be counted as part of the emir's portion.[28] Cowry and in-kind payments slowed to a trickle, interior granaries falling into disuse, eroding the *raison d'etre* of Sarkin Hatsi and Mai-Kudandan. While the latter title would eventually be allowed to lapse, Sarkin Hatsi's title would be retained, in part because the Native Treasury funded male slave activities in the palace, not female ones, allowing the emir to continue drawing on colonial funds. Initially, interim grain taxes were supplemented with grain purchased from the central city market; Abbas (1903–19), for example, purchased about one hundred sacks or taiki of guinea corn every Friday for palace use.[29] These grains, already threshed, were brought to and stored in Yelwa by Sarkin Hatsi and his men.[30]

Although Korama's market responsibilities initially and briefly expanded, changes in grain's importance as a tax and the rise of cash-cropping of groundnuts heralded the end of Korama's powers and position. The last Korama (Ayi) was appointed and turbaned by Emir Usman (1919–26). As was the custom, she was responsible for appointing subsidiary Koramas in other markets, such as Mandawari and Rimi. The aristocracy called upon the Korama Ayi's services extensively after the 1906 monetization decree and increase in colonial tax percentages; both measures placed pressure on the aristocracy to generate and use cash. The Madakin Kano (a high-ranking royal titleholder responsible for some city administration) visited the Korama weekly with palace-derived grains that the emir had commissioned her to sell for cash.[31]

Conserving Concubines

Despite early grain-related incursions into concubine spaces, palace concubine numbers initially doubled.[32] In part, this had to do with the fact that some concubines in the nearby Fanisau palace had apparently taken advantage of postconquest confusion and had taken lovers. Upon hearing this, Abbas punished them all by moving them to the central palace's confines where they were dispersed throughout the interior, except for Fanisau's unfortunate Uwar Soro, known as 'yar Fanisau (daughter of Fanisau). She was set apart from the others in an unwalled compound near the ward of Kacako, presumably to punish her (as the leading titleholding administrator) for the others' transgressions.[33] The relocation of Fanisau concubines, however, was probably also part of a general postconquest consolidation of rural concubine holdings, given the political uncertainties.

Concubine numbers also increased when some of Aliyu's concubines (who had fled with the emir) returned to become palace concubines under the new regime, a customary right and practice.[34] The mother of Hajiyya Mai-daki, one of the main cooperants of this study, for example, returned in this way. Concubine numbers additionally grew because of insecurities felt by palace slaves after the conquest, and because of British dissimulation and complacency about the institution. Palace slaves were, on the one hand, at risk of losing all palace-related wealth and power as a result of British scrutiny of and attacks on the institution of slavery as a whole. Palace slaves could mitigate potential losses by giving daughters to the king as concubines, a solution tenable because the British wholeheartedly endorsed concubinage, even priding themselves on their acceptance of it. Even though concubinage was slavery, the colonizers exoticized the institution as a private, domestic affair. Concubinage, after all, did not threaten British policies that promoted the creation of a free male class of landowners and waged laborers. Even as late as 1926, after special edicts against palace slavery in particular had been issued, then-Governor Bernard Bourdillon issued a circular, "Social Relations with Moslem Chiefs and Their Women Folk," encouraging European women to visit the king's "harem," which was cast as an important bastion of local culture.[35] In this sense, official British acceptance of concubinage pointed out to both British and local publics how much Native Rule honored traditional practices, when in fact concubinage had become one of the pathetically isolated and rare institutions wherein aristocratic privilege could assert itself. De-linked from traditional political and economic associations, concubinage became sexualized by direct and indirect rulers alike—a compensatory, biculturally intelligible sign of patriarchal authority. Incapacitated from becoming a power institution in its own right, concubinage became a mirror for both exoticized British patriarchal preconceptions of what the "harem" was, and local delusions of how to continue on in patriarchal grandeur. Thus, British blessings on concubinage, slave insecurities, and aristocratic needs sustained the institution, however altered. Concubinage hence became a source of social security for palace slaves and their kin in this generalized time of crisis and during especially difficult times such as the famine of 1913–14.[36] For palace bayi (slaves), concubinage was a potent means of streamlining themselves into the lineage-fabric of the royal family's ever-shrinking system of patronage.[37]

The Palace Slaves Exodus and Changes
in Colonial Tax Structures, 1919–30

After Abbas's death in 1919, his elder and ailing brother Usman, Wambai of Kano, was installed as his successor. Usman was a weak ruler, partly because he was chronically ill. Many of Usman's weaknesses derived, however, from colonial directives. Specifically, the British insisted that the traditional governance system whereby urban-resident Fulani overlords ruled provinces through male jakadu be dismantled. Overlords were instead to live in the rural places they represented, the geographical boundaries of these being somewhat arbitrarily and regularly redefined as the British experimented with various taxation and governance schemes. Usman had consequently lived much of his life and developed most of his political career in the rural district of Ringim. Usman's distance from the palace, like most of his noble, rural counterparts, removed him from the cultural manners of the city and court life. What this meant in practical terms is that by the time he was installed, neither he nor his household knew much about palace protocol or ritual. His concubines, for example, were supposedly confused by palace titles and ignorant about cikin gida administration and ceremony. In consequence, Usman and his family were derided by palace and city inhabitants alike.[38]

Worse, Usman was seen to be unforgiving, miserly, and insecure—expecting considerable expressions of obeisance. His reputation as a miser was somewhat unfair in that, like his predecessor, he could not control tax revenues and was constrained by his salary; unlike Abbas, Usman had few urban political or economic resources to mitigate his losses. His physical weaknesses accordingly assumed special significance and became a focal point for scorn. It was explained rather sarcastically by palace cooperants, for example, that Usman, not being strong enough to ride a horse on his own, eventually became so weak that he had to be carried to his council chambers.[39]

Usman's weaknesses provided an unexpected boon to the long-standing palace slave population: dan Rimi, Sallama, and Shamaki, the traditionally powerful slave triumvirate, assumed greater control over the administration of the emirate and palace life than had been obtained in the past. Palace slaves subsequently became even more insouciant, far beyond what was customarily accepted. When the three main state slaves disagreed with directives from the emir, they refused to carry them out.[40] Both the emir and British officials resented their behavior, the British reporting "that [palace] slaves were literally trying to seize power" (Ubah 1985, 72).

In 1920 colonial officials conducted a study of the palace slave system to determine its organizational structure, bemoaning the fact that they had not dismissed titled palace slaves earlier, upon Abbas's death. In 1921 the governor of Nigeria, Sir Hugh Clifford, and Acting Lieutenant Governor Palmer lobbied to outlaw palace slavery (Ubah 1985, 73), but it was only just prior to Usman's death in 1925 that they could mandate officially that the most powerful titled slave officials be removed from power and exiled to the palace's rural slave estates or *gandaye* (*gandu sing.;* Ubah 1985, 74). Sallama was sent to Gandun Gogel, dan Rimi to Gandun Zuri, Shamaki to Gandun Takai, and Ciroman Shamaki (a subordinate of Shamaki) to Gandun Fanisau. Jakadan Garko was also exiled.[41] Hundreds of slaves accompanied them, emptying out most of the palace's former slave grounds in the north, and thus the main labor force of the palace ciki.[42] The spatial and labor-related effects of the exile were compounded when palace slaves who had never liked the emir and/or who no longer had confidence in his ability to provide also left, and when the British insisted just after Usman's death that *all* palace slaves be freed, especially slaves born prior to 1903, persons hitherto grandfathered into slavery by previous stipulations in colonial proclamations affecting nonpalace-based slave populations in Nigeria. Each palace slave was now to be manumitted immediately and issued an official "certificate of freedom" through the newly established colonial Native Authority court system. Hence, Lieutenant Governor Palmer's telegraph message to the Resident of Kano, following Emir Usman's death: "please convey my regrets to the emir's family and council . . . also please have complete list of all emir's slaves made with view to complete manumission." [43]

Yet even more difficulties beset Usman's successor, Emir Abdullahi Bayero (1926–53). The British obliged him to abolish palace slave *titles,* which had been the main means of maintaining slavery informally.[44] To appease colonial sentiments, a palace slave titleholder might claim not to be a slave, but if that person held a palace title, carried out slave tasks tied to the title, assumed the title's customary position and powers, and was remunerated largely in-kind or through (palace-supported) Native Authority jobs and wages, that person effectively practiced and retained a slave identity. Palace slaves had, in fact, always been known by title, not name. Titles constituted, clarified, reproduced, and defined slave placement, labor, identity, and powers, allowing slavery-informed hierarchies to be maintained regardless of what abolitionist decrees the British stipulated. But without slave titles, the palace division of slave labor and the interpellative means of solidifying master-slave relations informally would be strained. It is not known if the palace community acquiesced to this British request, but it is clear that soon after assuming the throne Sanusi (1953–63) reinstated all of the exiled titleholders' titles. He could not, however, reinstate the exiled titleholders because they had since died. Thus he chose replacements for them from among those family members who had stayed in the palace, the new titleholders hence reassuming titular ownership over their traditional large palace households in the northern "male" slave domain. While the British strenuously objected, Emir Sanusi held his ground, arguing that all of the other emirates, especially Adamawa, Bauchi, and Katsina, had been allowed to retain these particular titles and titleholders.[45] Today, palace bayi maintain that they were never stripped of titles, it being impossible to imagine slave-derived positions dissolved by foreign decree.

Aristocratic livelihood was dealt another blow in 1926 when the British decreed that all men over the age of sixteen had to pay taxes, including palace slave men, who had hitherto been exempt. To meet these demands, the emir gave the grounds of his Nassarawa slave estate to former palace slaves with the understanding that they would use the land to generate cash crops to pay for their own taxes (Giginyu 1981). Henceforth, mostly groundnuts were grown, along with crops for household consumption.[46]

Within the first twenty-five years of rule, then, the British outlawed tax remittances in grain, implemented a new monetary head tax, manumitted and exiled the most important palace slaves to royal estates that formerly had produced palace grains, and indirectly fed a general palace slave exodus. All of these colonial interventions resulted in a devastating shortage of female labor in the palace cikin gida and the slowing down of in-kind grain revenues to a trickle. Many kuyangi followed their husbands, fathers, or uncles who left of their own accord in 1925 or went into exile with members of the slave triumvirate. Kuyangi farm plots and the female-guarded passageway leading to them became deserted and few persons remained to thresh and grind grain or carry out menial labor. Village women seeking waged work during the dry season, *cin rani* (eating the dry season), were consequently paid seasonal wages, or given room and board, to thresh and grind grain in Yelwa, and concubines and wives assumed somewhat heavier workloads.[47] The emir was also allowed to use male prison labor from the large colonial prison built nearby during Abbas's reign, a labor practice that continues today.[48] Like domestic slaves before them, prisoners performed the most menial of tasks, with food, but no wages, provided. Tasks included washing clothes in Shekar Yamma, maintaining the palace stables, and helping with building construction and maintenance.[49] The emir was also granted permission to use Native Treasury monies to hire "manumitted" bayi, many already housed gratis in the palace or in the old city. In any case, prisoners and former slaves (some of whom were salaried) became key players in carrying out colonially directed, Native Authority–funded, city and palace building projects. By the late 1920s another unexpected stream of labor accumulated in the palace—those persons of matrilateral slave descent returning "home" because of a poverty generated by the stock market crash and a global depression.

Voluntary Slavery and Slave Matrilaterality:
The Late 1920s and Beyond

A watershed event registered in the memories of elderly palace informants, though of less dramatic proportions than the slave exodus, was the voluntary return in the late 1920s and 1930s of persons of slave descent. I refer to these persons as *bayin sarki* (slaves of the king) or *bayi* (slaves) because they and their descendants did (and do) so.[50] This self-identification, of course, opposed British beliefs that slavery had been outlawed—beliefs subtended by their own assertions to that effect. Abolitionist decrees and assertions had, until then, been validated by creating colonial measures and indicators of social truth, such as the certificates of freedom. These and other artifacts— both material and symbolic—convinced the British that they had fundamentally changed the palace system. By contrast, those who sought legitimacy as palace slaves asserted the legitimacy of the palace slave framework. Palace slaves could best milk the colonial system of indirect rule by sidling up politically to the emir, a move that ironically kept the spirit of the master-slave patronage system largely intact. The bayin sarki's desires and needs for patronage, exacerbated during a global economic crisis, effectively rejected British assertions of freedom that had isolated these slaves and brought them poverty.

Similar continuity of servile status within the Bundunke Fulani community during the French colonial period is recorded by Clark in the Senegambia region:

> Bundunke Fulbe considered slave status hereditary and immutable. No one could be newly enslaved, but all descendants of ex-slaves retained their servile status in society. Persons of servile descent could leave, renegotiate ties of dependency, and engage in economic activities previously limited to free-born persons, but their social status of *maccube* [slave] did not change. (1997, 6)

Clark records that for similar economic reasons the Great Depression of the 1930s led to a resurgence of pawning ("the pledging of a person for a loan") in French West Africa (6). This continuation of slavery's affirmation by very particular sectors of slave populations despite British promulgations again demonstrates Sara Berry's contention that colonial and postcolonial states have been "intrusive rather than hegemonic" (in Cooper 1997, 21).

Not just anyone could claim they were a Kano palace *bawa* (pl. *bayi*), however: They had to prove their claim by verifying that their slave status derived matrilaterally. If they could do so, they could win traditional slave offices or assignments and would be beholden to display ritual forms of subservience. If they had never received the marks of slavery as children, they could opt to do so after the fact as adults. This conservation and cultivation of matrilateral slave ties after British abolition did not occur in non-palace contexts: in these cases, especially in poor rural households, there would be no reason for former slaves to claim a servile status. Generalized poverty among farmers and urban dwellers meant that palace slavery was unique, palace slaves historically constituting an entirely different class of enslaved persons, not unlike the elite classes of slaves that existed in ancient Rome. Commoners' slaves took advantage of the British presence by running away, seeking certificates of freedom, or by being integrated into the free community-at-large through a variety of means, including marriage (Hill 1977). Such integration was apparently unique to Kano; by contrast, slave-master relations elsewhere in Hausaland were transformed into relations of dependency as, for example, in northern Zaria (Smith 1960) and southern Niger (Cooper 1997).[51]

The voluntary return of palace slaves just years after Usman's death occurred not only for economic reasons, but because Emir Abdullahi, like Abbas, had tremendous informal political and economic resources at his disposal. He was conciliatory toward the British and had many friends in British administrative circles. In fact, some fifty years later, Abdullahi's sister, Mai-daki, would intimate somewhat critically that her brother was willfully subservient to British authority and culture.[52] His conciliatory approach, however, brought him important concessions, the use of prison labor being one of them. After all, British officials were aware of the hardships the emir faced as a result of abolitionist policies and salary restrictions. What was needed were alternative means upon which the emir could draw for labor and monies for carrying out colonial projects, whilst maintaining colonial illusions that traditional authority systems were still intact—a combination sustaining the dissimulative British ideology of indirect rule.

One means of colonial assistance given to Abdullahi, though initially of minor importance, was a salary increase. In 1926, upon his accession, his annual salary was raised from £4,800 to £5,000; in 1930 it was increased to £6,000.[53] His "establishment charge" of £1,000 also more than doubled in 1930, to £2,500.[54] Instituted in 1924 by Acting Governor D. C. Cameron and Secretary of State J. H. Thomas, the charge was intended to help defray expenses associated with the royal office. That the charge was mostly to be used to promote the legitimacy of British overrule is evident in the fact that the British first implemented it in 1925 for Usman to use in preparing for the Prince of Wales's historic visit. At this time, the British helped fabricate a dubious Kano "tradition"—the durbar, a series of ceremonial horse charges by the emir's sons and nobility, construed by the British as having local origins, but actually imported by them from colonial India. The durbar began with a formal parade of traditional leaders past a stand of colonial officers and guests at the Race Course in the British Government Residential Area, helping to convince the Prince that Kano royalty was authentically different, even oriental.[55] Abdullahi would later use his "charge" to purchase an automobile.[56]

Abdullahi's concessions brought him official British government recognition and regard. In the early 1930s, for example, he was invited to go at Native Treasury expense with the sultan of Sokoto, the emir of Gwandu, and a small entourage to England for an audience with King George V—an invitation he accepted. While there, the group visited the Zoological Gardens, the Royal Mint, Barclays Bank, Trafalgar Square, Piccadilly Circus, the Imperial Science Museum and Institute, Oxford Middle School, and various factories, most notably Port Sunlight, founded by Lord Leverhulme, who held substantial interests in oilseed production in Kano and West Africa.[57] Thereafter, on the occasion of Abdullahi's birthday, King George awarded him the CBE (Commander of the Order of the British Empire), a telegram of 5 June 1934 from Lieutenant Governor Brown congratulating the emir on his "birthday honour." Then, in 1946, Abdullahi was made CMG (Commander of the Order of St. Michael and St. George) in a public ceremony held on open grounds just north of the palace.[58] Despite the fact that his main function was to administer British policies in the emirate, the privileges, activities, and connections accorded Abdullahi gave him an aura of independence, strength, and progressiveness that he used to cultivate resources that would pay for traditional emblems of kingly munificence and power.

Two groups of persons responded to Abdullahi's apparent and real strengths: Wealthy, powerful persons needing the emir's patronage for political reasons and who cultivated his patronage by bestowing gifts on him in proportion to their wealth and needs; and, the poor or dispossessed in need of patronage for economic reasons, namely, to survive. The former group's interests and resources fed the latter's.

By this time, the poor included slaves dispossessed in the exile and exodus of 1925 and by the edict of 1926, and persons of slave descent who suffered during the global depression of the late 1920s and 1930s when revenues from groundnut and other cash-crop production plummeted (Shenton 1986). Another group returning would have been those adversely affected when in 1935 the British ordered that the homes of former royal slaves living and farming on nearby Nassarawa be burned down as part of a program of land expropriation and cleansing.[59] The large number of people returning to the palace during Abdullahi's reign derived from these and other disadvantaged groups. Royal patronage, considerably weakened under Usman, was thus revitalized temporarily, lessening royalty's difficulties in finding palace labor.

Slave homecomings might have led to a subversive efflorescence of palace slave life, had there not been an opposing social tendency, namely, the preference by men of slave descent (male bayi) to status climb by marrying free women. Slave men's prerogative to marry free women had historical precedents. Abdullahi dan Dabo (1855–83) was perhaps the most notorious in having granted palace slave men the right to marry the daughters of Fulani nobility, this decision setting off a furor in his administration (chapter 4). Two related and negative repercussions followed for the palace master-bayi system. First, the freeborn status of these men's children alienated them permanently from palace slavery entitlements (but see below), including concubinage. Second, their alienation meant that the palace's bayi labor pool was irrevocably depleted. The mixed marriages were significant, indicating that despite poor economic conditions, some palace bayi felt that freeborn children had more to gain from the non-bayi world beyond the palace than from slave patronage within it.

The Dissolution of Concubine Spaces

Given the net return of "volunteer" bayi and the partial revaluation of slave status in the 1930s, kuyangi and jakadu communities were made anew, along with the associated leadership positions of Uwar Kuyangi and Babban Jakadiya. At the same time, since many slave women's duties and places had become redundant, the need for domestic labor was mitigated. The granaries, for example, remained abandoned, such that no jakadu were needed as granary guards and rendering obsolete many women's duties once related to grain storage, disbursement, and preparation. The new kuyangi also never took up farming in Shekar Yamma, in large part because Abdullahi expropriated the land to create a modern orchard, at one point bringing in a Caterpillar tractor. The jakadiya-guarded passageway leading to the fields was additionally abandoned, along with the jakadiya's quarters leading to Shekar Gabas. And with southern colonial encroachment into the southern labyrinth, the jakadiya posted to the southernmost southern labyrinth passageway was replaced by a male guard.[60] As in the precolonial past, female bayi were remunerated through informal benefits and privileges, unlike male bayi drawn into modern waged positions financed by the Native Authority. On balance, a net negative outflow of bayi community members resulted, making female waged and prison labor vital to palace reproduction.

Despite Abdullahi's popular appeal, concubine numbers dwindled and with them, concubine spaces, the overriding factor being the growing prevalence of male bayi's marriages to freeborn women. As Mai-daki noted,

> When the Europeans outlawed slavery, the male slaves of the Emir married the [freeborn] children of men from out there, from the bush, and of the town, and they brought them here. So it was that we could not seclude very many because there were no second-generation slaves. (Mack 1988, 55)

Concubine-related structures consequently were abandoned and a growing number of concubine wards were partially or wholly demolished, razed, amalgamated, converted to serve other functions, or fragmented to serve different communities in adjoining areas.

The first ward affected was Yelwa, which was split into two. The most important titled concubines continued to inhabit its southern parts. The much smaller remaining portion was set apart as a residential area for migrant waged laborers, known as 'yan gindin turmi (children at the mortar base), who came from nearby villages during the dry season. These women ground palace grains into flour, a task formerly accomplished by kuyangi. The northern part seemed so far away from Yelwa's core that it was assigned a new name: Mil Tara, or Nine Miles (Figure 22). Yelwa's breakup was facilitated by the fact that food was no longer cooked communally. Instead, persons in each concubine ward and wifely place cooked for themselves, with palace bayi outside the interior largely responsible for procuring and cooking their own food. Over the next several decades, Soron Tuwo, the one-time hub of palace food production, would be progressively abandoned.[61]

Ka-Iya, the second largest concubine ward at the turn of the century, was also transformed. With the aging of the palace community, it slowly became an enclave for elderly former concubines or matan fada (women of the palace) from Abbas's era. By Emir Sanusi's reign, Ka-Iya, long abandoned, was razed, the current emir later building a medical clinic on the site. Other wards, such as Garko and Dutse, also became largely deserted, many buildings falling into disrepair. By the time the present emir assumed power in

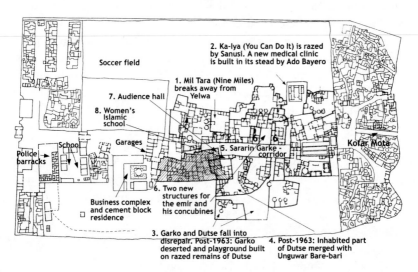

Figure 22. The palace landscape, circa 1990.

1963, Garko and part of Dutse were completely abandoned. To maintain a sense of community, the inhabited part of Dutse was merged into Unguwar Bare-bari. Today, with the exception of Yelwa, no concubine wards exist. A few important titleholders remain in Yelwa, but most live inside the places (wajeje) of wives, inside Babban Soro, or dispersed throughout other kingly quarters built by Abdullahi.

The Dissolution of Concubine Titles

Over the last fifty years the system of concubinage has been somewhat unconventionally maintained, partly as a consequence of Islamic and customary rules of concubine inheritance. Maliki law, for instance, stipulates that childless concubines can be inherited by the brother or successor of their master (chapter 1). Yet, by custom, any palace concubine (including those who had borne children) could opt to be taken as a concubine by a successor emir, provided she was not elderly or ready to be retired. Many palace concubines opted for the latter in the recent past: Aliyu's concubines returned to the palace to serve Abbas after Aliyu was exiled by the British; and Emir Sanusi sent most of his concubines back to the palace to serve under his successor-nephew, the current emir, after Sanusi was deposed. Not all of Sanusi's concubines, however, opted to stay. His leading titleholding concubine, Uwar Soro Wayo, is said to have wept so profusely and to have been so bereft at being separated from him that she was allowed to rejoin him, living with him until his death and eventually singularly honored by being buried in the palace cemetery.

As a result of Maliki inheritance laws, the reigning Uwar Soro Binta-Gaji and Mai-Soron Baki 'ya Hajiyya, and the recently deceased Uwar Waje Marya, all of whom were childless, collectively experienced concubinage across three reigns. While their experiences made them key repositories of knowledge of interior history and life, their presence meant that until 2002 no concubine from the present emir's reign had been given a chiefly title. Uwar Soro Aisha Delu, who reigned until her death in circa 1995, in 1990, for example, was inherited from the late Emir Inuwa (1963), as was 'ya Hajiyya and the late Uwar Waje Marya, whose title passed upon her death in 2002 to 'ya Duduwa, a concubine who first came to the palace during the reign of the present emir. After Uwar Soro Aisha died, Binta-Gaji (inherited from Emir Sanusi) was promoted from Mai-Soron Baki to Uwar Soro, 'ya Hajiyya hence promoted to Mai-Soron Baki. The Uwar Waje is today the only remaining member of the once formidable cadre of lower-level administrative concubines, the iya-yen waje. Uwar Waje's continuing administrative importance (heightened since the Mai Kudandan title lapsed) and her strategic placement in Yelwa have made her almost as powerful as the Uwar Soro. [62]

Who will hold the Uwar Soro title in the future is uncertain since the traditional processes through which the titleholder was chosen has been short-circuited. Historically, the Uwar Soro would have been a young palace slave girl given previously to the king when he was still a prince (and a favored son) by his predecessor-father. At this time she would be given the concubine title Uwar Gida Ma-Kulle and assume responsibility for the prince's household, thus gaining invaluable experience.[63] Whichever of the favored sons became king, his Uwar Gida Ma-Kulle would assume the Uwar Soro title and take up residence in the titleholder's quarters in Yelwa. For some reason Emir Abdullahi stopped this tradition, perhaps because there were no longer enough concubines to sustain the tradition and/or because he realized that few benefits obtained from concubinage. Nonetheless, the Uwar Soro title is administratively crucial to palace functioning and cannot die out unless concubinage as a whole collapses. The Mai-Soron Baki title is of similarly lasting relevance since someone is needed to maintain the emir's chambers and to arrange interior audiences with women and children.

By contrast, the last reigning Mai-Kudandan, also a childless concubine inherited from Emir Inuwa, was not replaced after her death, c. 1988, because her duties had become anachronistic: overseeing interior grain disbursement and communal threshing and cooking processes, all of which no longer exist. After she died, her keys to the modern dry goods store (which had come to assume ritual importance) were given to the Uwar Soro and Uwar Waje. Similarly, the Uwar Tafiya title lapsed sometime in the 1930s or 1940s, ostensibly because of its irrelevance: the titleholder prepared and administered concubines selected to accompany the emir onto a battlefield. These women cooked for the emir and his troops and attended to the emir's personal needs.

Intersecting Patriarchies and the Restructuring of the Cikin Gida, 1926–90

Abdullahi modernized certain parts of the palace landscape, and he capitalized on the traditional palace landscape's dissolution to compose experimental, "modern" spaces in collaboration with British male friends and officials. He cut down the baobab tree in the southern labyrinth, for instance, a tree as old as the palace itself and associated mythologically with the kingship. He additionally forbade cattle grazing in the palace on the grounds that cattle dung was unhygienic. He also rebuilt much of the southern "male" palace landscape to incorporate modern cement block police barracks and a middle school, and he used the cikin gida to experiment with new kinds of domestic spaces, including fireplaces, a large library, modern kitchens, and a modern garden and orchard, among many other things. Along the way, he increased the size of his interior domain and organized the female interior along a single linear vista at the apex of which were his main sleeping chambers in Babban Soro.

Creating the vista involved a mini-Haussmanization of the interior landscape and the destruction of key parts of the organic settlement pattern that had once mirrored that of the city-at-large. The cikin gida was divided into two long halves by creating a wide north-south trending corridor in the middle (see Figure 22, no. 5). The long, rectangular space that resulted was partitioned off from surrounding structures by a high curtain wall, creating an interior, building-free courtyard, Sararin Garke (Field of the Cattle Herds), so named because it was built on part of the large open field wherein Nassarawa cattle had once grazed.

To facilitate the corridor-building process, the granaries and compound of 'yar Fanisau were razed. The courtyard took on greater definition when two, large, two-story structures were built fronting it (Figure 22, no. 6). These latter served as private chambers for the emir and his concubines and substantially increased the emir's personal space, in Babban Soro.[64] The buildings, magnificently rendered out of adobe and covered in the highest quality traditional plasters, contained many modern features, including a library and fireplaces. Nearby, a stand-alone kitchen was built to cook for important British and other European guests. Abdullahi planned the form of these buildings with the assistance of a British friend and architect, who then worked and supervised construction within the cikin gida. The process involved architectural plans, an abstraction anathema to traditional practices wherein space was conceptualized between a builder and patron orally, the players tracing out minimal (if any) drawings on the ground.[65] Women were disallowed from the planning process and were warned when to keep out of workers' sight.

One of the end results of the courtyard-building process was the creation of a Versailles-like perspective emanating from the emir's audience hall (Soron Baki) in Babban Soro, the hall rebuilt to have two floors, heightening the emir's visual access to interior inhabitants and visitors. From his throne on the ground floor, the emir could now sit and survey anyone entering or leaving the cikin gida. Besides the fact that the new geometry required all persons entering the interior to navigate the corridor, the darkness of the audience chamber meant that visitors had no way of knowing if and when the emir might be seated inside. From Soron Baki's second floor, moreover, the emir could easily peer with binoculars into many of the women's sections.

Abdullahi also set up a Quranic school for palace women north of Babban Soro, along the corridor. Unlike the traditional religious school at the turn of the century, located in the first wife's waje (place) near the now-razed interior northern granaries, the new school was a stand-alone structure un-coupled from any household. As such, it represented a new kind of public space, albeit one within the palace interior.[66] Abdullahi built another modern place at the northeastern corner of the interior, linear corridor: a ward for elderly women, Dakata (Stop), its construction requiring that the final remains of the palace granaries be destroyed. All of the corridor-related changes made palace women feel that the interior had grown smaller. As Mai-daki laughingly recalled with 'yar Kutisa, "We [women] really thought the palace was shrinking" (Figure 22, no. 7, 8).[67]

Other modernization initiatives that affected interior life indirectly involved Abdullahi's injunctions that all of his concubines and wives give birth in the modern City Hospital, established with Native Authority money in the 1930s. By the end of Abdullahi's reign, most royal women were giving birth in the hospital, though many still demanded to be accompanied by midwives who administered limited amounts of herbs and other traditional remedies. Later in his reign, Abdullahi began large-scale, recreational gardening in the western and eastern fields of the cikin gida, a venture inspired by British precedents. Colonial officials had used prison labor to produce vegetables for themselves, additionally, experimenting with orchard planting to procure citrus and other tropical fruit familiar to the British; many of the orchard projects were linked to windmill schemes. Abdullahi's successors elaborated on the recreational spirit of his early efforts, by flower gardening.

Abdullahi's successor retained and elaborated upon many of his changes. Emir Sanusi was perhaps the greatest modernizer to follow Abdullahi, transforming one of Abdullahi's rooms in his private chambers along Sararin Garke into a modern medical clinic for women. Later, His Highness Alhaji Ado Bayero built a single-storied, rectangular, cement block medical clinic on the razed remains of the deserted concubine ward, Ka-Iya. Sanusi also welcomed automobiles more fully into palace life and protocol. He adopted the now-famous Rolls Royce as his official vehicle, creating new forms of ceremony around it, most noticeably a large police escort. Two cement-block palace garages were built for Sanusi's automobiles. The largest one was built just south of the cikin gida, on what remained of the old eunuch colony. To facilitate the entrance of vehicles into the northern part of the palace, another round of Haussmanization ensued: a long, linear, covered entrance called Kofar Mota (Gate of the Automobile) was carved through what had been the central northern residential area for eunuchs (Figure 22).

The current emir recently attempted to modernize children's play: he had the abandoned concubine ward of Dutsen Babba leveled and a playground built in its stead. Within months the area was again deserted, the playground equipment broken by children unfamiliar with and largely disinterested in what the playground had to offer. Today children play both traditional and modern games. Small boys ride makeshift stick-horses and push old tires with sticks, for example, while older boys play soccer in the palace fields just west of the cemetery. While some little girls engage in the play that small boys do, most girls engage in traditional play forms related to domesticity, such as pretending they are mothers by carrying dolls on their backs. Since older girls are married by their mid- to late teens, I saw no one from this age group at play in the palace's play spaces, and certainly none of them played soccer.

Most relict concubine wards today accommodate the elderly, especially retired concubines (matan fada), elderly or divorced royal women ('yan Fulani), and elderly helpmates or family members. One successful initiative realized about two years ago was building a Quranic school on the largely abandoned grounds of Dakata. Today, elderly royal Fulani women, palace concubines, and palace children attend the new school, which has become quite popular. In tandem with this initiative, Kofar Mota, the long modern entranceway built by Sanusi in the northern male slave domain for automobiles, was converted into a women's mosque in about 2000, the long linear covered structure having previously served informally as a place for women to gather to pray.[68] Although the cement block structure lies 100 meters or so from the main Friday mosque, women are forbidden from praying there, their presence reasoned as being distracting to men.

Postindependence: A Shifting Global and Domestic Economy

In the late 1970s, almost twenty years after independence, the current emir embarked on a seemingly mundane project that represented a profound break with tradition: He built himself a modern cement-block residential and business complex outside the cikin gida on the grounds of what had historically been the southern eunuch colony. For the first time in history, personal chambers for the emir were built outside the secluded interior in a newly manufactured "public" space in the southern "male" parts of the palace. What remained of the sixteenth-century eunuch colony was razed to accommodate the new structure, called Sabon Gida, now connected via a passageway to his old residence, Babban Gida. His newly built home boasted air conditioning, electricity, running water, and, later, a massive satellite dish, television and audio systems, faxes, and computers.[69] Moreover it was part of a large business complex dedicated to cultivating local and international economic and political interests. In the mid-1990s, large areas of Babban Soro were torn down and replaced by new, modernized cement-block structures. The emir's new place within a modern "male" public sphere and the need to leave the cikin gida to pursue international and local business interests shows just how far concubines have fallen from power in the new political economic order.

In the late 1980s a small trickle of bayi again returned voluntarily to make traditional claims to palace life based on matrilateral slave status.[70] This second round of returns occurred presumably in part because of the early 1980s global recession. Again, Clark records a similar kind of economically driven migration among slaves and freeborn men of the Sengambia region, "with the Sahelian drought of the 1970s and the lack of economic opportunities in the region in the 1980s" (1997, 11). Even where these slaves emigrated out of the country, they retained their servile status:

> *Maccube* [slaves] who migrated generally maintained ties to their related freeborn family. Migrants of servile descent sent remittances and gifts to their freeborn counterparts while away. . . . In Fulbe migrant communities in France, social divisions were strictly maintained, with *maccube* migrants doing certain chores for free-born migrants. (11–12)

Matrilateral slave status of Kano bayi, however, had by this time become more difficult to verify because of decades of intermarriage. Because of both groups' needs, however, bayi and royalty were more willing to stretch the truth. The late 'ya Dada, daughter of the reigning Uwar Kuyangi in 1990, for example, was first given by an emir (probably Abdullahi) as a concubine to a colonially appointed District Head. She bore this man several children and therefore, according to Maliki law precedents, should have been freed upon his death. Despite her being given her "freedom," however, she returned to the palace as a bayi for economic reasons, serving as a kuyanga under her mother. She thus remade herself into a domestic "slave." Similarly, another of Uwar Kuyangi's daughters was given by the emir (again, probably Abdullahi) to a District Head as a concubine. She had a son and was hence released into freedom upon her husband's death. She married again (as a freed woman) and bore Daraba, who, according to matrilateral slave rules was freeborn. Yet after Daraba's second husband died, Daraba returned to the palace as a kuyanga. A last case in point is Mero, whose father was the son of a palace kuyanga, which made him a slave. Mero's father, however, married a free woman (Mero's mother), giving Mero freeborn status. After Mero's marriage failed, she returned to the palace to serve as a kuyanga for several years, in 1990 remarrying and moving out of the palace. By contrast, there appears to be little stretching of the truth when it comes to concubinage, perhaps because concubinage today is considered to have few benefits and many restrictions. In the late 1980s, for example, the emir asked to be given the freeborn daughter of a palace bayi who had married a freeborn woman. The emir was refused on the grounds that the daughter was freeborn, a refusal unimaginable fifty years ago. At the same time, the emir's request signals a larger anxiety and points to a future crisis: if large numbers of concubines are not forthcoming (the only kind of slave currently legal), the condition of the monumental ciki grounds will suffer, as is presently the case.

What remains of palace concubinage today is used for modern political and economic ends. Three daughters of a single dogari (a traditional male slave bodyguard) and a female bayi, for example, were given away to wealthy local merchants, with another given to the wealthiest merchant in Kano. The high economic status of the men shows how much concubinage has changed. Instead of slave girls and royal daughters being exchanged among princes and nobility to effect political bonds, concubinage is forging kinship ties between the emir and wealthy men for whom these women are status symbols. The kinds of connections forged, and the reasons for them, show how devalued in their own right concubines have become. The emir's need for financial resources is real, for how else is he to maintain an anachronistic institution that supports thousands of people directly and indirectly—people who currently have few alternatives. Cultivating symbolic and political capital out of his traditional position will be essential to the palace's socioeconomic survival.

Conclusions

Colonialism eviscerated the economic and political basis for palace concubinage at the same time that it touted the existence of the institution as a sign of Britain's respect for traditional rulers within the system of indirect rule. At the same time, many palace bayi negotiated the economic hardships of what the British called, "freedom," through cultivating the lines of matrilateral slave descent. As Clark records for slavery generally in eastern Senegal, "Independence . . . had no discernible impact on servile status" (1997, 8). Additionally, his observation that "[i]n the early to mid-twentieth century, the precise meaning of the term *maccudo* [slave] in Pulaar [Fulani] changed among the Bundunke Fulbe from denoting 'slave' to signifying 'servile,' 'former slave' or 'person of servile descent,'" obtains analogously in Kano where palace *bayi* continue to negotiate their options and places in today's economy through their historical rights and positions as *bayi* (8). Nonetheless, concubinage flounders: no longer able to wage war and no longer sovereign since the colonial conquest, emirs have had few resources to support a system once embedded in a larger symbolic and practical system of fertility and a much larger institution of slavery.

British expropriation of emirate lands, subsequent monetization of the economy, concomitant changes in the currency of taxation, and the abolition of the palace slave and slave estate system spelled the demise of an interior landscape that once celebrated and expressed the fertility of earth and woman. Today, fertility is largely understood as an expression of an individual emir's physical and economic virility, disintegrated from territorial conquest and consolidation. Concubines have consequently become solitary figures of modern domestication, rather than the embodiment of territorial expansion, fertility, and wealth. Today most have little, if any, knowledge of the territories of their enslaved forebears, which in any case has little utility in today's political economy; nor do their procreative abilities produce the kinds of powerful connections they once did. Grain is now delivered by truckloads by men and offloaded to a large palace grain warehouse outside the palace interior, palace women having little idea from where the grains derive.

Conclusion

> [T]he tradition of respect for what is established and repeated, whether in oral or especially literary form, remains dominant, so that fresh thinking and new scholarship leads not so much to a reconceptualization of Hausa history but rather to a revised orthodoxy. (Sutton 1979, 181)

D rawing on a variety of new geographical resources and methods, this book proposes a number of hypotheses concerning state formation processes in Kano where I argue that culture and politics revolved initially around and depended on earthly and human fecundity. Perhaps most important, I suggest that the womb functioned symbolically and practically as a place wherein the state's primary currency was created: children. Royal children of the Kano monarchy were "paid out" in marriages that solidified territorial gains and brought knowledge of the outside world into the palace interior (ciki). There was no "gold standard" through which an individual child's value could be measured, but rather this value was sustained by faith—that the monarchy was powerful and that kinship and other ties to the monarchical system were useful and prestigious. Royal children hence had symbolic and practical functions, marriages with royal children producing the sought-after knowledge and kinship links between king and hinterland. I have also theorized that children were akin to grains, which were collected in the palace interior initially as the main form of state tax and used (in some instances) as currency or the basis of grain exchange (kwaru).

In large part due to women's procreational powers, the special category of slave woman—the concubine—was valued and collected in the Kano palace. Not coincidentally, the palace soon became a vibrant Islamicized center of the state, built as a suburb abutting the city chosen by Rumfa (1463–99) as the state's permanent capital, Kano. Islam helped to codify and systematize concubinage's importance, along with other state institutions, Islam being one codification system among many available at that time. Perhaps Islam's importance derived from the fact that it was regionally extensive (bringing many worlds within and beyond West Africa into the potential orbit of the king), and that, unlike other religions, it mapped paternity onto ownership of a slave woman (the concubine) such that the birth status of her child was transformed through the father from slave born to free. It was the freeborn status of the children that made them useful politically.

Concubines held additional value, given the imperial nature of the state, in that they represented and could relay information about their place of origin to the state and other interested parties, such as the Korama. Individual concubines held different political value depending on their pedigree. The captured daughters of royalty, important personages, or recalcitrant leaders, for instance, might assume considerable powers, allowing them to forge politically meaningful connections with the place from where they derived, aiding in that area's pacification and in the elaboration of their own (and the king's) powers. One marker of the importance of concubine *provenance* was the fact that concubines resided in a complex ward (unguwa) system, ward names often reflecting concubine places of capture or origin.

At the same time the livelihood of concubines and that of the state depended on amassing sufficient quantities of food, an activity often overlooked in state formation studies of early Hausaland. I theorize here that food sourcing was accomplished initially through centralizing grain taxation in large palace interior granaries managed by a specialized concubine-led slave hierarchy. My emphasis on the importance of grains to the state and to state political culture is in keeping with Sutton's hypothesis that Hausaland as a whole, extending from Bauchi and Garun Gabas in the east, to Kebbi and Yauri in the west, was settled through grain cultivation. Thus, he writes,

> [The] emergence of Hausa as an ethnic identity expanding from east to west across the Nigerian savanna has to be viewed ecologically. It was more than a matter of gradual migration and assimilation: it involved also Hausaization of the land, the conversion of bush and woodlands into parkland

and open savanna, with a marked reduction of the tsetse-infested areas, and the increasingly intensive exploitation of the land for seasonal grain cultivation and a fair degree of cattle-keeping. (1979, 183)

And that

[t]his Hausaization, as it proceeded from its old bases in eastern Hausa-land, would have been both a cultural and an ecological process, through which woodland would have been converted into more open and contin-uous savanna to support grain-cultivation and a denser peasant popula-tion. (201)

For Sutton, it is grain cultivation, then, that set the cultural ecology apart from the highlands and forests (with longer rainy seasons) to the south and the Sahelian region to the north. Within this ecological zone, Kano was central (183).[1]

The centralization of representation of the outside world "within" through palace concubinage and the ward system created a prototype for bod-ily and domestic interiority that over the centuries would be adapted and val-ued in different social contexts. Early on, for example, the nobility mimicked the palace's elaboration of seclusion (the ciki), a sociospatial creation that in the nineteenth and twentieth centuries would be adopted by commoners. Thus, sociospatial linkages of women and domestic interiority were forged with domesticity's and interiority's associations metonymically, practically, and symbolically mapped onto the stomach, food, and childbearing. At the same time, the ciki's incorporation of the outside world through the ward sys-tem and specialized concubine practices, such as bori (a syncretic practice representative of an ever-changing amalgam of conquered peoples) spoke to the internalization, domestication, and enculturation of conquered lands. In this way, the stomach and womb were mapped onto one another and were, in turn, mapped onto a sense that conquered lands were effectively "di-gested"; domesticated; brought "inside." Thus, the word for "eating" *(ci)* car-ried connotations at once bodily (ciki, as related to stomach or womb), spatial (e.g., mu ci gaba; let's go forward!), and imperial (ci; conquest).

I surmise that the organically derived value of children and grains, and thereby concubinage as an institution, was significantly eroded with the intensified growth of male-led regional trading networks and territorial con-solidations sometime in the eighteenth century.[2] In particular, when non-organic currencies such as cowries, cloth, and European monies came prominently to bear, certain economic activities of palace women and Kano women, generally, became somewhat circumscribed. Women both in the palace and beyond it were formally proscribed, for example, from participating in the lucrative indigo cloth-dyeing industry of the nineteenth century, the jihad of that time leading to a regional geopolitical consolidation that made concubinage and the mass production of royal children of lessened importance to territorial accretion and the acquisition of new knowledge. All of these processes meant that the nineteenth century saw a sharp decline in royal children and concubine numbers and in concubine powers.

My analysis is in keeping with Guyer and Belinga's attempt to rework solely kinship-based renderings of "wealth-in-people" arguments (1995); here, centralizing authority figures attain power simply by accumulating people (lineages) and resources quantitatively through, for example, conquest and slavery. Instead, drawing upon a case study specific to Equatorial Africa, they point to a more dynamic and synthetic understanding of wealth. Theirs depends upon the idea that the successful centralization of powers is accomplished through cultivating the *composition* (rather than accumulation in the strict sense) of socially disparate elements, developing knowledge through cultivating new social and material networks. As they write:

> Society is not integrated; it is a constant improvisation along a continuum from centrifugality to brilliant synergism . . . group structures and relations of inequality are ephemeral instantiations of singularity, multiplicity and connective receptivity whose operation—like musical conventions rather than authoritarian rules—infringe only conditionally and transitorily on the autonomy that makes personal singularity possible in the first place. (1995, 103)

Such improvisation and synergism were clearly present in the palace over the centuries. Creation of the concubine-led indigo dyeing yard in as early as the sixteenth century, for example, required the continual incorporation and adaptation of knowledge about dyeing practices and networks from outside the region, something initially accomplished presumably through the enslavement of those from cloth-dyeing regions to the southwest—either eunuchs or slave women. Dyeing practices, in turn, depended on continual innovation in large-pot technologies tied, in turn, to cooking-pot innovations—something needed given the massive palace population—and pot-based birthing rituals. Similarly, impressive sociospatial networks developed around the central market Korama, palace concubines, and regional grain production sites in the sixteenth century—networks redolent in the palace landscape: a large number of palace granaries linked to the central market via a special pathway along which women bartered grains. The regional knowledges of concubines captured from various regions in tandem with Korama's knowledge of regional grain production levels would have been essential to the seasonal levying of state grain taxes. Finally, in the early twentieth century, we find the king (emir) marrying the daughter of the chief blacksmith rather than the daughter of another chief or king, a move consolidating the latter's relationship to the most strategic industry of that time.

Guyer and Belinga end their analysis of how disparate knowledge and power are interrelated by suggesting how such interrelationships might be empirically studied. Their concern that "wealth in people" not be taken to imply a simple accumulation of kinship lines or labor leads them to foreground implicitly the importance of mapping out a person's social geography. In the specific context of elite polygyny, for instance, they write:

> To find a correspondence between numbers of wives and the structures of a growing trade system goes only part of the way towards understanding the meaning and power of the "accumulation" of wives. Ideally one would trace out . . . the different facets of power that each particular wife [or concubine] brought: links to a new territory or trade network; taps into the power of specialists amongst her kin and their personal qualities of strength of skill; control of a centrifugal home front . . . or pathways to the outside; access to agricultural or other productive and spiritual knowledge appropriate to different environment as groups migrated. And then there are the personal qualities of women themselves. (1995, 116)

The book's findings and conjectures also support the work of Musisi (1991), Kaplan (1997a), Bay (1998), and others, that challenge popular exoticized, eroticized, western notions of the "harem," cultivated since at least the seventeenth through early twentieth centuries (e.g., Alloula 1986; Apter 1990; Lal 2003; Pucci 1985, 1989). In Kano concubines constituted a hard-working managerial class that sustained everyday life in the palace, their duties taking them into larger realms of the marketplace and the body politic, not unlike royal wives in Dahomian, Benin, and Bugandan palace contexts.

The geographical methods deployed here produced invaluable new historical information, without which none of the hypotheses I have proposed here would be possible. Exploring the spatial organization of everyday palace life involved mining traditional sources for new kinds of empirical information, whether these be linguistic data, aerial photographs, archival photographs, the mapping of landscape details, or architectural analysis. In so doing, new empirical finds were made, including the large indigo dyeing yard, the "women's path" leading into the palace from the market, the sacred baobab tree and well outside the prejihadic king's quarters, the sixteenth-century eunuch colony, and so on.

It is hoped that this study's insights into the workings of concubinage (along with those from comparative African contexts) will lead to a re-examination of the institution's political importance in other cultural milieus. It is also hoped that the work will lead to new ways of thinking about currency—not only in the context of masculinist realms of exchange, but in terms of more organic currencies tied to the fecundity of earth and women. While the hypotheses presented here are tentative, the empirical directions outlined will hopefully shape comparative works in and beyond the region, in the process challenging this work in synergizing, productive ways.

Epilogue

I n late 2000 and 2003, I returned to the palace for two monthlong visits to review the book manuscript with the emir and other palace community members and to develop new research projects. The ciki had changed dramatically. Most notably, each wife's compound now hosted a large cement-block bungalow about 1,500 square feet in size, each one identical in design. The story behind these speaks complexly to how globalization and modernity have intersected changes in the palace interior since I left in 1990. The emir had married a fourth wife from Kano, Hajiyya Fatima Rabi'u, the "Kano wife." The emir's first wife had died, allowing him to remarry. Hajiyya Fatima (born 1969) is a modern woman who, just prior to her marriage, had completed a laudatory report about the Emir of Kano, titled "Sarkin Kano Alhaji Ado Bayero," as her master's thesis at Bayero University Kano. The first of the cement-block bungalows was built to honor her arrival and, presumably, to honor her as a modern figure. The modernity of interior and exterior of the new structure was unlike any other building, except for the emir's new quarters. It featured a large modern kitchen and large sliding glass doors facing a patio. It was furnished with modern accoutrements, such as armchairs and curtains. Upon learning that a bungalow was being built for her, the other wives demanded the same on the grounds that in Islam each wife must be treated equally. The emir accordingly built three more identical cement-block structures, one for each wife. None of the bungalows is used, except occasionally to receive western guests. Most palace women continue to live in traditional structures and to cook outside. The bungalows have given the four wives' estates an internationalized and somewhat disaffecting feel: largely unused cement-block structures alongside lived-in adobe ones from pre-jihadic, jihadic (Fulani), and British colonial times.

Several precolonial ciki structures have also been modernized, but in a hybrid way: the adobe bricks *(tubali)* of some traditional structures have been replaced in cement block and covered over with traditional plaster (or cement textured to look like traditional plaster). Parts of the Soron Malam–Turakar Dabo complex that ten years ago were dilapidated and deserted have since been rebuilt in cement block, with some of the structures' original shapes and styles retained. The complex has been divided into separate sections and divvied up among different groups of women. One part of Soron Malam was conjoined to the newest wife's quarters with a new modern kitchen addended onto it, while other parts of the complex were incorporated into adjacent residences for concubines and elderly women. Other traditional structures have simply been covered over in cement, including the one-time central kitchen (Soron Tuwo) and Shekara's house, these two structures now nearly unrecognizable from what they looked like ten years ago. Cement has been the material of choice because it is now impractical to build traditionally: producing building materials for royal structures takes what is today considered an inordinate amount of time and labor, making production of the most durable plasters and bricks much more expensive than cement; and those traditional materials that are less labor- and time-intensive are less long-lasting and hence require annual repairs. Given contemporary labor demands and needs (particularly wages), the chief royal builder, Sarkin Gini (who is nearly blind), cannot mobilize the massive amount of skilled labor that once carried out the palace's monumental and arduous building projects. There is little wage-based incentive for young people to learn the trade, royal builders receiving little in the way of remuneration. While the Sarkin Gini (King of Building) has learned to master the use of cement block and plasters, producing wonderful facsimiles of traditional shapes and geometric plaster and bas-relief forms, the form of cement block and the more consistent texture of cement plaster has given the reworked buildings a much more orthogonal, measured, and, hence, modern look.

Modernity is not only present in the material reconstructions of the landscape but is evinced in disparate kinds of interior palace practices. Parts of Shekar Yamma are used by young boys as a soccer field, and many palace women don the latest Saudi styles of Islamic dress and attend the modern new Islamic school for women and girls inside the palace ciki. The latter phenomena speak to the growing religious conservatism of the region, especially the widespread adoption of Shari'a law by states across most of (Muslim) northern Nigeria, including Kano state. One especially powerful sign that ideological times have changed is that no one wanted to acknowledge, much less discuss, "traditional" spirit practices, which had not previously been the case. Palace women with whom I broached the topic in fact denied that a spirit house ever existed in Yelwa. By contrast, many women emphasized the importance of Islam in their lives. One wife placed a large poster of the Ayatollah Khomeini on her wall in the mid-1990s (it has since been removed) and presently keeps her television tuned to Saudi religious instruction channels. At about the same time, Hajiyya Fatima celebrated her new marriage by having Quranic passages sculpted into the plaster of the interior walls and vaulted ceilings of her sitting chambers (featuring a very large oil painting of the emir propped up against one of the walls), forming a beautifully complex and colorful bas-relief. Both of these wives stressed how much more Islamic recent emirs had become, one sign of this being that each successive emir had chosen for moral reasons to have fewer palace concubines; hence, concubinage's decline. During my 2000 visit, one bori practitioner felt so uncomfortable talking about her work in one of the wives' quarters that she requested we meet in her home in the old city. It was also during this visit that Gogo Nani (one of the emir's sisters) and Gogo Mama (the so-called Illorin wife whose paternal ancestor was the brother of the Shehu) asserted that the female spirit living in Babban Soro was not related to bori but to Islam.[1] In particular, Gogo Nani noted that just after the jihad, the Shehu told the first and holiest of Kano appointees, emir Suleiman, that all palace spirits had now departed except for one crippled woman named Maimuna. Suleiman is said to have told the Shehu that he wanted her to continue living there and he therefore built her a home in the palace.

The Islamicness of this spirit (aljanna) is belied by the fact that the spirit house was allowed to fall into ruin because it was seen as representing un-Islamic practices, the emir only repairing it in time for me to photograph it. The late queen mother, Mai-Babban Daki Hasiya, was the last concubine to ensure that the spirit was cared for, the emir ending these activities upon his mother's death circa 1995. As one of the emir's daughters recalled, each Friday the late Uwar Soro Aisha Delu had mobilized certain concubines to clean and sweep the aljanna's quarters, and had fed the aljanna regularly with nono (milk) and white goro (kola nut), the concubines returning later to retrieve the empty utensils. The spirit room contained large bottles of perfume (turare) and a bed, upon which indigo-colored rugs (kilishi) were laid.[2]

The modern bungalows and building materials, the accommodation of soccer, the wearing of Saudi fashions, and the new institutionalized place for palace women's Islamic education hence contrast starkly with the deserted and ruinous conditions of the concubine wards, the overall waning and aging ciki population, and the circumscription of spirit worship practices and places. Today, what remains of palace concubine life is in some flux and disarray.[3] Yelwa nonetheless remains the center of concubine life, though its former hub, Soron Tuwo (The Hall of Porridge), has been abandoned. Most grains are today delivered via channels unfamiliar to palace women or even the King of Grain; concubines are now completely outside the circuits of grain procurement. Curious about certain recent interior landscape changes, Hajiyya Abba visited the southeastern edge of the ciki to see for herself a large new cement-block structure built just to the south, in Kofar Kudu, which palace concubines told her warehoused rice (which is imported) and maize. A friend additionally informed her that large bags of grain were regularly trucked into the oldest male slave section in the north, Kofar Arewa, where they were off-loaded into the Shamaki's quarters.[4] Sarkin Hatsi now performs mostly domestic servant functions and declined to comment on where the grains came from, noting ruefully that a titleholder known as the Wakili currently handles grain warehousing and disbursement, both activities located firmly beyond his purview and the interior domain of women.[5]

The ciki population continues to decline as royal children marry and move off the premises, as many elders die, and as new concubine replacements are not forthcoming. One concubine recently left the palace without officially negotiating her departure, while several years ago another concubine left with the emir's support, following lengthy discussions with him. In 1990 fifteen concubines populated the interior; by late 2003 there were twelve.

Given present political, ideological, and economic conditions, concubinage cannot be resumed on the monumental scale that characterized its past. At best, it will become a residual elite institution that says little about its historic power and influence. Palace girls of slave descent given away as concubines are valued today as status symbols and as practical extensions of the emir's political influence, enabling him in turn to enter new socioeconomic domains. Concubine children similarly bolster the emir's economic position: royal daughters who marry strategically help to create kinship links with those outside palace circles, especially those of the merchant class, while royal sons often find themselves employed in important political and economic places. How concubinage will be sustained in the future is unknown, especially since no royal prince has taken or been given a concubine. How the emir or the palace bayi community might deploy the institution to some economic or political advantage remains to be seen.

Notes

Prologue

1. Since then, this trend has been reversed, largely as a result of new technology-driven commercial and governmental uses of spatial information, especially those associated with GIS (geographical information systems) and remote sensing. In this sense, the growth reflects a return to mapping, most GIS practitioners not engaging in critical social and geographical analysis.

2. See for example, Necipoglu 1991 on the Topkapi palace in Istanbul built in the late 1400s, O'Fahey 1980 on court life and hierarchies in Dar Fur (Sudan), a sultanate originating in the mid-1600s, Spaulding 1985 on royal women in the Funj kingdom of northern Sudan in the mid-1700s and thereafter, and Zahan 1967 on gendered divisions in the palace of Mossi, a kingdom south of Songhay, in the 1500s. The nineteenth-century accounts of Bornu and Dar Fur court life penned by Nachtigal (1971, ii and iv) are similarly suggestive of royal women's powers, but still largely silent on them. Presumably his silence reflects his lack of cultural access to, and diminished interest in, royal women. One of the few works to concentrate explicitly on royal women is Bay 1998, in the context of Dahomey. Nonetheless, her work addresses an eighteenth- and nineteenth-century palace, at some historical remove from early Kano palace life. Musisi's 1991 work on gender and state formation in Buganda is especially provocative, elite polygyny developing in Buganda as a result of Saharan influences.

3. Ramadan is the Islamic month of fasting. Joseph Raccah was a famously successful Kano businessman who was very close to Emir Abdullahi Bayero (1926–52) and subsequent emirs, though he was eventually thrown out of the country. A Libyan Jew with a British passport, he first came to Nigeria as a child with his brothers. He eventually married a Christian Lebanese woman who had eight children and a Fulani woman who had at least two children. Rebecca Abd's

mother, Doris, was one of Raccah's eight children, later marrying a Christian Lebanese man, George Abd. Miriam Sielah was the child of the Fulani woman and married a Muslim Libyan man, Mustapha. Kano emirs apparently had a soft spot for Miriam because she was the daughter of a Fulani woman and a Muslim in an otherwise largely Christian family (Chidi, 27 April 1988; Gogo Abba, 13 October 1989; Lamido Sanusi, 24 February 2004).

4. In April 1906, the emir "was called upon to pay the Government share in cash. Government commenced receiving half share of their tax [half of the District's total taxes] in April 1906" (SNP 7/9/1538/1908). Prior to this time, most taxes were paid in cowries. Still, a significant amount of tax seems to have been rendered in grain. Thus, the Kano Province Annual Report of 1909 states that "Government [the British colonial government] share is brought to the Waziri on behalf of Government in *cash or kind*. In the former case it is at once paid into the Treasury; in the latter it is realised by the Waziri as promptly as possible with the same object in view" (SNP 7/472/1909, my emphasis). I have assumed that in-kind taxes were collected from both non-Muslims (as a state tax), and Muslims (as the Islamic grain tithe, or zakkat).

Traditionally, zakkat was to be given to malams for distribution to the poor and others in need. This study shows that it was additionally drawn upon by the emir to sustain the palace community. The British assumed that the religious tithe belonged legitimately to the crown as well. Hence the 1909 colonial report talks about how "[the Government has] been peculiarly fortunate in getting *our* zakka this year [my emphasis]." British expropriation of grain alms for the poor at best suggests that the British ill-understood this kind of tax. At worst, the expropriation represents colonialist pragmatism: most of "their share" was used as feed for the colonial mounted infantry's horses and for the needs of the transportation department and their garrisons! The British nonetheless discouraged the rendering of tax in grain.

Introduction

1. I reproduce here a précis of Leo Africanus's life by Hunwick (n.d., 1), both because it establishes Africanus's geographical and biographical background and because it addresses why some scholars doubt the authenticity of his work as a primary source (see also Imperato 1996): "Leo Africanus was born al-Hasan b. Muhammad al-Wazzan al-Zayyati, of a family of Granada in Spain which relocated to Fez in the wake of the Christian *reconquista*. At age 17 (between 1506 and 1510) he accompanied his uncle on a diplomatic mission to Songhay and is said to have made another journey a few years later. In 1518 on his return from a visit to Istanbul and a pilgrimage to Mecca, he was captured by Sicilian pirates and subsequently presented to Pope Leo X, who later baptized him and gave him his name. He stayed in Italy and wrote his *Description of Africa* (mainly concerning North Africa and Egypt), and an Arabic grammar. He also taught Arabic at the University of Bologna. His *Description* was first published in Italian in 1550, and later translated into French and English. Recent scholarship has thrown doubt on the historicity of his claimed journey to Hausaland and Borno, suggesting that he gained his information from other travelers whilst in Gao or Agades, but this is by no means established."

2. Though some scholars claim the kingdom of Dahomey may have been founded in the 1600s, there is no sure evidence for this (Bay 1998, 40).

3. See Necipolgu 1991 (23, 162, 165, 254) on the geopolitical power of concubines and black eunuchs in the renowned Islamic palace of Topkapi in Istanbul.

4. See chapter 2 for an extended discussion of kingly seclusion across Sudanic contexts, Muslim and non-Muslim alike. See Necipolgu 1991 on kingly seclusion in the Topkapi palace of the Ottoman Empire and Musisi 1991, 768, on kingly seclusion in Buganda.

5. Musisi (1991, 759, 771) theorizes that kingly accumulation of wives in Buganda occurred at a particular time in Buganda's state formational history. While prior to the thirteenth century clan heads ruled the territory, in time one clan head emerged as king. Over the next few centuries, clan lands would be confiscated by the kingship and placed under the king's centralized authority. To re-enfranchise those who had lost power under the new centralized regime, the king developed what she calls "elite polygyny." In so doing, the king could produce many children, marrying them off to clan heads who had lost power. In so doing, he *linked* (and made subsidiary) former clan heads' lineages to his own. In this way, a new ethic of subordination and societal restructuring obtained. Bugandan state formation depended on destroying the political economic basis of territorialized clan life and assimilating conquered peoples through a common state culture that eventually transcended differences in lineage, culture, and language—all of which depended on the kingly cultivation of *reproduction and elite polygyny*. It is tempting to surmise that something analogous occurred in Kano in the 1400s. Intriguingly, the geopolitical changes Musisi documents for Buganda were initiated just after Bantu-speaking inhabitants of the region were invaded by Nilo-Saharan peoples from the northeast (see Musisi 1991, 764).

6. Culling information from many secondary sources, Murdock (1959, 37–39) outlines what he sees as the special political-cultural characteristics of Sudanic absolutist monarchies, systems he deems "African despotism." Among the eighteen characteristics are "harems," his commentary noting that "[t]he ruler is invariably surrounded by a large number of wives and concubines." Most of the historical kingdoms and polities to which he refers were Islamicized ones, making it difficult to determine if the state concubinage to which he refers preceded or followed regional Islamization.

7. This respect for the procreational power of women, embodied in fertility images of earth and mother, also has a history in non-African agrarian contexts. See, for example, Lerner 1986.

8. The Maliki School was founded on the ninth-century writings of Malik, a third-generation jurist of the Prophet Muhammed. See Ruxton's 1916 English translation of the 1843 French translation and commentary of Perron on the *Mukhtasar*. Perron writes that "the most widely circulated and the most revered [juridical work of Sidi Khalil] is the *Muktasar*. Khalil devoted twenty-five years to its composition. . . . When Khalil died, the manuscript of the *Mukhtasar* was complete up to the chapter upon marriage, or about one third of the work. The remainder was found among his possessions, either on separate sheets, or, in the form of unedited copy. His disciples added the remainder, thus recovered, to what had already been finally put together by him; and in this manner, the book was finished" (Ruxton 1916, 10).

9. "Marriage is the most solemn act of civil life and a married man is more in the eyes of God than the most pious bachelor: 'Marry the women who please you, to the number of two, three, and even four'" (Ruxton 1916, 90).

10. "If an owner is unable to provide food for his slaves and live stock, they must be sold or given away. A *umm-walad* [concubine], who cannot be sold, must be given away in marriage or enfranchised" (ibid., 153).

A concubine-wife distinction in law and practice did not obtain in Dahomey where all women were known as *ahosi*, a designation connoting submission to kingly authority rather than conjugality. Female ahosi similarly derived from many sources, such as war, lineage levies, punitive measures, or as daughter offerings from the wealthy (Bay 1998, 18).

11. "If the master of a 'mother of offspring' becomes bankrupt, the slave-mother may be sold for the benefit of the creditors" (Ruxton 1916, 368).

12. These differences are crucial ones. In the non-Islamic kingdom of Dahomey, for instance, *all* palace ahosi were permanent residents who could not be "divorced," most of these women

never having a conjugal relationship with the king (Bay 1998, 19). For a synopsis of different types of concubinage across time and place, see the entry for "Concubinage" in the *Macmillan Encyclopedia of World Slavery* (1998), especially the entries on Ancient Rome (Hunt), the Islamic World (Mack), and China (Jaschok).

13. Other pertinent passages include, "If the slave becomes pregnant, she will not be sold, but will live with the father under the name of 'mother of offspring' [Arabic, *umm walad*], that is, a woman to be enfranchised owing to her motherhood" (Ruxton 1916, 100). And "The *umm walad* [concubine] remains as she was until the death of the father of her child is either proved or may be presumed" (142). Ruxton, in an editorial footnote, relays that "[a] *hadith* says: when a slave girl has a child by her master, she is free at his death" (100).

14. I use the word "accumulation" here not in the restricted sense, as described by Guyer and Belinga (1995), but in their expanded sense of *composition,* that is to say, as a kind of accumulation of resources that was dynamic, synergistic, and open. Or as Guyer and Belinga argue in the context of Equatorial Africa, "social mobilization was in part based on the mobilization of different bodies of knowledge, and leadership was the capacity to bring them together effectively, even if for a short time and specific purpose. We refer to this process as *composition* and distinguish it from *accumulation*" (120; my emphasis).

15. 'Yar Duduwa (a concubine) and the Uwar Soro Binta Gaji, the highest-ranking palace concubine and a former concubine of Emir Sanusi who chose to stay in the palace after he was deposed in 1963 (25 November 2000). She had this option because she was childless. Like any titleholder, the Uwar Soro is called by her title only. It was considered unusual for me to ask for her name, which is Binta, though prior to her appointment circa 1995 she was known by her nickname, Gaji. Gaji is short for Magajiya and Binta is from the Arabic "Bint" or daughter; both are nicknames for Fatima, the daughter of the Prophet Muhammed (Sanusi Lamido Sanusi, 2 November 2003). At any rate, the great-grandparents of Uwar Soro Binta Gaji, like the kinsfolk of Sanusi's Uwar Soro (Hajiyya Wayo), were Bornoan (from Maiduguri), captured as slaves and brought to the palace, probably in the 1890s. Uwar Soro Binta Gaji's parents, though part of the palace slave community, live outside the palace proper, in a compound near the northeasterly palace gate.

16. His Highness Alhaji Ado Bayero, 24 November 2001; Alhaji Ado Sanusi, 2 December 2003.

17. Gogo Nani with Hajiyya Abba, 12 November 2000; Alhaji Maitama Sule (dan Masani), 10 December 2003. Shekara's importance and residence are discussed in chapter 3.

18. Anonymous, November 2000.

19. Philip Shea put forward this reason for concubine children's succession, equating choice with "love" (personal communication, November 2000): That is, because a leader often chose his concubines, love came into play. A chosen concubine is consequently in a superior position vis-à-vis the royal wives to pressure a leader to choose her son as the successor. By contrast, a ruler's wives are chosen for him, making it less likely that kingly choice or womanly guiles could come into play. Shea's reasoning offers an interesting and apparently nonfunctionalist account of why concubine sons so often ruled.

20. I want to thank Sanusi Lamido Sanusi for suggesting this possibility (2 November 2003). Lamido's paternal grandmother was the highest-ranking concubine titleholder of the palace, Uwar Soro Wayo, during the reign of his grandfather, Emir Sanusi.

21. She writes: "They say, for example, that [the wealthy commoner] Adonon [a slave ahosi captured by a king reigning prior to Agaja] convinced Agaja to wage a war of revenge on Weme Jigbe, a town where a son of hers had previously been captured and killed. Her wealth is

suggested by the four families in the area of Abomey today that trace their ancestry to her, a sign that she controlled a large number of people. Moreover, there are still farms in and around Abomey that are managed in her name and from which the current Adonon, who inherited the estate through positional succession, derives income.... [A]t least by the nineteenth century, lineages began offering promising daughters to the king in the hope that they would do well in the palace organization" (1998, 76).

22. Bay writes, "Because of the centrality of the lineage in social life, individuals involved in the state always had divided loyalties. Faithful service to the king offered rich rewards, but one's material and spiritual past and future were tied up with the lineage. The tug of those loyalties can be imagined most easily for women within the palace, who were pledged to serve the king yet who stood to enrich themselves and their lineages if they managed their resources and opportunities well" (1998, 97–98).

23. Here, my conclusions depart from those of Mack, who asserts that the primary importance of concubinage to the patron (she refers specifically to the Kano palace) "was the potential it provided to increase the pool of offspring eligible as successors to the throne" (1998, 212). Lovejoy avers that in the nineteenth-century reformist Caliphate, concubinage was "a means of controlling women.... First, it concentrated women in the hands of the wealthy and powerful. Second, it increased the size of aristocratic and mercantile households as children were born to these women. Third, it helped consolidate the dominant [reformist] culture of caliphate society" (1983, 246). While his reasoning is generally correct, I would argue that by the nineteenth century concubinage was of limited political importance, having become more a sign of virility than a sign of female fertility power.

24. Lamido Sanusi, 2 November 2003.

25. Wigley 1992, for example, analyzes how the ancient Greek notion of *chora* informed notions of interiority in western architecture and households over time. Butler 1990 draws upon Plato's analysis of chora to think through relationships of substance and depth.

26. Hajiyya Abba asserted that children had to be born in the kudandan of Mai-Kudandan, who lived in the central concubine ward of Yelwa (Abundance; 11 November 2000). The head concubine, Uwar Soro, disagreed with this assessment and averred that children could be born in any of the kudanda located in Yelwa. This assertion nonetheless was made three years after the death of the last Mai-Kudandan. Field evidence from the Dutse palace shows that all royal children were born in the granary-house of that palace's respective Mai-Kudandan. In either case, what is important is the overlay of food and child-birthing functions in the same place, whether it be in Yelwa generally, or in Mai-Kudandan's quarters, in particular.

27. In 1990 I spoke with Jerome Barkow about his dissertation work with non-Islamic groups around Kano. He could recall no formal architectural strictures governing spatial relationships between men and women. No one, to my knowledge, has done a comprehensive comparative analysis on seclusion or gendered *spatial* divisions in non-Muslim Hausaland.

28. See Moore 1986 for what is still one of the most comprehensive anthropological discussions of gendered spatiality across cultural contexts. See also Spain 1992 for a useful summary of the many ways in which gendered differences in spatial prerogatives and practices have historically and in the present day worked to create and sustain social differences.

29. Azuonye drawing upon the published works of Marcel Griaule and Germain Dieterlen on the Dogon, summarizes the central symbolic importance of the human form thus: "the human form mirrors the entire universe, the earth, the society . . . and the female. . . . In turn, the family, the society, the earth, and the universe mirror the human form" (1996, 46). In this

way, the dichotomy order versus disorder was mapped onto the human body and the house, an order similarly transposed at the scale of the village. Disorder, in turn, was mapped onto an unknown and barbarous beyond (Michel-Jones 1978, 40–45).

The Dogon creation myth emphasizes the importance of fertility in an agrarian context not unlike that of Kano in the 1500s. According to the myth, the universe was born from the tiniest of seeds that exploded through its own internal vibrations. Its contents expanded to fill space, forming a large "egg of the world" out of which life emerged, not unlike the spatiality of the Hausa *ciki*. Here, the egg-world is maternal, the latter creating at a human scale the symbolic equivalent of what the egg-world brought forth at the scale of the universe (see Azuonye 1996, 24).

30. Any woman could become one of the "elite wives" or *bakembuga*. They fell, however, into one of three status categories: (1) freeborn women with titles who administered chiefs and taxation; (2) nontitled freeborn women; (3) and the daughters of lesser chiefs and peasants, and war captives. Women in category 3 were similar to domestic slave women in the Kano palace, performing the most arduous labor, many eventually being taken by the king as concubines. In Kano, then, palace women were defined partly through the practices and laws of Islam, which created three distinct juridical groups: wives, concubines, and slaves—each group having distinct rights (see chapter 1).

31. I talk about the KC in the singular as "the original text" for simplicity's sake. The historicity of the *Kano Chronicle* is complex. Lovejoy, Mahadi, and Muktar aver that there were up to four early versions of the manuscript, which they identify according to those who elicited or translated the document: "Wallace/Shaw ms, the Palmer ms., and the 'Dogon Lamba' (Temple) ms, [and] . . . a later manuscript, which Rupert East translated into Hausa around 1930" (1993). The version to which I normally refer is that translated into English by Palmer, the narrative of which ends during the reign of Muhammed Bello (1883–92). Occasionally, however, I also refer to the East 1971 (1930) manuscript, written in Hausa, because his transcription contains alternative spellings of key words. For example, in Palmer, the female titleholder Korama is rendered "Koremma." Similarly, Palmer spells one of the earliest sites of Islamic learning in the palace "Goron Pugachi," whereas East's translation renders it "Goron Fagachi." Goron Fagachi in current Hausa orthography is Goron Fagaci, transliterally, "Hill of the Sitting-in-Audience of a Chief." The phrase can thus be taken to refer to high ground where the king would hold court, an earthly precursor to the throne. *Fagaci* is also related to the word *fada*, the "chief's council chamber" (see Bargery 1934). Using East's renderings in tandem with modern place names allowed me to surmise where the high grounds were located. Lovejoy, Mahadi, and Muktar dismiss East's work as derivative, one written during Abdullahi Bayero's (1926–53) reign.

32. Starratt writes: "The informant, Malam Dauda Ali, said in an interview on July 23, 1987 that a history of Kano was dictated by Dan Rimi Nuhu to Malam Ali Rimin A'uu of Yakasai Quarter and that Nuhu's grandson Hassan dan Aminu sold it to the Sudanese teachers at the School of Arabic Studies" (1993, 153 n. 3).

And: "Shaikh Malam Nasiru Kabara, in an interview on April 4, 1987, said *The Kano Chronicle* was updated regularly by Malam Kabara until it was turned over to the Emir's Palace at the insistence of the Europeans" (153 n. 4).

33. See Starratt 1993 for a fuller discussion of oral traditions surrounding Al-Maghili's visit to Kano.

1. Grain Treasuries and Children

1. This spatial analysis clearly contradicts earlier assertions that the palace faced southward or in more than one direction, assertions based on secondary sources and present day features

of the palace rather than historical geographical data (e.g., Smith 1997, 131; Moughtin 1985). Similarly, Mack writes that the palace slave areas and stables are "in the back of the palace," indicating she believes the "front" of the palace is to the south, an entrance in fact created in the mid-1800s (1991, 121, 10).

2. This slave was responsible for the royal stables, including the spare horses that accompanied the king onto the battlefield. The title of this slave may have been Sarkin Dawaki Tsakar Gida, which transliterates as "King of the Horses of the Middle of the House." Significantly, this titleholder was among the appointees to the first Islamic all-male state council instituted by Rumfa—"The Kano Nine" (chapter 2). According to the KC, King Shashere (1573–82) was the first to award the title to a eunuch (see Palmer 1967 [1928], 115). The title was probably superceded by another, Shamaki (Stables), during the Kutumbi Dynasty (1623–48), the previous title then redefined and passed on to another slave or freeborn person. The title and duties of Shamaki exist today, the title Sarkin Dawaki being held by freeborn Fulani nobility (see Fika 1978, 11). The stable was inside the labyrinth, attached to, but distinctly south of, Shamaki's quarters. Shamaki may additionally have trained and housed sword carriers and armored soldiers and safeguarded palace armor. The stables' proximity to Shamaki's quarters and the positioning of both places along the path leading to the main city defenses of that time (the ramparts and moat) was clearly strategic, allowing for spatial streamlining of military activities.

3. I want to thank Philip Shea for discussing this aspect of Kano urban planning with me (personal communication, November 2000).

4. His Highness Alhaji Nuhu Muhammad Sunusi, 8 December 2003.

5. Gogo was an elegant, well-spoken elder who died in about 1996. Her mother was Emir Aliyu's concubine and, later (because she was childless), the first colonial emir, Abbas's concubine. Gogo, as a royal daughter, is therefore Fulani royalty, her status stemming from the fact that her father (the king) owned her mother (a concubine-slave). In the 1920s Gogo married the emir of Katsina, a nearby and historically competitive emirate, returning to the palace in the 1940s after his death (see Nast 1992, 224–25). Her life history is elaborated upon by Mack 1988.

6. My own work suggests that towns and agricultural estates dedicated to the palace fluctuated in number over time, with many established during the nineteenth century. Discussions with the late Madakin Kano Shehu, based initially on material provided in Yunasa 1976, 55–56, show that over thirty slave estates existed in Kano emirate by the late twentieth century, many created by Fulani emirs in the nineteenth century. Abdullahi dan Dabo, for example, built the Nassarawa estate, while Darmana was begun by his father (Ibrahim Dabo), Gogel by his brother (Usman), and Chiromawa, by his great-grandson, the current emir, His Highness Alhaji Ado Bayero (21 March 1990).

7. The main titleholding slave in charge of maintaining food supplies for the royal horses was Maje Sirdi, which roughly translates as "He Who Is in Charge of the Saddles." According to the present-day Maje Sirdi, before taxes were paid in cowries, they were paid in grain and known as *harajin hatsi* (25 November 2000). See also Garba 1986 for a summary of works dealing with taxation in Kano.

8. Even in places monetized much earlier, like Dahomey, grain tribute was important as late as the eighteenth century. Bay writes, for example, that "[p]ayments in kind made by prominent persons who had been given control over villages or plantations were also effectively tribute. They included foodstuffs and other provisions that were an essential part of the maintenance of the palace population and the preparation for Custom," an annual ritual wherein the king fed thousands of his subjects (1998, 122).

9. According to the KC, King Naguji (1194–1247) was the first king to exact a land tax, which equaled one-eighth or 12 percent of farm production. I have used 10 percent as a general figure, given that at least 2 percent of the 12 percent would have been taken up by local rulers and tax collectors as a kind of stipend. In later years, taxation levels in grain would be less than 12 percent collected, but there would have been a larger population and more rural slave estates dedicated to producing food for the palace.

10. Imoru notes that different sizes and types of granaries existed, some holding 100–500 bundles or dami, the largest holding 1,000. He claims to have seen the granaries of certain rulers (none in Kano) that contained 2,000 dami (Ferguson 1973, 64–65).

11. According to the 1908 Annual Report for Kano, the threshed weight of a dami was 33 pounds. If wastage was about 3:1, an unthreshed bundle would have weighed about 100 pounds.

12. I assume a per capita consumption of one pound/person/day based upon various estimates given in Hill 1972.

13. I read Hill's 1985 work after reading Cooper's 1997 allusion to it where she uses Hill 1985 to summarize differences between pre- and postjihadic forms of slavery: "The word rimji, which is used in Hausa to refer to slave village/plantations, is originally Fulani in origin. The rimji is set in contrast to the ruma, or the Fulani master's cattle encampment. . . . Hill emphasizes the difference between the 'Hausa' form of farm slavery, in which private farmers own and work alongside a small number of slaves, and the more 'Fulani' system of larger plantations owned by absentee aristocrat and merchant farmers, and shows that the vocabulary of the rimji form comes primarily from Fulfulde" (Hill 1985, 36, 40).

14. Spaulding writes, for example, that "[i]nsofar as it consisted of a levy upon crops, the sultanic treasury thus existed in the form of numerous storage granaries throughout the kingdom. During the first century and a half of the history of Sinnar, the perambulatory sultanic court had drawn upon these resources in its travels 'month by month, from station to station.' After the fixing of the capital in Sinnar, the widespread granaries still served to maintain national armies and agents as they moved through the provinces, but it is probable that the local lords, who exercised immediate oversight over the stored tax goods and received a fraction of them as a reward for their services as collectors, came to regard them with an increasingly proprietary air" (1985, 88). Indeed, in eighteenth-century Sinnar, there is evidence that state grain treasuries were used to support Islamic holy men, something similarly suggested by the special enclave of granaries controlled by Islamic malams in the Kano palace, malams traditionally depending upon the goodwill of their adherents.

15. See, for example, Garba 1986. Smith is one of the only scholars to surmise what happened to grain taxes after their collection, though he seems to underestimate the degree of their centralization in the capital or why such centralization would have been needed (1997, 52). Moreover, his discussion focuses on the last Hausa king, Alwali, by which time grain taxes were presumably of much less importance (see chapters 2 and 3). He writes: "Presumably some of these [grain taxation] stores were kept within the palace and in the adjoining compounds of [male slaves] . . . ; but customarily, the ruler left the bulk of grain in state granaries distributed throughout the country at compounds of the local chiefs who undertook its initial collection. These grain stores were mainly held as reserves against famine due to drought, locusts and other pests, or to devastation by enemies; but they were also drawn on by the chief to assist invalids and paupers or to provide subsistence for immigrants during the first year or two. . . . Finally these grain stores were scattered over the country at strategic points to serve as food dumps on which the army could draw when campaigning." In a twentieth-century appraisal of granaries in

Batagarawa, just outside Katsina city, Hill notes that several granaries were owned by women, though most were owned by men. She notes that the clay kudandami were raised off the ground on stones, helping to keep grains dry for up to several years. She also quotes several nineteenth- and twentieth-century sources on Hausaland granaries (1972, 254–55). Clapperton, writing in 1824, for example, asserts that granaries are made in the form of a large urn or pitcher and raised about three feet from the ground by stones (Denham 1826). Over one hundred years later, Cardew comments on the magnificence of Gobir granaries, located north of Kano, the largest able to accommodate eight to ten tons of dami. These granaries were raised to a height of sixteen feet, with a girth of over fifty-five feet and a wall thickness of only three and a half inches.

16. None of the younger palace inhabitants could recall the title. Older palace and market women and many older slave men who did, recalled with admiration her considerable prerogatives and powers in the royal court and her many accoutrements, especially her horse, turban, and alkyabba. See also Sa'id 1978, 52.

17. Jaggar records that the Sarkin Makera (King of Blacksmiths) in Kano city was also appointed in the palace by the emir who turbaned him and gave him a "large gown," though it is not clear if the gown was an alkyabba per se (1973, 17).

18. His Highness Alhaji Ado Bayero, 10 November 2000. High Highness Alhaji Ado Bayero stated that Korama came to court every day, not just on Fridays. The last Korama of the central market, Ayi, was turbaned by Emir Usman (1919–26). She died circa 1950, her grandson, Lawan jika Ayi (Lawan the grandson of Ayi), eventually taking over her duties, by this time greatly reduced. He relayed that a *malafa*, or broad-rimmed straw hat typical of the Fulani, was placed atop her turban, presumably a nineteenth-century Fulani addition (16 November 2000).

19. Lawan jika Ayi, 16 November 2000.

20. Hajiyya Abba notes the gendered sense of the word *korama*. She states, "*Korama* is when water flows with great fullness and force. It is a feminine word. The male equivalent is *kogi*" (10 November 2000).

21. Bargery's assertions regarding Katsina are contradicted by the present-day royal wife from the palace of Katsina, who holds that the title had always been Korama.

22. I employ the word *prostitute* diacritically to point to how the word karuwa has no exact western translation. Karuwai (*pl.*) did not hold lowly social positions, and often had long-standing extrasexual relationships with their partners. Karuwa were relatively free to move in and out of liaisons outside of marriage, and they could easily enter into marriage. If they divorced they could once again engage in external liaisons as karuwa. See Cooper 1997, 172, for a summary of the debates over this word and English-language writers' preference for the word *courtesan*; French-speaking Hausa persons in her field area translated the word as *une femme libre*. See Pittin 1983 for a discussion of the organization of *Katuwanci* in Katsina.

23. Smith's assertion may be historicized, however, to the extent that by the time he was interviewing, grain had much diminished importance. But even this is unlikely since very recently a Korama was elected in a lesser market by her peers (below). Smith also notes that her nineteenth-century duties included grain provision for state prisoners (1997, 63).

Like most Kano researchers, Smith says remarkably little about palace grains or the Korama. He also pays the title little analytical regard in his earlier work on Zaria (1960). The dearth of scholarly research on Korama reflects the gendered fact that grains were the preserve of women, a group of persons male scholars do not and often cannot interview. Similarly gendered patterns of interest and inquiry—and thus of historical reconstruction itself—are present in colonial documentation.

24. 4 December 2003.

25. Alhaji Nulu Muhammad Sunusi, 8 December 2003.

26. Uwar Kuyangi Adama, 9 November 2000.

27. There have been Koramas appointed in newer, modern markets outside Kano, but none have the state recognition they once did. I was accidentally instrumental in turbaning a Korama of the smaller Kano city market of Rimi: I had asked the Madakin Kano to send all the Koramas to Hajiyya Abbas's quarters so that we could interview them. Upon learning that none of them existed any longer, he decided to take a proactive stance. Apparently following historical precedents, he inquired from the handful of women grain traders in the Rimi market (a much more recent market than the central one) who they would like to have as their Korama. They elected a free Fulani woman, Hajiyya Binta Umar, who was delighted. Upon arriving in the palace for an interview, however, she made it clear that she had no idea what the Korama had traditionally accomplished or who she was. Hajiyya and I, therefore, discussed with her what history we knew, as inadequate as that might have been (Hajiyya Binta Umar, 12 November 2000). Much of the information I gathered about the Kano Korama was from discussions with Lawan jika Ayi, the grandson of the last Korama of the central Kano market, Ayi, interviewed in his grandmother's quarters in the old central Kurmi market (16 November 2000).

28. The present-day emir noted it was very possible for Korama to have had a direct role in grain taxation (10 November 2000). Hajiyya Abba, by contrast, expressed strong doubts.

29. Most palace women with whom grain bartering was discussed insisted that it was commonly accomplished up until several decades ago (e.g., Hajiyya Abba, 9 November 2000).

30. I believe Kofar Kwaru is the gate's original name, interviews with a number of persons suggesting gendered differences in understanding its place name and origins. Several palace women pointed out that the word *kwaru* is an archaic reference to grain bartering by women; though the word is rarely used today, they insisted that it was grain trading along the pathway to, and in, the market that gave the gate its name. Their explanation makes sense, considering that the gate was the fulcrum of the "female" pathway that led to the central grain market and that the pathway was used to exchange political intelligence between palace concubines and Korama concerning regional grain production levels. Recall that palace kuyangi would have used the Kwaru gate-path to follow through on palace-dictated market errands, including the exchange of treasury grains for other grains and/or the purchasing or taking of items needed in the palace.

There are competing interpretations for the gate name. Bargery 1934, for example, defined *kwaru* as the changing "of money to cowries." That this was its definition in the early 1900s intimates that its meaning with respect to bartering changed over time—perhaps as a result of the eighteenth-century monetization of the Kano economy or twentieth-century colonial directives that taxes be paid in sterling. Alternatively, Bargery may have obtained a gendered definition based on male uses of the term. As I often found in the palace, men's and women's naming of places differed based on their gendered understandings of the place. Thus, perhaps women retained the word *kwaru* for bartering long after men ceased to use it as such. A young Hausa man attending a presentation I gave at the Kano State History and Culture Bureau, Alhaji Danladi Saleh (21 November 2000), noted that primary school children in Kano are taught that the palace gate was named after a warrior, Kwairanga, who fought in the Damagaram War during the reign of the last emir, Aliyu. This popularized "male" war narrative fits in well with an interpretation offered by Philip Shea, a local scholar and historian of Kano. Shea relayed that he suspected *kwaru* was an archaic Hausa referent for war or drum, palace women vigorously denying all such masculinist interpretations (10 November 2000).

31. The information in this paragraph comes mostly from discussions with His Highness Alhaji Ado Bayero (10 November 2000), Lawan jika Ayi (16 November 2000), Nani Karaye (the emir's eldest sister, 9 November 2000 and 11 December 2003), Hajiyya Abba (11 December 2003), and Uwar Soro (25 November 2000), and Uwar Kuyangi Adama (9 November 2000). Excerpts from the interview with the Uwar Kuyangi follow: "Once there is work to be done here, she [Korama] comes with people. In those days, the floor was not cemented. The flooring was traditionally done. . . . She comes along with them [her recruits]. They come drumming and flooring. She, she sits down. . . . Every one of them [the laborers recruited by Korama] come along with a calabash of gravel [tsakuwa], each of them. . . . The gravel is spread for the traditional flooring, here. She sits down till they finish and they leave. If it is not finished, they come back the next day. Till it is finished. . . . Yes, they are given some [remuneration] amount. In the form of kola nut or money. It all depends on their luck. . . . [Then] they greet him [the king]. . . . When they [first] come in, they will be blaspheming and flooring. When they finish and are about to go, the king (sarki) comes out. They will greet him. But if he does not come out, they will continue the blaspheming [she gestures and hums and mimics someone dancing]. They will be beating the ground. They will be dancing, and dancing. Food is cooked. Food is cooked (repeated) . . . It's only when the flooring work comes up and she is invited that she comes. She is just at the market [and] her house. Once there is dabe work, then she is informed. On invitation each woman comes with a calabash of gravel on her head. The gravel is spread and water poured onto it. They will be singing, shouting, and dancing. . . . Like this. Singing and twisting at the waist. They finish and leave. They come the following day."

In keeping with the geographically restricted domains of informant knowledge, when Uwar Kuyanga was asked whether or not the Korama interacted with the emir, she replied, "I don't know. This does not affect me" and went on to talk about the floor pounding, her next sentences being, "But they come to do work even if it is for ten days, they do it. No, they come for a day and if they finish they go." When I again asked about whether or not Korama met with the emir regularly, Hajiyya Abba interjected, "Okay, but that time [in history], you know, is not her time."

32. Hajiyya Abba with the Mai-Kudandan of the late Emir Sanusi, 22 November 2000. Traditionally, Hausa persons measured time according to major events or the reign of kings. It is therefore hard to discern whether or not the palace concubine to whom Sanusi's Mai-Kudandan referred had a mother old enough to have reigned as Korama, before Ayi did so. Ayi was turbaned by Emir Usman and died during the reign of Abdullahi (1926–52), which means she may have been born about 1880 or so. If so, when she was appointed sometime during Usman's reign, she would have been about forty-five years old. While technically Ayi could not have been a concubine's mother, since Korama was a freewoman, making her children free, the children of freeborn women and palace slave men were in practice taken as concubines or other sorts of slaves. There is a slight chance that the concubine's mother was a "real" slave and not Ayi and that she served her term of Korama before Ayi did. If Ayi was born about 1880, the previous one was presumably born before that.

The emir's sister, Gogo Nani Karaye, relayed that there was in fact one Korama whom she remembers whose mother was a palace slave (11 December 2003). This Korama's junior sister, Giwa, was given to Emir Abdullahi Bayero as a concubine. When this Korama died, all her belongings (kaya) were brought to the palace: Giwa inherited one cow and two wrappers; a junior brother also received kaya. The emir took the rest. Gogo Nani suggested that perhaps the Mai-Kudandan of Sanusi confused the details of Korama's connection to the palace, mistakenly relaying that it was the Korama's daughter (rather than her sister) who was a palace concubine and that she was, moreover, the leading titleholder, Uwar Soro, rather than simply one of many palace concubines. Giwa had no children.

33. The Nupeland kingdom dates from the early 1400s and is located southwest of Kano (see Nadel 1965 [1942]).

34. As Nadel avers, Sonya's royal equivalent was the Sagi, a title bestowed on the king's mother, father's sister, elder sister, or daughter (1965). The word *Sonya* is related to the Hausa word *Sarauniya,* or Queen. Smith writes that in Abuja (the postjihadic successor state of Zazzau), the king's eldest daughter held the title Sarauniya, the Fulani equivalent being Magajiya, a title eventually abolished (1960). Malama Halima Sadiya, a bori adept, suggested perhaps the Kano Korama was equivalent to the Magajiya of Zazzau and Daura, which is unlikely, given that the Korama was of nonroyal birth (21 November 2000). In Daura, the Magajiya was the first daughter born *after the king acceded to the throne,* the Daura Korama being a separate title awarded to his first-born daughter, something not found elsewhere (Sarkin Daura, 4 December 2003). Perhaps, then, the Kano and Dutse Korama were equivalent titles for those of lesser birth, similar to the equivalences between the royal Sagi and the nonroyal Sonya.

35. Many Kurama villages came into existence in the nineteenth century, apparently in part for protective reasons, the Akurmi being a non-Islamic people. Indeed most villages were built on hill sites or in forests (Nengel 1988, 248). I thank Philip Shea for drawing my attention to his own research on the market and that of Nengel.

36. Rufa'i implicitly comes to a similar rendering of the meaning of Mai-Kudandan's title in that she tells us that twentieth-century information suggests she was the palace's "officer-in-charge of the grain store," the latter being a small modern storehouse where threshed grains were brought after market purchase (1987, 93). Mai-Kudandan was alive during Rufa'i's study, but died shortly thereafter. Note that Skinner's comparative work demonstrates that *mai* derives from Tangale, Mupun, and Mafa precedents located southward and to the east (the plateau area and Borno) and means "belonging to, that of" and "chief, king, head, leader, owner" (1996).

37. According to Bargery a *kuyanga* is "a female slave, usually, but not necessarily, young" (1934). The presumed youthfulness of a kuyanga is in keeping with the description of Imam Imoru, born in Kano in 1858 (Ferguson 1973) who, in reference to a man who has one wife, writes: "If he has the money, he purchases a female slave, *baiwa,* or redeems a beautiful young slave girl, *kuyanga.*" Imoru goes on to say that he redeems her in order to take her as a concubine, whereupon she is known as a *k'ork'ora.* In contrast, Lovejoy writes that kuyangi (plural) in nineteenth-century Sokoto were court messengers who had often previously been concubines (1988, 2). In Kano, once the king took a slave woman sexually, she was secluded and redesignated, as described by Imoru.

38. It is unclear whether or not this calling upon village women is an act of desperation that began during the colonial period, after palace slavery was outlawed. Gogo Maidaki asserted that the village women were paid (5 September 1989 and 25 October 1989).

39. Mack is therefore incorrect in her assertion that concubine tasks are "controlled by royal wives, each of whom directs the women in her vicinity and oversees activities" (1991, 126). She is partly correct in that a royal wife administers those concubines who arrived with her in the palace when she was a little girl. These concubines were traditionally gifts from her father to the king and acted as guardians and caretakers of the typically prepubescent wife. Even in this case the relationship was and is ambivalent in that the resident concubines were/are senior to the wife and raised her as a child. Because Mack worked in the 1980s in the palace she understandably

assumes that the last remaining concubine ward (Yelwa) in the center of the palace was the only one that ever existed historically.

Imam Imoru describes a very similar labor scenario in the context of everyday nineteenth-century life. He notes that different sizes and types of granaries existed, one of them known as a kudanda, and that there were different sizes of granaries, some holding 100–500 bundles or dami, the largest holding 1,000. He claims to have seen certain rulers' granaries (none in Kano) that contained 2,000 dami (Ferguson 1973, 64–65).

40. Hajiyya Abba Ado Bayero, 10 November 2000.

41. Almost everyone, including the youngest "Kano" wife, Hajiyya Fatima (b. 1969), remembered with fondness the palace tortoises that wandered about the women's domain (22 November 2000). The last tortoise died in the mid-1990s.

42. See, for example, Talbot, who surmises that throughout Africa, the tortoise is emblematic of femaleness, just as the snake is emblematic of maleness (1967 [1927], 5–9).

43. Relatively few persons live in the old Dutse palace, built in 1807. Most hark back to the previous emirship, the current emir living in more modern quarters. One of the few remaining palace slave titleholders, Sallama Alhaji Muhammad Ismail, took us to see the now-abandoned house of the last Mai-Kudandan, where he pointed out that her house was shaped like a granary, that she was responsible for distributing grains, and that it was in her granary-house that all royal children were born (8 December 2003). There is some conflicting evidence in the Kano context. The Mai-Kudandan of former emir Sanusi asserted that all royal children had to be born in her house (13 November 2000). The present-day Uwar Soro argued that royal children could be born in any of the residences of senior concubines in Yelwa (25 November 2000). I have taken the word of Mai-Kudandan in part because she would best have known her responsibilities and because of corroborating evidence that the same arrangement obtained in the old Dutse palace. Uwar Soro's point that children had to be born in Yelwa nonetheless points to the fact that Yelwa was the place where threshed grains were stored and cooked, forging equivalences between grains and children.

44. I have deduced that her quarters were shaped like a kudandan from nineteenth- and twentieth-century data. Bargery (1934, 628) relays that the word kudandami or kudandan could in fact be applied to describe a residence, the characteristics of which vary regionally. He thus writes that kudandami is also a "house built in the same way [as the granary type] and thatched." The kudandan, derived etymologically from kudandami, is said in Sokoto and Katsina to have consisted of a "round house built as the bin kudandami . . . and thatched, the opening being closed by a removable cap of thatch." In contrast, Bargery informs us that in Kano, a kudandan is a "round clay-built house with a mud, usually flat, roof," one linguistic variant in the town of Tasawa being kudundum. Regardless, I am suggesting that the fact that concubines charged with grain duties lived in this particular kind of house is significant.

45. See the emir of Dutse's Web site (www.dutseemirate.org) for references to intermarriage between ruling families of Kano and Dutse. For example, King Abdullahi Burja (1438–1452) is said to have married the daughter of a king of Dutse whom he had just defeated; and a nineteenth-century Dutse king married the daughter of the king he overthrew in addition to the daughter of a powerful Kano titleholder.

46. The last time bori was practiced openly in the palace was in the late 1950s (Alhaji Nuhu Muhammad Sunusi, 8 December 2003), though I was not able to verify this with palace women.

47. The concubine quarters of the aljanna were documented by both Rufa'i (1987) and me (Nast 1992). Today, royal women deny that such a place ever existed in Yelwa, though they

acknowledge openly the spirit location in the king's quarters. I am not sure how to interpret this discrepancy, since the Uwar Soro with whom both Rufa'i and I spoke died in about 1995.

48. The building of spirit houses is significant in many ways. As Masquelier points out in the context of bori practitioners in Dogondoutchi in present-day Niger, spirit houses are "an objectification of the interconnection of human and spirit worlds" (cited in Cooper 1997, 86).

49. Today, political tensions exist between Uwar Soro and Mai-Soron Baki, who, along with Mai-Kudandan, constituted historically the power base of concubine hierarchies. Mai-Soron Baki arranged audiences between women and the king and she trained young concubine recruits inside the king's personal chambers. It was her consistent proximity to the king, and her ability to arrange communications with him, that apparently fostered her rivalry with Uwar Soro, who today is the most powerful (Hajiyya Abba Ado Bayero, 11 November 2000).

50. It is not clear if the taxes constituted religious tithes only (zakat), or other taxes rendered in grain. Perhaps only a sampling of grains from each farmstead were brought before the king. I suggest this because it seems far-fetched to imagine all tribute and tax-related grains being sent to the king for inspection, given the vast amounts involved (Hajiyya Abba Ado Bayero and Sallama Aminu Dako, 7 November 2000).

51. Smith writes that prior to the nineteenth-century Fulani jihad, nobility or hakimai "administered their lands or fiefs through titled staffs of jekadu [jakadu] recruited from their kin, clients or slaves. On his appointment to the official staff of a hakimi [sing.] as a jekada [sing.], the subordinate (lawani pl., lawanai) usually received one of the titles derivatively attached to that of his superior. Thus, the Madaki's lawanai bore such titles as Barden Madaki Shentalin Madaki, Ciroman Madaki. . . . The designations of these subtitles corresponded with prototypes attached to the chief, but distinguished their holders by specific reference to the Madaki" (1997, 77).

52. The data of Smith apparently date from the reign of the last Hausa king, Alwali, the British, for strategic reasons, documenting only male slave institutions in the palace.

53. This is the main historical reconstructive bit with which Hajiyya Abba disagrees. She argues that female jakadu would never be allowed to engage in male affairs, and for her taxation was always a singularly male affair. I argue that female jakadu's contemporary powers are mostly residual ones. Hajiyya Abba also did not think at first that historical connections existed between palace women and the Korama, that royal children were born in Mai-Kudandan's kudandan, or that the word kudandan derived from a grain storage facility for dami. Nonetheless, with research, all the latter were shown to be true. Nonetheless, on this point, we each remain unconvinced of the other's conclusions.

54. In the mid-1800s a second labyrinth was built as a result of restructuring of the palace interior, whereupon a new southern entranceway was also built (chapter 4).

55. Two differences between the Kano and Dahomey palace guards are that a portion of the latter were armed with muskets, and they guarded the king outside the palace confines; one eighteenth-century observer noted that the guardswomen guarding the Allada palace entranceways were slaves (Bay 1998, 68). Bay points out that women are recorded as carrying swords as early as 1703 in what is now present-day Ghana, while the early nineteenth-century king of Oyo had a special unit of five hundred wives armed with spears (68). She also notes that eunuchs often served as the king's main bodyguard in Dahomey, suggesting that perhaps a similar relationship with eunuchs obtained historically in Kano (113).

56. One baobab tree near Yelwa and the western perimeter of women's precolonial farm fields is still considered magic. None of the women use its leaves for cooking, for it is said that the leaves would turn into hair; nor is the wood burned or the fruit eaten. Before, there were

many spirits in trees in the western fields. If these spirits were singing or drumming, the jakadiya would lock the passageway leading to the fields so that the slave women could not enter (anonymous comment, November 2000).

57. Soon after the British conquest, the farm fields were abandoned. In 1990 only a small, dilapidated portion of the guardwoman's chambers remained, rebuilt in cement in 2000 as a storage facility and tool shed for itinerant prison labor.

58. Traditionally, the four wives and Uwar Soro individually prepared large pots of tuwo (porridge) made from different grains for all nobility (hakimai) who came to greet the emir or ride a horse following him, on Sallah day. Each man received one pot of each of the prepared grains (three in total), each pot covered by a *faifai* or woven cover. These were loaded onto the heads of kuyangi who, led by jakadu, ritually visited the hakimai, delivering the food and receiving gifts in return. The ritual continues today, but the pots are small metal ones with lids (Hajiyya Abba Ado Bayero, 9 November 2000), their diminished size reflecting the palace's diminished powers, especially in regard to grains and concubines.

59. Carryovers of this tradition abound. During the current emir's reign, the highest-ranking Kano palace concubine, Uwar Soro, was called upon to cook for the governor of Kano. She prepared one hundred dishes, all different, and then had one hundred kuyangi carry the food in procession to the Governor's House (Hajiyya Abba Ado Bayero, 23 January 1990).

60. The Dahomey kingdom had a cadre of trained female fighters who may have been used in offensive warfare as early as the eighteenth century (Bay 1998, 138–39). There is no evidence to suggest that similar female soldiers existed in Kano.

61. Evidence for the ascendance of male jakadu was deduced partly from the fact that a new, grain-related, male slave hierarchy was created in the mid-1800s, led by the titleholder, Sarkin Hatsi. Royal concubines evidently lost out with this appointment, for Sarkin Hatsi was awarded a large estate in the middle of what had been concubine-occupied lands. Though he technically served Uwar Soro, he worked directly with Mai-Kudandan, a partnership that begs the important question of who carried out his grain-procuring duties previously, duties involving the receiving and storing of grain tithes and taxes. If it is assumed that Mai-Kudandan had done so, the mid-1800s onwards saw substantial circumscription of her powers (Yaya Duduwa, an elderly concubine, 25 November 2000; chapter 4).

62. A permanent capital and palace did not emerge in Dar Fur until the end of the nineteenth century.

63. Cooper cautions that associations between the Iya and *karuwai* ("prostitutes") are recent: "Much of the literature on . . . the iya . . . has assumed an automatic association . . . with karuwanci . . . and unmarried women, an association that seems to have resulted from the degeneration of the office . . . to a kind of representative of *karuwai* in post-jihad northern Nigeria. With the elimination of many titled positions of political power for women in the emirates, the [iya] . . . was often retained only to provide a liaison between the authorities and the karuwa population, for whom bori provides community, spiritual support, and material resources, and who often use bori dancing as a form of entertainment. In Maradi there is not now nor was there in the past any automatic association of the iya with women who practice karuwanci; in fact it was another titled woman, the magajiya, who was in charge of the courtesans. . . . The iya was . . . indirectly associated with them because bori cult members could . . . practice karuwanci on the side. A few rural women who prefer to remain unmarried for a time have nevertheless been housed and protected by the iya over the years particularly if they are . . . members of the bori cult toward whom she has a special responsibility" (1997, 27). Pittin asserts, however, that the person who was

"nominally or actively, leader of the spirit-possession cult" and who acted as a mediator and negotiator "between the masculine power structure and the *karuwai*," was the Magajiyar Karuwai, not simply a Magajiya, though the title may be been shortened to Magajiya in vernacular usage (1983, 298). Hence, perhaps the Magajiya to which Cooper (1997), Echard (1991), and others refer to was the leading titleholder within the structure of *karuwanci* itself? Indeed Echard writes that the title is "used in Hausa political chieftainships to designate the mother or the sister of a political chief" whereas in Ader "it denotes more commonly a woman who runs a house of prostitution" (1991, 116).

64. Sarkin Daura, 4 December 2003.

65. The Hausa word *magajiya* is the feminine counterpart of *magaji*, and means a "woman inheriting, heiress," a secondary definition being "elder sister" (Abraham 1962 [1946]). Abraham additionally cites two definitions for the title "Magajiya." The first is "title for Chief's mother or his elder sister or his father's younger sister," a definition harking back to matrilineal succession practices. The second is "title for senior procuress," perhaps pointing to the matrilineal power of arranging for extramarital and premarital sexual liaisons, prerogatives beyond paternal law or authority. Bargery 1934 has the additional entry, *magajiyar k'arya*, defined simply as an "official position and title amongst women." But the word *k'arya* is complex. Depending upon how it is intoned, it can mean, among other things, "a bitch," an "immoral . . . [or] quarrelsome woman," a "small hole dug where iron ore is found," or "a lie . . . [or] mistake" (Bargery 1934). The Sarauniya also attended to "all royal daughters with regard to marriage" and took responsibility for "other royal wives whenever they were away from the palace" (Mack 1991, 112). Bargery defines the latter title as "A female ruler, in her own right" or "An official position of a woman amongst devotees of bori" (1934).

66. Most top female officials lived in the palace and, according to Johnson, were "wives," even though they were not intimate with the king (1937 [1921], 63). These included the Iya Oba, a woman who represented (but was not) the king's biological mother, and the Iya Kere, a woman who guarded the king's treasures and whose tasks and powers were similar to the Kano palace concubine Mai-Soron Baki.

67. This passage is my paraphrased translation from the following passage in Lebeuf 1969, 127: "Elle l'accompagne dans toutes les reunion officielles, intervient dans la nomination d'un tres haut dignitaire, le Chef des Armees, et a son mot a dire dans les affairs de justice. Elle percoit les redevances d'un certain nombre de localites dont elle nomme directement les representants aupres du gouvernement central ; ce sont Guedaba, Nkarse et Guechi a Longone-Birni, Klessoum a Kousseri. Mais sa principale fonction est d'etre a l'entiere disposition du Prince."

68. In ancient Egypt, the second and third positions involved royal incest and were occupied by the same woman (Murdock 1959, 146).

69. This pattern whereby the most important royal female quarters are located centrally was also the case in the nineteenth-century palace of Dar Fur (see O'Fahey 1980, 25).

70. The Mai-Kudandan of Emir Sanusi, Amina Abubakar, born during Abbas (13 November 2000). A similar practice obtained in late-1500s Buganda where a chief chose certain "wives" (freeborn and enslaved) to accompany him on military expeditions where they "guarded the war gods, cooked, sharpened spears or reeds, performed religious rituals, and at times attended to the wounded" (Musisi 1991, 781–82).

71. Amina Abubakar noted that bori had always been done in Yelwa (13 November 2000). The present emir's wife from Katsina, Hajiyya Abba, noted that historically the Sarkin (king of) Bori in Katsina was turbaned by royal palace women, suggesting a similar scenario obtained in

Kano. At least after British colonization in 1903, Katsina women waited for the king (or emir) to leave before they engaged in bori practices. She noted that in Kano, royal women invited practitioners from bori to attend Katsina bori specialists and vice versa. More recently in Kano, royal concubines conducted bori services in Yelwa after the emir left for his nearby farm (Gandun Nassarawa) on Sundays. It is unclear if the Kano and Katsina women waited for their emirs to leave because the emirs would forbid bori (as an Islamic practice), or because it was customary to do so.

72. Spaulding goes on to say, "The image of the king as a serenely disinterested reapportioner of food was reinforced by the tenet of customary orthodoxy that he himself never ate. . . . Some of the imperfectly documented court rituals of Sinnar should probably be interpreted in this light. In the rainlands, for example, the lords lit the first fires of the year, which cleared brushland for farming. . . . The sultan, at least once at his coronation and perhaps yearly thereafter, broke ground for cultivation with his own hand, thus acquiring the title of Badi, 'farmer'" (1985, 127).

Imam Imoru similarly notes that in nineteenth-century Hausaland, "[t]here are many towns in which this day for sowing is a festive occasion because in Hausaland the rain announcing the time for sowing falls on one day. All the people of each land travel five, six, or seven days, and then all sow on the same day. On that day the ruler mounts his horse and rides with all his courtiers, slaves, wives, and young maid servants to his farm, *gandu,* where they sow the seeds as if it's a special ceremony. . . . [A]ny of these people who have no seeds ask the ruler for some, and he distributes them" (Ferguson 1973, 61). Here, food and the distribution of seeds are the symbolic basis of the kingship itself, to the extent that leadership derives from provision, and provision ideally involves the just distribution of earthly fruits. Grain food provisioning for all, then, is the mythical-practical basis of Sudanic kingship (see also O'Fahey 1980, 20).

Similar to many other Sudanic contexts, the mouth of a king was veiled, much symbolic importance attached to the invisibility of the ruler's mouth (see also Murdock 1959; O'Fahey 1980, 22; Rufa'i 1987, 144; Spaulding 1985). Might this covering-over of the mouth also be attributed in part to expressing divinity itself as the ability to do without food; that the ultimate provider-as-leader feeds all, but does not himself need to be fed?

73. His Highness Alhaji Ado Bayero, 24 November 2000. I want to thank Philip Shea, who alerted me to this ritual during a discussion on kingship and planting (14 November 2000). In about 1970, he attended what turned out to be the last of these planting rituals in Kano.

74. Dmochowski (1990, 47–48) describes these single women as "harlots," an impoverished term that occludes the sense of female fertility as divine *in and of itself.*

2. Fecundity, Indigo Dyeing, and the Gendering of Eunuchs

1. Indeed, the much larger amount of material available required that the nineteenth century be addressed in two chapters. Of course this is a common problem. Bay discusses a similar dilemma with respect to documenting the early history of Dahomey prior to the 1720s (1998, 40).

2. This discussion is based upon the works of Hunwick (1985, 1994), Last (1979, 1983), Palmer (1967), Barkindo (1983), Philips (1989), Clarke (1982), and Fage (1969), and is a condensed version of material presented in Nast (1996).

3. Population figures are taken from guesstimates presented in Frishman 1977, 210.

4. Sources used in this section include Palmer 1967 (1928), Fika 1978, and Lavers 1981. According to the KC, Rumfa authored twelve innovations in the city-state. These are listed here in abbreviated fashion in the order obtaining in the KC (only some of these are discussed): (1)

Built the palace-exurb; (2) expanded the circular city walls; (3) built the central market; (4) embellished on the state cavalry; (5) began the seizing of first-born virgins from the town of Indabo, southeast of Kano; (6) was the first to have 1,000 wives; (7) instituted wife seclusion; (8) created the Tara-ta-Kano (the Kano Nine), an all-male state council; (9) used long horns in kingly processions; (10) wore ostrich-feather sandals; (11) celebrated the Islamic festivals; and (12) appointed eunuchs to state offices.

5. I am grateful to Professor Michael Bonine of the University of Arizona, Tucson, for measuring the palace orientation for me (see Nast 1996, 73 for details).

6. My own calculations, given the areal extent of the Kano palace, is that no more than three to four hundred concubines could have been accommodated comfortably in the palace interior; most were set apart from the four legal wives. Though both groups had numerous slave girls at their disposal, concubines were also slaves. The KC's figure of one thousand may euphemistically refer to the total number of women residing in the palace interior, which could easily have reached one thousand. Visitors to the Dahomey palace in the early 1700s, for example, noted that the Dahomean king had more than two thousand wives in the palace; yet only a fraction of these women were conjugal with the king, many being either the king's servants or those of other important palace women (see Bay 1998, 51).

7. The introduction of clitoridectomies during Rumfa's reign is recorded in Rattray's translations of *Hausa Folklore Customs, Proverbs, Etc.* where Rumfa is disparaged as an un-Islamic king and where palace women remained uncircumcised until "learned men [the Fulani] were found in Kano, who had renounced the world, who feared Allah" (1913, 13, 22). Field evidence indicates that Kano palace women are circumcised, a sign of Islamic piety; whether or not clitoridectomies were introduced into the palace only after the Fulani took over is not known.

The practice of clitoridectomy was apparently introduced into Kano from Morocco and contrasts with the female infibulation practices of the Sudan. According to one informant, clitoridectomies make girls less libidinous and, therefore, of greater moral character than men. In the palace the procedure is done on the third day after an infant girl's birth, when her tonsils are removed. Janice Boddy (1989), working in a different and much later Sudanic and Islamic context, argues that female circumcision (in this case, the more radical procedure of infibulation) makes maleness and femaleness visibly and mutually exclusive, symbolically and practically: Protruding female parts (understood as male) are removed for the same reasons that the "female" folds on male parts are excised, the surgeries ritualistically purifying the two "sexes" in body and, hence, spirit.

8. Kingly seclusion was practiced, for example, in the fourteenth-century Sudanic kingdom of Dongola. The geographer al-Bakawi writes, for example, that, "it is among their customs to venerate their king as a divinity, and they observe the fiction that he never eats. Thus one brings him food in secret, and if any of his subjects sees him, he is killed instantly" (cited in O'Fahey and Spaulding 1974, 18). That the king may not be seen eating—also the case for an Asante paramount chief—resonates with an earlier point that the king in many Sudanic contexts is represented as a farmer and provider, and not a consumer, of grain (see chapter 1). Spaulding writes similarly that seventeenth-century Funj sultans "lived in a world of restricted access and circumscribed physical movement. Not only were the number of intimates with whom he had contact limited, but also many of them had access to him by virtue of their titled position in the state or family relationship rather than at his pleasure" (1985, 130). Bay records analogous practices associated with the non-Islamic kingship of Dahomey as early as the 1700s, including kingly seclusion and the donning of clothing that obscured the king's face, both

practices mystifying his person (1998, 67, 112). Musisi provides a more practical explanation in the context of Buganda: After various clan heads' geopolitical authority was usurped and centralized kingly authority instituted in its stead, "[n]ew laws forbade them [clan heads] from meeting the king face to face and from meeting in one place at the same time, thus inhibiting the growth of possible political plots to overthrow him" (1991, 769). See also Kaplan 1997a and Murdock 1959, 35–36.

9. Nineteenth-century data suggest that a Fulani ruler built a granary house (kudandan) abutting his quarters for a female spirit. It is unclear if he was rebuilding an earlier spirit house or if he was building something new, which is more likely, given the outcry that he practiced bori and the fact that he built a partition wall effectively shielding his quarters from those of resident clerics and scholars (chapter 3).

10. In this sense, Rufa'i's contention that the early nineteenth-century Fulani reformist, Emir Ibrahim Dabo, was the first to build a palace Quranic school in the Kano palace is partially correct (1987, 191). The school Dabo built seems to have been a reconstruction of the place first instituted by Kisoki. The nineteenth-century palace school in the Sudanic kingdom of Dar Fur was also rebuilt on a much older site by a sultan who, like Dabo, was reformist.

11. If Last's conjecture is correct, the marriage would have taken place after the Askia came to power in 1493, toward the end of Rumfa's reign.

12. The KC records that Auwa's brother, Koli, achieved considerable power and "was much respected by the Sarki [king]; he came to have power over the whole country" (113). His power suggests that matrilineal decision-making may have held considerable sway during and just after Rumfa's reign. When Kisoki's son, Yakufu, became king, tensions evidently flared between the Kano Nine and the Queen Mother, who had another candidate in mind, another one of her sons. Accordingly, in tandem with her brother (Koli), Auwa engineered a coup, initiating a short-lived civil war. Koli was killed and Yakufu was asked to re-assume power, but he refused. Yakufu's son was installed in his stead but he, too, was overthrown, presumably by Auwa's allies, since the next successor was Auwa's son, Abubakr Kado.

13. Madaki was perhaps the most important title held by a royal woman. It may initially have been reserved for the Queen Mother, though as of 1989, it was not; by then, the title was held by a royal widow (daughter of Abbas) who had been the late emir of Katsina's wife.

14. The four titled eunuchs assigned to be "chiefs of the treasury," Turaki, Aljira, Al-Soro, and Kashe Kusa, apparently held different responsibilities related to treasury goods, presumably not including grain storage and administration, which I hypothesized were overseen by palace concubines (chapter 1). The name *Turaki* may be related to the Katsina title Turaku. Bargery claims that the Kano derivative of this word was Sarkin Tike and that the official headed dealers of sheep and goats (1934). If so, this eunuch may have administered animals tendered in-kind to the king. The word *Aljira* arguably derives from the words *al* and *jira*. *Al* is used in many Arabic loan words in Hausa and represents the Arabic article. One of the most archaic meanings of *jira* is "keeping watch on (property)" (Bargery 1934), Skinner's comparative dictionary showing some affinity for this word with an Egyptian root that means "wait, remain" (1996). Thus, Aljira may have been he who kept watch over a particular treasury good or perhaps he who was given ultimate jurisdiction over treasury security. Al-soro would be "he who looks after the soro [room]." The exact nature of the room is unclear. It may have been the king's personal quarters wherein were stored some armaments or perhaps some sort of treasury room that held things given to the king specially as gifts. *Kashe Kusa* might refer to many things, depending, like most Hausa words, on how it is intoned, something not captured in Palmer's rendering of the KC. One

tonal rendering of the word *kashe* has to do with money and means "to spend" (see Robinson 1925). *Kusa*, on the other hand, refers to proximity or nearness, suggesting that this official was a, or the, palace accountant.

15. One of the KC's longer passages describing Rumfa's innovations states that he "began the custom of giving to eunuchs the offices of state, among them [the titles-offices of], Dan Kusuba, Dan Jigawa, Dan Tarbana, Sarkin Gabbas, Sarkin Tudu, Sarkin Ruwa, Maaji, Sarkin Bai, Sarkin Kofa. There were four eunuchs left without a title. He said to them, 'I make you chiefs of the Treasury.' The name of one was Turaki, another was Aljira; the names of the other two were Al-Soro and Kashe Kusa" (Palmer 1967 [1928], 112).

16. See Cohen 1977 and Kaplan 1997b for discussions of the importance of Queen Mothers in African Islamic and non-Islamic state systems. Cohen's work is particularly important in that it deals with a non-Islamic area just east of Kano, the Pabir kingdom of Biu.

17. Information on Queen Amina is generalized and contradictory. See, for example, Abubakr 1992 and Sweetman 1984.

18. The production of eunuchs in Africa was geographically dispersed since at least the eleventh century. Four major source regions for Mediterranean markets are identified by Hogendorn (2000): Ethiopia and Nubia; the east coast, as far south as present-day Kenya; the eastern Sudanic region, including such places as Baghirmi, Dongola, Dar Fur, Kordofan, and Sinnar; and the western Sudanic and Saharan regions of southern Algeria, northern Niger, Mali, and Nigeria. Most source regions were in non-Islamic areas, the eunuchs then transported to various Islamic markets.

19. See Hogendorn 2000 for a fascinating review of the different types and geographies of castration and eunuchism. Death rates were much higher in the warmer, moister climes of West Africa, with certain centers specializing in one of two forms of castration. The more radical involved removal of the penis and testicles, less radical forms involving removal of one or the other. After the eleventh century, sub-Saharan Africa became the leading source of eunuchs for Mediterranean Islam, leading to an interesting racialization of the castration process. Whereas the "white eunuchs" of the Ottoman Empire had typically undergone the less radical form of castration, black eunuchs underwent the most radical form of castration (Hogendorn 2000, 50–51).

20. The photographs had not been catalogued by the Royal Geographic Society and therefore had no content information.

21. For details on the landscape reconstruction process, see Nast 1996.

22. In Palmer's translation of the KC, the text reads *mainya*, a word nonexistent in all dictionaries consulted. I thus interpret the word as either *manya*, which means powerful, or *maina*, which derives from a Kanuri-derived Hausa word that refers to the son of a prince. East, translating the KC into Hausa, uses the term *manya* (1971).

23. The word *san* is a contraction of the word *Sarkin*, meaning "king of." Attaching *Sarkin* to these two Turaki titles bestows upon them special honors. See Shea's discussion and chart of all the ways in which the title Sarki is used in Hausa contexts (1975). The word *kuka* presumably refers to the large baobab (considered kingly and divine) that grew right behind the king's quarters. It would not have been unusual for the king to meet with his councillors under this tree.

24. According to the KC, Muhammad Zaki was the last Hausa king to award political power to the eunuch title Turaki Mainya, though the title and allusions to its importance are made until Fulani rule in 1807. The KC claims that it was not until the reign of the penultimate precolonial Fulani emir that a Turaki would again hold substantial power. In this case, however, the title was awarded to the emir's son and not a eunuch, a switching of entitlement between freeborn and

slave that occurred frequently throughout Kano history in accordance with changing political contexts and needs.

25. Hajiyya Abba remarked that tensions between eunuchs and royal women were common (13 November 2000). She relayed a story to illustrate her point: When she was growing up in the Katsina palace, there was a eunuch who did not cooperate with one of the palace concubines. The concubine complained bitterly to the emir of Katsina who counseled her: "Give him a *babban riga* (a male gown of prestige for men) and he will be your friend." She did so, and the problem was solved. It should be noted that in a patronage system gift-giving to someone from whom you desire political allegiance is expected. Nineteenth-century Kano palace data also indicate that eunuch–palace women relations could be strained. Elderly royal women and male slaves relayed stories of, for example, nineteenth-century eunuchs who tattled on, and physically disciplined, royal women; others spoke of how palace wives and concubines cultivated eunuch alliances through gift-giving.

26. Gendered differences among eunuchs was hinted at during discussions with a twentieth-century slave who held the powerful "male" eunuch title of Sallama. At one point, Sallama pointed out whimsically that a male slave title created in the nineteenth century and probably held at least initially by a eunuch (King of the Grain) was not for a "real" man. King of Grains lived in a compound in the "female" western side of the palace where he administered grain storage, traditionally the domain of royal women. Although at the highest level he was overseen by Shamaki, he reported directly to Uwar Soro.

27. According to Bargery the primary meaning of *Iya* is "[a] Mother, maternal aunt, or any female relative in loco parentis; also used in vocative to these and to any female about the same age as one's mother or older (= *inna; vide uwa*)" (1934). *Inna* was the most important female titleholder in Gobir. According to Skinner, *Inna* derives from *'iy* (mother) + *na* (my) (1996). The title *Iya* may originate from the Hausa kingdom of Daura, the mythic precursor of Kano (see Palmer 1967, 145), though its relation to the Yoruba female title Iya is unknown.

28. As Last's 1983 work makes clear, Palmer's English translation does not mention that the market was for eunuchs, whereas East's 1971 Hausa version does. Nonetheless, Last is incorrect in claiming that the text cites Madaki Auwa as creator of the market. Both Palmer and East cite Iya Lamis as the market's originator. It is not clear what kind of international purchase the market had, or if it merely served local aristocratic needs. Bay notes, for example, that by the early 1700s, troublesome female ahosi (dependents) of the king of Dahomey were sold off by the monarchy to the overseas slave trade (1998, 48).

29. Royal women's participation in commercial slavery was not uncommon. Bay notes, for example, that as early as the 1720s King Agaja and his wives tried to monopolize commercial slave trading, his ahosi (female dependents, not wives per se) traveling to and from the coast to complete transactions (1998, 104–5). Throughout the 1700s kingly patronage dependents (men and women) traded slaves in the Whydah market, the king normally garnering 10 to 38 percent of commercial slavery revenues.

30. Unlike other cultural or religious contexts, such as the Chinese or Byzantine, eunuchs in Islamic contexts were typically manufactured in regions beyond Islamic areas (Hogendorn 2000). Thus, while "male" eunuchs may have been manufactured from slave stock in the palace community, there is no evidence to suggest this.

31. Eunuchs were not used much in the Dahomey kingdom until after Agaja's death in 1740. Over the next half century eunuchs held considerable powers that were gendered. Those in closest attendance to the king wore female garb and worked in tandem with women in the palace

interior. Others served as tattletales and spies, still others holding titled positions of state (see Bay 1998, 113).

32. Royal female elders recalled at the turn of the twentieth century that they played amidst dye pit ruins, the majority of the area by then having been converted into a dynastic cemetery. Conversations with the Sarkin Gini (King Builder) and Maje Sirdi (Master of the Saddles) in November 2000 showed that the Fulani may have only briefly used the pits, later subsidizing men in commercial dye pit operations in the city.

33. Shea notes that the two most important plants used in Hausaland to dye cloth indigo were also used in Morocco and Thailand. He writes, "[T]he presumption is that the use of these plants began in the East Indies during ancient times and spread from there to much of the rest of the world. As early as 450 B.C. Herodotus described the use of indigo, and Marco Polo also reported about the use of indigo" (1975, 177).

34. In the late nineteenth century, King Njoya, in present-day Cameroon, used Hausa expertise and techniques to set up male-led indigo dyeing practices in front of his palace and, later, in the city. Some of the cloth was reserved for the queen mother. Earlier, indigo-dyed Royal Cloth was used in ransoms, rituals, and bridewealth, uses that hint at earlier uses of the cloth in the Hausa region (see Harris 1985, 165).

35. Clark provides no historical information about this practice, though from other comments it appears that the association of indigo dyeing with slave women is at least as old as the mid-nineteenth century (1997, 1999).

36. Slave women were apparently involved in many aspects of textile production since at least the mid-1800s. Slave women and children harvested the cotton, and slave women ginned, carded, and spun it (Clark 1999, 71, 72). The indigo, "grew principally along the Senegal and Faleme Rivers. A few agriculturalists, primarily Soninke, planted some bushes for local use. . . . [It] did not enter significantly into trade" (63). Elsewhere he writes, "Informants insisted that previously carding and spinning were done only by slave women who spent most of their dry season time in spinning to produce an adequate supply of cotton thread for the male slave weavers. . . . Weavers charged a small fee to weave the cotton. . . . The thread's owner then sewed together the strips. Dyeing, particularly indigo-dyeing, occurred in Soninke villages by Soninke women dyers, also of slave descent" (Clark 1997, 14).

37. Balfour-Paul records that "[t]he information obtained from the dyers of Almyu [a village in Morocco] probably applies to indigo dyeing throughout the rural region. The main task of the specialist indigo dyer was to dye wool yarn supplied to her at the weekly market by the weaver, who gave her skeins some distinguishing mark. . . . The dyer would take the yarn home for dyeing and return it to the weaver on the following market day. She would also dye small pieces of coloured cloth in indigo for headscarves" (1997, 1047). Balfour-Paul also notes that preparing the lye in the vats of urban Morocco (especially Marrakech, Meknes, and Rabat) was uniquely similar to techniques uses in "Nigeria, and other West African countries today," indicating the long-distance trade connections between the two regions (105).

38. Sadiya Ado Bayero, 28 November 2003.

39. Indigo-dyed Royal Cloth was the third of five most important textiles associated with the Jukun Court.

40. Analogously, Nachtigal noted in 1870 that the highest quality cloth of Borno never reached the market, as it was made by Hausa slaves (women?) working in private houses (Nachtigal 1971).

41. Sadiya Ado Bayero, November 2000, and 28 November 2003. Sadiya often peeked into the chambers when she was a child and in 2000 revisited it. Alhaji Ado Sanusi remembers puzzling as a young boy (also sneaking in) about the origins of the sand and what it meant, surmising that the sand came from a river (20 December 2003). The sand formed a sort of seven-by-nine-foot carpet in the middle of the room.

42. Imam Imoru provides some details for these other dyes (Ferguson 1973, 308–9). He relays that "[t]hey dye with the stalk of the *dafi* plant, *karan dafi*: it is a type of guineacorn with red bark, *bawo*. The bark is pounded, mixed with water, and then natron, *kanwa*, is added to it. When a white thing is dipped into the solution it immediately turns red. That is how red dye is made. A lot of this plant is grown in Hausaland because the dye is used frequently: tanners, *majema*, buy the stalks and dye leather red with them; and dyers color dum-palm fronds with it to decorate mats and large straw hats. Many other things.

"There is a plant called *turi*, which is also Canba, *dan Canba*, after a place in Bornu. It is used, [with?] lime juice, *lemo*, to dye things yellow, and they are very beautiful. When '*dan Canba* is mixed with water, natron, and lime juice, the mixture will dye things green.

"Yellow dye is also made from turmeric, *gangamo*, as well as from the *rawaya* root."

43. Class-based color restrictions are, of course, in keeping with the sumptuary prerogatives of many hierarchical societies.

44. Malam Nuhu Limawa, from Limawa village, Dutse emirate, 8 December 2003. According to him, any woman from Limawa could come to work in the dyeing yard, there being one woman in charge of it. One could approximate that there were at least one hundred pits in the yard, each one measuring about one meter across. Within the pits were set very long tubular pots, Malam Nuhu raising his hand high above his head to indicate their length. Dyeing apparently occurred here for many years, if not centuries, the yard's topography built up by pot shards and ash into a plateau-like area, similar to what we saw along the River Jambo. Today, the area is farmed, sorghum stubs poking up in between the dye pits/pots, now used as outdoor toilets. Malam Nuhu explained that men appropriated the dyeing yard during or after the Kano civil war (1893–94). When asked why they did so, he shrugged and said, "Sabo da sun fi karfe" (Because they are stronger). Perhaps this transpired because Dutse emirate sided with the rebels in Kano, Kano men sent to take over the Dutse region's female-controlled dyeing yards. Or perhaps Limawa men took them over due to the economic exigencies of the war.

45. Maje Sirdi's duties fall under the general jurisdiction of one of the three most powerful male titleholders, Shamaki, a position created by Kutumbi. See Stilwell's 1999 dissertation for additional information on primarily nineteenth-century male slave hierarchies in the Kano palace.

46. In traditional birthing rituals the kwatanniya would be set atop rocks and filled with water. Herbs, leaves, roots, and branches were boiled in the water, which would then be used as a medicinal bath. Beforehand, however, a good portion of the boiled water was set aside for the birth mother to drink. The mother drank the water for forty days after giving birth to purify her milk. Some women opted to drink the water for three months. The water remaining was then used to bathe in every morning and every evening for forty days. The water would be vigorously dashed onto the woman's body using branches of the nim tree to aid her recovery and to increase circulation. Today, few women carry out the ritual for forty days, if at all. Those few who choose to do so use plastic or other modern containers and rarely continue the process for more than two weeks. Most of this information comes from Maje Sirdi and Hajiyya Rabi'u (25 November 2000). See Ferguson 1973, 249–52, for Imam Imoru's nineteenth-century account of birthing

rituals in Kano and Wall 1988, 229–31, for a modern analysis of some medical dangers associated with Hausa birthing rituals.

47. Communal cooking disappeared after the British outlawed grain taxation and slavery. Slave estates had been crucial to securing adequate grain supplies for the palace (chapter 4).

48. Even though *karofi*—the term that first captured my attention—is understood to mean dye *pits*, there is some etymological evidence that the word bears earlier associations with indigo dyeing in *pots*. Shea, for example, surmises that *karofi* is a blend of two Mande words: *kara fye* (dye + place), which he interprets in the context of dye pits only (1975). Skinner's 1996 work, however, indicates that the Mande term *fye* refers *first* to "a calabash utensil" and only secondarily to an "open space," while *fi* means dark blue. If we then transliterate *karofi* to mean "dyeing + blue/calabash," we come historically closer to the origins of cloth dyeing, namely the use of calabash-like containers or pots for indigo dyeing. Over time, these containers were presumably replaced by large pots modeled after those innovated in the palace for the production of large food quantities and birthing ceremonies.

Skinner's work may also indicate links between the Hausa word for indigo (*baba*) and the correlative term in Nupe, *babari*. Recall that the first eunuchs (*babbani* pl.) given to Queen Amina in the 1400s from the king of Nupeland may have derived from the Malian empire. Might eunuchs and indigo have been introduced into Hausaland at the same time from the west, particularly Mali, via Nupeland? Renne notes that the Bunu Yoruba traded early on with Nupeland, indicating that women-run dyeing practices may have been introduced into Kano trade networks with the Nupe even earlier than when eunuchs were introduced (1995).

Though I am not arguing for an exclusively western provenance for the dyeing industry, I am wondering whether or not eunuchs, brought in during Islamization through Nupeland, did not bring with them certain dyeing traditions. Shea's comprehensive work makes it abundantly clear that influences on the industry came from both west and east. A large number of words related to dyeing, for example, derive from the Kanuri of the kingdom of Borno to the east, and from thence to Arabia and India. Shea writes: "The Sanskrit and Arabic roots of the Hausa word *rini* are also the roots of the word *analine* (indigo-derived chemicals) as found in English, and in slightly different forms, in several other European languages. There is thus a substantial case that the knowledge of using indigo for dyeing spread to both West Africa and to Europe through Arabic-speaking peoples" (1975, 146).

49. In Dal town, a servant of the village head known as King of Indigo, assisted by his own cadre of servants, supervised and certified sales of indigo in the central market. The King of Indigo received a commission on sales, but the village head received all indigo collected by the servants that had fallen onto the ground during the day. At the time, two thousand donkey loads of indigo was sold in one week, enough falling onto the ground to fill two dye pits. Might something similar have obtained in the palace, with the indigo collected being carried back by eunuchs or slaves from the market to the Kano palace dyeing yard?

50. Abandonment of the dye pits and other palace landscape changes affecting royal concubine's spaces and powers are discussed in chapters 3 and 4.

51. It seems that since at least the nineteenth century, cloth dyers were threatened by the thought of slaves carrying out cloth dyeing. Shea writes, "There was a slight prejudice shared by many against teaching slaves how to dye, or allowing them to do so, but in some of the areas which experienced rapid growth . . . slaves did do some of the dyeing" (1975, 202). Slaves and sons, however, would have been the primary labor deployed by women business owners.

52. From Liberia came meliguette. Hiskett notes in the case of Yorubaland and Nupeland that "a link of some dimension, however tenuous, did extend from Tripoli, through Hausaland and down to the Benue long before the 10/16 century, although, it is certainly not to be assumed . . . that there is now . . . an earlier date for the emergence of the major Hausa commercial centers [like Kano] than the 9/15 century" (1981, 74). Drawing on secondary evidence, he suggests that some sort of precursor route from the south to Kano may have existed as early as the 800s (75).

3. Great Transformations

1. Last comments on the jihadic leaders' assessments of sultanates near to where the jihad began, comments that just as easily speak to jihadic assessments of Kano: "Conditions in these eighteenth-century Sulanates are described only in sources committed to Islam and the jihad. Despite this, the charges of non-Islamic government laid against the Hausa states by the Shaikh [Usman dan Fodio] in *Kitab al-farq* are likely to be substantially true: the illegalities are familiar. The question is the extent to which these illegalities were practised. The question is unanswerable, and did not need an answer: illegalities are the way of the unbelievers. Clearly local practice overruled the Shari'a in several spheres, such as taxation, music and women, methods of justice, conscription and appointments of officials" (1967, lxviii).

2. See M. G. Smith's discussion of the jihad in Kano (1997, 185–270). See also Garba 1986. There were three main groups of Fulani involved in the jihad (Last 1967, xxii). The Toronkawa clan from which the jihadic leaders derived claimed to have more Arab ancestry and members of the clan were renown "as Islamic scholars throughout West Africa, becoming almost a caste in areas where caste-consciousness exists." The Sullabawa, in contrast, were said to be half Mandingo. Both groups, though not deemed Fulani, spoke Fulfulde and they shared "some Fulani characteristics, including a preference for marrying Fulani" (lxxii). The third group, the "cattle Fulani," was made up of various clans that had geographically distinct (though fluid) grazing areas. See Last 1967, lxxii–lxxv, for a detailed description of the clans and their interrelationships.

3. See Fika 1978 for a bibliography of early scholarly works on the jihad in Kano. His overview of the Fulani who participated in the Kano jihad is instructive: "During Rumfa's time and in subsequent centuries, there were at least twelve principal 'clans' [of Fulani] settled in Kano territory. There is evidence that the various clans were frequently on the move to or from Borno, Bagirmi and elsewhere but at the time of the jihad, as at present, the more important groups frequently took their names from the Habe towns near which the headquarters of the 'clan' was situated. Like the indigenous Habe and other immigrant groups, the Fulani were subject to the Habe chiefs. The less nomadic among them would seem to have intermarried with the Hausawa and in many cases had given up their nomadic life.

"At the outbreak of the Fulani jihad in 1804 only six of the principal Fulani or quasi-Fulani 'clans' participated in the uprising. As soon as the news spread of the Fulani victory against Gobir in June 1804, these clans sent a delegation to the Sheikh in Sokoto asking for a flag and his sanction for the conquest of Kano. The major groups involved were the Mundubawa or Modibbawa settled principally in Birnin Kano but of Borno origin (Fulata-Borno), their name derived from the Fulani word *Modibbo* or learned man; the Sullubawa who were the most numerous 'clan' with their main base at Kiru thirty-five miles south-west of Kano; the light-skinned Danejawa at Zuwa thirty miles south-west of Kano; the Yolawa—a section of the Ba'awa Fulani—from Yola to the east of Kano; the Dambazawa at Dambazau north of the city; and the Jobawa basd at Utei thirty miles east-south-east of Kano" (16).

4. Technically, only the Shehu or Sheikh was the "Amir al-mu'minin." As Burnham and Last (1994, 317 n. 4) explain, "In Fulfulde, the Amir al-mu'minin was Lamido Julbe, in Hausa Sarkin Musulmi [lit. King of Muslims]; only in English was that position termed 'Sultan.' 'Caliph,' for head of 'the Caliphate,' is somewhat of a neologism in Sokoto; 'the Sokoto Caliphate' was introduced in print only in 1966 (by Last) to describe what was otherwise apt to be labeled 'Fulani empire,' but it has since become standard usage."

5. See Kanya-Forstner and Lovejoy 1994, 8. While they deem the caliphate a "state," I prefer to consider it a quasi-state entity because it was so loosely consolidated and because key apparatuses of state (courts, the army, administrative structures) were autonomous across emirates.

6. The Fulani word for Hausa is *Habe*. According to Last, the terms *Hausa, Kado,* and *Habe* were almost never used in the literature of the jihad. Instead, the Fulani cast the Hausa as "Sudanese" and as "Black": "the term 'land of the Blacks' (bilad al sudan) had classical authority, being used in travellers' accounts and discussion on the state of Islam" (1967, lxxvi). Smith, in contrast, claims that the term *Habe* had specific utility in Kano, namely it applied to those non-Muslims denied participation in the Kano government and placed under Fulani chiefs (1997, 204–5). Those Hausa who allied themselves to the Fulani and who supported the jihad were called Hausawa and were not liable to direct administration or the harsh treatment given to the Habe. The Hausa who aided the Fulani on behalf of the Ciroma dan Mama were further distinguished by being nominated, Kutumbawa, a reference to the fact that the Ciroma was related to the previous Kutumbi dynasty. Today, the word *Habe* is used commonly to derogate someone whose Islam seems less orthodox than it should be, such that he or she is not recognizably a believer.

7. From the *Kitab al-farq* attributed to the Shehu and translated by Hiskett (1960), cited in Smith 1997, 206. See Last 1987 (1974) for an overview of changes in the Shehu's political-religious life and thought. In his early years he worked preaching Islam to a growing number of largely rural followers. Later, he became a militant and idealist jihadist, after the jihad adopting a more politically pragmatic stance on a number of extant, non-Islamic practices.

8. Last points out that the city of Sokoto was not associated with the jihad until twentieth-century colonial rule. He writes: "In the common phrases 'Sokoto jihad,' 'Sokoto empire,' the term 'Sokoto' is an anachronism. Founded as a camp late in 1809—over five years after the jihad began—the town of Sokoto for most of the nineteenth century was not the residence of the Caliph or his court. It did, however, have the houses of the Shaikh, of his sons and their councillors; it was the largest town in the area. It thus became in 1903 the headquarters of a province named after it. But the term is alien: the 'Sokoto jihad' is the jihad of the Shaikh, the 'Sokoto empire' is the Shaikh's Community; the 'Sultan of Sokoto' is the Commander of the Believers and the Sokoto townspeople are Kadirawa. Only the town is Sokoto" (1967, lix). See Last 1967, 42–45, for historical details about the two administrative divisions.

9. These authors go on to say: "Otherwise many simply kept traveling, only to settle once their learning and their reputation was established. . . . There were scholars in the cities, but they tended to be Wangara or Hausa, who also provided the various religious services the ruler and his court required. . . . Fulbe [Fulani] scholars might go to the towns to learn or to get books, but few took up permanent residence or employment there.

"The success of the jihad therefore posed two distinct questions for the Fulbe. First should they take over the great cities—Birnin [the walled city of] Kano, Birnin Katsina, Birnin Kebbi, Birnin Zazzau, Birnin Ngazaragamu—and move into the abandoned palaces of the Hausa kings and their councilors? Second, where there were no such great ancient cities, should the jihad forces now build new ones? The answer to both questions was an unequivocal 'yes.' The development of a distinct urban Fulbe . . . culture . . . was a matter of policy, consciously promoted. By settling the Fulbe and Tuareg pastoralists, 'Uthman's [the Shehu's] son Muhammad Bello sought . . . to secure the perimeter of the new state with a line of strongholds (*ribat; thagr*)" (326–27).

10. Burnham and Last (1994) make important distinctions in the political structures and qualities of states conquered by the Fulani, dividing them into four groups: Kano, Zaria, and Katsina (type Ia) are typified as having had well-developed urban and political infrastructures wherein office holders lived in the city and administered their domains through intermediaries. These three places are also characterized in part as having good levels of agricultural production and well-established industries and trade networks. What is discussed in the context of Kano, then, cannot be universalized for all states that made up the caliphate.

As these authors also note, the Shehu's successor and son, Muhammad Bello, hoped that by occupying and creating cities throughout the caliphate and intensifying the use of slaves for agricultural and other kinds of labors, he might "create, through education for a cadre now freed from herding and other manual work . . . the administrative, judicial, and military staff required to run the new caliphate."

11. This is not to say that the caliphate was not threatened internally or externally. Particularly in the latter half of the nineteenth century, many pressures on the caliphate came to bear including (1) the rise of the Sudanic Mahdi who found allies in leaderships centered in Borno and Adamawa, (2) the opposition of those living in contiguous territories, (3) the resistance of non-Muslims within the caliphate, and (4) colonial wranglings at the turn of the twentieth century (Kanya-Forstner and Lovejoy 1994, 9). Moreover, as Burnham and Last point out, the initial scale of jihadic conquest was small and "[l]arge areas of the Caliphate remained unsubdued: the watersheds that separated emirates even in central Hausaland were no-man's-land of great danger to Caliphal officials having to traverse them on government business" (1994, 329).

12. The Kano Chronicle relays that "[w]hen he became *Sarkin* [king of] Kano, the Fulani prevented him from entering the palace. He went into the house of *Sarkin Dawaki*'s [King of Horses—a slave title] mother. One of the remaining Kanawa said to Sulimanu, 'if you do not enter the *Giddan Rimfa* [House of Rumfa, a euphemism for the palace], you will not really be the Sarki of city and country.' When Sulimanu heard this he called the chief Fulani, but they refused to answer his summons, and said, 'we will not come to you. You must come to us, though you be the Sarki. If you will come to Mallam Jibbrim's house we will assemble there.' When they had assembled, he asked them and said, 'Why do you prevent me entering the *Giddan Rimfa?*' Mallam Jibbrim said, 'if we enter the Habe's houses and we beget children, they will be like these Habes and do like them.' Sulimanu said nothing but set off to Shehu Osuman Dan Hodio [Shehu Usman] asking to be allowed to enter the *Giddan Rimfa.* Shehu dan Hodio gave him a sword and a knife* and gave him leave to enter the *Giddan Rimfa,* telling him to kill all who opposed him. He entered the house, and lived there" (Palmer 1967 [1928], 127–28; Palmer's note: "A flag was also given him as well as a knife and sword. He did not go to Sokoto, but sent a message. Had he gone himself, he would never have regained his position").

Temple records in his 1909 "Notes on the History of Kano" that following the Sultan's appointment of Suleiman to the position of emir, Suleiman "continued to wander round Kano city without attacking it. Kano was by this time practically empty, and in the second year after being made *Sarki,* Suleimanu entered the town" (Lovejoy, Mahadi, and Muktar 1993, 33, 54).

There are numerous historical accounts of how and why Suleiman was appointed and the clan tensions involved in the appointment. See Smith 1997 for a summary and critical synthesis of these accounts. In any case, religious objections to Suleiman occupying the palace disguised larger political objections.

13. Smith, based on an analysis of many historical accounts of the jihad, suggests that it was the Shehu's son, Abdullahi, who nominated Suleiman (1997, 213). Abdullahi resided in Kano for about one year between 1807 and 1808. He probably thought Suleiman's appointment was strategic because he was an outsider and, as such, might still the rampant clan-based in-fighting amongst Kano jihadists. Moreover, Suleiman was well regarded as a pious liman who was religiously principled. At any rate, Smith avers that since the Shehu had proscribed any sort of Hausa state ceremony, Suleiman was not formally installed and there was no public pronouncement of his position. According to Smith, "[h]e remained poor, without followers, rural desmesnes, slaves, courtiers and the like" (1997, 213).

14. Four eunuchs were given major positions: Abu was made Wombai; Inusa was made Sarkin Shanu; Yaoji was made Dan Rimi, and Gorkori was made Dan Amar (Lovejoy, Mahadi, and Muktar 1993, 55).

15. According to Smith, Suleiman was proscribed by the Shehu from reinstituting Hausa titled offices (1997, 213–14). Smith avers that the only positions he reinstated were the liman for Kano city, eventually giving him territories and an assistant, and Sarkin Shanu, the official charged with levying taxes on nomadic Fulani. Smith writes that it is uncertain whether any of Suleiman's appointments were ever publicly witnessed, much less accepted by other Fulani leaders in Kano. His information conflicts with that in a recently discovered early twentieth-century colonial document concerning Fulani history, relayed by a palace insider (Lovejoy, Mahadi, and Muktar 1993). The document declares that Suleiman reinstated many titles: "He proceeded to make several appointments:—Mallam Bakatsene's son, Mandiko, was appointed Madawaki [Madaki], and subsequently Makama on the death of Mallam Bakatsene. Mallam Bakatsene became Makama. Limam, son of Mallam Jibbrin, who was younger brother of Mallam Goshi, was made Sarkin Dawaki Maituta; subsequently Ciroma, and subsequently Madawaki.

" . . . He made Dabo, younger son of Mallam Jemo, Galladima. Tsani, son of Dan Zabua was made Dan Iya. Balere, one of his relations, was made Sarkin Dawaki Tsakkar Gidda. Abu, his eunuch, was made Wombayi [Wombai]. Inusa, another eunuch, was made Sarkin Shanu. Yaoji, another, was made Dan Rimi. Gorkori, another, was made Dan Amar. Da Tua was made Alkali. Zaki was made Makama Gado da Masu. . . . Gulbi was made Sarkin Taramai. Dan Bazau was made Sarkin Bai. Salihi (a son of Dabo) was made Turaki Mainya. Zauno was made Barde. A man called Gajere was made Maiji" (54–55).

16. From the *Bayanul Bida'i*, 25, cited in Kaura 1990, 88.

17. This is not to say that the Shehu did not support women in other areas. He was, for example, a vocal proponent of women's education and women's Islamic rights, admonishing them to pay heed to Allah and not their guardian's vain attempts to control them (e.g., Sule and Starratt 1991, 36).

Recall also that local women in Dutse (an area located about sixty miles east-southeast of Kano) managed to retain control over indigo dyeing until the Kano civil war (1893–94), whereupon men overtook all of the area's dyeing yards. Given Dutse's support for the "wrong" side during the war, it is tempting to surmise that the takeover was retaliatory and accomplished by Kano-based interests.

18. I deduced that Suleiman abandoned this site based on two lines of evidence. First, I found clear evidence that Suleiman's successor, Ibrahim Dabo, built modest quarters for himself in the northwest part of the interior, far from the old Hausa seat of kingly rule, something discussed later in the text. I assumed that Dabo's move was in keeping with what Suleiman had accomplished previously, namely, a formal shunning of the place most intensely associated with Habe rule.

19. Stilwell (2000) avers that it was a powerful titleholding male slave from the former Habe regime, known as Barka, who was instrumental in reinstituting slave practices in the palace, beginning in the time of Ibrahim Dabo (2000).

20. Palace data indicate that women captured from royal contexts were taken as concubines or as wives, whether or not they had been living previously as a freeborn wife or slave concubine. Last similarly cites information provided by an early nineteenth-century traveler (Clapperton) that after Alkalawa fell (a key turning point in the jihad), at least one of the sultan's wives was captured. She was taken by the Shehu's son, Muhammad Bello, with whom she bore at least two sons (1967, 39 n. 99).

21. Bargery traces the origins of this word to *sa* (place in) and *daka* (house) (1934). But it may also derive from a play on words: *sadaka,* if intoned differently, means alms, especially a gift given to a malam.

22. Cited in Smith 1997, 217.

23. See ibid. for a detailed assessment of Dabo's reign. See Stilwell's discussion of the politics of key slave-emir relations after the jihad (2000).

24. Shehu Usman dan Fodio, who was much opposed to prejihadic state structures, died in 1817. He was succeeded by his son, Muhammad Bello, who reinstated a number of prejihadic state titles and practices, his knowledge of which had been culled from surrounding areas (see Smith 1997).

25. After the war, clan leaders that had participated militarily in the war moved into the state compounds of the Hausa state titleholders who had vacated these premises. As Smith points out, although Suleiman did not resurrect many titles, the fact that they lived in the former state compounds linked their lineages with the entitlement schemes of the previous regime (1997). Dabo, however, made it possible for them to have the titles and the compounds as state entitlements, legitimately and explicitly. At the same time, Dabo allowed them, as part of the state entitlement schema, to retain jurisdiction over lands they had de facto claimed, setting up a system of land administration tied to his centralized authority.

26. Since Dabo's death, Soron Malam has figured importantly into official accession rituals (see Rufa'i 1987, 136).

27. See Palmer 1967 (1928), 145. Smith offers a comprehensive summary of primary and secondary sources regarding the origins and duties of Daura's early queens (1978, 52–59). Most important, the first Magajiya is said to have been an ancestor of a Canaanite who migrated southward from Tripoli, nine women succeeding him as chiefs, one of whom was named Daura.

28. Smith provides some details about the marriages (1997, 236). He writes: "[H]e gave his daughter, the Magajiya Fatsumatu Zara, to Dabo Dambazau, the Sarkin Bai, with Kunci as her dowry. He gave Kumboto, another daughter, to the baYole Madaki Umaru, together with the town of Kumbotsu, five miles south of Kano, which was renamed in her honour. He likewise gave a daughter in marriage to the recognized leader of each of the senior Fulani lineages, to the Sarkin Dawaki Maituta, the Dan Iya, the Gyenamawa leader, the Liman, and others. Dabo likewise offered one of this daughters to the baJobe Makama Mandikko. Mandikko however refused to

accept Dabo's daughter as a bride, thus showing his hostility and contempt for Dabo, and in the context, implicitly challenged him to take disciplinary action."

29. See n. 11.

30. See Lovejoy 1996, 57, for Dabo, and Last 1987 (1974), 332 n. 11, for the Shehu and Bello.

31. I have no information on who this king (sarki) was, and it was not possible to deduce his identity from the historical record since details of the Fulani defeat of Daura are not well known. Apparently, however, the Fulani established themselves in the main palace of Daura city, while two other Hausa rulers established themselves in towns to the southeast of Daura town. There were therefore competing houses of rule, ruling different parts of the original Daura territory, after the jihad. As Smith explains: "When the British established their rule [in Daura] in 1901 to 1903, they found Fulani rulers at Daura and Hausa rulers at Zango and Baure. Despite the repeated inquiries of H. R. Palmer, Miller-Stirling, and others, less was learned about the Daura jihad than from Arnett's paraphrase of Sultan Bello's *Infaku'l Maisur*. As it is unlikely that the Fulani and Hausa consciously withheld such information, the campaign may have been forgotten or transformed into legend. No chronicles of Fulani Daura have since been found. . . . Perhaps the historical details of local struggles have been forgotten to emphasize the legitimacy and inevitability of Fulani rule as a requirement of Islam. Perhaps to justify the political result of these local campaigns, it has been necessary to stress their ideological significance to the exclusion of their historical details. The resulting inconsequential accounts of local conquests furnish examples of structural amnesia, one function of which was to legitimate Fulani rule on religious grounds, while another was to facilitate the mutual accommodations of conquerors and conquered to their new situation" (1978, 146).

32. Hajiyya Abba recalls that Shekara was kidnapped (29 October 1989), whereas Gogo Mai'-daki remembered that Shekara escaped from the Daura palace on her own and was later brought to the palace, presumably by her captors, when her pedigree was discovered (1988). Alhaji Maitama Sule (dan Masani, a well-known Kano palace slave descendent) says, by contrast, that he heard that it was Ibrahim Dabo's Galadima that found her after he officially visited and greeted the newly appointed Fulani emir who had taken over the old Daura palace (9 December 2003). While en route back to Kano, the Galadima's entourage met up with a powerful Fulani cattleherder who would not let Galadima's men water their horses until his cattle had finished. While the Galadima waited, someone came around to inquire into their origins and when he found out their royal provenance, he pointed to a young slave girl at the well drawing water with other girls for the cattle and intimated that the girl was of some former importance. He therefore urged the Galadima to beg the powerful Fulani cattleherder to give or sell the young girl to him. The Galadima begged accordingly and was successful in procuring her. He then delivered her to the palace where it was revealed that she was a princess from the pre-Fulani palace of Daura (9 December 2002). When I visited the Daura palace in 2003, however, no one had ever heard of Shekara, much less the Room of Shekara, suggesting that the palace from which she ran away and/or was eventually captured was in a successor state palace beyond Daura town, perhaps in Zango or Baure. More research is needed to clear up the details of Shekara's origins and Kano journey.

33. Dokaji Kano 1978 (1958), 44. See chapter 2.

34. Hajiyya Abba Ado Bayero, 9 November 2000.

35. Ibid., 18 November 2000. The Kano title associated with the queen mother is Mai-Babban Daki or Owner of the Big Room. Smith writes that upon Abbas's accession in 1903 as the first colonial emir, he "transferred Kura and its dependencies to his mother Hauwa, on whom he also conferred the long-vacant title of *Mai Babban Daki*" (1997, 406). It is not clear, though, what

span of time constitutes "long-vacant." Unlike Mack (1991, 113), I do not take this to mean three hundred years (the last time the title is mentioned in the KC) since it is likely that such a long absence would have effaced any memory of the office. Since her office and entitlements were well known by the time of Abbas, I instead interpret "long-vacant" as several reigns back in time, to Abdullahi's reign.

36. Gogo Mai'daki (n.d.) recalled that during her childhood at the turn of the twentieth century, ostriches lived, but never successfully reproduced, in areas near the granaries, feeding off kernels of grain littering the granary grounds. Sallama Dako remembered that ostriches were given to the emir as tribute *(gaisuwa)* and hailed from Borno, Zinder, or Damagaram (24 July 1990, now deceased). According to him, palace ostriches never bred in captivity, though they could lay eggs. If they wanted them to do so, they would lay a mortar down on the ground, the birds eventually stepping over it. Several days later, the birds would lay eggs, but these never hatched. Gogo Mai'daki recalled that they made jewelry items from the eggshells.

37. *Rimi* has many meanings, but according to Bargery, the silk-cotton tree is the most important. Within this context, the term can be applied to "a generous, open-handed person because when the pods of this tree burst, the contents become scattered far and wide" (1934, 857).

38. Madakin Kano Shehu averred that these three slaves were brought onto the emir's Executive Council (27 July 1990). Though the word *Sallama* technically means Peace, in Kano's Islamic context, a person must "do" Sallama before entering a house, that is, they must call out, "Sallama Aleckum" upon crossing the threshold. The act of doing Sallama is in other words the act of "seeking permission to enter." The title Sallama hence refers to the *act of doing Sallama* and indicates that the titleholder is the king's main gatekeeper between the inside and outside of the palace-house, all outside visitors having to go through him for an audience with the king (Lamido Sanusi, 22 November 2000). He is the only male titleholder (traditionally, but not always a eunuch) who attends personally to the king in his private chambers and he is the only one who can enter any palace building in the interior at will.

39. The word *house* needs to be approached with care. According to Last, earlier parts of the KC were written with a political agenda in mind, namely to create a history of a caliphate-like entity that would rival that of Borno (1983, 85). If this was the case, "then the Kano Caliphate had to have as impeccably unbroken a line of descent as that claimed by the Saifawa. . . . [T]he division of the Kano Chronicle into 'dynasties' would have run counter to the project." Last's project, in contradistinction, teases out the political tensions and non-linearity of descent, though his work is largely speculative. For him, a broader political definition of dynasty might be more suitable, for example, "as a faction allied by common interests and ties of patron-clientage as well as marriage and kinship . . . also a possible ideological basis, with *gida* [house] implying a school of thought or party with a particular programme . . . *gida* represents a 'set' of rules" (1983, 85).

40. See Last 1983 for a discussion of Kutumbi's importance in the evolution of Kano's political culture.

41. Maje Sirdi, 25 November 2000.

42. Culling a number of secondary sources (Giginyu 1981; Yunasa 1976; Sa'id 1983; Garba 1986; Palmer 1967 [1928]) and field data (Madakin Kano, 16 June and 21 July 1990; Hajiyya Abba, 19 November 2000), I was able to draft a preliminary list of thirty-four royal slave estates (many with palaces) and towns founded for military reasons, the former ranging from less than two acres in size (Gwagwarwa Rafin Sarki) to over 300 acres (Giware). The Fulani were especially productive in both endeavors. Dabo founded the town of Dambatta as a ribat (military fortress) and the small slave estate of Darmana (16 acres). His son Usman created the second-largest slave

estate of Gogel, consisting of more than 150 acres and hosting over 400 slaves. Gogel was contiguous with the largest slave estate of Giware (more than 300 acres), probably commissioned much later by either of his successors and brothers, Abdullahi or Bello. Usman also built a series of resthouses along two routes to Sokoto, at least one of them (Shanono) part of a very large slave estate complex. Abdullahi additionally built a pastoral slave estate and farm at Nassarawa just outside Kano's city walls, and a palace at Takai, 88 kilometers southeast of Kano. Takai's town walls were possibly built first by Sharefa (1703–31).

43. The definitive text on the history and diffusion of the cowry shell, particularly those from the Maldives (*Cypraea moneta*) is still that of Hogendorn and Johnson (1986). In their chapter dealing with "Cowries in Africa," they write that although cowries are first recorded to have appeared in Kano in the 1500s, they were not used in any systematic fashion for purposes of taxation until the 1800s. In particular, they assert, "Cowries were apparently an earlier arrival in Hausaland than previously believed. There is a recently unearthed reference (Anania's *La Universale Fabrica del Mondo*) to their use in Kano and/or Katsina in the sixteenth century. According to the *Kano Chronicle*, which almost all scholars of the cowrie have depended upon, they arrived in quantity only during the time of Emir Sharifa in the first half of the eighteenth century. The original assumption was that these shells were of trans-Saharan provenance, and the new evidence of their sixteenth century use in Hausaland does indicate introduction from the west and importation across the desert. Hiskett argued that they reached Hausaland from the south rather than the north and west, and indeed the reference in the *Kano Chronicle* may mean that Sharifa's raiding and conquests caused a shift in the source of supply to the Guinea coast.

" . . . With most of the region under the sway of the Sokoto Caliphate from the first decade of the nineteenth century, cowries soon came to figure in the nexus of tribute payments, in particular from the more southerly emirates. Soon several sorts of taxation were both calculated and payable in shell money, which, as the taxpayer had to earn the cowries in the first place, served to encourage the spread of a cash economy decades before the colonial authorities were said to have introduced taxes to speed monetization" (Hogendorn and Johnson 1986, 104–5).

Tambo summarizes: "By the early nineteenth century, the Caliphate, with the exception of Adamawa, was an integral part of a common cowrie currency zone which extended north to Agades, south to the coast and west nearly to Senegambia. The zone gradually expanded eastward during the course of the century, cowries being introduced into Bornu around 1848, and into Adamawa between 1860 and 1880" (1974, 3).

44. See Fika 1978, Lovejoy, Mahadi, and Muktar 1993, 55 n. 115, and Stilwell 2000.

45. Establishing the dual treasury was probably linked to problems encountered by Dabo in receiving his share of taxes. In particular, Fulani and non-Fulani chiefs in control of taxation flows refused to send to Dabo his tax share, causing him to write to the caliph for permission to control tax collection himself, giving local chiefs leave to take a proportion of taxation proceeds. The caliph agreed, fueling further revolts against Dabo.

46. See Fika 1978, 11–12, Garba 1986, and Smith 1997 for some of the many reviews of the evolution of the Hausa taxation system, most of the data of which are taken from the KC (Palmer 1967 [1928]). None of these studies, however, broach the sixteenth and seventeenth centuries or the political economic and political cultural processes attending the shift from grain taxes to cloth and cowries.

47. Burnham and Last (1994, 328) state, "We know that the number of concubines increased, and births of children soared," providing no references for this assertion or any sense of geographical context: did the numbers soar across the caliphate? or only in certain places therein?

Similarly they write of a "demographic explosion among the royals," asserting that the Shehu had thirty-seven children and that his successor and son had seventy-three children. While these numbers may have been high for the Fulani, they were hardly unusual for any royal or wealthy African household. As I will show, below, at least in the Kano palace, concubine numbers declined relative to the numbers that had been kept by pre-Fulani regimes.

48. Cooper hypothesizes that as a result of the jihad, the Sokoto Caliphate, "found itself faced with the dual tasks of absorbing and acculturating large conquered populations while meeting defense needs. Slave settlements strategically placed along defensive borders could be used to answer both needs at once and could be patterned after the slave villages established by Fulani herders" (1997, 6). If this is so, it begs the questions of what the Hausa leadership did when similarly intense slave raiding took place in the past; or if such slave-raiding intensity had ever taken place historically.

49. Again, this arrangement was needed in part because Dabo had determined that local headmen charged with levying taxes were forwarding to the capital only 10 percent of what was collected, leading Dabo to ask the sultan if he might collect his own taxes. After Dabo received the sultan's permission, he turned the tables; local chiefs were allocated 10 percent plus horses and arms. The sultan received 30 percent of the emir's earnings (Lovejoy, Mahadi, and Muktar 1993, 56).

50. The late Madakin Kano Shehu averred that two kinds of male jakadu existed: those appointed directly by the emir (who were presumably somewhat independent) and those under the leadership of Shamaki and dan Rimi (23 July 1990).

51. Shamaki may have accomplished this particular distribution task through a Sarkin Hatsi appointee. As Smith claims, Shamaki had "responsibility for supplying grain and foodstuffs through the *Sarkin Hatsi* to the palace staff" (1997, 247). He does not reference the sources he used for this conclusion. In contrast, palace informants I interviewed affirmed that Sarkin Hatsi was first appointed during the reign of Dabo's son, Abdullahi. Accordingly, the Sarkin Hatsi title is discussed in chapter 4.

52. Smith writes: "The Shamaki's function became a polite imperial joke. It was said that whatever the Sarkin Musulmi (caliph) demanded for himself or anyone, the stables *(shamaki)* of the Sarkin Kano contained. But in his roles as paymaster and quartermaster, the Shamaki had also to keep Dabo informed about state stocks of war weapons, and cash for purchasing more" (ibid., 246).

53. Smith writes that the Ciroma Dan Mama's identity is not known, but that he probably helped counsel the dynastic segment of rule represented by the last ruling king, Alwali (1781–1806), additionally ministering to important parts of the territory (ibid., 171–72). When the Shehu or Sheikh Usman dan Fodio sent a letter to Alwali asking him to submit to the jihad, Alwali was apparently on the verge of doing so. Smith writes: "According to local tradition, Alwali wanted to write, accepting the Shehu's message; but his Ciroma Dan Mama first dissuaded him and then, or shortly afterwards, personally wrote the Shehu, offering to support his affairs at Kano. Alwali knew nothing of Dan Mama's treachery. Indeed, he appears to have accepted Dan Mama's advice against his own inclination. . . . Dan Mama remained at court in the city throughout and after the jihad. According to one report, Dan Mama was then in charge of Rano, Karaye, Bebeji, Tofa, Aujara, Jahun, Dambarta and Sankara . . . [constituting] a substantial portion of the chiefdom" (ibid., 188).

54. See Smith for details of the benefits and positions awarded him by Dabo and how the latter relegated his progeny to obscurity by giving them a title that was highly circumscribed

(ibid., 239–40). In Temple's "Notes on the History of Kano," Dan Mama is referred to as "Chiroma (the traitor to Alwali)" (Lovejoy, Mahadi, and Muktar 1993, 58).

55. Alhaji Ado Sanusi, 2 December 2003; Gogo Nani, 12 November 2000 and 11 December 2003; Sarkin Gini, 14 November 2000; and the late Madakin Kano Shehu, 21 July 1990. According to Madakin Kano Shehu, mostly royal women and children are buried in the cemetery since they frequently die within the palace's confines, burial at the place of death being the norm. The elderly Uwar Kuyanga, 'Ya Adama, the titleholding leader of the kuyangi, declared that no slave would ever be buried there, nor any concubine (12 November 2000). Indeed, His Highness avers that traditionally all concubines were buried outside the palace except for a Mai-Babban Daki (the Queen Mother), but only if she survived her ruling son (5 December 2003). If a Mai-Babban Daki died before her son came to power, she would be buried outside the palace. Alhaji Ado Sanusi (2 December 2003) noted that a large exception occurred when Uwar Soro Wayo was buried there: She was the famous leading concubine of Emir Sanusi (1953–63), who died with him while he was in exile in Wudil. Her son, Ciroman Kano, is also buried there. Beginning with Ado Bayero's reign, all wives, concubines, and children are buried in the palace cemetery (Alhaji Ado Bayero, 5 December 2003). Grown sons and daughters are buried in their own houses.

56. Usman lived in the eastern part of Yelwa (Madakin Kano Shehu, 26 July 1990).

57. See Rufa'i 1987 for a lengthy description of the accession ritual. The late Madakin Kano Shehu noted that Usman was the one who built up his mother's quarters as a kind of shrine, calling upon the genius of an architect-builder known as Babban Gwani (23 July 1990).

4. Concubine Losses and Male Gains

1. The last Mai-Kudandan was an informant of Rufa'i (1987). By the time I began interviewing palace women in 1989, Mai-Kudandan had passed away and I was told that the emir would not be appointing a new titleholder.

2. See chapters 1 and 2.

3. Sarkin Hatsi, 2 December 1988 and 28 October 1989. Sarkin Hatsi is a traditional village title, the holder of which administered the harvest (John Lavers, personal communication, 2 March 1990). It is therefore not the title itself, but its accommodation inside the palace, which was new.

4. The emir encouraged me to interview the three remaining Koramas in Kano: one in Kasuwar Kurmi and the other two in Kasuwar Rimi and Kasuwar Mandawari (10 November 2000). I don't know how old the last two markets are, but Barth mentions visiting the Mandawari market, though he curiously never alludes to the large grain-selling areas in any Kano market (1965 [1857]). Upon investigation, I found that the Korama title had lapsed in all of the markets, the grandson of the last Korama in Kasuwar Kurmi presiding under the assumed title of Sarkin Hatsi, while a new female Korama was appointed to Kasuwar Rimi by the Madakin Kano the next day (11 November 2000), expressly so that I could interview her! Lesser Koramas were not turbaned, but were appointed by the Kasuwar Kurmi Korama in consultation with grain sellers in those markets.

5. The last Korama of the central market died circa 1950, thereafter the Korama title like Mai-Kudandan, being allowed to lapse. The information here was obtained from the last Korama's grandson, Lawan jika Ayi (16 November 2000) who assumed her responsibilities after Korama's death and the death of an interim male successor. Both the latter and he ironically hold the same title as the titleholder placed in charge of palace grain during Abdullahi dan Dabo's reign, Sarkin Hatsi. Relatively little grain is sold in the central market today.

6. This figure is taken from estimates made by nineteenth-century travelers, tabulated by Frishman (1977, 214). Whereas in 1924 Clapperton had estimated that Kano city proper contained between 30,000 and 40,000 persons (Denham 1836), by 1851 Barth (1965) moved the upper limit to 60,000 and in 1885 Staudinger (1990) estimated the city's population to be between 60,000 and 80,000. Despite seasonal differences in populations, these and other nineteenth century figures suggest significant population increases during the nineteenth century.

7. Both Garba 1986 and Mack 1988 refer to but do not elaborate upon the timing or reasons for the removal of women's authority in the city grain market.

8. Ward and place names and locations, along with the division and placement of interior labor, were obtained primarily through discussions with Hajiyya 'yar Mai-Tilas and Gogo Kahu (daughters of Emir Aliyu), Mai-daki and Gogon Ita Dambatta (daughters of Emir Abbas, 1903–19), 'yar Kutisa (formerly a concubine of Emir Abdullahi Bayero, 1926–53), Hajiyya Abba Ado Bayero (currently the first wife of Emir Ado Bayero, 1963–present), Malam D'au (a son of Emir Aliyu), Sallama Dako, Sarkin Hatsi, Galadima Rumbu, Alhaji Baba dan Meshe (a present-day "eunuch" who is impotent, but not castrated), and the current emir, His Highness Alhaji Ado Bayero. Discussion data were integrated with previously derived map data and verified in the field with one or more of the cooperants. Some ward and place data conflict with more contemporary data presented by Rufa'i (1987), who did not take into account the historical dynamics of place production and the changing titles and hierarchies of male and female slaves.

9. The KC relays that Kutumbi was the first king to collect taxes from the nomadic Fulani, paid in-kind in cattle. He was also the first ruler to designate an official to oversee state holdings of cattle: "He was the first Sarki of Kano who collected the *Jizia* [tax] from the Fulani which is called *Jangali*. He collected a hundred cows from the Hafunawa, the chief clan of Fulani, seventy from the Baawa, sixty from Dindi Maji, fifty from the Danneji, and others too numerous to mention. When he had collected the cattle, he said to his slave Ibo, 'I make you Sarkin Shanu.' Hence, the latter was called 'Ibo na Kutumbi'" (Palmer 1967 [1928], 119). I could not determine, however, where these cattle were kept and if they were brought regularly into the Kano palace to be milked.

Smith provides details on how Maliki law computes a cattle tax, noting that though originally it was rendered in kind (as zakat), no explicit proscriptions exist against converting it into its exchange value in the form of, say, cowries (1997, 53–56). By the time of Alwali, the tax was paid in-kind by locally resident pastoralists, but in cowries from migratory groups entering Kano during the dry season.

10. Slaves were captured from areas outside Kano, such as Warji, Yola, and Damagaram, and from villages in the Kano region, including Garko, Jahun, Gurjiya, and Sankara (Giginyu 1981, 111–12, 115, 140).

It was primarily from the Nassarawa palace that concubines streamed into the central palace after the British conquest, suggesting that a permanent cadre of concubine managers, at the very least, lived in and maintained that palace interior throughout the year.

Ibrahim Dabo and Usman also created estates much further from the city, making it implausible that concubines would have resided there unattended.

11. Madakin Kano (26 July 1990) claims that Babban Gwani also built Turakar Dabo, the sleeping quarters of Dabo (26 July 1990). Indeed the style of the vaulted arches inside the turaka is reminiscent of the work of Babban Gwani. It is not clear, however, if Babban Gwani built the turaka of Dabo during his reign or rebuilt it after his death during his reign of Abdullahi.

12. According to Hajiyya Abba Ado Bayero and Gogo Maidaki (25 October 1989), only two palace buildings hosted second floors at the turn of the century: Soron Malam, the study

chambers of Ibrahim Dabo, which Madakin Kano (26 July 1990) averred was also built by Babban Gwani; and Babban Soro, which Abdullahi commissioned Babban Gwani to build on the site of Hausa kingship. My research suggests that after Abdullahi, it was not uncommon for emirs to build second stories onto the first floors of their personal chambers in the ciki.

13. The late Malam D'au, a son of the last precolonial emir, averred that palace spirits lived in a kudandan in Yelwa (recall the association of this term with grains; chapter 2) called *danki* (18 November 1989). See also Rufa'i 1987, 61, whose informants, since deceased, included Uwar Soro Umma and Fulanin Dandago. Interestingly, all wives and concubines I queried in 2003 denied that any such spirit or spirit house ever existed, perhaps a sign of the recent fundamentalist times (spirit worship is anathema to Islam) and concomitant politicized criticisms about the religoius purity of the ruler and the aristocracy generally.

14. According to Rufa'i, the structure known as Babban Gwani underwent a name change to Katon Gwani during the reign of the last precolonial emir, Aliyu, in deference to him: Aliyu's nickname was Babba, making it inappropriate to utter the name of the building (1987, 55). She describes the building as follows: "*Katon Gwani*—(literally, the huge expert) is another important building in this [the king's residential] section. It was named after a popular builder Muhammadu Durubu who was nicknamed *Babban Gwani* (the great expert). [He] . . . not only built this section but also other sections at the palaces in Katsina and Zaria. In the traditions of the palace, the guardian *Aljana* (spirit) of the palace lives in *Babban Gwani*. Her room is well decorated with *Kayan daki* (various things used to decorate the room of a woman)—such as plates, dishes, a bed and bodings etc. It should be noted that *Kudandan* in the *Uwar Soro*'s section also belongs to the same *Aljana*. . . . *Babban Gwani* is not used by anybody in the palace. Only the belongings of the guardian Aljana of the palace are kept there. They are constantly being washed and rearranged by the Sadaku [Concubines] especially on special occasions like *Sallah* celebrations." While my research supports Rufa'i's findings, I am increasingly uncertain that the *same* spirit inhabited both rooms. Some evidence suggests that Katon Gwani is a much younger structure. Moreover, while it is built onto the emir's quarters (opening up directly onto them via an internal entrance), it also has a "public" entrance that opens up onto one of the open courtyards of what was characteristically (though not always) the first (senior) wife's quarters. During my 2000 field season, the first wife stressed that the spirit was that of a saint who first came to the palace during the reign of the first Fulani ruler, Suleiman. If so, this may explain why this particular spirit/place is still acknowledged, though in a much subdued fashion. That its placement was/is adjacent to the quarters of a Fulani wife is strikingly dissonant with the placement of the other (presumably older) spirit house in Yelwa, though both were shaped like granaries and involved pre-Islamic forms of spirit worship and symbology.

15. Abdulkadiri had been given the highest ranking title and state office, that of Galadima, a vizier-like post that Abdullahi had held previously under his brother's reign, Usman, and a post typically held by an emir's successor. Abdulkadiri was unhappy with the way he was sidelined politically when Abdullahi was away on military campaigns, during the early years of office. During these times, another state titleholder had been left in charge, Sarkin Shanu, in keeping with precedent. But even when Abdullahi returned to reside in the capital, the Galadima was not used as the sort of advisor that Abdulkadiri expected. His complaints reached Abdullahi who, angered, used Abdulkadiri's allegations of spirit worship to remove him from office.

16. Smith claims that Abdullahi was so religious that he would never have done such a thing, field data from this research indicating otherwise (1997, 284). Within the caliphate structure, the

emir could not dismiss the holder of the Galadima title without permission from the caliph. Abdullahi would later dismiss Yusuf from the Galadima post.

17. Recall that Rumfa appointed four eunuchs to take care of the treasury, one of whom was entitled Turaki. Over time, the title proliferated as an honorific prefix conjoined to other titles. Recall also that Turaki Kuka (Turaki of the Baobab) was one of Shashere's (1573–82) two most favored eunuchs, a title that probably refers to the baobab tree outside his quarters where the king may have held court historically.

As Last points out, the Fulani reformists objected to what they considered to be pagan practices, some of which involved trees: "although Islam was common by the end of the eighteenth century . . . non-Muslim cults were still strong. From twentieth-century accounts and from collections of folk-tales, it appears that the main characteristic of non-Muslim belief was a reverence for a large number of spirits localised particularly in trees; stones, wells and rivers are also mentioned. Although these spirits become identified with jinns [Islamic spirits], practices connected with them, such as possession ceremonies and sacrifices, are still polytheistic" (1967, lxix). See Rufa'i's discussion of the importance of baobab and silk trees in defining the extent of a pre-Rumfa site of rule, Gwammaja (1987, 20–22).

18. The mosque was probably an original feature of the palace that was first rebuilt after the attempted assassination of Mohammed Shashere (chapter 2).

19. Malam D'au, son of the last precolonial emir, Aliyu, claims that Ibrahim Dabo and not Abdullahi dan Dabo built the mosque, whereas Rufa'i claims that it was Bello (1987, 67). I have chosen to rely upon my own informants and the KC, which states: "He [Abdullahi] rebuilt the mosque and house of the Turaki Mainya [a chief eunuch] early in his reign. They had been in ruins for many years" (Palmer 1967 [1928], 131). The explorer Clapperton passed through Kano in 1824 and visited the palace, declaring that the palace "even contains a mosque," which points to several possibilities: Clapperton did not notice that the mosque was in disrepair; Ibrahim attempted to rebuild the mosque, but it fell into disrepair during the reign of his son, Usman; or that Ibrahim began rebuilding the mosque but never completed it. The KC hints that early on the mosque may have been rebuilt by Ibrahim Dabo when it notes that he was the first to build up southern areas in the palace. The latter may also suggest that it was Dabo who built the turbaning hall, given that it was he who instituted formal turbaning during the Fulani era, Abdullahi perhaps elaborating on it later.

Abdullahi built a number of other male-dedicated structures in the southern palace, which I discuss elsewhere (see Nast 1992). These included Soron Giwa (see also Sa'ad 1985, 13, Rufa'i 1987, 65, and Ahmed 1988, 68), in honor of his father who was called the "Bull Elephant" in praise songs, and Soron Cafe (the Room of Plaster), named perhaps after the town cafe or because of its façade of plaster etched with ornate geometrical designs. He may also have built the Quranic study room Soron Makaranta (Hall of the School), and the dining hall for Fulani children, probably young boys (Soron 'yan Fulani, Hall of the Fulani Children). Again, both structures had northern labyrinth equivalents, the latter structures built during the reign of Ibrahim Dabo.

20. Rufa'i assumed that council meetings (fada) were held weekly, as they were during the colonial period (1987, 153). They were only held weekly in the latter period, however, because the nobility had been forced by the British to live in the countryside, making daily fada a logistical impossibility.

21. The KC writes that the title of Sarkin Dogarai (King of Bodyguards) was created during Kutumbi's reign. See Fika 1978, 11. According to Layi-Layi (22 January 1990), titleholding

dogarai at the turn of the twentieth century included Sarkin Dogarai, Galadima Dogarai, Madakin Dogarai, and Makaman Dogarai. Only the last titleholder resided in the palace amid approximately eight to ten households, totaling about one hundred persons. The latter figure was only a small portion of the total number of bodyguards, who according to Sarkin Dogarai numbered about 250, most of these persons presumably living in the city ward of Dogarai (25 October 1985, cited in Rufa'i 1987, 99, 122).

22. The late Sallama Dako, 27 October 1989.

23. Even up through Aliyu's reign some commoners paid taxes *(haraji)* in grain, though by this time most grains derived from the estates and zakat. Workers threshed estate grains *before* bringing them to the palace, such that the grains were delivered not in dami or bundles (though bundles were sent to the stables), but in *buhu* or bags (Maje Sirdi, 25 November 2000).

24. Al-Maghili outlined for Muhammadu Rumfa an Islamic treatise on taxation for Kano (Gwarzo, Bedri, and Starratt 1974/77). Technically, only Muslims were to pay the zakat and this was to be the main tax. But in practice other taxes were levied, the zakat being a regressive tax unable to support a large bureaucracy. There has been no detailed study of Kano taxation, except for Garba 1986, which summarizes secondary sources, especially the KC. Imam Imoru details how zakat was understood by malams and ideally practiced in the nineteenth century: "The fourth pillar is the religious tax, *zaka*. When a person has wealth and the year has ended, he will count it, bit by bit, and then give alms, *sadaka*, because of God, not because of man. The *zaka* is not much: if the value of a man's possessions is 100,000 cowries, he gives 2,500. Likewise, when he harvests ten bundles, *dami*, of cereal, he gives one because of God. If he has had to irrigate his farm, he gives one bundles for every 20 harvested.

"If a person has domestic animals, *bisashe*, he gives *zaka* because of God: for five camels, he gives one goat as *zaka*; for 30 cows he gives one cow as *zaka*; for 40 goats and sheep, he gives one.

"There is no *zaka* for horses, donkeys, or slaves. There is no *zaka* paid on garments—even if they are expensive—and none is paid on jewelry made by smiths, *k'erek'eren ado*.

"There is the 'bowl tax,' *zakar nono*, which is also called the 'eating tax,' *zakar ci*. On the morning the fast is finished, *safiar salla*, every Muslim gives four measures, *mudu*, of cereal, because of God, to any commoner he likes; the recipient must be a Muslim, for nothing is given to an animist, *kafiri*. This tax is given for a man, his wife, and the rest of his family. That is *zaka*" (Ferguson 1973, 170–71).

25. However, see Ubah, who writes that "the extension of *taki* [a colonial tax] assessment meant in effect the abolition of *zakka* [*sic*] as a separate tax and the removal of the necessity to stock pile millet and guinea corn. Even the opposition on sentimental and religious grounds to the payment of *zakka* in cash did not last very long. In 1911/1912 the *zakka* was paid in cash. By 1913 payment in kind was said to have become unpopular among many people who now preferred to pay the 9d per bundle: probably the removal of the burden of transferring thousands of bundles of grain to Kano had helped to facilitate the change" (1985, 175).

Ubah relies entirely on colonial reports in his analysis of the zakat. Informants, however, recalled that some zakat grains were delivered to the palace for the first several decades of colonial rule.

26. Imoru describes some of the tensions among "palace malams" and two other groups whom Imoru calls "malams of the hide" and *malaman kundi*, the last category dealing in magic (Ferguson 1973, 229). Palace malams "have little to do with the commoners, *talakawa*, who fear them. The malams of the hide look down upon the palace malams as people who are not God-fearing, but there are, indeed, God-fearing men among them" (227). In contrast, if "a malam has

read many books, and knows them well, he is said to be erudite, *babban malam*. He remains in his house which becomes a school, and whoever wants to read for knowledge comes to him, and he teaches that person because of God. . . . This type of malam is called the 'malam of the oxhide,' *malamin k'irigi*, or the 'malam of the mat,' *malamin shinfida*. He has nothing to do with the ruler, because he is God-fearing and he has no other dealings apart from teaching" (265). These and other Fulani malams were exempt from paying taxes, at least through the reign of Usman (Sa'id 1983, 118).

27. The full passage reads: "As soon as he became Sarki he collected stores of 'Gero' [bull-rush millet] and 'Dawa' [guinea corn] in case of war and famine. Nevertheless famine over-took him."

28. Sallama Dako, 26 October 1990.

29. The Kilishi personally attended to the emir, ushering him into and out of the rooms in which he sat. Imam Imoru identified Kilishi as the seventh most important attendant to the king (Ferguson 1973, 210). My informants asserted Kilishi was a eunuch, as did the informants of Fika (1978), though Smith asserts that Kilishi was a freeborn appointee (1997, 289), which seems unlikely given his responsibilities with women.

30. Elsewhere he writes, "[T]he *kilishi* talks to female plaintiffs and returns alone to tell the king because women do not appear before the king in his chamber" (Ferguson 1973, 212). He claims that most female plaintiffs won their cases. He recounts that "[w]hen a woman takes a case to the king, he helps them: he thinks these women are probably right because it is very dif-ficult to come to the king. If she is not deceived, she will be able to go there, and that is why the king gives these women favorable judgments" (Ferguson 1973, 238).

31. Hajiyya Abba Ado Bayero and Gogo Nani, 12 November 2000.

32. During the reign of Aliyu, cattle grazed at the pastoral estate and elsewhere. A number of cows were tethered at night inside concubine wards in the eastern part of the interior and after milking in the early morning would be led southwards back to the estate (Gogo Madaki, Gogon Ita, Gogo Kahu, 23 and 27 August, 1989).

33. Hajiyya Abba Ado Bayero, 23 January 1900. Her culinary skills are similarly mentioned by Imam Imoru (b. 1858). He writes, "There is an office, held by a woman, called 'mother of the inner room,' *uwar soro:* the king's many female slaves are with her. She prepares various kinds of food and small fried cakes: when the king wants to make a gift of food, he sends to her house and she gives what is requested. If they cannot get the food from her, she has done the king a great disservice and she is removed from office" (Ferguson 1973, 213).

34. The name of the room, like that of many others, is gendered, in this case used only by men (see Nast 1992, 41). Women call this chamber Rumfar Kasa, the same name given to a func-tionally similar court room for men located in the present day southern male slave domain (see Nast 1994, 67 n. 64).

35. I found Imoru's description of this and related nineteenth-century rituals relevant for the colonial period and much of today. He notes, "Great kings—like those of Kano, Katsina, and Zaria—have a special house built called the 'king's chamber,' *fagaci*. It is a big rectangular room: the floor is beaten to make it hard and a platform, *tugufa*, is made: on top of the platform is placed the king's couch and hide mats on which he sits every day." The "house" to which he refers in the Kano context consisted of a number of large court chambers located in the labyrinths (described elsewhere in this chapter) and known as Rumfar Kasa, Kudandan, or Soron Hakimai. They lay outside the ciki. Imoru continues: "A similar room is built in the palace: it is called 'the resting place,' *mashayar iska*, or the 'inner room,' *soron ciki*." Women refer to this room either as

Rumfar Kasa or Soron Baki. Imoru avers that after the palace household ritually greeted the emir, his slave officials (*manyar bayi*, literally, the *big* slaves), and eunuchs (*babani*) entered: "the eunuchs enter first and are followed by the slave officials. There are seven of these officials and, while their names differ, they are found in every capital." These officials included Shamaki, Dan Rimi, Sallama, Ka-sheka, Turakin Soro, Abin Fada (a title unfamiliar to me), and Kilishi. "These seven officials are called the 'slaves of the inner house,' *bayin cikin gida*. When they greet the king in the morning, they sit and talk with him in a very attentive manner: one does not talk nonsense and there is no joking." These seven are the only ones allowed into the ciki for regular meetings. My research shows that thereafter the emir proceeded to an adjacent chamber in one of the labyrinths, accompanied by female jakadu who ritually cautioned the emir as he walked, with the refrain "takkawa sannu" (walk with care). These women delivered him to his male bodyguards, who then accompanied him to his outer court chamber to meet with nobility; see Imoru in Ferguson 1973, 210, for an accurate description of the "passing over" of the king from one group of guards (women) to another (men).

36. Her duties resemble those of the king of Kotoko's highest-ranking wife, the Gumsu. Like Mai-Soron Baki, she lived in quarters facing his bedchambers. And like Mai-Soron Baki, the Gumsu was not expected to engage in the communal labors expected of other "wives" (both freeborn and concubines), but to devote herself to the needs of the king (Bay 1998, 127).

37. Hajiyya 'yar Mai-tilas and Gogon Kahu, 25 August 1989.

38. The last Uwar Tafiya was the mother of one of my informants, the late Malam D'au.

39. Musisi 1991, 781–82. Unfortunately, she does not provide dates, though it can be deduced from other information in the text that such practices occurred after the adoption of elite polygyny sometime in the late 1500s, this polygyny involving scores of freeborn and enslaved women.

40. Her house, along with that in Emir Abdullahi's quarters, were built with a domed ceiling, an architectural flourish and innovation developed in the nineteenth century (see Sa'ad 1981).

41. See Nast 1994 for a discussion of the duties of these two groups of slave women.

42. See Nast 1992 and Stilwell 2000.

43. Smith writes, "Abdullahi was fortunate in having many sons. However, this fortune created its own problems as Abdullahi's sons replaced Usman's in princely positions" (1997, 285).

44. Lovejoy notes that in postjihadic Sokoto, "being a wife was preferable to being a concubine" (1983, 247). At least two qualifications need to be made here. First, titled royal concubines in particular held tremendous powers in relation to freeborn royal wives prior to the jihad; hence the latter's postjihadic powers were unique. Second, some concubines were undoubtedly princesses prior to their capture or kidnapping (like Shekara was) and may have outranked particular wives.

45. Smith recounts a story about another of the caliph's daughters that has uncanny resemblance to what I present here, but in a very different context (1997, 273). In particular he writes that the caliph's Waziri Abdulkadiri, the religious advisor sent from Sokoto to Kano to announce Usman's successor, had a tense encounter with Abdullahi, who forced his hand in giving him the throne. In appreciation for his skill in handling the situation, Smith avers that the caliph gave Abdulkadiri one of his daughters as a wife, also named Saudatu, their son eventually acceding to his father's office.

46. See also Boyd and Last, who remark that after she was widowed she returned to Sokoto to help with the educational work of her sister, Asmau, married to the Waziri of Caliph Muhammad Bello (1985, 295).

47. Ordinarily, Islamic law would never have permitted Sanusi to marry Usman's widow. Usman was Abbas's brother and Abbas was Sanusi's grandfather. However, it seems that Usman was too old to consummate the marriage—he assumed the throne at age eighty-two (Sanusi Lamido Sanusi, 8 January 2003)—such that he never had any children with her (Alhaji Ado Sanusi, 2 December 2003).

48. I am grateful to Sanusi Lamido Sanusi (Emir Sanusi's grandson) for singing and later writing down this praise song for me during my visit to Kano in November 2000.

49. Gogo Sokoto, 22 November 2000; Sanusi Lamido Sanusi, 1 and 22 November 2003.

50. Gogo Sokoto, 22 November 1990. She noted that just after she married the emir, Mai-Soron Baki made a special visit to deliver the emir's prayer mat and inform her that the emir would visit her quarters to say his Friday prayers. At this time she was to bring out his mat, later storing it safely.

51. Ibrahim Dabo married Mariam, the daughter of the leader of the jihad, Shehu Usman dan Fodio. After Dabo's death, Mariam married the son of a councilor of the late Muhammad Bello and played a major part in reconciling Abdullahi to the newly appointed caliph, Ahmadu Rufa'i (Smith 1997, 290).

52. Interestingly, Halima had been married previously during which time she'd had a son, Musa. She bore the emir no children (Gogo Ya'ya, 31 August 1989, who served as her kuyanga).

53. Jaggar emphasizes the prerogatives awarded to city versus rural blacksmiths by Kano rulers: "[R]ulers clearly favoured the City blacksmiths by exempting them from payment of tribute which was levied on those of the villages. The relationship between the authorities and the smiths of the City was characterized by mutual respect. In a society where agriculture was the major economic activity, and whose rulers were almost constantly engaged in warfare, from a utilitarian point of view the blacksmiths had no equals and represented an indispensable section of the community" (1973, 21).

54. The ward name suggests that iron-based armaments and farming implements had been produced here historically for the palace. Settlement pattern analysis shows that Rimin Kira is located *outside* the original rectangular ex-urban walls that Rumfa built, indicating that it was created after the suburb wall was abandoned. Jaggar's comprehensive work shows that blacksmithing took place in fifteen wards in the city, blacksmithing activities controlled by the patriarchs of families having distinct ancestries (1973). As Jaggar notes, military activities took place during the dry season "and the army conscripted a number of blacksmiths into their ranks" (19). His interviews with blacksmiths show that the Kano palace placed their order for armaments yearly with the Sarkin Makera who, if the order was unusually large, would gather his men under a "specially built grass shelter *(runfa)* erected in a convenient space, either just to the east of the Central Mosque, or in Rimin Kira ward, or the north side of the City prison" (20). Jaggar asserts that no guns were ever produced in Rimin Kira, the simple technology of the times allowing for them only to repair imported muskets; but see n. 56.

55. As Smith points out, not all eunuchs were castrated (1997, 295). Some were impotent or disinterested in women. Sallama Barka, Abdullahi's favored eunuch, for example was not castrated, but ostensibly disinterested, a state of affairs that eventually was reversed, leading him astray. My own field data indicate that later colonial sanctions against slavery and castration were avoided in part by employing impotent men and hermaphrodites (identifying primarily as men) as eunuchs.

56. Madakin Kano Shehu, 16 June 1990; Malam D'au, 4 November 1989; and Sallama, 27 and 28 October 1989. According to Madakin Kano, by the time of Emir Aliyu, blacksmiths

working in Sallama's house were manufacturing Dana guns there, a kind of long-barreled musket. Sallama apparently lived in this house through much of the colonial period. One of Stilwell's titleholding informants, Mai Tafari Hussaini, averred in 1998 that his father earned the Mai Tafari title through skills attained in Sallama's house: "What really led him to the title and [skills with] guns *[bindiga]* was a result of the fact that he grew up in the house of the Sallama. The house of Sallama was the house in charge of the guns and the work associated with guns [blacksmithing etc.]" (Stilwell 2000, 149, his brackets). His father probably served under Emir Usman or Sanusi, the latter bringing Sallama out of exile in the 1950s and into the palace's northern "male" slave domain (Malam D'au, 18 November 1989). By contrast, Jaggar asserts that guns were never produced in Sallama's blacksmithing facility because the technology there was limited (1973, 20).

57. Rufa'i erroneously assumes that Sallama's house was made into an arms depot only during the colonial period (1987). Sallama Barka of Abdullahi's time is not to be confused with Dan Rimi Barka, who was the confidante of Abdullahi's father, Ibrahim Dabo (see Stilwell 2000, 128, and Fika 1978, 19).

58. Technically, there is nothing to prohibit a slave man from setting up a household with a nonslave woman. The palace slave practice of marrying free women was nonetheless forbidden by Emir Bello in a bid to exert greater authority and control over royal slaves (see Fika 1978, 56). Among commoners, however, a slave man had, unlike a palace slave, almost nothing to offer a freeborn wife. Thus, the nineteenth-century malam Imam Imoru writes, "A freeborn woman, *'ya*, will not consent to marry a slave unless she is a good-for-nothing" (Ferguson 1973, 230). Any benefits to be had accrued in any case largely to slave men. Slave men were the ones whose prestige increased, and their children were born free.

59. Sumptuary codes are part of every culture. Harris has an especially interesting discussion of the Royal Cloth of Cameroon: who could wear it and when and why King Njoya in the early twentieth century issued a law allowing any person to wear "any garment he liked in his kingdom even if he, the king, had not given the garment to the person" (Harris 1985, 169). Similarly, Martin 1994 offers a fascinating account of social hierarchies and changing sumptuary codes in colonial and precolonial Brazzaville.

60. Slaves of high status could wear other clothing as well, but such slaves could also be forced to wear the loincloth as a form of punishment and public humiliation. This happened in the early twentieth-century palace (see Nast 1994) and was recalled by Imoru for slaves, generally. Imoru noted that "[i]f the slaveowner feels like it, he may make a handsome slave with a full beard and grey hair—undress and go to the market with only a loincloth on" (Ferguson 1973, 231).

61. Stilwell avers that it was Dabo who developed the uku-uku to distinguish his children from those of slaves. Stilwell nevertheless notes that a different oral slave tradition attributes the practice to Abdullahi (2000, 133). My informants additionally claimed it was Abdullahi, which I think makes the most sense (e.g., Sallama Dako, 28 October 1989): Abdullahi had numerous slaves and there had been considerable controversy over the marriage of male palace slaves to free Fulani women, begging the question of how these women's freeborn children might be distinguished from those born into slavery around them. This periodization is also consistent with Yunasa's guess, based on fieldwork in the early 1970s, that the uku-uku was introduced in the second half of the nineteenth century (1976, 47). His palace slave informants relayed that it was done because the emir could not distinguish between slave children and his own. However, this "problem" was a centuries-old one, nineteenth-century Fulani emirs having far fewer children (and concubines) than was previously the case. I suggest that the uku-uku was instituted not so much because emirs were befuddled, but because certain nobility whose daughters were mar-

ried to palace slaves were anxious that their grandchildren living among palace slaves would be mistaken for slaves. The personal concerns of the emir, relayed by Yunasa's informants, would thus be of allegorical significance. Maje Sirdi offered yet another theory for the uku-uku: that the emir didn't want his people to get lost, presumably a euphemism for runaways (25 November 2000).

62. Less commonly, free daughters might be given to slaves. Drawing upon the *Gwarzo District Notebook*, for example, Stilwell notes that a niece of Emir Bello was given as a wife to a slave captured from Borno.

63. Hajiyya Abba with Gogo Nani and Bagadede, 12 November 2000; Uwar Soro Binta, 25 November 2000. As Hajiyya Abba later noted, "they [already] have the knife" out for the tonsillectomy and circumcision procedures, so it makes the greatest sense to make the uku-uku marks then (19 November 2000). Female infants in the palace still undergo clitoridectomies, though a minority of princesses are beginning to contest the practice with respect to their children. The popular wisdom of female elders is that uncircumcised girls will be out of control sexually, and that circumcision gives them greater rationality than men, allowing them to control men through "sex."

64. It seems that some time after the uku-uku was instituted this particular scarification became prestigious. Adults desiring to be scarified thusly could do so as long as they were servants of the court and received the emir's permission (Maje Sirdi, 25 November 2000), presumably, the markings giving them considerable prestige. It was possibly also used historically to "brand" adult slaves who were particularly difficult or who had run away.

65. During my visit in November 2000 I heard in passing that the uku-uku of palace slave women was considered sexy by men outside the palace, perhaps a relic of how the unique marks of palace bondage became historically and publicly sexualized.

66. If so, perhaps concubinage became a more sexualized or exoticized institution overall. Given the Sokoto leadership's strictures against women operating in public, one might expect Sokoto women to have been particularly domesticated and sexualized. Accordingly, erotic control over men may have become a central and legitimate avenue for women to pursue, there being little else women might cultivate socially. Indeed, during a 1990 stay with a Fulani aristocratic woman in the northern city of Kaduna, we were visited by a woman specialist in female aphrodisiacs. I was told that Sokoto women held the most knowledge in this regard. Their knowledge may be a measure of both the sexualization of women's bodies generally, and how women developed creative domestic means for using sex to their political advantage under now more limited spatial circumstances.

67. The nineteenth-century caliphate structure dissolved many pre-existing political boundaries, allowing merchants to travel with greater ease. Trade networks consequently grew, facilitating slave trading. Most slaves obtained from within the caliphate were supplied by Adamawa, Bauchi, and Gombe, while many of those imported from outside the caliphate hailed from the lower Benue River region (where slaves were traded for iron) and Zinder, the latter sending most of its slaves to Kano. By Abdullahi's reign, slaves were also imported from places east of the caliphate and were bought with cowries. Abdullahi's reign coincided with the decline of trans-Atlantic slave exports from the caliphate and the realignment of export paths to southern coastal areas where they might be deployed on plantations (Tambo 1974, 16–18; see also Bay 1998). Most slaves exported southward out of the caliphate were slave men who traveled the Kano-to-Zaria-to-Rabba route, from where they (along with Nupe slaves) might be sent to Yorubaland, the port cities of Badagry, Porto Novo, and Lagos, or southward to Iboland and the Delta region ports.

Slaves exported out of Kano northward traveled to Ghat and from there to Ghadames (leading onward to Tunis or Tripoli and Constantinople) or from Kano eastward to Bornu and from there to Fezzan, Tripoli, and Constantinople. The largest number of slaves exported northward out of the caliphate came from Kano, with the majority of those exported out of Kano through Bornu being young females. The beginning of Abdullahi's reign saw the decline of the Kano-Bornu-Fezzan-Tripoli-Constantinople route due to banditry, such that the one leading directly out of Kano northward grew in importance. Figures from the early 1850s show that perhaps 2,500 slaves were exported per year.

Interestingly, not only were the majority of northbound exports composed of young girls, but the value of girls was much greater than that of boys, the ratio of female to male value declining northward. Hence, circa 1850, a young girl and boy captured and sold in the Kano area fetched 32 and 10 Maria Theresa dollars, respectively, whereas in Constantinople, the price of a young girl and boy from Kano was 130 and 90–100 Maria Theresa dollars, respectively (Tambo 1974, 24). Young female slaves held greater market value than their male counterparts because of their reproductive potential as concubines. Their value was in fact largely measured by the shape and condition of their breasts (e.g., full, sagging, or old). Girls' higher value starkly contrasts with their lesser value in the Americas where male-led production was more valued. At the same time, the decline in the female-male price differential between Kano, North Africa, and the Ottoman Empire (where fairer-skinner slave women held greater value) may have to do with how beauty was racialized (Tambo 1974).

68. Fika lists the following original members of the council, though he provides no indication of his sources: (1) Galadima; (2) Madaki; (3) Wambai; (4) Makama; (5) Sarkin Jarumai (Chief of the Brave Ones); (6) Sarkin Bai; (7) Barde; (8) Sarkin Dawaki Tsakar Gida (King of the Horses in the Middle of the House); and (9) Turaki (1978, 9). Since that time, these positions and the status of those holding them have shifted and changed, in keeping with the prerogatives and logics of various rulers. The KC relays, for example, that Kisoki took the Barde title off the list completely, replacing the title with a new one: dan Iya (the Son of Mother). This change was presumably done at his mother's behest for dan Iya was his full brother, their mother known as Iya (Mother) Lamis. The KC relays that "Kisoki ruled the town with his mother Iya Lamis and his grandmother Madaki Auwa, and Guli, the brother of Madaki Auwa" (Palmer 1967 [1928], 113). Later, the Turaki was taken off the list and replaced by the titleholder, Ciroma.

It is unclear how exactly the Kano Nine changed under Fulani rule, except that all positions were given to various Fulani clansmen. Different scholars claim different changes, largely with respect to the three lowest positions. All agree that the top four positions were remade by Dabo to include: (1) Madaki; (2) Makama; (3) Sarkin Dawaki Mai-Tuta (King of the Flag-bearing Horse; newly created); and (4) Sarkin Bai, filled by men of the Yolawa, Jobawa, nonroyal Sullubawa, and Dambazawa clans, respectively, though Fika avers that the third position was held by royal Sullubawa (Fika 1978, 21, 33; Sa'id 1978, 170; Ubah 1985, 12; Madakin Kano Shehu, 27 July 1990). There is also agreement that the next two positions, Galadima and Wambai, were filled by Sullubawa clansmen. Madakin Kano Shehu (27 July 1990) and Fika also agree that dan Iya was held by the Sullubawa, the Madaki explaining that Dabo originally gave the title to the Danejawa who sided with the Tukurists in the civil war; Aliyu in retribution consequently claimed the title for his own clan. Sa'id, meanwhile, claims that dan Iya was not on the council; the Turaki was. Moreover, the last two positions Madaki notes (the Magajin Malam and Gado da Masu) are not included in the lists drawn up by Fika and Sa'id, who claim that the last two were Ciroma and Sarkin Dawaki Mai-Tuta, both given to the Sullubawa. These and other differences have much to do with informants: when they were born, when they were interviewed, how reliable their memories are, under whose reign they served, to whom they are allegiant, and what version of history they want the historian to record. Ubah, for example, drew on the memories of Maje Abdu (the Turakin Kano from Jakun), Malam Hamza from Kano, Malam Isyaku, and Barden Kano (Alhaji Ibrahim Bayero), the District Head of Gwaram, interviewed on 29 July, 25 August, and 27 August 1972, and 3 August 1971, respectively (1985). Fika interviewed informants from the royal Sullubawa in 1970 (1978). My interviews took place twenty years later with the Madaki, who hailed from the Yolawa clan.

Barth lists only members on the emir's council, eight, including Sarkin Bai, Sarkin Dawaki (it is unclear which one), Galadima, Alkali, Gado, Ciroma, Barde, and Sarkin Shanu, the last entry and the Alkali being titles not listed by the other sources (1965 [1857]).

69. Drawing on earlier works, Fika relays some evidence of the tensions that accompanied Bello's decision: "[Bello] directed all the leading cucanawa (palace-born slaves) to divorce their free-born wives and retain as wives only women of slave descent like themselves. The cucanawa were resentful . . . for marrying free-born women had the effect of boosting their social status and making them almost indistinguishable from the non-slave dignitaries in the emirate. Apparently some of the important cucanawa tried to resist the ruler's directives but Muhammad Bello acted firmly. . . . Salama Barka is said to have been so outspoken that he was deprived of his title. It is also narrated that two other slave dignitaries . . . were so incensed . . . that when on one occasion they accompanied him [the emir] . . . to Sokoto, they complained to the Sultan . . . Even though the Sultan did not take up the matter, the emir came to know about it. . . . Jiga-Allah committed suicide to avoid what could only have been a horrible end. The second man, Dankumatu, was tortured, beheaded and then mutilated on the return of the emir to Kano" (1978, 57). See also Smith 1997, 303.

70. Centuries earlier, prior to the ivory trade, elephants were commonplace in the region. As Hiskett explains, the source of ivory traded in Kano in the 1500s A.D. only partly derived from the Ivory Coast: "No doubt some of it was obtained from herds in the Chad area and the upper Benue valley. Indeed, one cannot discount the possibility that there was a significant elephant population in Hausaland itself in the 10/16 century. But Professor Mahdi Adamu has drawn attention to the fact that the country lying between the Benue and the Cameroons was the source of the bulk of the ivory exported from the Niger Territories in the 13/19 century" (1981, 77).

5. British Colonial Abolition of Slavery and Concubinage

1. In Muffet 1964, 92.

2. There are discrepancies between data provided by different informants. His Highness Alhaji Ado Bayero (December 1988) claimed that the British entered from the southeast, whereupon a fierce skirmish took place below a kind of tower that formed part of the arsenal in the personal chambers of the emir established by Emir Abdullahi (Nast 1993). This direction of entry would make sense given that they had entered the city from the south. In contrast, Madakin Kano claimed that the palace was entered from the northeast and that the British met with intense resistance from the second floor of a guardswoman's chambers in the northern labyrinth that also served as a palace arsenal. Most data support the latter.

3. Mai-daki, April 1989.

4. There are conflicting accounts of why Emir Aliyu left Kano to go to Sokoto in the first place (given that he probably knew that the British would attack) and why he took so long to return (see, for example, Muffett 1964, 95–96, and Sa'id 1978).

5. In Muffett 1964, 92.

6. Mai-daki noted the location of the ritual and later confirmed her claim using landmarks visible in a photograph of the event presented in plate 46 of Lavers 1985.

7. These can be transliterated, respectively, as: "Behind the Son *of* the Soro," "son" referring to a small room behind the emir's much larger quarters known as Babban Soro or Soro for short, where this wife's estate was located; Field of the Cattle Herd, in reference to the fact that cattle commonly grazed there; Sokoto, where the daughter of the caliph of Sokoto lived; and Ward of the [Royal] Fulani Woman of the House referring to the first wife. The last name contains an honorific title that refers to the wife's ethnicity, Fulani, an ethnicity generally believed to be emblematic of religious purity, in contradistinction to the presumed heathenness of concubines.

8. That the estates of wives were characteristically designated *wajeje* (places) whereas those of concubines were *unguwoyi* (wards) is significant. "Place" refers to "ownership" by a single person. Wajen 'yar Sokoto, for example, means "the place of the wife from Sokoto." Each waje consisted of a large single-family compound built and organized to cater to the particular wife and her children. Smaller rooms therein housed live-in sadaku concubines and their children; unmarried domestic slave women lived in interstitial spaces (hallways, entranceways, the floors of large rooms). In contrast, unguwa connotes a communal shared space that belongs to the group. These spaces were densely settled. The residential differences between wives and concubines were one means of underscoring and making visible the lesser status of the latter.

9. A preliminary study indicates that thirty or more slave estates lay outside Kano city in the nineteenth century. At least two additional estates were built by Abdullahi Bayero and the present emir, Ado Bayero, including Fanda and Chiromawa, respectively (see also Yunasa 1976). Many of these estates were associated with country palaces, though only two were known to house concubines.

10. Ward and place names and locations were derived primarily from discussions with the late Hajiyya 'yar Mai-Tilas and Gogo Kahu (daughters of Emir Aliyu), the late Mai-daki and the late Gogon Ita Dambatta (daughters of Emir Abbas), the late 'yar Kutisa (formerly a concubine of Emir Abdullahi), Hajiyya Abba Ado Bayero (the second wife of the current emir), Malam D'au (a son of Emir Aliyu), the late Sallama Dako, Sarkin Hatsi, Galadima Rumbu (a slave assistant to Sarkin Hatsi), the late Alhaji Baba dan Meshe (a "eunuch" who was actually only impotent), and the current emir, His Highness Alhaji Ado Bayero. Discussion data were integrated with previously derived map data and verified in the field with one or more of the cooperants. Some ward and "place" data conflict with more contemporary data presented in Rufa'i 1987, which did not take into account the historical dynamics of the production of places and the changing roles, titles, and hierarchies of male and female slaves.

11. The emir's main chambers were in Babban Soro, built by Emir Abdullahi, and the Turakar Dabo-Soron Malam complex built by Abdullahi's father, Ibrahim Dabo (chapter 4).

12. Gogo Madaki, Gogon Ita, and Gogo Kahu, 23 and 27 August 1989.

13. Roughly transliterated, the title means "Woman of the [Emir's] Room."

14. Hajiyya Abba Ado Bayero, 23 January 1990. The political importance of Uwar Soro's culinary abilities in impressing important guests is additionally noted by Imam Imoru (Ferguson 1973) and Giginyu 1981.

15. The name of this room, like that of many others, is gendered in that it is used only by men. Women know it as Rumfar Kasa, the same name given to a functionally similar courtroom for men located in the nineteenth-century southern male slave domain. The room is sometimes called Soro (Hall) in reference to the emir's compound, Babban Soro of which it forms part. In

this sense, Soro needs no qualifier—it is part of *the* soro. Imam Imoru refers to this building as soron ciki, or hall of the "inside," it lying inside the cikin gida (Ferguson 1973, 209).

16. Those seeking an audience included women living in the cikin gida and any women from the emirate-at-large. Recall, for example, when freeborn Fulani women came seeking an audience with Emir Abdullahi to complain about the Fulani marriage partners to whom they had been betrothed. Abdullahi was away on a military campaign, for which reason the women were accommodated in the palace interior until his return.

17. Mai-daki and Hajiyya Abba, 5 September 1989 and 24 October 1989.

18. 'Yar Kutisa, 1 September 1989. I was told that kuyangi could use their crops in whatever manner best suited them. This arrangement whereby dependent women were given control over the yields of small fields awarded to them is similar to what Cooper describes in the context of the mid-twentieth-century Maradi (1997, 49). Whereas earlier, women had worked on the family farm (gandu), they also had their own restricted farm land *(gamana)* along with vegetable plots near their houses, both of which provided food for the family during the dry season; after French colonization, women assumed the right to use the proceeds of their production as they saw fit, the man now being recast in Islamic terms as the year-round provider of family food needs. As Cooper notes, aristocratic women (in this case from Gobir and Katsina) did not farm. The difference in the Kano context, of course, is that the palace was so large that kuyangi did not have to leave the palace's secluded "female" domain to cultivate their crops. Cooper points out that gourds were traditionally grown by women. If this was the case in the palace, it explains from where palace calabashes (dried gourds) derived (1997, 50).

19. A kuyanga wanting to farm her plot had to request permission from the guardswoman to enter the area ('yar Kutisa, 1 October 1989).

20. In November 2000, a burial mound west of the checkpoint leading to Shekar Yamma was pointed out to me. This was the place, I was told, where the executed lover of a concubine had been buried as a warning to other concubines (anonymous, November 2000).

21. Mai-daki, Gogon Ita Dambatta, Gogo Gandi, 1 September 1989. Wheat was a dry season crop that had to be grown under special conditions. Accordingly, it was mainly used by the aristocracy and featured during celebrations. It was used to cook a homemade form of couscous (actually dough flicked off with the thumbnail into a bowl to look like couscous grains), *talia* (spaghetti, probably obtained hundreds of years ago through trans-Saharan trade), *alkaki* (a fried sweet dough), and other specialties. With the postcolonial introduction of massive irrigation schemes, this would change (see Andrae and Beckman 1985).

22. A fuller description of colonial changes made to male slave domains is found in Ubah 1985, Nast 1992, and Stilwell 1999.

23. The king's bodyguard was reintroduced soon thereafter and was given bright red and green uniforms to wear. Traditionally, royal bodyguards wore white robes and turbans (Lavers 1985, plate 24). According to Sallama Dako, the men were so humiliated at having to wear such brightly colored robes that Emir Abbas donned the robes to cajole his men into wearing them (Sallama, 28 October 1989). Whether or not this story is true, it demonstrates how something as simple as colonial aesthetics impacted how a group of palace slaves felt about themselves.

24. See also Shenton 1986; Ubah 1985.

25. See Giginyu's reference to biyayya and the colonial demise of royal slavery on the Nassarawa pastoral slave estate (1981, 171).

26. Before the 1930s, most public works projects involved road and railway building and construction of colonial institutions, such as a large central prison, city and district court houses,

housing for colonial officers and schools (Ubah 1985, 184). The conscription of royal builders (who had slave status but lived outside the palace) for these projects is noted by Sa'ad (1981) and was investigated informally further by the author in 1989.

27. Ubah writes: "At the very beginning of the colonial administration all taxes were brought to the emir who converted them into cash and paid the agreed proportion to the Resident acting on behalf of the colonial government. Under [Resident] Cargill's re-organization, the district heads paid government's share in cash or cowries direct to the Waziri who then negotiated the cowries for silver and paid the whole lot to the Resident; at the same time the *hakimai* [nobility] paid the emir's share to his treasurer. Under [Resident] Temple it was made obligatory on the district heads to convert their taxes into cash before paying to the emir who then undertook to pay the usual percentage to the Resident" (1985, 176).

28. NAK/SNP7–8/1538/1908; Bello 1982. Ubah has a slightly different chronology. He writes: "At first all of the taxes were inevitably paid in kind or in cowries, which were the general currency of the emirate, and there was considerable difficulty in converting them into silver. It was known . . . that cowries would soon cease to be legal tender, and there was increasing demand for coins. . . . So long as cowries continued to be accepted regardless of the depreciation, the major sufferer was the [traditional] treasury because taxes paid in cowries or kind had to be converted into silver. . . . In December, 1910, a discussion between the [British] Resident and the emir led to an agreement that . . . [taxes] should be collected in coins—except in [several] . . . districts where these were difficult to obtain. . . . With the *zakka* the problem was more difficult. Since this tax was always computed in terms of bundles of grain there seemed to be no conceivable way of making the payer feel the impact of the depreciation so long as the principle was honoured. Each bundle was valued at 9d, but with the depreciations . . . *zakka* became a thorny issue. To demand it in cash was considered . . . a very risky matter. Palmer deliberated . . . with the emir and a decision was arrived at that . . . the [zakat] grains should be stored and then gradually sold off. . . . In 1911/12 the *zakka* was paid in cash. By 1913 payment in kind was said to have become unpopular among many people who now preferred to pay the 9d per bundle; probably the removal of the burden of transferring thousands of bundles of grain to Kano had helped to facilitate the change" (1985, 175).

29. A taiki is a very large leather sack used to carry grain on pack animals. The sack has an opening cut along the middle of its width, such that when it is placed atop an animal's back with the opening facing upwards, it forms two adjacent pocket-like spaces (Ferguson 1973, 324).

30. Mai-daki, 24 and 25 October 1989.

31. Lawan jika Ayi, grandson of the late Korama Ayi, 16 November 2000. That the Madaki was engaged in this "ritual" suggests that the palace was receiving zakat and possibly other grain taxes at this late date. Prior to 1909, the emir or the Waziri converted the emir's tax portion of cowries or grains into cash, requiring the sort of transaction Madaki engaged in. However, by 1909, district heads submitting the taxes were responsible for the cash conversion of all in-kind payments. Ubah avers that Palmer conferred with the emir and they jointly decided to sell off zakat grains, and that by 1912 zakat was collected entirely in cash (1985, 175). Garba argues, however, that payment of zakat did not end as easily as the colonizers said it did (1986, 112–13). Indeed many palace inhabitants recall zakat being received in the palace for decades after the conquest.

32. Malam D'au, December 1989.

33. Emir Abbas apparently was not good at monitoring the private lives of his wives and concubines, his frustration leading him to issue a mandate: all women entering the palace ciki had

to bare their faces by removing their outermost headcover or *lullubi*, hence allowing jakadu and others to ascertain if men (impersonating women) were unlawfully entering the interior (see Rufa'i 1987, 149).

34. According to Islamic precedents (see chapter 1), a concubine remains a concubine until her death, although if she has borne a child, she can be freed upon her master's death. A concubine, unlike a wife, cannot be divorced and is entitled to being cared for until she dies. Customarily, however, a royal concubine could opt to become the concubine of the king or emir who succeeded her master. Aliyu's concubines did not stay with him presumably because the emir no longer had the means to sustain them. Their returning, or Aliyu's sending them back, to the palace ensured their well-being and also allowed for knowledge about interior administration to be passed from one emir to the next. In this sense, concubines were similar to other important titleholding palace slave men who lived in the palace during, and served, successive administrations. Emir Sanusi also sent his concubines back to the palace after he was deposed in 1963 (below).

35. NAK/KANPROF 1836.

36. Christelow reasoned similarly that juridical claims for children's freedom by their parents virtually ceased after 1913 because their parents could not sustain them during the famine: "parents of slave children were reluctant to give up claims on the master's support, and masters, should claims arise, would not contest them, since the child's freedom would diminish claims upon his resources" (1985, 65).

37. Wealthy households had other means for securing concubines, presumably because, as Cooper argues, other kinds of slavery had been outlawed, allowing concubines to be used to pick up the labor slack. In particular, British colonial courts allowed unrelated men to "redeem" slave girls (1997). In reality, these men were using the colonial system to procure young girls as concubines (see Lovejoy 1988, 264–65, and Christelow 1985).

38. Hajiyya Abba and Mai-daki, 24 October 1989. Rural dwellers are traditionally characterized as uncultured and dull (see Sa'ad 1981).

39. Sallama Dako, 27 October 1989.

40. Mai-daki, 16 and 24 October 1989.

41. Alhaji Ado Sanusi, 2 December 2003.

42. Mai-daki, 24 October 1989; Sallama, 28 October 1989.

43. NAK/KANPROF 4164.

44. Ubah 1985; His Highness Alhaji Ado Bayero, 23 January 1990.

45. Alhaji Ado Sanusi, 2 December 2003.

46. This decision by the emir to give the Nassarawa lands over to his slave dependents parallels similar decisions described by Cooper for heads of households generally in Maradi where French colonial policy disrupted previous familial farming arrangements: "The fragmentation of landholdings resulted, thus, in part from a strategy on the part of household heads to reduce the tax burden they faced to pay the taxes of their junior male dependents. By permitting younger men to set up independent households on family land, older men could shift tax burdens to juniors" (1997, 46).

47. Cooper writes similarly in the context of the Nigerien population after French abolition of slavery. In this case, junior wives took over the tasks once carried out by slave women (1997, 13). Christelow's (1985) perusal of colonial court records in Kano for the years 1913–14 reveal in analogous fashion that slave girls born prior to the 1901 slave proclamation (who were hence not free) were often redeemed in courts by men who "freed" them. While he theorizes that this

was done so that they could become their legal Islamic guardians and thereby control the dowry associated with marriage-related transactions, it is also probable that many were redeemed by men who desired them as concubines. See also Lovejoy 1988, 264 n. 58.

48. Christelow writes, "Indeed, it is ironic that the British, who prided themselves on bringing freedom to Nigeria . . . introduced this new form of unfreedom. . . . A man whose brother had been sent to prison . . . [said that] 'imprisonment is not the same thing as killing, but as the prisoner is worn out, he dies without dying'" (1985, 71).

49. Malam D'au, December 1989.

50. I have never heard a bayi refer to themselves as a "servant" (bara or bawan yarda), which would be a linguistic option. Just as the former ruling class maintained a level of authenticity by assuming titles that had little to do with colonial and postcolonial realities so, too, palace bayi assumed authenticity by retaining their linguistic options. Whereas the British happily supported retaining aristocratic titles, claiming these were the basis of indirect rule (and allowing them to claim publicly that they held respect for local hierarchies), they disapproved of palace bayi titles. Their disapproval stemmed from the fact that the ties between master and elite palace slave threatened colonial agendas, slaves often attempting to subvert colonial policies. By outlawing palace slavery and palace slave titles, the British inverted the power hierarchy: the British were now an "aristocracy" and the aristocracy their dependents.

51. Cooper's work on marriage in Maradi, Niger, provides a different perspective. She found that even though slavery was much less prevalent than in the Sokoto caliphate, it provided sufficient additional labor to create considerable tensions in post-abolition society (1997; see especially her chapter 1). In particular, women's participation in farming intensified and senior wives and representatives delegated the most arduous labor to junior wives. Because slavery was most prominent in urban areas, it was here that the tensions were most noticeable. As she describes: "In the city, however, slave and free women were more readily distinguishable, not primarily because of veiling, but because of their different duties and because of substantial differences in wealth. The leisure made possible by the use of female slaves enabled aristocratic women to spin cotton thread, a significant source of income and prestige. . . . Aristocratic urban women therefore had to find ways to retain or replace the captive domestic labor that had freed them from onerous household duties in the past. The simplest solution, of course, would simply be to redefine the slave women as concubines and junior wives, women whose labor could then be controlled by senior aristocratic women as senior wives and mothers-in-law" (9).

52. 24 October 1989.

53. NAK/KANPROF 4164; Ubah 1985, 182.

54. NAK/KANPROF 4164.

55. NAK/KAN/LA/140; KANPROF 1926. An earlier durbar was held on New Year's Day in 1909, which Ubah refers to as a "Lugardian tradition" (1985, 66). Although Kano leaders had traditionally been saluted by ceremonial military charges in the past, the durbar demilitarized, formalized, and staged these salutations into an aestheticized, public time and space. The durbar has since become an annual popular event held at the end of Ramadan and celebrated on open grounds just north and south of the palace.

56. NAK/KANPROF 1744.

57. NAK/KANPROF 1081/vll; Shenton 1986, 83–92.

58. NAF/15/1939; NAK/KANONA 152.

59. The plan was to incorporate the area into the British Government Reserved Areas (Giginyu 1981).

60. The area south of the labyrinth was made into a public, male domain of state to accommodate British administrators, apparently making the southernmost labyrinth passageway off-limits to female guards (Nast 1992).

61. Mack is therefore incorrect when she states that palace "women began preparing food only for those for whom they were directly responsible" when "the task grew to impossible proportions" and that "traditionally, the entire palace community was fed from a central kitchen" (1991, 118). It was, in fact, constrictions in the sources of grain and labor during the colonial period that led to the dispersion of cooking duties, with the palace population steadily in decline. Moreover, a wife had always personally overseen food production for all persons living or serving her in her individual personal estate (waje), concubines carrying out the required labor tasks under her watchful eye, there being the general fear that concubines might poison a wife and her family to prevent her sons from succeeding to the throne.

62. Sadiya Ado Bayero, 3 December 2003; Alhaji Ado Sanusi, 2 December 2003; Lamido Sanusi, 13 November 2000. Aisha's nickname was Delu. 'Ya Hajiyya's real name is Hasiya. Because the late Queen Mother held the same name, the name cannot be spoken, out of respect for her. Instead all persons (including one royal daughter) named Hasiya are called 'ya Hajiyya. 'Yaya means "senior sister." In the tradition of the palace, any concubine instated ahead of another is called 'Yaya, for example, 'Yaya Mai-Soron Baki. Palace children customarily refer to all concubines as 'Yaya except the Uwar Soro who is called 'Umma (Mother). Rufa'i 1987 places Uwar Waje on par with the other three titleholding concubines, whereas Mack is unaware of the historical presence and importance of Mai-Kudandan (1988, 76).

63. Uwar Gida Ma-Kulle transliterally means "Woman of the House of Those [Women] Locked Up [Secluded]." A similar practice obtained in Buganda where the king's father was expected to supply him with a senior (administratively skilled) wife (Musisi 1991, 777).

64. By this time, Turakar Dabo near Kacako, and Turakar Usman in Yelwa were no longer in use.

65. See Sa'ad 1981 for a discussion of how spatial abstraction in the practices and content of traditional building increased over colonial time. Jaggar similarly documents how blacksmith control over in-palace carpentry and metalworking was superceded by the Public Works Department of the Native Authority, a modern intervention partly responsible for the decline of the blacksmithing guilds (1973, 23).

66. The school was instituted at a time when the British were pushing for girls' schools in the city and region.

67. 5 September 1989.

68. Sadiya Ado Bayero, 3 December 2003.

69. The wives' and concubines' quarters are fitted with fewer luxuries. None of them had air conditioners, faxes, phones, or computers in 2000, for example, and water was obtained from standing pumps distributed throughout the palace interior. By 2003 one wife had a cell phone, the finances for which she handled independently.

70. Hajiyya Abba Ado Bayero, 1990.

Conclusion

1. Sutton continues: "Thus Hausaland . . . has during the present millennium come to support denser populations than both the drier Sahel to its north and also most of the 'middle belt' with longer rains but more woodland to its south. . . . Being Hausa implied belonging to a wider, more open and receptive system, rural indeed but not rustic, one in which the countryside could

support and interact with semi-urban centers where markets gradually developed and political power was increasingly focused" (184).

2. My arguments that increasing commoditization negatively impacted the originally organically derived powers of concubines in the eighteenth through twentieth centuries resonate with arguments made by Cooper (1997, 155–57) with respect to Hausa marriages in twentieth-century Maradi. Cooper claims that marriage for women traditionally carried much symbolic imagery associated with fertility. The sadaki payments made by men, for instance, were often rendered in livestock and cowries, the former allowing for social reproduction and the latter redolent of female pregnancy. Moreover, most gifts given to the young bride to decorate her marital home were objects made through women's labors, symbolic of fertility, and tied to reproduction. Calabashes, for instance, were made out of gourds—grown by women and then dried and decorated by them. Symbolic of the womb and female pregnancy, calabashes were used as food utensils. With the monetization of the economy, women found themselves in a difficult position. Marginalized from the most lucrative forms of trade, they struggle to give gifts that have exchange value (beds or enamel bowls), a form of wealth divorced from their own productive endeavors, but which point to the bride's worth and the strength of her social networks. Cooper's argument that women's double alienation (from a valuation of their own labor and the intrusion of the market) weakened them politically during the colonial and postcolonial period parallels the gist of my arguments with respect to the decline of palace concubines' powers over several centuries.

Epilogue

1. Gogo Mama's great-great-great-grandfather was named Alimi. The Shehu sent him from Sokoto to conquer Ilorin, which he did. He settled there and was made emir. Gogo Mama considers herself Fulani (Gogo Mama, 21 November 2000). While I believe the spirit house may date from the nineteenth century, I am more inclined to see it as part and parcel of Abdullahi dan Dabo's re-creation of the old Hausa kingship site and his engagement with pre-Islamic practices. The practices relate to bori sensibilities. Gogo Nani, 25 November 2000.

2. Sadiya Ado Bayero, 23 November 2000.

3. Although many older "male" structures in the palace have similarly deteriorated or become outdated, many modern buildings are being constructed in their stead.

4. Hajiyya Abba, 9 November 1990.

5. Sarkin Hatsi, 25 November 2000.

Bibliography

Abraham, R. C. 1962 [1946]. *Dictionary of the Hausa Language.* London: University of London Press.

Abubakr, Sa'ad. 1992. "Queen Amina of Zaria." Pp. 11–23 in *Nigerian Women in Historical Perspective,* ed. Bolanle Awe. Lagos: Sankore.

Ahmed, Bello Nuhu. 1988. "Kano Emirate Palaces: An Architectural and Historical Study. B.Sc. honors thesis, Architecture, Ahmadu Bello University, Zaria, Nigeria.

Alloula, Malek 1986. *Colonial Harem.* Minneapolis: University of Minnesota Press.

Amadiume, Ifi. 1997. *Reinventing Africa.* New York: Zed Books.

Andrae, Gunilla, and Bjorn Beckman. 1985. *The Wheat Trap.* London: Zed Books.

Apter, Emily. 1990. "Colonial Fiction and Architectural Fantasm in Turn-of-the-Century France." *Ottagono* 97:97–107.

Awe, Bolanle, ed. 1992. *Nigerian Women in Historical Perspective.* Ibadan, Nigeria: Bookcraft.

Ayalon, David. 1979. "On the Eunuchs in Islam." *Jerusalem Studies in Arabic and Islam* 1:67–124.

Azuonye, Chukwuma. 1996. *Dogon.* New York: Rosen Publishing Group.

Backwell, H. F. 1969. *The Occupation of Hausaland, 1900–1904.* London: Cass.

Balfour-Paul, Jenny. 1997. *Indigo in the Arab World.* Surrey, England: Curzon Press.

Bargery, Rev. G. P. 1934. *A Hausa-English Dictionary and English-Hausa Vocabulary.* London: Oxford University Press.

Barkindo, Bawuro. 1983. "The Gates of Kano City: A Historical Survey." Pp. 1–31 in *Studies in the History of Kano,* ed. Bawuro Barkindo. Ibadan, Nigeria: Heinemann Educational Books.

Barkow, Jerome H. 1972. "Hausa Women and Islam." *Canadian Journal of African Studies* 6:317–328.

Barth, Dr. Heinrich. 1965 [1857]. *Travels and Discoveries in North and Central Africa Being a Journal of an Expedition Undertaken under the Auspices of H.B.M.'s Government in the Years 1849–1855.* Vol. 1. London: Frank Cass and Co.

Bay, Edna. 1998. *Wives of the Leopard: Gender, Politics and Culture in the Kingdom of Dahomey.* Charlottesville: University of Virginia Press.

Bello, Sule. 1982. "State and Economy in Kano: A Study of Colonial Domination." Ph.D. diss., Ahmadu Bello University, Zaria, Nigeria.

Boddy, Janice. 1989. *Wombs and Alien Spirits: Women, Men and the Zar Cult in Northern Sudan.* Madison: University of Wisconsin Press.

Boyd, Jean, and Murray Last. 1985. "The Role of Women as 'Agents religieux' in Sokoto." *Canadian Journal of African Studies* 19(2):283–300.

Burnham, Philip, and Murray Last. 1994. "From Pastoralist to Politician: The Problem of a Fulbe 'Aristocracy.'" *Cahiers d'Etudes africaines* 34 (1–3):313–57.

Butler, Judith. 1990. *Gender Trouble.* New York: Routledge.

Christelow, Alan. 1985. "Slavery in Kano, 1913–14: Evidence from the Judicial Records." *African Economic History* 14: 57–74.

Clark, Andrew F. 1997. "'The Ties That Bind': Servility and Dependency among the Fulbe of Bundu (Senegambia) circa 1930s to 1980s." Draft paper, Department of History, University of North Carolina–Wilmington.

———. 1999. *Economy and Society in the Upper Senegal Valley, West Africa, 1850–1920.* Lanham, Md.: University Press of America.

Clarke, Peter B. 1982. *West Africa and Islam.* London: Edward Arnold.

Cohen, Ronald. 1977. "Oedipus Rex and Regina: The Queen Mother in Africa." *Africa* 47(1):14–30.

Coles, Catherine, and Beverly B. Mack. 1991. *Hausa Women in the Twentieth Century.* Madison: University of Wisconsin Press.

Cooper, Barbara. 1997. *Marriage in Maradi: Gender and Culture in a Hausa Society in Niger, 1900–1989.* Portsmouth, N.H.: Heinemann.

Crary, Jonathan. 1992. *Techniques of the Observer.* Cambridge: MIT Press.

Denham, Dixon. 1826. *Narratives of the Travels and Discoveries in Northern and Central Africa, in the Years 1822, 1823, and 1924 by Major Denham, Captain Clapperton, and the late Dr. Oudney. Extending across the Great Desert to the Tenth Degree of Northern Latitude, and from Kouka in Bournou, to Sackatoo, the Capital of the Felatah Empire.* London: John Murray.

Dieterlen, Germaine. 1982. *Le titre d'honneur des Arou (Dogon-Mali).* Paris: Musée de l'Homme.

Dikko, Sande. 1982. "The Role of Women Title Holders in the Zaria Political Setup." B.A. thesis, Bayero University Kano, Kano, Nigeria.

Dmochowski, Z. R. 1990. *An Introduction to Nigerian Traditional Architecture,* vol. 3. London: Ethnographica.

Dokaji Kano, Alhaji Abubakar. 1978 [1958] *Kano ta Dabo Cigari.* Zaria: Northern Nigerian Publishing Company.

Dunk, Thomas W. 1983. "Slavery in Hausaland: An Analysis of the Concept of the Slave Mode of Production, with Special Reference to Kano Emirate, Nigeria." M.A. thesis, Department of Anthropology, McGill University, Montreal.

East, R. M. 1971 [1930]. *Labarun Hausawa da makwabtansu: Littafi na biyu.* Zaria, Nigeria: Northern Nigerian Publishing Company.

Echard, Nicole. 1991. "Gender Relationships and Religion: Women in the Hausa Bori of Ader, Niger." Pp. 207–20 in *Hausa Women in the Twentieth Century,* ed. Catherine Coles and Beverly Mack. Madison: University of Wisconsin Press.

Fage, J. D. 1969. *A History of West Africa.* Cambridge: Cambridge University Press.

———. 1978 [1958]. *An Atlas of African History.* 2nd ed. London: Edward Arnold.

Ferguson, D. 1973. "Nineteenth-century Hausaland Being a Description of Imam Imoru." Ph.D. diss., Department of History, University of California, Los Angeles.

Fika, A. M. 1978. *The Kano Civil War and British Over-rule, 1882–1940.* Ibadan, Nigeria: Oxford University Press.

Frishman, Alan Ivan. 1977. "The Spatial Growth and Residential Location Pattern of Kano, Nigeria." Ph.D. diss., Economics, Northwestern University, Evanston, Ill.

Garba, Tijjani. 1986. "Taxation in Some Hausa Emirates, circa 1860–1939." Ph.D. diss., Centre for West African Studies, University of Birmingham, England.

Giginyu, Sa'idu. 1981. "History of a Slave Village in Kano: Gandun Nassarawa." B.A. (honors) thesis, Ahmadu Bello University, Zaria, Nigeria.

Grosz, Elizabeth. 1990. "Inscriptions and Body-maps: Representations and the Corporeal." Pp. 62–75 in *Feminine-Masculine and Representation,* ed. Terry Threadgold and Anne Cranny-Francis. Sydney: Allen and Unwin.

Guyer, Jane I., and Samuel M. Eno Belinga. 1995. "Wealth in People as Wealth in Knowledge: Accumulation and Composition in Equatorial Africa." *Journal of African History* 36:91–120.

Gwarzo, Hassan I., Kamal I. Bedri, and Priscilla E. Starratt. 1974/77. "Taj al-din fima yajib 'ala al-muluk or The Crown of Religion Concerning the Obligations of Princes." *Kano Studies* 1(2):15–28.

Harris, Moira Flanagan. 1985. "The Royal Cloth of Cameroon." Ph.D. diss., The Graduate School, University of Minnesota, Minneapolis.

Hill, Polly. 1972. *Rural Hausa.* London: Cambridge University Press.

———. 1977. *Population, Prosperity, and Poverty in Rural Kano, 1900 and 1970.* London: Cambridge University Press.

Hiskett, Mervyn. 1981. "Reflections on the Location of Place Names and on the 10/16 Century Map of Hausaland and Their Relation to Fatauci Routes." *Kano Studies,* n.s. 2(2):69–98.

Hogendorn, Jan S. 2000. "The Location of the 'Manufacture' of Eunuchs." Pp. 41–69 in *Slave Elites in the Middle East and Africa,* ed. Miura Toru and John Edward Philips. London: Kegan Paul.

Hogendorn, Jan S., and Marion Johnson. 1986. *The Shell Money of the Slave Trade.* New York: Cambridge University Press.

Hunt, Peter. 1998. "Concubinage: Ancient Rome." Pp. 210–11 in *Macmillan Encyclopedia of World Slavery.* New York: Macmillan Reference USA.

Hunwick, John. n.d. "Leo Africanus on the Hausa States." Unpublished manuscript.

———. 1985. "Songhay, Borno and the Hausa States, 1450–1600." Pp. 323–72 in *History of West Africa,* 3rd ed., ed. J. F. A. Ajayi and Michael Crowder. London: Longman.

———. 1994. "A Historical Whodunit: The So-called 'Kano Chronicle' and Its Place in the Historiography of Kano." *History in Africa* 21:127–46.

Imperato, Pascal James. 1996. *Historical Dictionary of Mali,* 3rd ed. Lanham, Md.: Scarecrow Press.

Jaggar, Phil. 1973. "Kano City Blacksmiths: Precolonial Distribution, Structure, and Organisation." *Savanna* 2(1):11–25.

Jaschok, M. H. A. 1998. "Concubinage: China." Pp. 213–15 in *Macmillan Encyclopedia of World Slavery*. New York: Macmillan Reference USA.

Jell-Bahlsen, Sabine. 1997. "*Eze Mmiri di Egwu*, the water monarch is awesome." Pp. 103–34 in *Queens, Queen Mothers, Priestesses, and Power*, ed. Flora Kaplan. New York: New York Academy of Sciences.

Johnson, Dr. O., ed. 1937 [1921]. *The History of the Yorubas: From the Earliest Times to the Beginning of the British Protectorate by the Reverend Samuel Johnson, Pastor of Oyo*. Lago: C.M.S. (Nigeria) Bookshops.

Johnston, H. A. S. 1967. *The Fulani Empire of Sokoto*. London: Oxford University Press.

Kanya-Forstner, A. S., and Paul E. Lovejoy. 1994. "The Sokoto Caliphate and the European Powers, 1890–1907." *Paideuma* 40:7–14.

Kaplan, Flora E. S. 1997a. "*Iyoba*, the Queen Mother of Benin: Images and Ambiguity in Gender and Sex Roles in Court Art." In *Queens, Queen Mothers, Priestesses, and Power*, ed. Flora Edouwaye S. Kaplan, 73–102. New York: New York Academy of Sciences.

———. 1997b. *Queens, Queen Mothers, Priestesses, and Power*. New York: New York Academy of Sciences.

Kaura, J. M. 1990. "Emancipation of Women in the Sokoto Caliphate." Pp. 75–103 in *State and Society in the Sokoto Caliphate*, ed. Ahmad Mohammad Kani and Kabir Ahmed Gandi. Zaria, Nigeria: Gaskiya Corporation.

Kriger, Colleen. 1993. "Textile Production and Gender in the Sokoto Caliphate." *Journal of African History* 34:361–401.

Lal, Ruby. 2003. "Mughal India: 15th to Mid-18th Century." *Encyclopedia of Women and Islamic Cultures*. Leiden, Netherlands: Brill Academic Publishers.

Last, Murray. 1967. *The Sokoto Caliphate*. London: Longman.

———. 1979. "Early Kano: The Santolo-Fangwai Settlement System." *Kano Studies* 1:7–23.

———. 1983. "From Sultanate to Caliphate: Kano ca. 1450–1800." Pp. 67–93 in *Studies in the History of Kano*, ed. Bawuro Barkindo. Ibadan, Nigeria: Heinemann Educational Books.

———. 1987 [1974]. "Reform in West Africa: The Jihad Movements of the Nineteenth Century." Pp. 1–47 in *History of West Africa*, vol. 2, 2nd ed., ed. J. F. A. Ajayi and Michael Crowder. London: Longman.

Lavers, John. 1981. "The Walls of Kano City." *History Today* 3:54–56.

———. 1985. *A Guide to the Gidan Makama Museum Kano*. National Commission for Museums and Monuments, Lagos, Nigeria.

Lebeuf, Annie M. D. 1969. *Les principautes Kotoko : Essai sur le caractere sacre de l'autorite*. Paris: Université de Paris, Editions du Centre National de la Recherche Scientifique.

Lefebvre, Henri. 1991. *The Production of Space*. Translated by Donald Nicholson-Smith. Cambridge, Mass.: Blackwell.

Lerner, Gerda. 1986. *The Creation of Patriarchy*. Oxford: Oxford University Press.

Lingis, Alfonso. 1994. *Foreign Bodies*. New York: Routledge.

Lovejoy, Paul E. 1988. "Concubinage and the Status of Women Slaves in Early Colonial Northern Nigeria." *Journal of African History* 29(2): 245–66.

———. 1990. "Concubinage in the Sokoto Caliphate (1804–1903)." *Slavery and Abolition* 11(2): 159–89.

Lovejoy, Paul E., and J. Hogendorn. 1993. *Slow Death for Slavery: The Course of Abolition in Northern Nigeria, 1897–1936*. Cambridge: Cambridge University Press.

Lovejoy, Paul E., Abdullahi Mahadi, and Mansur Ibrahim Muktar. 1993. "C. L. Temple's 'Notes on the History of Kano' [1909]: A Lost Chronicle on Political Office." *Sudanic Africa: A Journal of Historical Sources* 4:7–76.

Mack, Beverly. 1988. "Hajiya Ma'daki: A Royal Hausa Woman." Pp. 47–77 in *Life Histories of African Women,* ed. Patricia Romero. Madison: University of Wisconsin Press.

———. 1991. "Royal Wives in Kano." Pp. 109–29 in *Hausa Women in the Twentieth Century,* ed. Catherine Coles and Beverly Mack. Madison: University of Wisconsin Press.

———. 1992. "Harem Domesticity in Kano, Nigeria." Pp. 75–97 in *African Encounters with Domesticity,* ed. Karen Tranberg Hansen. Atlantic Highlands, N.J.: Rutgers University Press.

———. 1998. "Concubinage: Islamic World." Pp. 211–13 in *Macmillan Encyclopedia of World Slavery.* New York: Macmillan Reference USA.

Madauci, Ibrahim, Yahaya Isa, and Bello Daura. 1985 [1968]. *Hausa Customs.* Zaria: Northern Nigeria Publishing.

Malami, Hussaini Usman. 1998. *Economic Principles and Practices of the Sokoto Caliphate.* Sokoto, Nigeria: Institute of Islamic Sciences.

Martin, Phyllis M. 1994. "Contesting Clothes in Colonial Brazzaville." *Journal of African History* (35):401–26.

Masquelier, Adeline. Forthcoming. "How Is a Girl to Marry Without a Bed? Weddings, Wealth, and Women's Value in an Islamic Town of Niger." In *Situating Globality: African Agency in the Appropriation of Global Culture,* ed. Wim van Binsbergen and Rijk van Dijk. Leiden, Netherlands: Brill.

Massey, Doreen. 1984. *Spatial Divisions of Labour: Social Structures and the Geography of Production.* London: Macmillan.

Matory, James Lorand. 1994. *Sex and Empire That Is No More: Gender and the Politics of Metaphor in the Oyo Yoruba Religion.* Minneapolis: University of Minnesota Press.

Michel-Jones, Francoise. 1978. *Retour aux dogon: Figures du double et ambivalence.* Paris: Le Sycamore.

Moody, H. L. B. 1967. "The Walls and Gates of Kano City." *Kano Studies* 3:12–26.

Moore, Henrietta L. 1986. *Space, Text and Gender.* Cambridge: Cambridge University Press.

Moughtin, Cliff. 1985. *Hausa Architecture.* London: Ethnographica.

Muffett, D. J. M. 1964. *Concerning Brave Captains.* London: Deutsch.

———. 1971. "Nigeria-Sokoto caliphate." Pp. 268–99 in *West African Resistance: The Military Response to Colonial Occupation,* ed. M. Crowder. London: Hutchinson.

Murdock, George Peter. 1959. *Africa: Its Peoples and Their Culture History.* New York: McGraw-Hill.

Musisi, Nakanyike B. 1991. "Women, 'Elite Polygyny,' and Buganda State Formation." *Signs: Journal of Women in Culture and Society* 16(4):757–86.

Nachtigal, Gustav. 1971. *Sahara and Sudan.* 4 vols. Translated from German, with introduction and notes by Allan G. B. Fisher and Humphrey J. Fisher with Rex S. O'Fahey. Berkeley: University of California Press.

Nadel, S. F. 1965 [1942]. *A Black Byzantium: The Kingdom of Nupe in Nigeria.* London: Oxford University Press.

Nast, Heidi J. 1992. "Space, History, and Power: Stories of Spatial and Social Change in the Palace of Kano, Northern Nigeria, circa 1500 to 1990." Ph.D. diss., McGill University, Montreal.

———. 1993. "Engendering 'Space': State Formation and the Restructuring of the Kano Palace Following the Islamic Holy War in Northern Nigeria, 1807–1903." *Historical Geography* 23:62–75.

———. 1994. "The Impact of British Imperialism on the Landscape of Female Slavery in the Kano Palace, Northern Nigeria." *Africa.* 64(1):34–73.

———. 1996. "Islam, Gender, and Slavery in West Africa circa 1500: A Spatial Archaeology of the Kano Palace, Northern Nigeria." *Annals of the Association of American Geographers* 86(1): 44–77.

———. 2000. "Mapping the 'Unconscious': Racism and the Oedipal Family." *Annals of the Association of American Geographers* 90(2):215–55.

———. 2001. "Nodal Thinking." *Historical Geography* 29 (Special issue: Practicing Historical Geography):74–76.

Necipoglu, Gulru. 1991. *Architecture, Ceremonial and Power: The Topkapi Palace in the Fifteenth and Sixteenth Centuries.* Cambridge: MIT Press.

Nengel, John Garah. 1988. The Impact of the Sokoto Jihad on the Kurama People of Eastern Zazzau, c. 1800–1900. *Afrika und Uberser* 71:245–65.

Newman, Roxana Ma. 1990. *An English-Hausa Dictionary.* London: Yale University Press.

O'Fahey, R. S. 1980. *State and Society in Dar Fur.* London: C. Hurst and Company.

O'Fahey R. S., and Jay Spaulding. 1974. *Kingdoms of the Sudan.* London: Methuen.

Paden, John N. 1973. *Religion and Political Culture in Kano.* Berkeley: University of California Press.

Palmer, H. R. 1967 [1928]. *Sudanese Memoirs Being Mainly Translations of a Number of Arabic Manuscripts Relating to Central and Western Sudan.* London: Frank Cass and Co.

Philips, John E. 1989. "A History of the Hausa Language." Pp. 39–59 in *Kano and Some of Her Neighbors,* ed. Barwuro Barkindo. Zaria, Nigeria: Ahmadu Bello University Press.

Pittin, Renee. 1983. "Houses of Women." Pp. 291–302 in *Female and Male in West Africa,* ed. Christine Oppong. London: George Allen & Unwin.

Plumer, Cheryl. 1971. *African Textiles: An Outline of Handcrafted Sub-Saharan Fabrics.* East Lansing: African Studies Center, Michigan State University.

Pucci, Suzanne Rodin. 1985. "Orientalism and Representations of Exteriority in Montesquieu's *Lettres persanes.*" *Eighteenth Century: Theory and Interpretation* 23(3): 263–79.

———1989. "Letters from the Harem: Veiled Figures of Wiring in Montesquier's *Lettres persanes.*" Pp. 114–34 in *Writing the Female Voice,* ed. Elizabeth C. Goldsmith. Boston: Northeastern University Press.

Rattray, R. S. 1913. *Hausa Folklore Customs, Proverbs, etc. Collected and Transliterated with English Translation and Notes by R. Sutherland Rattray . . . with a Preface by R. R. Marett.* Oxford: Clarendon Press.

Renne, Elisha P. 1995. *Cloth That Does Not Die.* Seattle: University of Washington Press.

Robinson, Charles Henry. 1925. *Dictionary of the Hausa Language.* Cambridge: Cambridge University Press.

Romero, Patricia. 1988. *Life Histories of African Women.* Madison: University of Wisconsin Press.

Rufa'i, Mrs. Ruqqayatu Ahmed. 1987. "Gidan Rumfa: The Sociopolitical History of the Palace of the Emir of Kano with Particular Reference to the Twentieth Century." M.A. thesis, History, Bayero University, Kano, Nigeria.

———. 1995. *Gidan Rumfa: The Kano Palace.* Kano: Triumph Publishing.

Ruxton, F. H. 1916. *Maliki Law: Being a Summary of French Translations of the Mukhtasar of Sidi Khalil.* London: Luzac and Company.

Sa'ad, Hamman Tukur. 1981. "Between Myth and Reality: The Aesthetics of Traditional Architecture in Hausaland." Ph.D. diss., 2 vols., University of Michigan, Ann Arbor.

———. 1985. "Continuity and Change in Traditional Kano Architecture." Paper presented to the second conference on the History of Kano, Sept. 16–20, 1985. Bayero University, Kano.

Sa'id, Halil Ibrahim. 1978. "Revolution and Reaction: The Fulani Jihad in Kano and It's Aftermath, 1807–1919." Ph.D. diss., Department of History, University of Michigan, Ann Arbor.

———. 1983. "Notes on Taxation as a Political Issue in Nineteenth-century Kano." Pp. 117–25 in *Studies in the History of Kano*, ed. Bawuro Barkindo. Ibadan, Nigeria: Heinemann Educational Books.

Schuh, R.G. 1983. The Hausa Language and Its Nearest Relatives. Unpublished paper, Bayero University, Kano.

Schwertdfeger, Friedrich. 1982. *Traditional Housing in African Cities*. New York: Wiley.

Shea, Philip James. 1975. "The Development of an Export Oriented Dyed Cloth Industry in Kano Emirate in the Nineteenth Century." Ph.D. diss., History, University of Wisconsin, Madison.

———. 1986. "Reconsideration of the Term *Kasuwar Kurmi*." Postgraduate seminar paper. History Department, Bayero University, Kano.

Shenton, Robert. 1986. *The Development of Capitalism in Northern Nigeria*. London: James Currey.

Skinner, Neil. 1996. *Hausa Comparative Dictionary*. Cologne, Germany: Rudiger Koppe Verlag.

Smith, Mary. 1954. *Baba of Karo: A Woman of the Muslim Hausa*. London: Faber.

Smith, M. G. 1960. *Government in Zazzau*. London: Oxford University Press.

———. 1967. "A Hausa Kingdom: Maradi under dan Baskore, 1854–75." Pp. 93–123 in *West African Kingdoms in the Nineteenth Century*, ed. Daryll Forde and P. M. Kaberry. Oxford: Oxford University Press.

———. 1978. *The Affairs of Daura*. Berkeley: University of California Press.

———. 1983. "The *Kano Chronicle* as History." Pp. 31–57 in *Studies in the History of Kano*, ed. Bawuro Barkindo. Ibadan, Nigeria: Heinemann Educational Books.

———. 1997. *Government in Kano, 1350–1950*. Boulder, Colo.: Westview Press.

Spain, Daphne. 1992. *Gendered Spaces*. Chapel Hill: University of North Carolina Press.

Spaulding, Jay. 1985. *The Heroic Age in Sinnar*. East Lansing: African Studies Center, Michigan State University.

Starratt, Priscilla Ellen. 1993. "Oral History in Muslim Africa: Al-Maghili Legends in Kano." Ph.D. diss., History, University of Michigan, Ann Arbor.

Staudinger, Paul. 1990. *In the Heart of the Hausa States*. Translated by Johanna E. Moody. Athens, Ohio: Ohio University Center for International Studies.

Stephens, Connie. 1991. "Marriage in the Hausa *Tatsuniya* Tradition." Pp. 221–31 in *Hausa Women in the Twentieth Century*, ed. Catherine Coles and Beverly Mack. Madison: University of Wisconsin Press.

Stilwell, Sean. 1999. "The Kano Mamluks: Royal Slavery in the Sokoto Caliphate, 1804–1903." Ph.D. dissertation, York University.

———. 2000. "The Power of Knowledge and the Knowledge of Power: Kinship, Community, and Royal Slavery in Pre-colonial Kano, 1807–1903." Pp. 117–56 in *Slave Elites in the Middle East and Africa*, ed. Miura Toru and John Edward Philips. London: Kegan Paul International.

Sulaiman, Ibraheem. 1986. *A Revolution in History*. London: Mansell.

Sule, Balaraba B. M., and Priscilla E. Starratt. 1991. "Islamic Leadership Positions for Women in Contemporary Kano Society." Pp. 29–49 in *Hausa Women in the Twentieth Century*, ed. Catherine Coles and Beverly Mack. Madison: University of Wisconsin Press.

Sutton, J. E. G. 1979. "Towards a Less Orthodox History of Hausaland." *Journal of African History* 20:179–201.

Sweetman, David. 1984. *Women Leaders in African History.* London: Heinemann.

Talbot, P. Amaury. 1967 [1927]. *Some Nigerian Fertility Cults.* London: Frank Cass and Co.

Tambo, David Carl. 1974. "The Sokoto Caliphate Slave Trade in the Nineteenth Century." M.A. thesis, History, University of Wisconsin, Madison.

Ubah, C. N. 1985. *Government and Administration of Kano Emirate, 1900–1930.* Nsukka: University of Nigeria Press.

VerEecke, Catherine. 1988. "From Pasture to Purdah: The Transformation of Women's Roles and Identity among the Adamawa Fulbe." *Ethnology* 28(1):53–75.

Wall, L. Lewis. 1988. *Hausa Medicine.* Durham, N.C.: Duke University Press.

Wigley, Mark. 1992. "Untitled: The Housing of Gender." Pp. 327–89 in *Sexuality and Space,* ed. B. Colomina. Princeton, N.J.: Princeton Architectural Press.

Yunasa, Yusufu. 1976. "Slavery in Nineteenth-century Kano." B.A. honors thesis, History, Ahmadu Bello University, Zaria.

Zahan, Dominique. 1967. "The Mossi Kingdoms." Pp. 152–79 in *West African Kingdoms in the Nineteenth Century,* ed. Daryll Forde and P. M. Kaberry. Oxford: Oxford University Press.

Archival Documents

Abbreviations

NAF, Native Authority Files.

NAK, National Archives, Kaduna.

KAN/LA, Kano Local Authority.

KANONA, Kano Native Authority.

NAF/15/1939. General correspondence regarding the Kano palace, 1939–65. Kano: Kano State History and Culture Bureau Archives.

NAK/KAN/LA/140. "H.R.H. Prince of Wales, Durbar in Honour of, Invitations to Officials and Non-officials, 1925."

NAK/KANONA 152. "Installation of the Emirs, Northern Provinces," 1946.

NAK/KANPROF 1744. "Kayan Sarauta (Appurtenances of Office)," 1923.

NAK/KANPROF 1836. "Social Relations with Moslem Chiefs and Their Women Folk," 1936.

NAK/KANPROF 1081/VII. "Emir of Kano, Visit to England," 1934.

NAK/KANPROF 4164. "Emir of Kano, 1926–45."

NAK/SNP 7–8/1538/1908. "Kano Province Annual Report for 1907."

NAK/SNP17/k105/vll. "Kano Province Annual Report for 1926."

SNP 7/472/1909. "Kano Province Annual Report for 1908."

SNP 7/9/1508 1908. "Kano Province Annual Report for 1907."

Index

Abakyala, 50–51

Abasame, Dauda (1565), 65

Abba, Emir (1903–1919), xxi

Abba, Hajiyya, xxiv, xxv, xxvii, xxviii, 181n26

Abbas (1903–1919), 31, 140, 148, 150

Abdullahi, Emir (1499–1509): eunuch market establishment and, 37; Nupeland weavers and, 83; as successor to King Rumfa, 65

Abomey palace: concubine mobility of, 8; date built, assumed, 2; female bodyguards, 44; grain-related responsibilities, 40; Islamic law and, 62; territorial benefits of captured women, 10; women governing, 2, 8

Abubakar, Mamman Siya, 33

Adonon, 180–81n21

Africanus, Leo, 2, 60, 178n1

Agricultural estates, 26, 183n6

Ahmed, Bello Nuhu, xxvii

Ahosi: Abomey palace governing by, 2; Adonon, 180–81n21; children of, 10;

divorce and, 179n12; kingly, 2; rise in power of, 10; as signs of owner's military prowess and virility, 8–9; as submission to kingly authority, 179n10; territorial conquests and, 10. *See also* Wives

Aku (Forest People), 37

Aliyu, Emir (1894–1903), xxi, 139, 140

Aljanna (spirit): as important female palace spirit, 41–42, 128, 189–90n47

Al-Maghili, 20

Alwali, King (1781–1807), 31, 102, 108, 124, 184n15

Amadiume, Ifi, xx, 54

Amina, Queen, 68, 71, 83

Aphrodisiacs, 219n66

Auwa, Madaki: influence of, 18, 65, 101

Babban Gwani, 117, 118, 211nn11–12, 212n14

Babban Jakadiya: and indigo-dyeing practices, 45

Babban Soro, 126, 127, 140, 142, 160, 222n7, 222n11, 222n15

Heidi J. Nast is associate professor of international studies at DePaul University, Chicago. She coedited and contributed to *Places through the Body* and *Thresholds in Feminist Geography.* She has exhibited her photographs of the Kano palace and is now working on a photographic history of the palace. She has written extensively about the social construction of race and the intersection of political economy, race, and sexualities.